Government and Political Life in England and France, c.1300–c.1500

How did the kings of England and France govern their kingdoms? This volume, the product of a ten-year international project, brings together specialists in late medieval England and France to explore the multiple mechanisms by which monarchs exercised their power in the final centuries of the Middle Ages. Collaborative chapters, mostly co-written by experts on each kingdom, cover topics ranging from courts, military networks and public finance; office, justice and the men of the church; to political representation, petitioning, cultural conceptions of political society; and the role of those excluded from formal involvement in politics. The result is a richly detailed and innovative comparison of the nature of government and political life, seen from the point of view of how the king ruled his kingdom, but bringing to bear the methods of social, cultural and economic history to understand the underlying armature of royal power.

CHRISTOPHER FLETCHER is a senior research fellow at CNRS (National Centre for Scientific Research) at the University of Paris I (Panthéon-Sorbonne). His publications include *Richard II: Manhood, Youth and Politics, 1377–99*.

JEAN-PHILIPPE GENET is professor of Medieval History at the University of Paris I (Panthéon-Sorbonne). His publications include *La genèse de l'état moderne. Culture et société politique en Angleterre* and *Les îles britanniques des origines à la fin du Moyen Âge*.

JOHN WATTS is professor of Later Medieval History and fellow and tutor in History at Corpus Christi College, University of Oxford. His publications include *Henry VI and the Politics of Kingship*, *The Making of Polities: Europe, 1300–1500* and the edited collection *The End of the Middle Ages?*

Government and Political Life in England and France, *c.*1300–*c.*1500

Edited by

Christopher Fletcher

CNRS – University of Paris I (Panthéon-Sorbonne)

Jean-Philippe Genet

University of Paris I (Panthéon-Sorbonne)

and

John Watts

University of Oxford

CAMBRIDGE
UNIVERSITY PRESS

CAMBRIDGE
UNIVERSITY PRESS

University Printing House, Cambridge CB2 8BS, United Kingdom

One Liberty Plaza, 20th Floor, New York, NY 10006, USA

477 Williamstown Road, Port Melbourne, VIC 3207, Australia

314-321, 3rd Floor, Plot 3, Splendor Forum, Jasola District Centre, New Delhi - 110025, India

79 Anson Road, #06-04/06, Singapore 079906

Cambridge University Press is part of the University of Cambridge.

It furthers the University's mission by disseminating knowledge in the pursuit of education, learning and research at the highest international levels of excellence.

www.cambridge.org
Information on this title: www.cambridge.org/9781107461758

© Christopher Fletcher, Jean-Philippe Genet and John Watts 2015

First published 2015
First paperback edition 2020

A catalogue record for this publication is available from the British Library

ISBN 978-1-107-08990-7 Hardback
ISBN 978-1-107-46175-8 Paperback

Contents

Contributors

MICHELLE BUBENICEK, University of the Franche-Comté

CHRISTINE CARPENTER, University of Cambridge

VINCENT CHALLET, University Paul-Valéry, Montpellier

FRANCK COLLARD, University of Paris-Ouest, Nanterre

GWILYM DODD, University of Nottingham

CHRISTOPHER FLETCHER, CNRS – University of Paris I (Panthéon-Sorbonne)

IAN FORREST, Oriel College, University of Oxford

JEAN-PHILIPPE GENET, University of Paris I (Panthéon-Sorbonne)

DAVID GRUMMITT, Canterbury Christ Church University

STEVEN GUNN, Merton College, University of Oxford

ARMAND JAMME, CNRS – Universities of Lyon II and Avignon

JEAN-FRANÇOIS LASSALMONIE, Ecole normale supérieure

AUDE MAIREY, CNRS – University of Paris I (Panthéon-Sorbonne)

OLIVIER MATTÉONI, University of Paris I (Panthéon-Sorbonne)

RICHARD PARTINGTON, Churchill College, University of Cambridge

SOPHIE PETIT-RENAUD, University of Versailles, Saint-Quentin-en-Yvelines

BENJAMIN THOMPSON, Somerville College, University of Oxford

MALCOLM VALE, St John's College, University of Oxford

JACQUES VERGER, University of Paris IV (Paris-Sorbonne)

JOHN WATTS, Corpus Christi College, University of Oxford

Preface

The research group France-Îles Britanniques was sponsored by the CNRS from 2000 to 2008. It harboured several projects, and organised and published a series of Franco-British conferences, such as those edited by Lachaud, Lescent-Gilles and Ruggiu; Chassaigne and Genet; Bates, Gazeau, Anceau, Lachaud and Ruggiu; and Genet and Ruggiu. The book we present today is the result of the work of a subgroup, convened by Jean-Philippe Genet, Malcolm Vale and John Watts, which met for the first time in September 2002 to discuss what was to become this project and then regularly met for four years, mostly in Oxford, usually at the Maison Française, and once at Fontevraud. From the beginning the aim of the project was to write a detailed comparative analysis of the ways in which France and England were governed in the later Middle Ages. For most chapters, two authors were selected, and they exchanged their views and their opinions during the meetings. We made the assumption that French and British specialists would deal with the history of their own country, since they had the command of both the sources and the historiography. Many drafts were exchanged between the authors until they could agree on a common text. By December 2007, most of the half-chapters had been sketched out, or even written. But at this point it became apparent that the task of fusing together these pieces into single chapters was much more formidable than had been expected, especially since we were attempting to finalise two interdependent versions, one in English, and one in French. By 2010, several chapters had been completed, but some others were far from being in publishable form. This is where Christopher Fletcher, hitherto author of one of the two single-authored chapters, stepped in, to help us in the editing process and to finalise the English text. Without him there would be no book at all.

In the course of these years, we have benefited from the help and the support of several institutions, and most conspicuously that of the Maison Française in Oxford, to which we owe a special gratitude, a gratitude which extends to its directors, Jean-Claude Sergeant and Jean-Yves Tadié. Gilbert Balavoine, Jacques Chevalier and the office of the

Scientific Councillor of the French Embassy in London have also been most helpful. Several colleges in Oxford helped us in one way or another, especially St John's College, Corpus Christi College and Merton College. We would also like to thank the Centre Culturel de l'Ouest for its hospitality in Fontevraud, which was in many ways the high point of the enterprise, and Martin Aurell for introducing us to the Centre. But our greatest thanks must go to the authors, who remained committed to this time-consuming enterprise until the end, and to the translators, Christopher Fletcher and Nicole Genet.

Jean-Philippe Genet and John Watts, with Christopher Fletcher

1   The government of later medieval France and England: a plea for comparative history

Jean-Philippe Genet

On 30 May 1420, a solemn assembly, in which the three estates of the kingdom of France were represented, met in Paris to confirm the new treaty concluded at Troyes between the King of England and the King of France. Once a direct line had been established through the French king (whose son, the future Charles VII was disqualified because of his crimes) and the English one, by the marriage of Henry V with Catherine de Valois, daughter of Charles VI, the two kingdoms of France and England would belong to the heir of this marriage and his own heirs, that is:

the same person who will be, for the time, King and sovereign lord of both king-doms, as said earlier, keeping nevertheless in all other matters to each kingdom his rights, liberties, customs, uses and laws, without subjecting in any way one of the said kingdoms to the other[1]

The double reign of Henry VI was a double failure, but the geographical and historical proximity of the two kingdoms was such that the per-sonal union under the imperium of one man of France and England was thought to be a political structure worth trying. The two kingdoms were, however, to be kept strictly separated, each governed according to its own particular laws and traditions.

    Close, if distinct: such were France and England in the eyes of their governing elites in 1420–2, a view which nearly two centuries of academic (but nationally based) historiography has obscured by dividing what had been a common history into two parallel and distinct national histories. It is worth remembering that, at one time, it seemed common sense to teach and study British and French histories together: 'the histories of France and England from the reign of Edward the Confessor have been so constantly and closely connected by all international relations of peace and war that they would naturally collect themselves into one province',

---

[1] Cosneau (1889), p. 111.

advised the Oxford Regius professor of Modern History, Henry Halford Vaughan, in his *Memorandum to the Parliamentary Commissioners* in 1856.[2] This is why we wanted to reconsider the history of the French and English political space, concentrating our examination on the problem of government. In this brief introductory chapter to the volume, I intend to justify this project, by establishing to what extent it is possible to describe England (or the British Isles) and France as a common political space; why we have chosen to explore it through the theme of government; and what some of the methodological implications of such a choice were. It is worth noting that I shall not attempt to give a narrative of the events of the period, though it might have been useful for some readers. In the introduction, it will only be possible to combine efficiently the two traditional national perspectives. In his conclusion, John Watts offers a general survey in the light of the findings of this book.

I

On another occasion, I have described France and England as a couple.[3] They are obviously two states and two nations with a long and turbulent history, but at least for the medieval segment of this history, it is mostly a common history: the Saxon tribes were next to the Frankish ones in the queue to breach the *limes*; the Normans did, after all, conquer England; and the Norman and Plantagenet kings of England ruled over a much larger slice of French territory than their Capetian counterparts for quite a long time. True, in the later Middle Ages, from the last decade of the thirteenth century onwards, war was the dominant link between the two countries, but the English still governed significant parts of France until 1453 and they kept Calais (1347–1558) and later on Boulogne (1543–6) until the middle of the sixteenth century. As we have seen, the double kingdom of France and England had some reality between 1422 and 1435, at least. The marriages between the two royal dynasties were so frequent (Henry II married the divorced wife of Louis VII; Henry III and Saint Louis were brothers-in-law; Edward I, Edward II, Henry V and Henry VI had Capetian or Valois wives) that one could nearly say that one and the same family ruled both countries. Despite all this, the dream of the double monarchy vanished, although it is difficult to know what would have happened had Henry V, by far the best soldier of his times, lived longer than he did. All the same, the loss of Guyenne and Normandy did not erase France from the English agenda. Calais was still in English hands, and Burgundian Low Countries could still offer

---

[2] Bill (1973), p. 266.   [3] Gazeau and Genet (2012).

a powerful alliance (at least until 1475 when Edward IV crossed the Channel). And after the Battle of Pavia, Henry VIII was quick to suggest to his nephew Charles V that he should get rid of Francis I and recognise himself as the true King of France to ensure a lasting European peace.

Be it a peaceful one, or a warring one, the relation between these two entities has always been intense and it is all the more surprising that the two histories have usually been written in the rigid framework of national historiography imposed by the nineteenth century on the emerging scientific history. There were some good opportunities for crossing the Channel, especially with the so-called debate on the 'Norman yoke', but they proved unequal to the task of diverting historians from the main road of national history. Indeed, it is only recently with David Bates and the late Marjorie Chibnall that British historians really came back to Normandy to write in depth the history of the Conquest from where it began.[4]

Mutual interest has, however, always been keen, although not synchronic. English nineteenth-century historians sought a model in the Prussia of Stein and generally speaking in Germany, while their French counterparts, whether Orleanists – such as Thiers and Guizot – or Republicans, were fascinated by the history of England: they valued highly a political system which seemed able to prevent the violent political upheavals experienced by France. There is a distinctly Whig flavour in the French approach to English history. Henry Wallon (who introduced the word 'République' into French parliamentary legislation in 1875 and is therefore, at least formally, the founder of the Third Republic) was an Anglophile who wrote a history of the reign of Richard II, while André Réville (1867–94), the son of a French minister at Amsterdam, was the author of a history of the 1381 rising which is still useful today.[5] This tradition was continued by Charles Bémont[6] (1848–1939); Charles Petit-Dutaillis (1868–1947), who was brought to English history by the editing of his friend Réville's work and later edited the translation by his own pupil, George Lefèvre, the future great historian of the French Revolution, of Bishop Stubbs' *Constitutional History of England* (to which he added the *Studies and Notes*, prefaced by Powicke);[7] and Édouard Perroy (1901–74).[8] All these men knew what force was driving them to English history: the love of freedom. Petit-Dutaillis was jailed for a time

---

[4] See Bates, (1969–80).   [5] Réville (1898), (1892), pp. 1–42.
[6] Bémont (1884), (1892).
[7] Stubbs (1913); Petit-Dutaillis' comments, mostly taken from his edition, were published as *Studies and Notes Supplementary to Stubbs' Constitutional History* . . . (Petit-Dutaillis (1908–28), with several re-editions.
[8] Perroy (1933a) and Perroy (1933b).

at Fresnes by the Gestapo, and Perroy had an important role in the Resistance, writing his *Guerre de Cent Ans* while on the run in the mountains of Forez, and coming close to being the first 'préfet' of free France at Saint-Étienne in 1944. Marc Bloch had the same political sympathies and died a martyr at the hands of the Nazis in 1944 and we now know, thanks to François-Olivier Touati, that he had developed strong intellectual links with his fellow contributors to the *Cambridge Economic and Social History of Europe*, M. M. Postan and Eileen Power.[9] But after this, while contemporary historians such as François Crouzet and François Bédarida continued in the same tradition, English history appears to have disappeared as such from French medieval historiography. Younger historians such as Bernard Guenée and Philippe Contamine were very learned in English history and historiography, but did not work on English sources. French historians with some curiosity for countries other than the motherland have now deserted the United Kingdom, flocking to the French schools and institutes in Rome and Madrid, or following the government's incitements to study German history – long neglected, it is true, for obvious reasons.[10]

With the end of the Second World War, however, it was now time for the English to cross the Channel and they indeed introduced new perspectives on French history. Several of these young historians were exceptionally well prepared to work in France, thanks to the teaching of diplomatic and palaeography provided by Pierre Chaplais in Oxford.[11] These views were not always welcomed – though their exponents were – but they have in the end deeply affected French historiography, and this is also one of the reasons why this book had to be written. Roughly speaking, there are two areas in which they have been most influential: the first is the export of the 'McFarlane legacy', which made historians realise that 'bastard feudalism' was not restricted to England, but that money and contracts, though disguised as 'alliances' were just as common in France – and in many other places – as they were in England.[12] Peter Lewis is mainly responsible for this and he has written what remains one of the best and most innovative histories of later medieval France.[13] The other area is a tactful but well-grounded revision of the degree of cohesion and unity of the French kingdom, too often taken for granted by French historians. While Ferdinand Lot, Robert Fawtier and their collaborators in their epoch-making *Histoire des Institutions de la France* drew – and not

---

[9] Touati (2006).   [10] For a survey, see Genet (1991).
[11] On his role see Sharpe (2012). His *English Diplomatic Practice* (Chaplais (1982–2003)) is a monument, with unfortunately no counterpart for France.
[12] Britnell and Pollard (1995). See also Hicks (1995).   [13] Lewis (1968).

so long ago – a sharp line between the *Institutions royales* and the *Institutions seigneuriales*,[14] in which category they dissolved beyond recognition the princely states of the later Middle Ages, British historians produced superb studies of the governments and societies of these principalities: Christopher Allmand[15] (Lancastrian Normandy), Michael Jones[16] (Brittany), Malcolm Vale[17] (Gascony), Richard Vaughan[18] or Graeme Small[19] (Burgundy) to name but a few of the British historians working on the period under scrutiny in the present book, have amply demonstrated the amount and the vitality of state-building activities emulating but also opposing the French kings.

A consequence of these historiographical developments is that we are now in a better position to deal with France and England as a common political space. The French historians mentioned above had simply complemented their British colleagues' views on the twelfth and thirteenth centuries, but the new emphasis on the importance of the principalities and the state-making activities of the princes by British historians has deeply altered the perception of France itself and more generally of a European west as dominated by the great 'national' monarchies. Precisely because they were fast-growing organisations, these monarchies appeared fragile and precarious: several English and Scottish kings were deposed and murdered, and France faced disintegration at least twice. But we must face the consequences of this new vision for a comparison between France and England. On the English side, principalities were not a problem: England was more weakened by Fortescue's 'overmighty subjects' than by its peripheral principalities (the principality of Wales, the duchies of Lancaster and of Cornwall, the County Palatine of Chester) since they were used more often than not as royal power bases against aristocratic unrest. However, it must not be forgotten that Aquitaine and Normandy can be seen at times as English principalities, which greatly enhanced the status of the Black Prince, John of Gaunt[20] or the duke of Bedford: princes indeed they were, and their weight in English politics depended on this status. More recently, the question of 'Britishness' has been introduced, the winds blowing not from France but from Wales and Ireland, under the impulsion of the late Sir Rees Davies[21] and of Robin Frame.[22] But the problems of these territories did not affect the administrative machinery and the government of England to the same extent.

---

[14] Lot and Fawtier (1957); see Ferdinand Lot, quoted in the Introduction as saying 'À dire vrai, en France, comme ailleurs dans l'Europe occidentale, il n'existe qu'une seule institution; c'est la Royauté.' (p. ix).
[15] Allmand (1983).   [16] Jones (1970, 1988, 2003).   [17] Vale (1970, 1990).
[18] Vaughan (1970a), (1973a), (1979).   [19] Small (1997).   [20] Goodman (1992).
[21] Davies (1986), (2000), (2009).   [22] Frame (1995).

Ireland remained an external problem, though it could be used as a power base by magnates just as much as Aquitaine or Normandy; the Welsh, on the other hand, were gradually integrated in the English political society after the failure of Owain Glyn Dŵr's revolt.[23] Welsh problems proved less dangerous for England than they had been previously, even during the so-called Wars of the Roses,[24] because of the decline of the Marcher Lordships, would-be principalities of thirteenth-century England. The case of Scotland must be left to further investigation, since we are facing here a quandary similar to the Franco-British one, perhaps even worse, that of two unduly 'national' histories for a largely common historical space.

If the 'British turn' in English historiography can be left aside for a Franco-English comparison without too much damage,[25] the re-evaluation of the importance of the principalities presents more difficul-ties for France, which had several principalities or would-be principalities developing on her vast territory. Several of these also had large dominions outside France, providing their masters with resources outside monar-chical control. Even if we discard as inconsistent the conglomerates of lordships of the two rival houses of Foix and Armagnac, and consider the dukes of Anjou (with their lands in Provence and later in Lorraine, not to speak of their Italian pretentions), Bourbon[26] and Alençon, as less lethal at the time, at least two of these principalities were well advanced in the process of becoming autonomous, if not independent, states by the mid-dle of the fifteenth century: Brittany[27] and Burgundy.[28] Burgundy was especially dangerous, since besides their French demesnes (Burgundy, Flanders, Artois) the dukes had secured a large slice of Imperial territory (most of the Low Countries, the County of Burgundy, part of Alsatia). Charles the Bold when he died was both trying to impose his authority on the Imperial ecclesiastical principalities on the Rhine and to unite the two main nuclei of his lands at the expense of the duke of Lorraine. Had he succeeded in wresting a royal title from the impoverished emperor, he would have been a formidable challenge for the legitimacy of the French king. Though he did not succeed, the ultimate result of his involvement with the Empire was the transfer of the most valuable Burgundian lands to the Habsburgs who, since they soon also became kings of Spain, were later able to encircle France. It was not in 1453, when an uncertain peace was re-established between France and England, but much later, after Charles the Bold's death in 1477 on the battlefield at Nancy and the

[23] Davies (1995).   [24] Griffiths (1991).   [25] But see now Brown (2013).
[26] Mattéoni (1998), (2012).   [27] Kerhervé (1987).
[28] Prevenier and Blockmans (1999); Schnerb (2005).

subsequent collapse of his 'state', or even later on, in 1488, when the government of Anne de Beaujeu had tamed the duke of Orléans (the future Louis XII) and brought Brittany under French control by marrying her brother Charles [VIII] to the heiress Anne de Bretagne, that France re-emerged as a unitary and consistent monarchical state.

At this stage, a reminder of the general situation in Europe may be useful. It is worth pointing out that in 1479, the crowns of Castile and Aragon were united in the persons of Ferdinand and Isabella; that in 1487, at the Battle of Stoke, Henry VII disposed of the last Yorkist competitor to receive strong aristocratic support (Lambert Simnel; Perkin Warbeck, eliminated in 1497, was chiefly backed by foreign powers); and that in 1489 James IV put an end to chronic rebelliousness in Scotland. But before this monarchical turn in the last decade of the century, in a period in which the general prevalence of wars, feuds and civil unrest in the two great kingdoms of France and England drew into their rivalry nearly all adjacent powers from Scotland to Spain, including the principalities of Western Germany, the Swiss and Italian regional states and the Iberian kingdoms, the sinews of power were operated at regional or factional level, if not below.

This means that during most of the fifteenth century, political action has to be followed at infra-state level as well as at state level. Franco-English relations in the years 1412–13, for instance, are a complex web of negotiations, first between the Prince of Wales [the future Henry V], his associate the earl of Arundel and the Burgundians, and later between Henry IV and his second son Thomas [Clarence] with the leaders of the Armagnac party, producing two raids in France on opposite sides.[29] Until 1472, at least, Franco-English relations in the reign of Edward IV are best described as a highly volatile game of four parties – Lancastrians (attracting the previously Yorkist Warwick affinity); Yorkists (soon reduced to the king and his in-laws); Louis XI; and the Burgundians – with constantly changing alliances. English and French princes were also involved outside their respective kingdoms: John of Gaunt dreamt of being King of Castile, and the Valois dukes of Anjou fought for the kingdom of Naples and later in Catalonia or in imperial Lorraine. As we have already mentioned, the dukes of Burgundy were at least as much involved in the Empire as they were in France, while the dukes of Brittany long held the earldom of Richmond in England. It is no surprise that the crime of treason became one of the main political tools developed by the French kings.[30] For monarchies did survive in the end, and though we have to take into account the somewhat dislocated structures of both

[29] Favier (1980); Allmand (1992).   [30] Cuttler (2003).

polities, we are left with the impression that a certain degree of continuity existed and that it was strong enough to allow us to follow the thread of central government, despite the convulsive state of the political societies of France and England. A consequence of this is that we shall be focusing on the kingdoms of France and England: in the pages which follow there is almost no Wales, no Ireland and no Scotland, there is no Burgundy, no Gascony, no Brittany: there are only France and England and, while we are quite conscious that this is a distortion of reality, we have had to accept it as the only way of making a comparative study manageable.

II

As we have seen, though English and French historians were perfectly able to write history with minds alerted and informed by a deep knowledge of a different model, and though we have in both countries excellent 'national' histories,[31] they have on the whole fought shy of a truly comparative history. Though comparison between France and England used to be a well-established tradition in the Middle Ages – it is enough to remember Forstecue's *Governance of England* and *Le débat des hérauts d'armes de France et d'Angleterre*[32] – Charles Petit-Dutaillis may have been the first to have attempted such a comparative history with his study of the feudal monarchies of France and England.[33] Even so, it was left to Marc Bloch to make the first methodological breakthrough with *Seigneurie française, manoir anglais*, though there is not much left of his conclusions, the book being but notes for a lecture delivered in 1936 but published only in 1961, thanks to Georges Duby:[34] it is a daring attempt to use comparative history as a method to explore the rural structures of the two countries. However, a more wide-ranging attempt at writing a comparative history has come from the American medievalist Richard Kaeuper, who produced an impressive account of the development of the governing of both France and England in the fourteenth century, starting from the enterprise of war, in which he saw a kind of *primum movens*, moving then to taxation and credit, ending with justice and the maintenance of order.[35] Our approach, however, is different: we have

---

[31] See for instance Bove (2009) for France and Harriss (2005) for England – but see also Carpenter (1997) for the second half of the fifteenth century.

[32] *Le débat des hérauts d'armes*, ed. Pannier (1877); for Fortescue, see Fortescue (1997), pp. 83–123. There is also the extensive literature of confrontation between the two kingdoms: see for instance '*L'honneur de la couronne de France*', ed. Pons (1990) and Taylor (2006).

[33] Petit-Dutaillis (1936), a translation of the French edition published in 1933.

[34] Bloch (1960): see the review by Robert Fossier, *Bibliothèque de l'École des Chartes*, 119 (1961), pp. 361–3.

[35] Kaeuper (1988).

mostly concentrated our own work on the fifteenth century, and we never intended to produce a continuous narrative. But to write a comparative history, we had first to choose between two contrary approaches, either to compare structures, which would have led us to compare two societies, or to concentrate on dynamics, which opened other perspectives.

Against the first approach, it must be admitted that the present state of historiography makes it extremely difficult to write a comparative history of French and English societies. This is due to some obvious discrepancies (the sheer size of France makes it more heterogeneous, while the centralised structure of the old English state which survived the Conquest contrasts with the segmented nature of power in feudal France). But the main obstacle is historiographical. A kind comment would be that French historians have a highly centralised perception of their decentralised medieval past, while English historians have a highly localised perception of their centralised medieval past. But the fault is not entirely with them, since it is also a consequence of the configuration of the sources of each country. In England, we have excellent sources for the central machinery of government, sources which historians and antiquaries have tapped at least from the second half of the sixteenth century, while in France a large amount of these central archives has been destroyed from early on, either by accident (the burning of the *Chambre des Comptes* in 1737) or during political troubles such as the French Revolution and the Paris Commune. Enough survives to give us a clear idea of the working of the central administrative and judicial machinery (the *Parlement* of Paris has kept most of its archives), but it remains very difficult to track in any detail the relations of the centre with the regional administration and localities, not to speak of individuals, which is a *forte* of the English archives. On the other hand, the French Revolution confiscated religious and noble properties, including their archives, for which the *Archives Départementales* were immediately created, and the County Record Offices, created much later, pale in comparison (indeed, the spoils of the monasteries had already been dispersed by the end of the sixteenth century!).[36] Therefore it is possible to write in England what cannot be written in France, that is, extremely coherent and well-documented histories of the elites (nobility, gentry, town oligarchies) from the central archives,[37] while for the medieval peasantry we depend upon estates' archives. A striking consequence is that elites

---

[36] See Leitch (2011); Kitching (2011); Ruggiu (2011).

[37] A good example is the trilogy devoted to the Paston family by Colin Richmond (1990, 1996, 2001): the Paston Letters, in itself an exceptional source, is completed by the central archives to achieve with a *microstoria* precision the portrait of a gentry family; compare with, for instance, Charbonnier (1973) for a French counterpart.

are studied apart from the peasants, and that there are no regional studies that explore society in the round; histories of the elites are either centred on a town or on a county, peasant histories on estates.[38] The result is quite different in France, where the monumental French *thèse d'État* is ideally suited for good town and regional studies. This is why the pillars of French medieval historiography are the splendid regional studies produced by a long line of historians, from Georges Duby to Guy Bois,[39] a line that the demise of the *thèse d'État* seems to have brought to an end, to the despair of some.

The problem for us is that, given the regularity of structures in the limited space of the kingdoms, English local studies, whether they deal with aristocracy, towns or peasantries, are additive, while in France only town histories are; the regional studies never are, because the structures are too different from one part of the country to another. To come back to social history, it makes sense to speak about the English nobility or about the English peasantry, but they have no reliable French counterparts: the only social group for which some comparison is possible is urban oligarchies, because most French towns have a similar relation to the monarchy, and because town archives often provide what is lacking elsewhere (for instance, Bulst's epoch-making history of the *États généraux* in 1468 and 1484 has been written from this kind of material).[40] But neither for the peasantry nor for the nobility can we boast of a synthesis similar to that achieved by Bernard Chevalier for the French towns.[41] If we put alongside one another Bruce McFarlane's classic essay on the English nobility[42] (to which could be confidently added a selection of county-gentry studies) and Philippe Contamine's essay on the French nobility, the contrast is fascinating. Thanks to parliamentary summons, McFarlane knows precisely how many noble families existed at any given time; and from Warwickshire and other English counties,[43] we get impressive lists of gentlemen, with their retinue affiliation, the offices and commissions they received, and not too bad an idea of their income, thanks to the *Inquisitions post mortem*. On the other side of the Channel, Contamine struggles valiantly with his sources, or rather his absence of sources, and with an inadequate secondary literature to get the best of them, but he ends up with a patchy and indecisive survey, concluding that only 1% of them could belong to the higher nobility (perhaps the would-be French

---

[38] Hilton (1966) is an exception, and it may be worth stressing that Hilton was a Marxist historian.

[39] Bois (1976), highly relevant for the present project. (After all, the English *were* in Normandy.)

[40] Bulst (1992).   [41] Chevalier (1982).   [42] McFarlane (1973).

[43] Saul (1981); Payling (1991); Carpenter (1992), to quote but a few.

'Barons', although no list is available); 15% of the total were knights, and the remnant, some 84%, could be described as simple gentlemen. But these proportions change from one province to another, and the data on the income and, worst of all, on the wages and salaries which these men could draw from administrative or military functions remain totally inadequate.[44]

This is why to try and base a comparison between England and France on a social approach would have been difficult and, it is to be feared, unfruitful in the end: if it were not impossible, it would have been premature, to say the least. Different national research agendas would have to be made compatible, which will take time: this is precisely one of the aims of the CNRS group which has nurtured this cooperative project. However, social history cannot be reduced to taxonomy,[45] and social processes remain everywhere fundamental, including in one of the other possible (and easier) fields open to us, the political one. Here, we have the opportunity to start from below, while tracing individual trajectories and networks permits a dynamic approach. And it is a field in which we can draw inspiration both from Peter Lewis' seminal work and from previous collaborative programmes on the origins of the modern state,[46] in which several French and British historians (including some of the authors of this book) were involved, accumulating material and ideas for the present project. We knew what we did not want to do: a static comparison between institutions, or a flat reproduction of what classic textbooks (such as Bernard Guenée's *States and Rulers*)[47] have already described. What we wanted was to analyse the ways in which two already different political societies reacted to their respective governments, which implies keeping an eye both on the impulse coming from above through officers and holders of commissions and, as we said, on the reactions and the moves coming from below. In other words, we wanted to start from tangible and concrete elements, not from preconceived social or political premises. Our project has been planned as a purely empirical enterprise, avoiding abstract theoretical points of view, such as those provided by the bastard feudalism tradition or the model of the 'origins of the modern state'. Some of the participants made it quite clear that they did not share my views or those of Wim Blockmans about this model. John Watts has given a critical but fair and balanced analysis of it, in which he details

[44] Contamine (1997), pp. 134–5: 'sur ce point capital, la documentation ne permet pas de trancher, même pour la période 1450–1500, et ce malgré des sources notoirement plus abondantes'.
[45] See the contribution of S. H. Rigby to Horrox and Ormrod (2006), a book which has no French counterpart.
[46] Genet (1990), (1997).   [47] Guenée (1985).

his reservations, while delineating his own views on the structure and situation of the late medieval European polities.[48] Neither the 'origins of the modern state' nor 'the making of polities' have been imposed on the authors of the following chapters, who have been totally free in the writing of the part allotted to them, and their views have only been modified through common discussion and exchange during the many meetings we had in Oxford or in Fontevraud.

Nonetheless, even if the method was empirical, the choice of the governmental approach is not in itself entirely devoid of a theoretical bias. Though historians use the words 'govern' and 'government' as if they referred to timeless activities, it is worth noting that these words emerged in the vernacular precisely in our period.[49] Although the image of the mariner king governing the ship of state goes back to Plato, and Aquinas (as well as his continuator Ptolomeo de Lucca) is fond of this metaphor in his *De Regno*,[50] the words commonly used in medieval Latin were *regere* and *regimen*. These words are not easy to understand precisely: Michel Senellart's brilliant study of the political theory of *Fürstenspiegel* literature insists upon the close association between the political *regimen* and the pastoral *regimen animarum* as defined by Gregory the Great in his *Liber Pastoralis*.[51] It is, however, possible to distinguish between two ages in the use of *regimen*. The first age, until the thirteenth century, understands *regere* on the lines exemplified by Isidore of Seville's well-known definition of the king (*reges a recte agendo uocati sunt*), itself a complex construction since it results from a combination of Gregory and Augustine's views. It is mostly concerned with the moral value of the king, a man like all other men, who has to struggle victoriously against sin and vice to lead his people to salvation through justice.[52] Justice remained an essential component of the king's image, and the king's grace gives him the right to pass over in some cases the limits inherent to human justice: the kings of France, also more keenly attached to sacred kingship, made much more of it than their insular colleagues, even until the modern

---

[48] Watts (2009), pp. 26–34.

[49] The word is not used by Fortescue (*The Governance of England* is an editor's title) but see, for instance, *Mum and the Sothsegger*, ed. Dean (2000), or its frequent use in the Wycliffite *Tractatus de Regibus* or in *The III Consideracions right necessarye to the good governaunce of a Prince*, both in *Four English Political Tracts*, ed. Genet (1977).

[50] Aquinas (1979): words with the root 'gubern' have ninety-nine occurrences in 69, 246 words, among which twenty are for *gubernatio*.

[51] Senellart (1995), p. 27.

[52] This definition is to be found in the *Sententiae* III, 48, 7. That of the *Etymologiae* IX, 3, 4 (*Reges a regendo uocati*) is slightly different, closer to Augustin (*regere* associated with *corrigere*): see references and discussion in Reydellet (1981), pp. 550 and 576.

period.[53] But, and this is stressed by Senellart, things changed with Giles of Rome's *De Regimine Principum*: the king did not correct anymore, he directed; that is, he governed,[54] though Giles does not make much use of the word.[55] We may not be concerned at that stage with the implications of the theory of government and the concept of '*gouvernementalité*' developed by Michel Foucault in his 1978–80 lectures in the Collège de France, because he thinks that its main consequences became tangible only in the eighteenth century, with the Enlightenment, but it is clear now that Senellart had them in mind when he wrote his analysis.[56]

This change from correction (or regulation) to direction was not only a consequence of the consolidation of stronger monarchical centres from the twelfth century onwards, it also illustrated a change in the nature of kingship, which had far-reaching consequences, two of which must be mentioned here. Through the process of government, a relationship of mutual dependence developed between the ruler and the subject, a relationship which created the necessity of an articulate communication between them within a given political society, and this relation could take many forms: this is precisely the object of a new research programme of the European Research Council (SAS).[57] It was a relationship more and more managed through administrative processes and routines, implying the use of the written word and of documents alongside the old feudal system of direct personal relations. This was a slow, long-term process, which started in the twelfth century and was far from being complete in the fifteenth. The impact of the administrative process had another incidental effect, that of transforming the relationship between church and state, which became less competitive and more collaborative, since clerics were from early on the pillars of royal administration both in France and in England; things only started to change significantly in the fifteenth century. Thus, both in respect of communication within political

---

[53] Gauvard (1991).   [54] Senellart (1995), p. 30.

[55] Words with the root 'gubern' have ninety-nine occurrences for 158, 990 words, among which forty-two are for *gubernatio* in the *De Regimine*: but there are only two for *gubernatio regni*, against twenty-eight for *gubernatio domus*.

[56] The text of these lectures has now been edited from tapes by Michel Senellart himself: see especially the lectures for 1977–8, 1978–9, 1979–80, respectively 'Sécurité, territoire, population' (2004), 'Naissance de la biopolitique' (2004), and 'Du gouvernement des vivants' (2012).

[57] Details are on the LAMOP site: www.//lamop.univ-paris1.fr. One volume has been published in isolation: Gamberini, Genet and Zorzi (2011). Others will be part of the collection 'Le pouvoir symbolique en Occident', published in Paris and Rome. Already issued are: vol. I, Genet (2014); vol. V, Gaffuri and Ventrone (2014); vol. VI, Genet and Mineo (2014); vol. VIII Boucheron and Genet (2013); vol. X, Barralis, Boudet, Delivré and Genet (2014).

society and of administrative growth, we face complex processes which are at the centre of vivid historiographical debates: even if we leave aside the task of unravelling the flux of events, including the Hundred Years War[58] and the Wars of the Roses,[59] even if we restrict the model to a rump France deprived of its principalities and to a non-British England, our choice of a governmental approach required us to clarify our positions on several issues, three of which may now be explored in more detail.

III

The first one to be considered is the need to take seriously the notion of political society. This is not a new concept in itself, since it can be traced back to Thomas Frederick Tout in England and to Raymond Cazelles in France and it has been more recently revived by Philippe Contamine and Gerald Harriss, among others.[60] All these authors have in common a similar view of a political society more or less restricted to the social elites, but Gerald Harriss has introduced an important element which adds dynamics to the concept:

Far from entrenching the power of the Crown, the growth of the political nation enhanced it, adding new fiscal and military resources, extending its authority in the localities, and introducing new techniques into government. Correspondingly, as political society grew, so it needed the monarchy more, not less: to distribute patronage and power, to regulate and harmonise its tensions, and to provide a sense of direction and authority.[61]

I should like to go farther, and extend this notion of political society to all those whose conditions of life are affected in one way or another by the development of the state. It involves all those who pay taxes, who have to go to courts, or who take part in wars or suffer from them. In the end, that amounts in fact to all the subjects.[62] Representation grew in efficiency during the fifteenth century in most countries, with the possible exception of England, where some would argue that it declined with the Tudors: in any case England was well ahead of France. When representation failed or was not available, revolts and rebellions of all kinds erupted, but these outbursts are indeed proof of the existence and vitality of this political society: the governments' strategies for the return of order are to be understood as answers in this uncomfortable but real dialogue. The same reasoning drives John Watts to conclude that:

---

[58] But see Allmand (1988).   [59] Hicks (2010).
[60] Contamine (1998); Harriss (1993).   [61] Harriss (1993), p. 56.
[62] Genet (2007), pp. 90–1.

the stronger polities of the later fifteenth centuries were forged as much from below, or from within, as they were from above: mechanisms of representation and dialogue, means of upholding order and distributing social and political goods were just as important as the new tools of authority in creating the more integrated states of the period.[63]

This applies to France and England, and this sense of a larger political society pervades the following chapters, most notably those on the masses, on representation and, perhaps more unexpectedly, on grace and favour.

But to deal with this society, even under the restricted angle of the political society, could have brought us back to the problem we had been trying to avoid, that of social taxonomy. This is where, I think, our approach pays dividends, because we start not from preconceived ideas or concepts, but from what really happened in everyday social life. To put it simply, it was not the English gentry who produced a common law which was so different from the French judicial system; rather, it is because the two systems are different that they induced different evolutions in the social groups concerned with them. The common law and the French judicial system were two different answers to a similar question that both kingdoms had to face. The English answer came earlier, the French later; the English king ruled a unified political and social space, while the French king ruled over a much larger territory with at least two completely different judicial systems, and with varying levels of authority: the two answers could not be similar. With the use of French in the courts, with a system based (at first) upon previous judicial decisions, English lawyers did not need a university education; and when the growth of legislation and of reports of judicial proceedings made schools an alternative to apprenticeship, the continued use of French – now for reasons opposite to those of the twelfth century – precluded a university education: hence the inns of court. A common 'technology', to use Max Weber's word (his phrase: 'an empirical highly developed technology'),[64] gave the group its ethos and its cohesion. But the *robin* is not a French equivalent of the English lawyer. In France, *la robe* is defined in relation to *l'épée*, and this distinction only makes sense in respect of the French obsession with nobility. Were there French lawyers? Probably, and regional studies such as those of Bernard Guenée[65] or, to a lesser degree, René Fédou,[66] could prove it. Recent work on the culture of this social group has unearthed striking similarities between France and England in a field which was long thought to be an English monopoly,

[63] Watts (2009), p. 378.   [64] Weber (1978), pp. 976–8.
[65] Guenée (1963).   [66] Fédou (1934).

theatre. The link between the inns of courts, the revels and drama in the sixteenth century is well known, but the relations between the *basoche* (students and junior staff in the courts) and the theatre (mostly farces), though not ignored previously, have been recently re-evaluated.[67] On the status side, the social impact of the emergence of the justices of the peace could be paired with the long survival of seignorial justice in France to rethink the place of the lawyers and of the *gens de justice* among the elite, but many other occupations, such as the medical or the military, could present us with the same kind of contrast. But this can be done only by scrutinising practice, leaving aside preconceived notions of status.

Indeed, the same is true, but with an opposite evolution, for the army and the military: the French fought on their soil, the English fought – for most of the time – outside, with an extensive use of foreign soldiers, including their Welsh archers, though their participation in the wars was an important element in anglicising them (or making them British, if one prefers). The situation was at first not very different in France, where, paradoxically, foreign soldiers, mostly Bretons or Gascons, became in the end entirely French, and all the more dangerous for that when serving princes. Once the Hundred Years War was over, English armies were not needed any more, except for short periods. The French kings, on the other hand, needed armies not only to expel the English, but even more to check their own princes' ambitions, and they were soon to be involved in constant warfare against the Habsburgs and then in Italy: a permanent standing army and an artillery exceptional in size for the period had thus to come into being. If the lawyer is an English specificity, the soldier is a French one. The monarchy turned the French noble into a soldier,[68] while war remained simply an element of class distinction and a way of life for the English gentleman. Thus, the opportunities available to those men, often on the fringes of the established gentry, who turned to war for a living, or, if one prefers, as a profession, ended by being rather different; and it is this evolution which produced in the end differences between two groups which had earlier much in common, not least in their names, for the same word, gentleman/*gentilhomme* exists in both languages. To sum up this discussion, I should like to stress the fact that English historians use one word, which is conspicuously absent from French historiography, that is the word 'profession';[69] and in England professions proved pivotal in the dynamics of the elites, ensuring the integration of diverse social groups in the gentry. Since they are absent from French historiography,

---

[67] Bouhaïk-Gironès (2007).   [68] See Deruelle and Gainot (2013).
[69] Clough (1982).

the comparison remains difficult, but the approach through government is at least a possible strategy.

And it is precisely the need to secure the consensus of such social groups which makes communication such an important matter in the later Middle Ages, both in England and in France: an efficient communication system is the precondition for the existence of a political society. This may be too complex a problem to be surveyed in depth here, since we are not simply alluding to information or propaganda when discussing communication, but to a much larger range of activities. A brief survey is nonetheless indispensable. The new importance of cultural history means that the main components of any system of communication have been the subject of challenging revisions and new insights in the past few years: images, music, education, literacy, language, performance, rituals and information . . . Regretfully, we have had to leave aside the two first elements, but otherwise, these new advances have been taken on board. The rapid evolution of literacy, a concept masterfully imported from anthropology to medieval history by Michael Clanchy some thirty years ago,[70] and the consequent development of pragmatic literacy[71] are prerequisite to the positions assumed in late medieval societies by the *gens de savoir*, to use Jacques Verger's phrase:[72] by the clerics, the lawyers and the officers and administrators. Another field which appears essential for the study of communication is that of the development of languages, a point made by Dante himself at the beginning of the fourteenth century, and we are fortunate in having a remarkable and comparative study of the French language[73] which also throws light on the English language, a subject otherwise extremely well documented. All this is important not only for the chapters which deal with these social and professional categories, but also for those which are more precisely concerned with communicational problems (such as petition or literature, especially these texts which belong to what Janet Coleman once called 'the literature of protest').[74] However, unequal developments in French and British historiography, often caused by discordance at source level, have created distortions: there is no French equivalent to Nicholas Orme's work on primary and grammar schools in England,[75] and we still lack a systematic survey of a possible French literature of protest. The fact that this kind of writing is so prominent in England may also come from the existence there, in contrast with France, of a strong heretical movement, the Wycliffite and Lollard 'sect',[76] which, though it finally faded away in obscurity in

---

[70] Clanchy (2012).   [71] Britnell (1997). A recent survey is Chastang (2008).
[72] Verger (1998); Cobban (1988).   [73] Lusignan (2004).   [74] Coleman (1981).
[75] Orme (1973), (2006).   [76] Hudson (1988).

England, was to have a decisive impact on the religious history of Europe.[77] A third element which has more recently emerged and influenced our conception of communication is the reflexion initiated by Patrick Boucheron and Nicolas Offenstadt in Paris, very much at the moment we were starting to work on the Franco-English project, on the application of Jürgen Habermas' *Öffentlichkeit* ('public sphere') to medieval studies.[78]

Despite all these precautions, we are still left with the problem of that insidious form of national prejudice which is the product of historiographical tradition and from which no historian can easily free himself. To avoid this danger, we took a radical option and decided, as a rule, to have pairs of historians working together on each chapter. There was only one exception to prove the rule: Malcolm Vale's chapter on courts, because the author is an expert both on French and English history and since he has a European command of the subject. Another chapter (on representation) appears as single-authored, but this is due to reasons beyond our control, and Chris Fletcher has benefited from the experience and advice of his intended co-author, Neithard Bulst, who took part in most of our meetings. And for the last chapter, we made the unorthodox choice of two French authors, because we hoped that the methodological specificities of Aude Mairey's approach[79] could strike a new note in a field so rich in brilliant insular contributions that the selection of only one English contributor was well-nigh impossible (although this was also partly the result of Simon Walker's untimely death). This left us with a group of twenty-one scholars for which we were able, thanks to the CNRS research group *France-Iles Britanniques* to arrange several meetings in Oxford and one, appropriately, in Fontevraud. These meetings offered a good occasion for discussing and implementing new orientations in the field of political history which could affect a comparative approach. We thought that we would need two years to write the book. That was in 2002 . . .

BIBLIOGRAPHY

1. INTRODUCTION

Allmand, C. T., 1988. *The Hundred Years War. England and France at War c.1300–c.1450*, Cambridge.
    1992. *Henry V*, London.
Bove, B., 2009. *Le temps de la guerre de Cent Ans, 1328–1453*, Paris.

---

[77] Van Dussen (2012).
[78] Boucheron and Offenstadt (2011). See Watts (2004) for the situation in England.
[79] Mairey (2007).

Brown, M., 2013. *Disunited Kingdoms. Peoples and Politics in the British Isles, 1280–1460*, London.

Carpenter, C., 1997. *The Wars of the Roses. Politics and the Constitution in England, c.1437–1509*, Cambridge.

Chevalier, B., 1982. *Les bonnes villes de France du xive au xvie siècle*, Paris.

Davies, R. R., 2000. *The First English Empire. Power and Identities in the British Isles, 1093–1343*, Oxford.

Guenée, B., 1985. *States and Rulers in Later Medieval Europe*, Oxford.

Harriss, G. L., 2005. *Shaping the Nation. England 1360–1461*, Oxford.

Kaeuper, R., 1988. *War, Justice and Public Order: England and France in the Later Middle Ages*, Oxford.

Lewis, P. S., 1968. *Later Medieval France. The Polity*, London.

Prevenier, W. and Blockmans, W., 1999. *The Low Countries Under Burgundian Rule, 1369–1530*, Philadelphia.

Touati, F.-O., 2006. *Marc Bloch et l'Angleterre*, Paris.

Watts, J. L., 2009. *The Making of Polities: Europe, 1300–1500*, Cambridge.

2. SOURCES CITED

Aquinas, Thomas, *Opera Omnia*, Rome, 1979.

Chibnall, M. (ed.), *The Ecclesiastical History of Orderic Vitalis*, 6 vols., Oxford, 1969–80.

Le débat des hérauts d'armes de France et d'Angleterre suivi de The Debate between the Heralds of England and France by John Coke, ed. L. Pannier, Paris, 1877.

Fortescue, Sir John, *The Laws and Governance of England*, ed. S. Lockwood, Cambridge, 1997.

Four English Political Tracts of the Later Middle Ages, ed. J.-P. Genet, Camden Fourth Series, 18, London, 1977.

'L'honneur de la couronne de France'. *Quatre libelles contre les Anglais (vers 1418–vers 1429)*, ed. N. Pons, Société d'histoire de France, Paris, 1990.

Mum and the Sothsegger, ed. J. M. Dean, Kalamazoo, 2000.

3. FURTHER READING

Allmand, C. T., 1983. *Lancastrian Normandy, 1415–1450. The History of a Medieval Occupation*, Oxford.

Barralis, C., Boudet, J.-P., Delivré, F. and Genet, J.-Ph. (eds.), 2014. *Église et État, Église ou État?*, vol. X, Paris and Rome.

Bates, D., 1982. *Normandy before 1066*, London.

Bémont, C., 1884. *Simon de Montfort, Comte de Leicester*, Paris. (Trans. Engl. by E. F. Jacob, 1930, Manchester.)

(ed.), 1892. *Chartes de liberté anglaises 1100–1305*, Collection de Textes pour servir à l'enseignement de l'Histoire, Paris.

Bill, E. G. W., 1973. *University Reform in Nineteenth-Century Oxford. A Study of Henry Halford Vaughan, 1811–1885*, Oxford.

Bloch, M., 1960. *Seigneurie française, manoir anglais*, ed. G. Duby, Cahier des Annales, 16, Paris.

Bois, G., 1976. *Crise du féodalisme. Economie rurale et démographie en Normandie orientale du début du 14e siècle au milieu du 16e siècle*, Paris.

Boucheron, P. and Genet, J.-Ph. (eds.), 2013. *Marquer la ville*, 'Le pouvoir symbolique en Occident' Series, vol. VIII, Paris and Rome.

Boucheron, P. and Offenstadt, N., 2011. *L'espace public au Moyen Âge: débats autour de Jürgen Habermas*, Paris.

Bouhaïk-Gironès, M., 2007. *Les clercs de la Basoche et le théâtre comique: Paris, 1420–1550*, Paris.

Britnell, R. H., 1997. *Pragmatic Literacy. East and West, 1200–1330*, Woodbridge.

and Pollard, A. J. (eds.), 1995. *The McFarlane Legacy: Studies in Late Medieval Politics and Society*, Stroud.

Bulst, N., 1992. *Die französischen Generalstände von 1468 und 1484*, Sigmaringen.

Carpenter, C., 1992. *Locality and Polity. A Study of Warwickshire Landed Society, 1401–1499*, Cambridge.

Challet, V., et al. (eds.), 2007. *La société politique à la fin du xve siècle dans les royaumes ibériques et en Europe*, Valladolid and Paris.

Chaplais, P., 1982–2003. *English Diplomatic Practice*, 2 vols., London.

Charbonnier, P., 1973. *Guillaume de Murol, un petit seigneur auvergnat au début du XVe siècle*, Clermont-Ferrand.

Chastang, P., 2008. 'L'archéologie du texte médiéval. Autour des travaux récents sur l'écrit au Moyen Âge', *Annales HSS*, 63, 245–70.

Clanchy, M.T., 2012. *From Memory to Written Record, 1066 to 1307*, 3rd edn, Oxford.

Clough, C. H. (ed.), 1982. *Profession, Vocation and Culture in Late Medieval England, Essays Dedicated to the Memory of A. R. Myers*, Liverpool.

Cobban, A. B., 1988. *The Medieval English Universities: Oxford and Cambridge to 1500*, Aldershot.

Coleman, J., 1981. *English Literature in History. 1350–1400, Medieval Readers and Writers*, London.

Contamine, P., 1997. *La Noblesse au Royaume de France. De Philippe le Bel à Louis XI*, Paris.

1998. 'Le concept de société politique dans la France de la fin du Moyen Âge: définition, portée et limite', in S. Berstein and P. Milza (eds.), *Axes et méthodes de l'histoire politique*, Paris, pp. 261–72.

Cosneau, E., 1889. *Les Grands Traités de la guerre de Cent Ans*, Paris.

Cuttler, S. H., 2003. *The Law of Treason and Treason Trials in Later Medieval France*, Cambridge.

Davies, R. R. (ed.), 1986. *The British Isles 1100–1500: Comparisons, Contrasts and Connections: Colloquium*, Edinburgh.

1995. *The Revolt of Owain Glyn Dŵr*, Oxford.

2000. *The First English Empire. Power and Identities in the British Isles, 1093–1343*, Oxford.

2009. *Lords and Lordships in the British Isles in the Late Middle Ages*, Oxford.

Deruelle, B. and Gainot, B. (ed.), 2013. *La Construction du militaire*, Paris.

Favier, J., 1980. *La guerre de Cent Ans*, Paris.

Fédou, R., 1934. *Les hommes de loi lyonnais à la fin du Moyen âge: étude sur les origines de la classe de robe*, Annales de l'Université de Lyon, Lettres, 37 Lyon.

Foucault, M., 2004a. *Securité, territoire, population*, ed. M. Sennellart, Paris.
    2004b. *Naissance de la biopolitique*, ed. M. Sennellart, Paris.
    2012. *Du gouvernement des vivants*, ed. M. Sennellart, Paris.
Frame, R., 1995. *The Political Development of the British Isles 1100–1400*, Oxford.
Gaffuri, L. and Ventrone, P. (eds.), 2014. *Images, cultes, liturgies*, 'Le pouvoir symbolique en Occident' vol. V, Paris and Rome.
Gamberini, A., Genet, J.-Ph. and Zorzi, A. (eds.), 2011. *The Languages of Political Society. Western Europe, 14th–17th Centuries*, Rome.
Gauvard, C., 2010. *'De grace especial': crime, état et société en France à la fin du Moyen Âge*, 2nd edn, Paris.
Gazeau, V. and Genet, J.-P. (eds.), 2012. *France – Îles Britanniques, un couple impossible?*, Paris.
Genet, J.-P., 1990. 'L'État moderne; un modèle opératoire?', in J.-P. Genet, *L'État Moderne: Genèse*, Paris, pp. 261–81.
    1991. 'L'Angleterre médiévale', in M. Balard (ed.), *L'Histoire médiévale en France. Bilan et perspectives*, Paris, pp. 441–53.
    June 1997. 'La genèse de l'État moderne: les enjeux d'un programme de recherche', *Actes de la Recherche en Science Sociales*, 118, 3–18.
    2007. 'Les langages de la propagande', in V. Challet, J.-Ph. Genet, H. Rafael Oliva and J. Valdéon Baruque (eds.), *La société politique à la fin du xve siècle dans les royaumes ibériques et en Europe*, Valladolid-Paris, pp. 89–109.
    2014. *La légitimité implicite*, 'Le pouvoir symbolique en Occident' Series, vol. I, Paris and Rome.
    and Mineo, E. I. (eds.), 2015. *Marquer la prééminence sociale*, 'Le pouvoir symbolique en Occident' Series, vol. VI, Paris and Rome.
    and Ruggiu, F.-J. (eds.), 2011. *Du papier à l'archive, du privé au public. France et îles britanniques, deux mémoires*, Paris.
Goodman, A., 1992. *John of Gaunt. The Exercise of Princely Power in Fourteenth-Century Europe*, Harlow.
Griffiths, R. A., 1991. *King and Country: England and Wales in the Fifteenth Century*, London.
Guenée, B., 1963. *Tribunaux et gens de justice dans le Baillage de Senlis à la fin du Moyen Age*, Strasbourg, Publications de la Faculté des Lettres de Strasbourg, 144, Paris.
Harriss, G. L., 1993. 'Political Society and the Growth of Government in Late Medieval England', *Past and Present*, 138, 28–57.
Hicks, M., 1995. *Bastard Feudalism*, London.
    2010. *The Wars of the Roses*, New Haven.
Hilton, R. H., 1966. *A Medieval Society. The West Midlands at the End of the Thirteenth Century*, London.
Horrox, R. and Ormrod, W. M. (eds.), 2006. *A Social History of England, 1200–1500*, Cambridge.
Hudson, A., 1988. *The Premature Reformation: Wycliffite Texts and Lollard History*, Oxford.
Jones, M. C. E., 1970. *Ducal Brittany 1364–1399. Relations with England and France During the Reign of Duke John IV*, London.

1988. *The Creation of Brittany: A Late Medieval State*, London.

2003. *Between France and England: Politics, Power and Society in Late Medieval Brittany*, Aldershot.

Kerhervé, J., 1987. *L'État Breton aux xive et xve siècles: les ducs, l'argent et les hommes*, Paris.

Kitching, C., 2011. 'Changing Patterns of Access to Public and Private Archives in England, 1838 to 2005', in J.-P. Genet and F. J. Ruggiu (eds.), *Du papier à l'archive*, Paris.

Leitch, D., 2011. 'The Archival System of Britain and France: Similarities and Contrasts', in J.-P Genet and F.-J. Ruggiu (eds.), *Du papier à l'archive*, Paris.

Lot, F. and Fawtier, R., 1957. *Histoire des institutions françaises au Moyen Âge. Tone I: Institutions seigneuriales*, Paris.

Lusignan, S., 2004. *La langue des rois au Moyen Âge: le français en France et en Angleterre*, Paris.

McFarlane, K. B., 1973. *The Nobility of Later Medieval England*, Oxford.

Mairey, A., 2007. *Une Angleterre entre rêve et réalité. Littérature et société en Angleterre au xive siècle*, Paris.

Mattéoni, O., 1998. *Servir le prince: les officiers du duc de Bourbon à la fin du Moyen Âge (1356–1523)*, Paris.

2012. *Un prince face à Louis XI: Jean II de Bourbon, une politique en procès*, Paris.

Orme, N., 1973. *English Schools in the Middle Ages*, London.

2006. *Medieval Schools: From Roman Britain to Renaissance England*, London and New Haven.

Payling, S., 1991. *Political Society in Lancastrian England: The Greater Gentry of Nottinghamshire*, Oxford.

Perroy, E., 1933a. *L'Angleterre et le Grand Schisme d'Occident*, Paris.

1933b. *The Diplomatic Correspondence of Richard II*, Camden 3rd Series, XLVIII, London.

Petit-Dutaillis, C., 1908–28. *Studies and Notes Supplementary to Stubbs' Constitutional History Down to the Great Charter*, 3 vols., Historical Series, 7, Manchester.

1936. *The Feudal Monarchy in France and England from the Tenth to the Thirteenth Century*, Eng. edn, London.

Réville, A., 1892. 'L'abiuratio regni: histoire d'une institution anglaise', *Revue Historique*, 1, 1–42.

1898. *Le soulèvement des travailleurs d'Angleterre en 1381*, Paris.

Reydellet, M., 1981. *La royauté dans la littérature latine de Sidoine Apollinaire à Isidore de Séville*, Rome.

Richmond, C., 1990. *The Paston Family in the Fifteenth Century: The First Phase*, Cambridge.

1996. *The Paston Family in the Fifteenth century: Fastolf's Will*, Cambridge.

2001. *The Paston Family in the Fifteenth Century. Endings*, Manchester.

Ruggiu, F.-J., 2011. 'Defining Public and Private Papers in England. The Work of the Historical Manuscripts Commission and of the National Register of Archives', in J.-P. Genet and F.-J. Ruggiu (eds.), *Du papier à l'archive*, Paris, pp. 41–58.

Saul, N., 1981. *Knights and Esquires: the Gloucestershire Gentry in the Fourteenth Century*, London.

Schnerb, B., 2005. *L'État bourguignon*, new edn, Paris.

Senellart, M., 1995. *Les arts de gouverner. Du 'regimen' médiéval au concept de gouvernement*, Paris.

Sharpe, R., 2012. 'Pierre Chaplais (1920–2006)', *Biographical Memoirs of the British Academy*, 11, 115–50.

Small, G., 1997. *George Chastelain and the Shaping of Valois Burgundy: Political and Historical Culture at Court in the Fifteenth Century*, Woodbridge.

Stubbs, W., 1913. *Histoire constitutionnelle de l'Angleterre*, trans. Fr. by G. Lefèvre, 3 vols., Paris.

Taylor, C. (ed.), 2006. *Debating the Hundred Years War: Pour ce que plusieurs (La loy salicque) and A Declaration of the Trew and Dewe Title of Henry VIII*, Camden 5th Series, 29, Cambridge.

Vale, M. G. A., 1970. *English Gascony, 1399–1453. A Study of War, Government and Politics During the Later Stages of the Hundred Years War*, Oxford.

1990. *The Origins of the Hundred Years War. The Angevin Legacy 1250–1340*, Oxford.

Van Dussen, M., 2012. *From England to Bohemia: Heresy and Communication in the Later Middle Ages*, Cambridge.

Vaughan, R. 1970a. *Philip the Bold: The Formation of the Burgundian State*, London.

1970b. *Philip the Good. The Apogee of Burgundy*, London.

1973a. *Valois Burgundy*, London.

1973b *Charles the Bold: The Last Valois Duke of Burgundy*, London.

1979. *John the Fearless: The Growth of Burgundian Power*, London.

Verger, J., 1998. *Les gens de savoir en Europe au Moyen Âge*. 2nd edn, Paris.

Watts, J. L., 2004. 'The Pressure of the Public on Later Medieval Politics', in Linda Clark and Christine Carpenter (eds.), *The Fifteenth Century. IV. Political Culture in Late Medieval Britain*, Woodbridge, pp. 159–180.

Weber, M., 1978. *Economy and Society. An Outline of Interpretative Sociology*, ed. G. Roth and C. Wittich, Berkeley.

2   Courts

Malcolm Vale

The one-word title of this contribution, to a colloquium devoted to 'Governing', may give rise to potential misunderstandings, and I shall attempt to correct them straight away. The 'courts' to which the title refers are not courts of law or courts of justice. They are those gatherings of influential, and not-so-influential, people who formed the entourages of rulers in both formal and, in the context of 'governing', informal settings. The quasi-institutional court co-existed with much looser, more informal bodies which filled the space around later medieval rulers. To 'hold court' had of course for a long time been a regular, recognised feature of kingly and princely rule, and the occasional, 'full' or 'solemn' court was a normal accompaniment to the celebration of the major feasts of the liturgical calendar.

But we can perhaps legitimately extend the term to apply to a much wider range of types of gathering around a ruler. Courts could – as they do today – consist of informally invited advisers, favourites and cronies. The Hutton Inquiry (2004) built up a picture of 'governing' in Britain today: where 'network' was clearly more important than 'office' (especially elected or ministerial office), while 'idea' (if, by that, political ideas are meant) seemed virtually non-existent. When we look at fourteenth- and fifteenth-century courts, however, we may find that similar informalities in the style of governing are evident, or at least implicit, in what the records tell us. We may not find quite the same kind of sitting-room sofa government going on, but it is clear that some government was conducted by later medieval rulers in their bedrooms, at the hunt, on the road, while they were getting up or being shaved, or on their way to and from Mass. So Edward II of England (1307–27) could, on Wednesday 16 August 1312, tell two of his closest *curiales* (Aymer de Valence and Hugh le Despenser) that John Sandal, the treasurer, had met him on the road between Canterbury and Faversham, bringing favourable news from the papal court. They were to be at Faversham to hear the king's will the next day 'bien matin a nostre lever'.[1] As the matters to be dealt with included the negotiation of a loan from the pope and support against the baronial Ordainers, Edward had every incentive to rise early on that occasion. As a test case, we can use evidence largely derived from the reign of Edward II and his French contemporaries, mainly because it is so rich in certain kinds of documentation, especially diplomatic and other memoranda, drafts, newsletters and other correspondence. Before going any further, however, we need, very briefly, to define our terms a little more precisely and try to establish the underlying structures beneath this level of political society.

A number of questions need to be asked about the court and its nature in the later Middle Ages. It might be worthwhile to rehearse some of them here. First, was the court simply an occasion, or event, or can the emergence of a more durable, formal body with its own structures, personnel and procedures, be observed at this time? Or were those infra-structures still simply provided by the household? Secondly, when, where and why does a distinction between an 'upper' (that is noble and clerical) and 'lower' (that is domestic and menial) household appear? Answers to these questions can be found, but they will necessarily differ according to time and place. But what seems abundantly clear, in all instances, is that the court was indeed formed and shaped by the ruler's household. Its spine or backbone was composed of household offices. But the ruler's permanent domestic establishment, that is, the household consisting of its various departments or *metiers* – hall, chamber, buttery, pantry, stable, wardrobe and so on – by no means coincided with the full extent of the court. This could be a much larger, or indeed much smaller body, as occasion demanded.

Yet tendencies towards a more formal stratification within the house-hold seem to be emerging during the thirteenth century. King's clerks, king's knights and king's squires begin to form an upper household, retained as they were with fees and liveries of robes and furs on a regular, seasonal basis. The lower, or service household – the true 'below stairs' – comprised a less fluid body of officers and servants, represent-ing the origins of what became known in fifteenth-century England as the *Domus* Providencie, as opposed to the ceremonial, upper *Domus Magnificiencie*.[2] It also seems that the chamber, rather than the hall, *chambre* rather than *salle*, provided that part of a king's or prince's domes-tic establishment from which a formal upper household began to grow. A distinct rise in the status (and wages) of the chamber personnel is

---

[1] The National Archives (TNA) (formerly PRO), SC 1/49, no. 12.
[2] See Morgan (1973), pp. 2–4.

visible in England under Edward I, and chamber knights are clearly evident under Edward II and Edward III (1327–77). In France, the ever-growing body of *chambellans,* many of noble origins, suggests that the holding of a household office was now an important element in the career patterns of young nobles at the court of France.

By the mid-thirteenth century, moreover, in both England and France, the old hereditary officers of the royal household – seneschal, constable, marshal, butler and so on – performed occasional service only at plenary, 'full' or 'solemn' courts, while the king's daily needs were met by the permanent personnel of the household. This did not mean that the hereditary officers were politically unimportant, or that their duties and rights could be ignored – as Edward I (1272–1307) discovered in 1297. But the increasing size of the permanent staff around the ruler commands our attention. This consisted of the clerks who had formed the nucleus of princely courts since a very much earlier date, together with a secular group of chamberlains, knights and squires who formed an elite normally retained for life in peace and war. The king's knights could, of course, spend quite long periods out of court, busily engaged on the king's business and their own. They provided an increasingly valuable source of experienced and often talented representatives of the ruler, whose functions, as we shall see, were not exclusively military.

With the rise, during the thirteenth century, of the practice whereby regular, seasonal, carefully graded liveries of cloth, robes, fur and cash were distributed at Christmas, Easter, Pentecost and other feasts, a court society was in the process of formation. In 1301, for example, Edward I gave liveries to 60 king's knights, banneret and bachelor; Edward III was distributing livery to nearer 160 by the 1340s.[3] The quality of the cloth and furs given to them was one of the defining features whereby members of the upper household could be identified before the introduction, in the course of the fourteenth century, of badges, heraldic insignia and livery collars. Yet the 'full' court came together only on specific occasions, normally coinciding with the liturgical feasts – above all, Christmas and Pentecost – and this fundamental rhythm of court life did not die with the later Middle Ages. The 'occasional' court, characterised by heightened ceremony, often associated with special events or anniversaries in the life of a ruling house, was a hallmark of European imperial, royal and princely culture until its end under the houses of Habsburg, Hohenzollern and Saxe-Coburg-Gotha, later known as the House of Windsor.

If we consider courts in the frame set out for this project – that is, of 'governing' – some obvious points can be made. The part played by

---

[3] See TNA, E.101/361/17; 371/21/60, 61, 88, 90; and 383/4.

members of courts, or of court circles, in internal or domestic government perhaps needs little comment. That seems abundantly clear – a ruler was bound to seek advice from, listen to rumours voiced by, and advance the causes of those who had his ear. The consequences of this could of course be disastrous – both for the favourites, *mignons* and cronies themselves and, in the English case, for the ruler himself. Edward II, Richard II (1377–99), Henry VI (1422–61) – all fell victim to the consequences of alleged abuse of power and position by members of their courts. French kings were not subject to such violent behaviour, sacral beings that they were, but the fate of household men such as Enguerrand de Marigny in 1315 closely parallels that of Piers Gaveston in 1312, both of them chamberlains-in-chief to their respective monarchs. But what is sometimes less obvious is the role of such people, often holding household offices, as intermediaries *between* European courts. We have, however, first of all to establish who was 'in power' at a given court at a given time – the ebb and flow of patronage and favour could lead to a confusing kaleidoscope of 'ins' and 'outs' at court. When such records as minutes and memoranda of council meetings, or notes of decisions taken and by whom, tend not to survive, how can we be sure who held the reins of power, or at least was close enough (changing the metaphor) to the captain of the ship of state to play a significant part in steering it through what could be extremely rough seas? The metaphor was not unknown, by the way, in the fourteenth century: in 1314, one of Edward II's proctors at the *Parlement* of Paris spoke of the affairs of Aquitaine in just this way, referring to the intractable problem of Gascon appeals from the king-duke's authority to the Crown of France. 'Gascon business,' he said, 'is rightly called a great and dangerous sea, full of shipwrecks, with no safe haven.'[4] Who then were the ship's officers, responsible under their captain for negotiating that sea?

One means of establishing who may have influenced whom, and how, has often been traced to such surviving records as lists of witnesses to certain transactions or decisions, or the endorsement of writs and warrants with such phrases as 'teste me ipso', ' par le roi' or 'par le chancelier', plus a list of others present, sometimes named, sometimes not, often incomplete and ending simply with the words 'and many others'. These are not much good for discovering who was most likely to have the king's ear or to possess real political clout with the ruler. More helpful are, perhaps, the increasingly large number of letters sent from one ruler's court to another's, of which copies or versions were also dispatched to a number of named individuals apart from the ruler. Recent events in this country

---

[4] TNA, E 175/2/5/1 cited in Chaplais (1981), Chapter VIII, p. 61.

have shown the significance of those to whom emails are copied among the governing elite. In the fourteenth century, correspondence between the papal chancery and secular rulers, for instance, as well as the letters issued by those rulers' administrations, reveal the common practice of copying or circulating missives to members of the court circle as well as the king.

In October 1318, for example, Pope John XXII was attempting to defend his Gascon kinsman, Jourdain de l'Isle, from prosecution by both Plantagenet and Capetian authorities for his (Jourdain's) crimes, and was trying to stop his forthcoming trial by combat with Alexandre de Caumont. On 25 October 1318, the pope wrote to both Edward II and Philip V (1316–22) of France, urging clemency. The papal letters were copied, with suitable changes and endorsements, to Aymer de Valence, earl of Pembroke and Thomas, earl of Lancaster, at Edward's court; and to Louis d'Evreux and Henri de Sully, hereditary *grand bouteiller* of France (on whom, more later), at Philip's.[5] They were requested to use their influence with their respective monarchs. No doubt the papal intelligence service, through its nuncios and other agents and plants, knew exactly who was 'in' at court in both England and France at this juncture. It was not that the pope felt that the only way of getting anything done by Edward II was to solicit the aid of his courtiers – Philip V was similarly treated and there are many other examples of the practice. In May 1317, for instance, we find Edward II himself writing to Philip V of France and others at his court, appealing to their sense of honour so that Aymer de Valence, who had been captured in France, might be released. The other addressees included Charles of Valois, Louis d'Evreux, Gautier de Chatillon, John of Brittany (a useful Anglo-French intermediary), John of Luxembourg, Charles, count of La Marche and Anselme de Geneville.[6] Yet, as we shall see, there were certainly signs that Edward II's interest in, and application to, the business of government was not all it should have been.

In the conduct of relations between rulers, the existence of inter-mediaries who could command the confidence and trust of both sides was essential. Those with important connections at the courts of both parties were especially valuable. As Pierre Chaplais has shown, the constant diplomatic use by Edward I, Edward II and their successors of men who often had multiple loyalties, with a sure command of other languages, was very common. Some of these were clerks, but there were also laymen. One means of retaining and rewarding such 'foreign' representatives as

---

[5] 'Documents pontificaux sur la Gascogne' ed. Guérard (1896), nos. 70, 71, 75.
[6] See *Foedera*, ed. Rymer et al. (1816–30), vol. II, pp. 329–30 (10 May 1317).

Maurice and Amaury de Craon; Henri de Sully; Alphonse d'Espagne; Otto, Lord of Cuijk; or Hartung von Klux was to give them pensions, fees or annuities, and household positions.[7] These men all became English king's knights, although they were liegemen of other princes, while the last of them – the German knight, Hartung von Klux – was created a member of the Order of the Garter by Henry IV and went on to serve the Lancastrians as a trusted envoy and negotiator until 1440. They in effect joined a court circle, while retaining their places in the courts and allegiances of other rulers. The Craon family are a particularly good example of this practice. On 4 November 1323, Amaury III, Lord of Craon and Sablé, last hereditary seneschal of Anjou, Maine and Touraine, wrote to Edward II voicing his profound anxiety about the state into which Anglo-French relations had degenerated. The outrage at St-Sardos in the Agenais threatened to precipitate war between Edward and Charles IV (1322–8) and, such was his concern, that he immediately spoke to both Alphonse d'Espagne, Lord of Lunel, and Mathieu de Trie, marshal of France, both of whom he knew to be well-disposed towards Edward. Amaury went on:

Je vous escris a ce qe pur Dieu vous y purveiez du bon conseil et remede, qi y sount necessairs, a la fin deschuyre le contenz pereillous dentre vous, et pur nurrir lamur et la pees de vous deux ensemble qil voudroit garder, sicome je lay peu sentir avaunt ces choses avenues, si en vous ne defaut, en la separacion de la quele poet gesir la tresgrant doute pereillouse de la plus grant partie de tote crestienete.[8]

The Lord of Craon, knowing where power lay at Edward's court, also wrote on the same day to Hugh le Despenser the younger, copying his letter to the king to him, but also adding a substantial supplement of information and advice. He offered his services as a go-between, given that he was writing from his lordship of Sable in Anjou and that Charles IV had been holding his All Saints court at Angers. This must have been where Amaury had spoken to both Alphonse d'Espagne and Matthieu de Trie so soon after receiving the news of the St-Sardos incident. In interestingly affectionate terms, he told Despenser:

Cher sire et tres grauntz amis. Vous savez qe tres grant affeccion de cuer ne se puet tenir de ruser et esloigner de tout son poair le mal et le peril de ce qil aime. Et, sire, ce me fait enhardir de escrire a mon seignur le roi Dengleterrre en la manere contenue en ceste copie.[9]

---

[7] For their careers see Chaplais (2003), pp. 69–73.

[8] B[ritish] L[ibrary], MS Cotton Caligula D.III, no. 7/1; printed in *The War of Saint-Sardos*, ed. Chaplais (1954), p. 1.

[9] BL, MS Cotton Calig. D.III, no. 7/2; printed in *The War of Saint-Sardos*, ed. Chaplais (1954), pp. 1–2.

The reasons for Amaury de Craon's concern are not hard to find. He was one of the last representatives before the Hundred Years War of that class of French noble, who held lands within the kingdom of France, but also served the Plantagenet king-duke of Aquitaine – one of the greatest peers of France – in his French lordships. His pedigree could hardly have been more distinguished nor eminent. The family of Craon had produced a long line of Angevin and Lusignan office-holders and soldiers, including a hero of romance (Maurice de Craon), and it was natural that they should be drawn upon by the Plantagenets. His father, another Maurice, had served both Edward I and Philip III (1270–85) of France as an envoy and household officer, while Amaury himself had been appointed seneschal of Aquitaine by Edward II in July 1313, as one result of the amicable meetings between the family and court circles of France and England at Paris and Poissy of that year. He was a king's knight of Edward II, with a retaining fee and a salary as seneschal of the duchy. This was a high-ranking office, with extensive powers, demanding of its holder a wide range of skills: military, legal and diplomatic, although a small council at Bordeaux necessarily assisted him in fulfilling those functions. Amaury de Craon's service to the king-duke was thus performed both at the *Parlement* of Paris, where he was involved in Gascon cases, and in the duchy itself, where he proved a competent and hardworking officer, founding the new settlement or bastide of Créon (in the Entre-deux-Mers) in 1315, but also serving militarily in Flanders for the Crown of France in 1316. He left office as seneschal in that year, only to be reappointed for a second term of office (an unusual occurrence) in July 1320, serving for a further two years. The fact that he had feet in both camps – Capetian and Plantagenet – and was on terms of easy familiarity with men such as Despenser, Aymer de Valence and other *familiares* of Edward II, as well as their opposite numbers in the Capetian court, did not, however, make him exceptional or unique.

It is one of the paradoxes of Anglo-French relations in this period that beside the many instances we have of Anglo-French friction and conflict, very strong affinities existed between their ruling classes, often filtered through the courts of both rulers. Culturally these people were more or less one – francophone, chivalric, cosmopolitan in tastes, highly status-conscious, well versed in the courtly attributes of *courtoisie, debonairete, largesse* and, perhaps above all else, persuasive speech. Enguerrand de Marigny and Aymer de Valence were both noted as 'beaux parleurs', just as later figures such as Pierre de Breze at the court of Charles VII (1422–61) were. Marigny and De Valence were, to judge from their surviving correspondence and recorded behaviour, on extremely good terms. Moreover, the rise of king's (and queen's) chamberlains (*chambellans*) in both England and France, and the increased status of the office of the chamber from the early fourteenth century onwards, saw the emergence of chamber knights and chamber squires into the limelight of politics and diplomacy. Besides Amaury de Craon, king's knight of both Edward II and Philip V, other French nobles – of equally high and distinguished status – served both crowns. One of the best examples of a household officer of the Capetians who also acted for the English Crown was Henri de Sully, hereditary butler of France. Like Amaury de Craon, he became embroiled in the events leading to the outbreak of Anglo-French war in October 1324. He had been acting as an envoy for both Philip V and then Charles IV when, in October 1322, he was captured and ransomed by the Scots at Byland. Edward II paid most of his ransom (1,000 marks). He was retained at court by Edward with a pension of 400 pounds per year for as long as he stayed there (*quando in curia est*). He was back in England in July 1324 and, on his departure for France as an envoy at a particularly fraught period of Anglo-French tension, he was given the gift appropriate to his status by Edward: two silver bowls with silver-gilt bases, enamelled with the English royal arms, and issued from the treasury in the Tower of London.[10] It was on the occasion of this mission that he wrote to Hugh le Despenser (on 7 September 1324) about the failure of his attempt to appease Charles IV's indignation and prevent the invasion of Aquitaine by a French army. His letter gives us a glimpse of the realities of Anglo-French tension at the highest level:

Je alai par devers monseignur le roy de France a Mont Pipeau pres de Orliens, et li baillai la lettre du roy Dangleterre, monseignur, de creance et li dis les besoignes en la presence de son conseil le mieux que jai peu ne sceu... A ce, sire, me fu respondu que on avoit bien oi et entendu ce que je disoie, ni autre response ne me fu faite. Lors, sire, je demandai sil estoit mestiers que je attendisse plus pour poursuire response, ou en quel temps il voudroient que je retournasse pour ce mesmes. *Me fu respondu, sire, que je pouaie bien aler a mes besoignes.*[11]

In other words, Sully was dismissed without a further hearing and Edward's other clerical envoy, Master John Shoreditch, was not granted an audience at all. The war had in fact begun. In his proclamation to the inhabitants of the duchy of Aquitaine of 30 September 1324, Edward laid the full responsibility for the war at Charles IV's feet, referring to Sully's treatment at the hands of the king and his council.[12] But Sully was at pains to continue in both Despenser's and Edward's good grace,

---

10   TNA, E 101/381/4, m.4r; *The War of Saint-Sardos*, ed. Chaplais (1954), pp. 57–8.
11   TNA, SC 1/50, no. 45, printed in *The War of Saint-Sardos*, ed. Chaplais (1954), pp. 56–7.
12   TNA, C.61/36, m. 24r; printed in *Foedera*, ed. Rymer et al. (1816–30), II (i), p. 572.

as well as that of Charles IV, and offered to act as a source of news and assistance:

Sire, se nulles autres nouvelles me viennent dont je ferai mon pouair continuel-ment sanz cesser, Dieux le sceit, je le vous ferai savoir par mon propre message, non une foiz, mais pluseurs, toutes foiz que li cas si offrera, et je porrai avoir congie de passage. Sire, je vous pri que vous me veuillez recommender a mon trescher seignur monsire le roy Dangleterre, et vous plaise a moi tenir pour si vostre comme je sui et doi estre.[13]

This paid off because, when the Anglo-French agreement (*concordia*) which ended hostilities was drawn up in November 1325, Sully was acting as Charles IV's seneschal in Aquitaine, and delivered the duchy back to the young Edward, duke of Aquitaine, earl of Chester, count of Ponthieu and Montreuil (later Edward III), who performed homage for it. The fact that terms were agreed so relatively quickly was in part due to the role played by men such as Sully. He was among those with whom Isabella, queen of England, had dined at Corbeil on 26 May 1325 during her peace-making mission to France. His accommodating behaviour over the submission of Edward II's officers in Aquitaine, and their immediate reinstatement, was praised by the hard-nosed and often dyspeptic former constable of Bordeaux, the clerk John Travers. He told Edward II:

Et sire, . . . quant il [Sully] ad este avise par vostre counseil sur le mieux pur vous, il ad fait tant qen cea en si avise et aimable manere ceo qil poei[t], qil semble a moi qil eyme molt cherement vostre honur et profit.[14]

Accommodation, compromise, reciprocity, mutual understanding – these were the hallmarks of effective Anglo-French diplomacy, and it was entrusted as much to these knightly, courtly laymen as to the learned ecclesiastics and clerks. And it was not confined to formal appointments to diplomatic missions by either side – informality was again a constant feature of this world. Encounters at tournaments, jousts, great feasts, smaller-scale dinners and all kinds of broadly 'social' occasions marked the daily conduct of what we rather grandly style 'Anglo-French rela-tions'. But the advent of a new royal house in France after 1328 tended to have a disruptive effect, and the old *modus operandi* underwent changes which, if anything, produced more opportunities for abrasion and fric-tion. The House of Valois had already begun the process under the later Capetians: anti-Plantagenet sentiment, fuelled by Charles of Valois' resentment of Edward I's arbitrations of Franco-Aragonese affairs, were

[13] TNA, SC 1/50, no. 45; printed in *The War of Saint-Sardos*, ed. Chaplais (1954), pp. 56–7.

[14] TNA, SC 1/34, no. 190; printed in *The War of Saint-Sardos*, ed. Chaplais (1954), p. 240.

already visible by the later 1280s; Enguerrand de Marigny paid for his relative anglophilia, among many other things, with his life; and the war of St-Sardos was as much the war of Charles, count of Valois as it was of Charles IV, king of France.

Governing made demands upon later medieval rulers which some were clearly unable or simply unwilling to meet and discharge. There could be courts without kings at certain times, not merely because those kings were infants, invalids, absentees or lunatics. Although he might be physically present – as were Henry III (1216–72), Edward II or Henry VI – the king's application to the business of government, and enthusiasm for it, could be distinctly lukewarm. Something of the varying degrees of royal assiduity, or effective abrogation of responsibility, can be learnt from the part played by monarchs themselves in the petitioning process. In circumstances of royal inattention, or of disinclination to rule, the members of court and household assume central roles – under Edward II, the Despensers, their allies and clients, in effect governed. Departments of state could be bypassed, their officers suborned or bullied, and the distribution of favour and patronage effectively usurped by the dominant interest at court. The king's *familiares* would naturally move centre stage in such circumstances. They appear to have encouraged the very behaviour which removed the king from the action of the play. There is some archival evidence to support the chroniclers' assertions that Edward 'undervaluing the society of the magnates . . . fraternised with buffoons, singers, actors, carters, ditchers, oarsmen, sailors and others who practised mechanical arts'.[15] According to the interrogation of a royal messenger in July 1314, the king could not be expected to win battles (such as Bannockburn, 28 June 1314) when he spent his time 'idling and occupying himself in making ditches and digging and other improper occupations' (*alia indecencia*).[16]

A rare, surviving daily account or 'journal' for Edward's chamber (April 1324 to March 1325) is revealing in this respect. In January 1325 he was at least overseeing the digging in and planting of beans in his garden at King's Langley; he paid one of his carters and one of his coopers for 'playing' (probably dancing) before him at Mortlake; and a near-obsession with boats and boating, including the payment of a group of female singers from Lambeth who sang 'on the Thames' during boating parties in May and June 1324, is evident.[17] They had been secured by one of his *familiares*, the Gascon squire Bourgeois de Tilh. What these men actually did, as chamber squires, is tantalisingly described in an

[15] Higden (1865–86), pp. viii, 298.   [16] Cited by Johnstone (1933), p. 267.
[17] TNA, E 101/380/4, ff.. 22v, 24r; E 101/375/8, ff. 8r, 9v.

entry on 12 February 1325 which tells us that Bourgeois de Tilh and Giles d'Espagne, both chamber squires, 'played' before the king and sustained burns on their thighs and buttocks, for which they were given money gifts by him.[18] Was this an early, English version of the notorious *bal des ardants* at the court of Charles VI (1380–1422) of France? What form this 'playing' took is unclear but it gives rise to some suspicion, especially in view of Edward's known *penchant* for male actors and dancers, fifty-four of whom danced naked before him at Pontoise during his French visit of June 1313.[19] The difficulties which some of his officers encountered in getting replies to their letters out of Edward also suggests that the business of governing was not always uppermost in his mind. Hence Amaury de Craon, as seneschal of Aquitaine, could write to the king, 'with due reverence', from Bordeaux on 18 December 1315 about Gascon affairs which were threatening to lead to appeals before the court of France if something was not done about them. Although Edward had written from York on 25 July, saying that he would be communicating his wishes to the seneschal by 15 August, nothing had been received by mid-December. The king was urgently requested by Amaury 'to write to me, in so far as your honour – which may God augment – [is concerned] and so that this business ... shall in no way be devolved outside your court of Gascony through default of justice'.[20] Further delay would lead to recourse to Paris, as had been the case in other recent instances as a result of Edward's inordinate delay in replying to such requests.

We cannot, perhaps, examine the processes of governing in later medieval England and France without also looking at misgovernment or non-government. As a major vehicle of dysfunctional governing the court plays a significant role. The more successful and effective monarchs seem to have been careful to deal with their immediate entourages in a more even-handed fashion (as did Edward III of England) and to ensure that the magnates were summoned, as was their right, to the assemblies of formal courts at the great feasts of the year.

Above all, the retaining of a broadly based array of king's knights and king's squires, receiving the king's livery, whose numbers and distribution might also represent the status of the magnates by whom they were in turn retained, became increasingly essential to the stability of English political society. The court of Edward III, wrote the Liégeois chronicler Jean le Bel, drew more knights and squires to it than that of Philip VI (1328–50) of France because 'he loved his knights and squires and rewarded them well'.[21] So much depended upon the informal checks

---

[18] TNA, E 101/380/4, f. 24v.   [19] TNA, E 101/375/8, f. 30r.
[20] TNA, SC 1/55, no. 43.   [21] Le Bel (1904–5), pp. i, 155–6.

and balances which competent rulers were able to operate. The court remained a power-centre because it was simply where the ruler was, and those with whom he most frequently came into contact had easier access to that power. Familiarity can breed contempt, or indifference, but it can also offer a key to power and influence. To get the ear of a courtier was becoming as important as getting the ear of the ruler, state bureaucracies notwithstanding. But perhaps things had always been like that in the world of the great and powerful.

Although this contribution has tended to concentrate upon the reigns of the three Plantagenet Edwards and their French contemporaries, it also raises more general issues about the role of the court in later medieval government and political society. First, problems will always arise concerning both the nature of courts and their evolution: it could be argued, for instance, that differences between courts (in both space and time) simply embodied and reflected differences between rulers and their styles of government. Courts tended to be personality-driven bodies, often supplying arenas in which the ruler was perhaps freer to operate than in any other. It is, therefore, often difficult to discern any very clear linear progression in the court's evolution, or any obvious place for it in the onward march of the modern state. Its historiography has been very much influenced by theses such as that of Norbert Elias, and by the formulation of models derived essentially from the permanent, resident establishments in those monumental piles at Versailles, Vienna or Potsdam. The peripatetic, mobile court of the later Middle Ages was a rather different phenomenon. In this context, more and better itineraries of rulers are needed – Louis XI (1461–83) of France remains the exception which proves the rule. Further efforts to construct more accurate accounts of the movements and displacements of rulers and their followings are essential if we are to be able to generalise, especially from the French evidence. Throughout our period the 'centre' (that is, the king's court and household) constantly came to at least some areas of the 'periphery', as well as attracting the 'periphery' to the 'centre'. The great liturgical feasts continued to draw the politically powerful to the ruler's presence in plenary gatherings of the occasional court. As a counterpoint to this, the court moved, throughout the year, around a ruler's territories. It was not simply a question of the aristocratic bees buzzing around a Versailles-style honeypot, or honey-trap, during our period.

Secondly, the question of the nature of the relationship between court and household inevitably arises. Could there be courts without households? The answer would appear to be a negative one, because the household and its offices provided a structure or backbone for every court, whether those offices were exercised actively, honorifically, ceremonially or occasionally. Sometimes these categories overlapped and coincided, sometimes not. A potential source of difference between court and household could, however, be found in the degree of public accountability for household expenditure which is seen in England, for example, under Henry IV, Henry VI and the early Tudors, from which the court seems to be exempt. But, yet again, overlap could occur and household expenditure, especially on the upper household, could in effect represent court expenditure. There does not seem to be the equivalent of this level of conciliar and parliamentary scrutiny, and apparent control, in France.

Thirdly, power and its location must be a crucial theme in any study of later medieval government and of the role of the court in that process. Where did power lie, in the court or in the household? The evidence suggests that it lay, generally, in the court, because the actions of a ruler in his court could often cut across, and sometimes bypass, the more formal institutions of government. Members of the lower household, and even domestic servants, could occasionally be promoted to higher office and consequently gain political power and influence (such as Marigny under Philip IV) but that could be very dangerous both for monarchs and for the *mignons* themselves. It has been pointed out that, in some cases, the French evidence indicates that there could be a substantial degree of overlap between court, household and council. This can be found among the *conseillers et chambellans du roi*, particularly from the second half of the fourteenth century onwards. Also, in the earlier part of the century, the rise of the chamber and of the office of chamberlain/*chambellan*, as a higher-status position, could be emphasised in this context.

Fourthly, the significance, throughout this period, of members of courts and households as important intermediaries should be emphasised. They were intermediaries in two senses: between rulers and subjects, and between rulers themselves. Courtiers were go-betweens on both the domestic and international – or rather, inter-kingdom or inter-principality – stages.

In domestic politics, the petitioning process, whereby a dialogue between ruler and subjects was established and perpetuated, did not always involve only two parties: it could be a three-party nexus. Access to a ruler's ear, through the enlisting, retaining and/or bribing of a *curialis*, clearly carried important political and material benefits for all kinds of subject, both clerical and lay. A ruler's familiars, such as Pierre de Breze (d. 1465) under Charles VII of France, or some of the English king's knights and king's squires in the fifteenth century, formed an increasingly significant element in that dialogue. A further intermediary function was fulfilled by courtiers: in inter-state relations. Far more work is required to be done on these court and household milieux in the context not only of diplomacy, but also of other kinds of relationship between powers – political, social and cultural. The personnel who served in England's continental possessions, for example, were often drawn from the ranks of the household to provide expertise in these matters. Further prosopographical studies are called for in this area. There may well be career patterns here that need to be charted.

Fifthly, the role of the court as a centre, or platform, for propaganda and representational culture, and its part in state formation, have yet to be properly investigated. Irrespective of the person and personal eccentricities of the king, the court, when formally and ceremonially assembled, had a certain presence and existence of its own. In England, that came about on 'the festival days, or when estate should be showed'.[22] As an agent of state formation, however, the court's role could be offset by its function as a medium for essentially dynastic propaganda, and for the formation of royal ideologies which were not necessarily 'national' in their content. In English and French national mythologies, the distinctly non-English St George stood beside St Edward the Confessor; the distinctly non-French Saint-Michel beside Saint-Denis. In some ways, the court played as important a role in state *de*formation as in state formation – retarding in some respects the emergence of impersonal, publically accountable government. The court, it could be argued, contributed as much to dysfunctional rule, and to the prolongation of the household's functions in both government and administration, as to the promotion of modern bureaucratic government or the continuity of the state. The grand narratives of, among others, Elias and Elton, have to be deconstructed.

Last but not least, two further points emerge from the discussions accompanying the project: first, the continuing military importance of the court, reflected in the household's role as a source of military personnel – as apparent under Henry VIII of England as under Edward I. In France, recipients of royal pensions and annuities also enjoyed household membership and could perform significant military functions, as in Valois Burgundy, while household departments, such as wardrobe or chamber, could still facilitate and organise war. Secondly, the image of the court as a den of iniquity opens up a huge area of discussion, given the large volume of anti-curial literature, some of it entirely based on long-standing *topoi*. But it may also have had some impact upon perceptions of the court in the wider world of disaffected noblemen and disgruntled subjects, all of whom remained a constant feature of later medieval political society.

[22] Myers (1959), pp. 84–5.

BIBLIOGRAPHY

1. INTRODUCTION

Bumke, J., 1991. *Courtly Culture: Literature and Society in the High Middle Ages*, tr. T. Dunlop, Berkeley.

Elias, N., 1983. *The Court Society*, Oxford.

Scattergood, V. J. and Sherborne, J. W. (eds.), 1983. *English Court Culture in the Later Middle Ages*, London.

Vale, J., 1982. *Edward III and Chivalry. Chivalric Society and its Context, 1270–1350*, Woodbridge.

Vale, M., 2001. *The Princely Court. Medieval Courts and Culture in North-West Europe, 1270–1380*, Oxford.

2. SOURCES CITED

Foedera, Conventiones, Literae..., ed. T. Rymer et al. Records Commission Edition, 4 vols., London, 1816–30.

'Documents pontificaux sur la Gascogne', ed. L. Guérard, *Archives Historiques de la Gascogne*, 2nd Series, vol. 2, 1896; vol. 6, 1903.

Higden, R., *Polychronicon*, ed. C. Babington and J. R. Lumby, 9 vols., London, 1865–6.

Le Bel, Jean, *Chronique*, ed. J. Viard and E. Déprez, 2 vols. Paris, 1904–5.

Myers, A. R. (ed.), *The Household of Edward IV: The Black Book and the Ordinance of 1478*, Manchester, 1959.

The War of Saint-Sardos (1323–1325). Gascon Correspondence and Diplomatic Documents, ed. P. Chaplais, Camden 3rd Series, LXXXVII, London, 1954.

3. FURTHER READING

Armstrong, C. A. J., 1977. 'The Golden Age of Burgundy: Dukes that Outdid Kings', in Dickens, A. G. (ed.), *Courts of Europe*, London, pp. 54–75.

Asch, R. G. and Birke, A. M. (eds.), 1991. *Princes, Patronage and the Nobility: The Court at the Beginning of the Modern Age, c.1450–1650*, London/Oxford.

Autrand, F., 1989. 'De l'enfer au purgatoire. La cour à travers quelques textes français du milieu du xive à la fin du xve siècle' in P. Contamine (ed.), *L'Etat et les aristocraties, xiie–xviie siècle. France, Angleterre, Ecosse*, Paris, pp. 51–78.

Baron, F. (ed.), 1981. *Les Fastes du Gothique: le siècle de Charles V*, exhib. catal., Paris.

Binski, P., 1995. *Westminster Abbey and the Plantagenets: Kingship and the Representation of Power, 1200–1400*, New Haven/London.

Cauchies, J.-M. (ed.), 1998. *A la cour de Bourgogne. Le duc, son entourage, son train*, Turnhout.

Chaplais, P., 1981. *Essays in Medieval Diplomacy and Administration*, London.

1994. *Piers Gaveston: Edward II's Adoptive Brother*, Oxford.

2003. *English Diplomatic Practice in the Middle Ages*, London.

Contamine, P., 1994. 'Pouvoir et vie de cour dans la France du xve siècle: les mignons', in *Academie des inscriptions et belles-lettres. Comptes rendus des séances*, Paris, pp. 541–54.

Duindam, J., 1995. *Myths of Power: Norbert Elias and the Early Modern European Court*, Amsterdam.

Given-Wilson, G., 1986. *The Royal Household and the King's Affinity. Service, Politics and Finance in England, 1360–1413*, New Haven/London.

Gonzalez, E., 2004. *Un prince en son hôtel. Les serviteurs des ducs d'Orléans au xve siècle*, Paris.

Gunn, S. J. and Janse, A. (eds.), 2006. *The Court as a Stage. England and the Low Countries in the Later Middle Ages*, Woodbridge.

Harriss, G. L., 2003. 'The Court of the Lancastrian Kings', in J. Stratford (ed.), *The Lancastrian Court*, Donington, pp. 1–25.

Horrox, R., 1995. 'Caterpillars of the Commonwealth? Courtiers in Late Medieval England', in R. E. Archer and S. Walker (eds.), *Rulers and Ruled in Late Medieval England: Essays Presented to Gerald Harriss*, London, pp. 1–15.

Johnstone, H., 1933. 'The Eccentricities of Edward II', *EHR*, 48, 264–7.

Kruse, H. and Paravicini, W. (eds.), 1999. *Höfe und Hofordnungen, 1200–1600* Sigmaringen.

Lachaud, F., 1996. 'Liveries of Robes in England, *c.*1200–*c.*1330', *EHR*, 111, 279–98.

Lalou, E., 1996. 'Le fonctionnement de l'hôtel du roi du milieu du xiiie au milieu du XIVe siècle', in J. Chapleot and E. Lalou (eds.), *Vincennes: aux origines de l'état moderne*, Paris, pp. 91–127.

La Selle, X. de, 1995. *Le service des ames à la cour. Confesseurs et aumôniers des rois de France du xiiie au xve siècle*, Paris.

Marchandisse, A. and Kupper, J.-L. (eds.), 2003. *A l'ombre du pouvoir. Les entourages princières au Moyen Age*, Liege.

Mattéoni, O., 2013. 'Les cours en France (seconde moitié du xive-fin du xve siècle)', in W. Paravicini, T. Hiltmann and F. Viltart (eds.), *La Cour de Bourgogne et l'Europe. Le rayonnement et les limites d'un modèle culture*, Ostfildern, pp. 421–38.

Moeglin, J.-M., 2002. 'Les recherches françaises sur les cours et les résidences au bas Moyen Age', in J.-C. Schmitt and O. G. Oexle (eds.), *Les tendances actuelles de l'histoire du Moyen Age en France et en Allemagne*, Paris, pp. 357–8.

Morgan, D. A. L., 1973. 'The King's Affinity in the Polity of Yorkist England', *TRHS*, 5th Series, 23, 1–25.

1987. 'The House of Policy: The Political Role of the Late Plantagenet Household, 1422–1485', in D. Starkey (ed.), *The English Court: from the Wars of the Roses to the Civil War*, London / New York, pp. 25–41.

Paravicini, W. (ed.), 1994. *Die ritterlich-höfische Kultur des Mittelalters*, Munich.

(ed.), 1995. *Alltag bei Hofe*, Sigmaringen.

(ed.), 1997. *Zeremoniell und Raum*, Sigmaringen.

(ed.), 2005. *Die Hofordnungen der Herzoge von Burgund, 1: Herzog Philip der Gute, 1407–1467*, Ostfildern.

Patze, H. and Paravicini, W. (eds.), 1991. *Fürstliche Residenzen im spätmittelalterlichen Europe*, Sigmaringen.

Piponnier, F., 1970. *Costume et vie sociale: la cour d'Anjou, xive–xve siècle*, Paris/The Hague.

Robin, F., 1985. *La Cour d'Anjou-Provence*, Paris.

Vale, M., 1998. 'The World of the Courts', in M. Bent and A. Wathey (eds.), *Fauvel Studies: Allegory, Chronicle, Music and Image in Paris, Bibliotheque Nationale, MS français 146*, Oxford, pp. 591–8.

2013. 'England: Simple Imitation or Fruitful Reciprocity?', in W. Paravicini, T. Hiltmann and F. Viltart (eds.), *La Cour de Bourgogne et l'Europe. Le rayonnement et les limites d'un modèle culturel*, Ostfildern, pp. 439–56.

3 Kings, nobles and military networks

Steven Gunn and Armand Jamme

the king entered . . . fully armed,
as though clothed with the power to act as he willed
P. Commynes, *Mémoires*[1]

Many historians, sociologists and political scientists have argued that war was the main impetus behind the growth of the modern state and that the development of military institutions played a central role in state formation. Yet the later medieval French and English monarchies responded differently to the pressures of war. Despite their long struggle with one another and their parallel experience of civil war, they emerged from our period with dissimilar military systems. Philippe Contamine has underlined the differences in a brief comparison between the two in the mid-fifteenth century,[2] but no systematic long-term comparative treatment has been made. To understand the nature and causes of this divergence, we must consider first the evolution of French and English military institutions, then noble attitudes towards royal military policy, thirdly the wider means by which kings drew men to their service in war and finally the impact of military service on the values and political networks of the nobility. Our starting point is the late thirteenth century, the age of Philip IV and Edward I, when France and England made war by generally similar means despite the large difference in the size and population of the kingdoms. Each had fiscal and administrative systems capable of supporting large armies and, on occasion, navies, yet neither had significant permanent forces. Paid service was steadily replacing unpaid and each king had access to international markets to recruit skilled soldiers. But chivalrous values and feudal obligations were still important in inspiring noble service; towns were sometimes summoned to provide contingents

---

[1] *Sur Charles VIII et l'Italie, Livres VII et VIII*, ed. and trans. Dufournet (2002), p. 119: 'tout armé, comme revêtu du pouvoir d'agir à sa guise'.
[2] Contamine (1987).

41

for royal armies at their own cost; and custom bound the general population, however brief their service and doubtful their military effectiveness, to fight in local defence.

1.   Institutions and policies

In France the growth in the number of troops available to the king bore testimony to the power of the monarchical edifice. In 1346–7, 31,280 men spread through the kingdom were in the pay of Philip VI. In the last two years of Louis XI's reign, 45,000 men were in the king's service, at the cost of an enormous financial effort 'resting on the obsessive and tyrannical will of a single person'.[3] In 1523, Francis I considered that to re-conquer the duchy of Milan he would need 50,000 men. It is true that this growth was facilitated by economies of scale. In the fourteenth century the general trend was for the development of costly mounted forces, but in the course of the fifteenth century, the infantry tended to become more and more numerous, as men began to fight *en masse* rather than in line abreast. Nevertheless, detailed analysis of the troops that could be mobilised by the kings of France between 1300 and 1550 brings out variations that cannot be explained merely by their objectives or by demographic circumstances.

Until 1356 the French monarchy made use of the feudal summons of the *ban et arrière-ban*, which applied to all men fit to fight between the ages of 15 and about 60. It made it possible to gather in one place all or part of the contingents which could be raised by the higher and middling nobility, *baillis*, *sénéchaux* and towns. At the musters units would be combined into *routes*, of variable sizes, which were then integrated into *batailles*, twelve of them in the host of Bouvines in 1340, for example.[4] The classification of combatants, made afresh each time the host was gathered, had to take into account both military requirements and questions of precedence. The assembly of a large army was thus a political matter and the king could measure the prestige of his authority and the acceptability of his ambitions by the response of the men of his kingdom.

The Black Death, the financial difficulties of the Valois and new military thinking bred from defeat brought about the abandonment of summons of the *arrière-ban* after 1356. The direction of the war was now carried out from the palace, by a king who disliked adventurism, and who consequently favoured regulation, and thus to a certain extent

---

[3] Contamine in Contamine (1997), p. 232: 'reposant sur la volonté pathétique et tyrannique d'une seule personne'.

[4] Contamine (1972), p. 79.

encouraged the bureaucratisation of warfare. The strategy chosen by Charles V together with his family's grip on senior commands revealed the king's mistrust of the high nobility. Charles relied on an army of volunteers, who performed two different functions during operations. Some lords, knights and esquires were paid together with their retinues to ensure the defence of their own lands, especially in those regions under greatest threat, while others led companies of a standard size, manned with experienced soldiers, in campaigns against the English positions. An ordinance of 1374 set out that the king would retain *routes* or *compagnies* of 100 men-at-arms, each divided into 10 *chambres*.[5] Thus recruitment was justified by professional demands and no longer by socioeconomic arguments. The origins of those serving the king were likewise a matter of secondary importance, foreigners receiving the same wages as those born within the kingdom. This experiment may be considered the first attempt to establish a permanent army in France.

Once Charles V's re-conquest was successful, however, the scheme was abandoned, both for financial reasons and because military policy changed in the absence of a single overriding aim. In the following decades large, mobile armies were assembled quite frequently for expeditions to Italy, England or Castile, but these were less often serving the king directly than supporting his relatives in their conquest of lands for themselves.[6] These years were also characterised by a resurgence in chivalrous ideals that may explain the reluctance of French rulers to develop archery. Between 1390 and 1415, indeed, the most striking difference between English and French expeditionary forces was the ratio of archers to men-at-arms: one archer to two men-at-arms in France, three archers for one man-at-arms in England.[7]

After Agincourt, the military crisis of the monarchy was manifest in its inability to assemble strong armies. The summons of the *arrière-ban* in 1418, intended to recall the people to obedience to the king, was a total failure. The direction of the war was abandoned to a handful of officers, who amalgamated men-at-arms, archers and crossbowmen into units of variable size.[8] The siege of Orléans was typical of this state of affairs: the French army was of indeterminate size, held no musters and included no great lords or high officers like the Constable. Nevertheless, the outcome of the siege – apparently proving that the spirit of combatants could overcome mere problems of organisation[9] – reversed the course of

---

[5] Contamine (1972), pp. 142–5.   [6] Fowler (2001), p. 155ff.
[7] Contamine in Contamine (1997), pp. 182–3.
[8] Contamine (1997); de Medeiros (1998); Allmand (1999).
[9] Contamine, Bouzy and Hélary (2012).

history and drove back into the king's service ever-larger numbers of men, who then had to be organised.

Between 1445 and 1448, four ordinances provided new military structures for the French monarchy. The first aimed to reduce the number of professional soldiers in the king's service, subject them uniquely to royal authority and secure them regular pay. It established 15 companies of 100 lances, each composed of six men: a man-at-arms, two archers, one *coutilier*, one page and one valet. The second ordinance assigned lodgings to these 9,000 men, who were billeted on the local population, in private homes, inns and religious houses all over the kingdom. The third ordinance reorganised the service of the communes, who were now to furnish the king with one archer for every parish, who was to be exempted from the *taille*. The fourth ordinance reasserted the obligation of all nobles who held fiefs or sub-fiefs to serve in the defence of the kingdom.[10] Charles VII's military organisation was thus based on a strong body of professional soldiers with a dual function – to defend the kingdom and maintain order – and on reserves of archers and cavalrymen which had still to be potentially huge, because the professionals were insufficiently numerous to defend the kingdom in the case of a wide-ranging war. This tripartite articulation survived in the decades that followed, as French military structures had reached a relative equilibrium. From this moment the history of the royal army was characterised above all by the numerical and structural evolution of these three military institutions.

The strength of the *gendarmes de l'ordonnance* increased step by step, reaching 4,000 lances in 1481–3, until financial crisis and peace with Maximilian of Habsburg drove the number of lances back down to 2,500. Thereafter it rose again slowly: in 1490, there were 3,200 lances in 60 companies. An ordinance of 27 July 1498 modernised the *gendarmerie*'s structures and regulated the *gendarmes*' relations with the king's subjects in precise terms. The *gendarmes* kept the same organisation into the sixteenth century, at the price of such adaptations as the diminution of the number of men in each lance, the introduction of firearms and modifications to their plate armour. But the institution progressively closed in upon itself. An ordinance of 1549 restricted access to the nobility and fixed a minimum age for recruitment, while the companies' strength fluctuated between 3,000 and 3,500 lances until the peace of Cateau-Cambrésis in 1559.[11]

The infantry, meanwhile, were more radically transformed. At the end of the Hundred Years War, the *francs-archers* numbered about 8,000.

---

[10] *Construire l'armée française*, ed. Bessey (2006).
[11] Contamine in Contamine (1997), p. 248.

Louis XI doubled their number, placing them under four general captains; but the corps was dissolved after their deplorable conduct at Guinegatte in 1479. They were replaced by battalions of archers, pikemen and halberdiers regrouped in permanent camps in the north. In 1487, the system of the *francs-archers* was restored, now including pikemen and halberdiers. The frequency of reforms points to the rapid evolution of the tactical functions of infantry and to the hesitation between permanent infantry forces and those merely summoned for campaigns. In 1534 the creation of a national infantry of seven legions of 6,000 men each, recruited in the most threatened provinces of the kingdom (Brittany, Normandy, Picardy, Champagne-Burgundy, Lyonnais-Provence, Languedoc and Guyenne), attempted to resolve the issue in a distinctive way. The officers were regularly paid, but the legionaries – pikemen, halberdiers and arquebusiers – were paid only in time of war.[12]

As for noble service, the monarchy refused to renounce its rights despite the increasingly negative results produced by the feudal summons. Louis XI was particularly demanding. In 1467, he named permanent paid officers to lead the noble cavalry, and frequent musters and inquiries into the value of fiefs gave him quite accurate information about the numbers and capacities of those liable to serve. His ordinance of 1481 made the revolutionary demand that noblemen serve as foot soldiers. Although they were to wear armour, their lances and swords were to be replaced with pikes and long daggers. The king failed in this attempt to create a heavy infantry comparable to the Swiss. The *Instruction* of 1485 instead renewed the customary use of the feudal summons, which was used several times between 1487 and 1492, with uninspiring results. So, when Charles VIII decided to conquer the kingdom of Naples, the royal council decided it would be more efficient not to rely upon the *arrière-ban*, but to nominate individuals – 120 barons, 200 knights and 600 gentlemen – to take charge of the defence of France. In 1503, a general inquiry, based upon impressive documentation, was undertaken to determine exactly in what measure the nobles had to serve the king in war.[13] Francis I linked nobles' service obligations to the level of their revenues. But the general levies actually ordered during the first half of the sixteenth century showed that a large part of the nobility liable to military service was exempt, because already serving the king in the *ordonnances* or in the royal household, or for economic reasons. Thus by mid century

---

[12] *Construire l'armée française*, ed. Bessey (2006).
[13] Contamine (1972), pp. 373–8.

the *arrière-ban* could raise only two or three thousand horsemen in the poorly equipped and much-mocked *bandes des nobles*.[14]

The English monarchy, on the other hand, never developed significant standing forces for land warfare in this period. The Crown maintained regular garrisons only at Calais, Berwick and Carlisle, and these totalled hundreds rather than thousands of men. The English military establishment in Ireland was tiny before the mid sixteenth century. Only Calais represented a permanent and substantial reserve of military expertise and equipment. Before 1453, it is true, there were at times English garrisons several thousand strong in Normandy, and, on a smaller scale, in Gascony and Brittany, plus companies attached to the households of the regent or lieutenants of France, and some men made a career of serving continuously in them. But they could do so only by staying away from England, just as their fourteenth-century predecessors had stayed on the continent to make war on their own account in the English Free Companies when truce or peace interrupted their service to the king. Later, Englishmen entered Burgundian or Habsburg service after their own kings made peace with France in 1475 and 1550. But English soldiers professional enough to serve as mercenaries abroad were always comparatively few.[15]

The English made no attempt to establish institutionalised native infantry forces. Their only equivalent to the *compagnies de l'ordonnance* as a standing force of native heavy cavalry was not set up until 1551 and was abolished within two years because it was too expensive. It took the boyish enthusiasm and Tudor self-confidence of King Edward VI to believe that, as he wrote to his friend Barnaby Fitzpatrick at the French court, having watched a muster of these men, one might 'see in Fraunce none like' them.[16] Yet the English could raise forces of significant size for individual campaigns. Armies fighting in France, Scotland, Ireland and elsewhere were assembled when needed by the indenture system developed in the later thirteenth century, by which captains drawn from the nobility and gentry each contracted with the king to raise a company to serve at his wages for the duration of the campaign. These companies usually combined well-paid men-at-arms and humbler footsoldiers, the latter mostly mounted archers in the Hundred Years War, but also spearmen before the 1340s and billmen or pikemen from the Wars of the Roses on. The forces raised in this way to attack France or Scotland attained a maximum size of 10–15,000 men for the major campaigns of the fourteenth and fifteenth centuries, from Edward III's in 1333 to

---

[14] Contamine in Contamine (1997), p. 250.
[15] Fowler (2001), pp. 15–21; Meek (2001).   [16] Norris (1995), p. 102.

Henry VII's in 1492. The armies Henry VIII led to France were larger, at about 30,000 in 1513 and 40,000 in 1544, but those he and his son sent against Scotland were of similar size to those led there by earlier kings.[17] The assembly of effective armies by these ad hoc means was facilitated by the fact that every able-bodied adult male was in some sense a soldier: as ambassador Charles de Marillac put it in 1541, 'you will understand well enough that all Englishmen are skilled in war after a fashion'.[18] The Statute of Winchester of 1285, reinforced by proclamation in 1511, ordered that every man should have arms and armour suitable to his social rank and be prepared to use them in militia service. Repeated royal ordinances and parliamentary statutes from 1363 prescribed archery practice to ensure that all would be suitably trained and at least from the early sixteenth century there is evidence that such practice was widespread. It is true that the proportions of men noted as competent archers in muster certificates fell from one in three in 1522 to one in four in 1557, but from 1573 regular training with firearms was introduced in the effort to keep the militia viable as a modern military force. In the fourteenth and fifteenth centuries local levies were mustered at times and came into action to drive off raiding forces. In the sixteenth century musters were held with increasing regularity and in 1522 a survey aimed to list every man in the country with his wealth and his weapons. By 1545, Henry VIII could mobilise more than 100,000 militiamen to face a French invasion and soon the militia took over from the indenture system as the main means to raise English armies for service abroad. The scale of the mobilisation of 1545 is brought home when one realises that a similar levy in France would have produced a force the size of the *Grande Armée* of 1812.[19]

If the growth of permanent military institutions and the employment of military professionals is to be seen as a sign of the development of state power in England anywhere in this period, then it is not on land but in the navy. Before the late fifteenth century, English royal fleets waxed and waned with the wealth or enthusiasm of successive kings: strongest under Henry V at thirty-four ships by 1417 and twenty-eight retained sailing masters; comparatively weak even under great warriors on land such as Edward I and Edward III. With the exception of the traditional service of the Cinque Ports of Kent and Sussex, attempts to make towns provide warships when the king could not afford to maintain his own had only intermittent success, and that mostly in building galleys for local

---

[17] Bell et al. (2013).
[18] Potter (2001), p. 156: 'vous entendrez assez que tous les Anglois sont doctz à la guerre d'une sorte'.
[19] Goring (1975).

defence. Normally fleets for transport or fighting – indeed fleets capable of winning major victories such as those at Sluis (1340) and Winchelsea (1350) – were assembled by commandeering ships from English traders and hiring foreign merchant ships or, very occasionally, galleys from Genoa or Portugal. Naval administration and facilities were impermanent, the responsibilities of successive clerks of the king's ships varying dramatically and John's base at Portsmouth and Henry V's at Southampton disappearing after the deaths of their founders. Under Henry VII, however, large royal ships were built again and Henry VIII drastically expanded the fleet to about seventy vessels, established new dockyards and storehouses and created the Council of the Marine. Here were built the foundations of a permanent royal navy, absorbing some 10 per cent of the state budget in peacetime by 1551–3.[20]

In France, the birth of a permanent nucleus of royal warships dated from the reign of Philip the Fair. From 1294–5 he made considerable efforts to counter the power of the English king at sea. Yet his reorientation of the monarchy's naval investments from the Mediterranean to the Channel did not mark the end of Genoese input, which remained fundamental to the development of the *clos des galées* at Rouen. The vast logistical and technical support provided there rapidly energised the ports of the Norman and Picard coasts and enabled the royal fleet to become a serious challenger to the English: on the eve of the Battle of Sluis, indeed, Philip VI was capable of gathering a fleet slightly larger than that of Edward III. Charles V undertook to restore the monarchy's naval strength, but his efforts were compromised by the negligence of the government of his son's uncles and at length completely undone by the English conquest of Normandy and the scuttling of the ships in the *clos des galées*.[21]

French naval policy always formed part of an entirely land-based strategic conception: there was no clear will to control a maritime space of its own. In consequence the king moved easily from the construction and maintenance of a state navy, to which requisitioned merchant ships could be joined for certain operations, to phases of more or less complete renunciation of such schemes, marked by recourse to fleets supplied by allies and by the development of privateering. In the fifteenth century the monarchy relied heavily on this last expedient, which allowed it to operate at sea at minimum cost, sometimes even profitably, while preserving its theoretical control of war-making.

It was a return to Mediterranean priorities that encouraged the reconstruction of French naval forces. The Italian Wars dynamised ports

---

[20] Rodger (1997), pp. 61–237.   [21] Merlin-Chazelas (1977–8), pp. 27–32, 78–9.

all over the realm: though Louis XII's ships were concentrated in the Mediterranean for operational purposes, they were built at the king's command by a wide range of towns. The multiplication of France's enemies under Francis I further stimulated naval development in all the western and southern ports and made it necessary to integrate naval costs into the state budget. The missions with which his fleets were charged, ever-more independent of campaigns on land, asserted royal power at sea in such ventures as d'Annebaut's attempted attack on Southampton in 1545. Before the outbreak of the Wars of Religion the French royal navy had thus become a serious challenger to the English, both in terms of technical innovations, such as the invention of gunports, and in numerical strength.[22]

French forces on land, then, and the naval forces of both kingdoms showed a similar evolution towards permanency and institutional consolidation, marked though it was by many reverses or changes of direction. English land forces, in contrast, retained their temporary character and their dependence on non-professional militias throughout the period.

2.   Nobility and military service

Obligations based on the feudal land tenure of the nobility underlay many, though not all, of the military arrangements we have been discussing. The French and English nobilities both saw themselves as military castes and were seen as such by others, though the point was more insistently made in France because of the relationship between the military service of the French nobility and its exemption from taxation. Military service therefore expressed and shaped both the general relationship between king and nobility and the relations between individual noblemen that helped to constitute the frameworks of local politics and government in both kingdoms.

In France the nobility's strong claim to private privileges made evident the pre-eminent role it wished to play in the kingdom. The leagues of 1314–15 were born amidst disputes over service in the feudal host. The charters granted by Louis X and Philip V to the nobles of Normandy and Burgundy not only recognised their right to conduct private war, but also bound the king to respect the feudal hierarchy by not issuing summons for service directly to the nobles' vassals.[23] The army's organisation into *bannières* and *routes* of varying strength, each totally subject to its *chevetaine*, who was often also their suzerain, corresponded with the nobility's social ideals and interest in the maintenance of its authority.

---

[22] Mollat du Jourdin in Contamine (1997), pp. 167–8, 287–90.   [23] Brown (1981).

No doubt the nobility was also behind the social stratification of wages, by which a knight banneret received twice the pay of a squire banneret or a simple knight, a simple knight twice that of a simple squire.[24] As noblemen collected the wages due to the units they commanded – including a bonus in case of *bannières* of great size – the system displayed and reinforced the power of the established nobility each time the host was summoned; indeed, this practice was perhaps an indispensable means to make nobles come to the place selected for the army to gather. In terms of command, in terms of the payment of wages, the army was the aggregate of the social structures directed by the high nobility. The great lords considered the feudal host as an emanation of the entire kingdom, embodied as a community over which they claimed a natural share in government.

The increasing frequency with which the host was summoned in the first part of the Hundred Years War and the succession of French defeats led to a declining turnout. It was said that martial spirit decreased after Poitiers, and that the nobility turned instead to domestic affairs, and Christine de Pizan, for example, shows a certain contempt for the 'sleeping knighthood of France'. But this apparent disaffection with royal service is better explained by the demographic and economic consequences of the Black Death, which diminished the number and wealth of the nobility, by their need to resist the attacks of the Free Companies on their own estates, and by the limitations placed on recruitment by the monarchy for economic and tactical reasons. Perhaps Charles V did, as Christine wrote, wake up his nobility by his prudent policy, 'restored to very great boldness and good fortune'.[25] But in reality, though wages of war were still stratified by social rank, in other respects the military role of the nobility had significantly changed by his time. It was particularly important that simple esquires, often without noble estates, had taken on command roles: land and power over men were no longer the indispensable foundations of military authority. Professional experience, competence and renown gave certain individuals the chance to gather numerous men around themselves. By such means the captain emerged fully-formed, a famed leader of professional soldiers, though not without some political weight. This was the moment at which a simple knight such as Guillaume de La Penne, relating the feats of a cousin of Bertrand du Guesclin, Sylvestre Budes, could refer to the 'craft of arms', managed by a 'master' and practised by his 'companions', who had taken an oath

---

[24] Contamine (1972), pp. 620–6.

[25] de Pizan (1977), vol. I, p. 185: 'endormie chevalerie de France'; de Pizan (1958), p. 141: 'remise sus en très grande hardiesse et bonne fortune'.

'to be with him under his pennon'.[26] This adoption of the language of a guild or craft points out the limits of Christine de Pizan's reflections as noble life and military life began to diverge. The poetry of Guillaume de La Penne revealed the professional soldier's desire for social recognition and gratitude at a time when the growing marginalisation of military society was linked to the question of the Free Companies. Military activity was thus considered as a profession, one regulated by chivalrous values, long before it was effectively organised upon this basis by the monarchy.

This revision of the criteria for access to martial activity did not entirely throw into question the role the nobility had traditionally played in it. Yet that role was greatly modified, as military authority no longer flowed uniquely from landed power and royal favour, but instead rested on the control of a certain number of professional soldiers tied to their leader by contract and oath. Adjustment to these changes produced in the 1370s a 'refeudalisation' of the military units which had proliferated under the leadership of a myriad of ambitious captains. Captains who had broken their oaths of loyalty were beheaded, those most deserving of reward were granted lands and the soldiery were dispersed in expeditions outside the kingdom, all part of an overall policy of sanitising the military environment.[27] The power of the princes of the blood at the end of Charles V's reign was the direct consequence of their military responsibilities in the war against the English. Even if the captains he employed were recruited and paid by the king, through war Louis, duke of Anjou, became their real master: after the re-conquest of Guyenne, he could send them out once in the service of Enguerrand de Coucy, twice in the service of Pope Gregory XI and finally in his own service to conquer the kingdom of Naples. This appropriation of contingents paid by the king was accentuated in a partisan way during the madness of King Charles VI and reached its apogee in the civil war between Armagnacs and Burgundians.

When Charles VII wanted to restore the military power of the monarchy, he needed first to forbid the princes to raise armies without his permission. The ordinance of 1439 to that effect provoked the Praguerie, a rebellion that made visible the networks of allegiance binding the armed men of the kingdom. The rapid defeat of the revolt, together with the need to improve military organisation for the re-conquest of the last provinces occupied by the English, facilitated reforms about which the nobility was apparently unenthusiastic. The creation of the *gendarmerie*

---

[26] Jamme (1996), p. 161: 'métier d'armes', 'mestre' 'compainions' 'd'estre o lui souz son pennon'.

[27] Contamine (1981).

was effectively an official recognition of the professionalisation of military activity and staked the claim of the king, who now fixed his men's wages in relation to their functions, to exclusive control of its exercise. The nobility of the kingdom initially held the *gendarmerie* in contempt, regarding it mostly as a means to relieve the countryside from excessive numbers of plundering professional soldiers. But within a few decades noblemen found that by participation in this new structure they could regain their central position in military affairs.[28]

It was the appropriation of this institution by the native nobility that ensured that it put down roots in French society. Though wage rates in the *gendarmerie* were determined by military function rather than social status, the high cost of a man-at-arms' equipment, some 150–180 *écus* now that full plate armour was the norm, restricted the job mostly to nobles, though many of them were bastards. Normally these men served for 15 to 20 years, often in the same company throughout. The typical entrant started with the rank of page, becoming next an archer, then a man-at-arms; with talent and the support of patrons he could finish his career as a company lieutenant. This noble colonisation of the *gendarmerie* also meant that some of the distinctive values of a society structured by multiple loyalties perpetuated themselves through the institution: on the eve of the War of the Public Weal, and again in 1468, the desertion of some captains and their men to join the king's enemies showed the vigour of the factious spirit so characteristic of the nobility.[29] On a number of occasions, too, the way of life of the *gens de l'ordonnance* called down the disapproval of that parsimonious king, Louis XI.

In the course of the sixteenth century, the choice of a professional military career seems to have become a less decisive criterion in the life of the men-at-arms of the *ordonnance*, especially those engaged in a company posted in their native region. In the first half of the sixteenth century in Champagne, despite its front-line status in the war with the Empire from 1521, noblemen's service in the *ordonnance* might be a transitory prelude to marriage or inheriting land.[30] During the Italian wars, the martial spirit of the men of the *ordonnance* seems to have diminished with the years. Blaise de Monluc lamented that, although leave periods were limited to three months, a quarter or even a third of effectives might be absent from any operation.[31]

By then a place in the *ordonnance* was considered by the nobility in the same way as any other office. Noblemen's military service was strictly linked to an office-holding title, one that might appear on their

---

[28] Contamine (1972), p. 399ff.   [29] Lassalmonie (2001).
[30] Bourquin (1994), p. 33.   [31] Corvisier in Contamine (1997), p. 311.

gravestone beside a reference to their lordship. Several indicators show that the position rapidly became subject to venality and sometimes to tenure in plurality, building new bridges between civil and military service to the king. In some ways, the fact that military service was connected to an office, conferred on nobles who could gain money and titles through its exercise, corresponded exactly with what the nobility had been demanding from the monarchy for centuries. As Philippe Contamine put it, 'in this way the monarchy subsidised its nobility, for a fully-equipped lance earned 360 *livres tournois* a year, equal to the clear income of a small barony'.[32] In this sense, the companies of the *ordonnance* may have served as one of the monarchy's main instruments to domesticate the French nobility, intelligently harnessing its potentially most disruptive members in the service of the state, even if this was not their original purpose in the mid fifteenth century.

In England, personal acquaintance with the king and a sense of the social duty of their order made military service almost universal among the high nobility. In 1415, eleven out of a total of seventeen earls and dukes accompanied Henry V to France, while others guarded Gascony or the north. In 1513, twenty-three parliamentary peers plus three heirs standing in for aged fathers served in France, nine fought against the Scots and one in the fleet; three were too old or incapacitated to fight, leaving only one nobleman over the age of 19 unaccounted for. Statistics for service abroad by the next rank of the nobility, the county gentry, are less impressive. Something like one in three gentry families in England may have had a representative amongst the men-at-arms of Edward III's great French campaign of 1359 and even in the fifteenth century most knights and esquires probably expected to serve the king in war at some point in their careers, if only while waiting to inherit their fathers' lands and position in local affairs. But one attempt by Henry V's commissioners to mobilise the gentry of Yorkshire for paid service found that of ninety-six men approached, over seventy excused themselves, usually on grounds of financial incapacity or sickness: eight pleaded that they had served in earlier campaigns, two that they had lost sons in the king's wars, nine that they had brothers or sons currently serving the king at their expense. Only five agreed unequivocally to serve the king.[33]

The demilitarisation of the gentry was neither sudden nor total, but is suggested by several types of evidence. The number of knights in

---

[32] Contamine in Contamine (1997), p. 221: 'la monarchie subventionnait de la sorte sa noblesse, puisqu'une lance fournie touchait 360 livres tournois par an, l'équivalent du revenu net d'une petite baronnie'.

[33] Goodman (1981); Payling (1991), pp. 60–2, 137–40.

England fell steeply from the thirteenth to the fifteenth century. Men-at-arms did not have to be knights, but the proportion of men-at-arms to archers in English armies also fell sharply, from one to one in Edward III's time to one to three on the Agincourt campaign and one to nine in the later 1440s. The bearing of heraldic arms, closely linked to military experience in 1300, was no longer so by 1500. In these changes strategic factors interacted with social and political conditions. It was harder to combine the local office-holding expected of the gentry with service in the continual garrisons of Lancastrian Normandy than it had been with participation in Edward III's *chevauchées*. As local government expanded and landlords drew together to face the challenging economic circumstances of the decades after the Black Death, gentlemanly status became increasingly a matter of office-holding and landownership and decreasingly a matter of bearing arms. The Tudors still expected their gentry to raise troops and fight when called upon, and at least the greater gentry liked to appear in armour on their tombs, but few could match the real military expertise that was widespread amongst Edward III's knights, esquires and men-at-arms.[34]

It is possible that high participation rates from the mid fourteenth to the mid fifteenth century are attributable to the function of paid military service as a financial rescue package for landlords at a time of economic difficulty after the Black Death. Cash levied from the peasantry in direct taxation or drawn out of the wool and cloth trades through the customs was paid over to noble captains who may not have been able to extract equivalent sums in rent – though actually English landlords seem to have coped quite well with the post-plague situation – and may have found liquid cash especially valuable at a time of constricted money supply. But payment was often slow coming through from the exchequer to captains who had in the meanwhile to equip themselves and sometimes advance money to their men from their own resources. Under Henry VI in particular the Crown built up huge debts to some commanders. Any significant profits from the war were probably made at the expense of the French at times of English success, all the more so as the king took only one-third rather than one-half of the spoils of war of English men-at-arms from the 1370s. However, it seems unlikely that the spoils of war substantially modified the economic position of the English nobility and gentry. They were too readily spent on fine chantry chapels or tombs or more frivolous forms of conspicuous consumption and could be lost again through capture and ransom or a few fruitless campaigns. In any case, it seems that many men-at-arms and archers who served frequently were

[34] Keen (2002).

not established men desperate to maintain their position, but those on the margins of peacetime society: heirs awaiting inheritances, younger sons and bastards of the gentry, criminals awaiting pardon, perhaps yeomen uninterested in entrepreneurial farming.[35]

The networks through which English military service was articulated were for the most part the ordinary social and governmental networks of the day. The general sense that the nobility and gentry should serve the king and the attraction of his wages was such that feudal obligation was scarcely, if ever, used to secure noble service after 1300. The militia was organised by commissioners of array, later commissioners for musters, named by the king from amongst the lords and gentry who served on other local commissions. When companies were raised for service overseas or in civil war by nobles and gentlemen, then the obligation of tenants to serve their landlords and household servants to serve their masters seems to have been generally recognised. Towns likewise used the general defensive obligation of all inhabitants to raise contingents for royal armies when called upon to do so. The pre-existing connections between members of the small retinues and sub-retinues, each combining men-at-arms with archers, put together to form English armies, underpinned the tactical cohesion so necessary to English success on the battlefield, where dismounted men-at-arms and archers fought closely together.

Of the various social relationships contributing to recruitment, that which has attracted most attention from historians is the retaining by noblemen of knights, esquires, gentlemen and yeomen for service in peace and war. Such retaining used to be seen as the central feature of 'bastard feudalism', a social system organised for military purposes which was in the eyes of the nineteenth century a morally degenerate descendant of classic feudalism: for fiefs, homage and knight service it substituted cash payments and transferable contractual allegiances. A persuasively simple argument presented itself, in which the needs of the English Crown for soldiers to fight the Hundred Years War encouraged the construction of noble affinities of military followers retained by indentured agreements and the payment of fees. Those followings, unemployed after defeat in France, then turned on one another in the Wars of the Roses and crippled the English polity, until the Tudors' attack on retaining and on the over-mighty subjects it created restored stability with a new social and political order. A century of debate and detailed study of local political society has exposed the inadequacies of this picture, but makes

---

[35] Morgan (1987), pp. 174–8.

it harder to see clearly the relationship between structures of military service and wider political trends.

It now seems that bastard feudalism evolved less as a military system than as a response to the needs of gentry society to secure its landholding interests and of noblemen to secure their leadership in local affairs in the face of changing structures of royal authority and landed power. Indentured retaining in which military service was exchanged for payment of a fee was less fundamental to the operation of noble power than was the exchange of good lordship and protection for multi-faceted service and submission. Horizontal relationships amongst the gentry members of an affinity were as important to its effective operation in local politics as the bond between lord and follower. The great affinities retained by indenture that were first studied by historians turn out to have been exceptional. Those of John of Gaunt and of Edward the Black Prince were too diffuse to lend them much control in local politics but were very suitable for the military needs of royal princes with political ambitions on the European stage. That of William, Lord Hastings, was concentrated in counties away from his landed power-base in Leicestershire and was related to his need to raise troops as captain of Calais and his exercise of delegated royal authority in areas of dense Crown land-holding rather than his personal authority as a lord.[36]

The military retinues most noblemen led to France were very different in composition from the affinities they led in English county society. Indentured retainers were an important foundation for many contingents, but to recruit a sizeable force noblemen and knights had to appeal to their tenants, gather short-term retainers by distributing livery or giving temporary household membership, and negotiate sub-contracts with small groups of experienced soldiers who passed from captain to captain. Meanwhile the lawyers and men of business who played an important part in locally dominant affinities were better left at home than taken away from county administration, all the more so if the lord himself were to be absent. Very few of the captains or men-at-arms contracted to serve in the retinues of John Talbot, earl of Shrewsbury, in Normandy between 1420 and 1450 were linked to him in England, and these feed retainers and estate officers were outnumbered ten to one by those who attached themselves to him in France or acted as sub-contractors on the open recruitment market in England.[37]

It seems that the repeated civil wars of the later fifteenth century, with their need to raise large but politically dependable contingents quickly for

---

[36] Bean (1989); Carpenter (1992); Walker (1990); Green (2000).
[37] Pollard (1983), pp. 68–101.

short campaigns over limited distances, changed this situation. Already in 1484 Richard III was asking his lords to submit the numbers of men they would hold ready at all times to march to his assistance. In 1504, Henry VII forbade all retaining by statute and then licensed his trusted supporters to retain men to serve him when called upon to do so. The list of 1,365 retainers submitted to the king's secretary under this scheme by Sir Thomas Lovell, chancellor of the exchequer and treasurer of the royal household, survives. Many were the leading inhabitants of towns and villages of which Lovell was steward for the Crown or for ecclesiastical lords, most strikingly seven past and future mayors of Walsall. Some were his own estate officers or richer tenants, or those of his noble brother-in-law, who had conveniently been declared insane by the king and his lands entrusted to Lovell. Sub-contingents were organised by his fellow justices of the peace in the counties where he exercised influence, or by his subordinates in the administration of the Crown estates or the exchequer. These were precisely the men he and the king relied on in the day-to-day government of their communities. That was why they were valuable members of his affinity, seen as an instrument of local political control. If the fighting they were required to do consisted of occasional short campaigns against similar English forces or small invasions, they were also quite acceptable as a military retinue. As a draft licence to retain probably associated with this scheme put it, they were intended 'as well to resist outward attempts of hostility when the case shall require, as also to conserve our realm and subjects in good order of justice, tranquillity, and good obedience'.[38]

Presumably the recruitment of such pillars of the local community into retines was one factor that enabled Henry VIII to take armies to France two or three times the size of those led by Henry V, while drawing on a population not very much larger than that of the early fifteenth century. Certainly urban communities were drawn upon more systematically for contingents from the Wars of the Roses onwards, York for example sending out some 5% of its adult male population each time Henry VIII asked it for troops, though admittedly in southern towns the proportion levied was between 1% and 2%. But forces composed in this way were more brittle instruments for cross-Channel conquest than those of Henry's predecessors. Ellis Gruffydd, a Welsh veteran of the Calais garrison, could only watch despairingly as the army with which he campaigned in France in 1523 dissolved as winter set in. The mutiny, he grumbled, was led by 'the men of Essex and Suffolk, among whom

---

[38] Goodman (1981), pp. 119–52; Gunn (1998), pp. 117–19, 139–49; Dunham (1955), p. 96.

there were many wealthy farmers, who used this confusion to urge on the poor men to go home'.[39]

Although at the end of the thirteenth century, the military role of the nobility was in the end rather similar on both sides of the Channel, by the middle of the sixteenth century it was very different, largely because of changes in France. Here, adaptation to royal ordinances had led to the submission of the middling strata of the nobility to the control of the monarchy, from whom they received military office. In England, on the other hand, the high nobility and those who fought for the king kept their commanding position by way of their retinues and the commissions of array.

3.   Kings of war?

Wars prosecuted the king's personal rights – the English kings' claim to the French throne, for example, or the French kings' claims to Naples and Milan – and rested on the king's conscience. Kings such as Philip the Fair, Edward III, Philip VI, Henry V, and Francis I led the way in hand-to-hand combat as well as strategic planning and the largest armies were always those led by kings in person. Many ties beyond those of formal military institutions brought men to serve the king in war and kings in turn used various means to equip those who served them to do so to best effect. We thus need to examine those elements in the person and attitude of the king which led large numbers of men to join his service. The existence of a group of major military officers, the cultivation by the king of a martial spirit even in the organisation of his household, and the recruitment which he carried out abroad, must all be examined to understand the image which he hoped to project.

In the feudal army of the French king, the senior commander was the *sénéchal*, but this post remained vacant after 1191. Instead, command of operations was generally given to a wide variety of high-ranking nobles, frequently relatives of the king. Though the insignia granted by the king to the constable was a sword, this officer exercised no function of command over the whole military body: during the fourteenth and fifteenth centuries, he was in charge of limited operations. But like the *sénéchal*, he normally had a place in the royal council, could not be dismissed and received a very substantial fee, all of which made him a powerful officer. At court, he was indeed one of the focal points of the political game. Bernard d'Armagnac, for example, was murdered in the Burgundian uprising in Paris in 1418, and Raoul de Brienne and Louis de Saint-Pol

---

[39] Davies (1944), p. 41.

were decapitated in 1350 and 1475 respectively. To lessen the influence of the high nobility, French kings chose to give the office to nobles of lower rank, like du Guesclin, or to foreigners, like Carlos de La Cerda or John Stuart, or decided to leave the constableship vacant, as in 1458–65, 1475–83, and 1488–1515.[40]

The other offices in the French high command structure were granted to men of experience. The two *maréchaux de France* might be dismissed from office, and their job, given by grant of the *bâton*, was much more technical than that of the *sénéchal* or the *connétable*. They controlled all the musters and the payment of compensation (*restor*) for horses lost in action. Their court settled disputes between men on the king's service or those following the host. To cope with expanding numbers of cases, the *maréchaux de France* made increasing use of *prévôts*. By the later fifteenth century, the latter were settling differences between the king's men-at-arms and his subjects, and acquired a following of soldiers for that purpose: an embryonic military police.[41] The *amiral de la mer*, later *amiral de France*, was until the later fourteenth century an officer of middle rank, recruited amongst foreigners, frequently Italians, on the basis of professional competence. Afterwards this office seems to have reached a level equivalent to that of the marshals, the admirals being members of the established nobility, mostly natives of the non-coastal regions of the kingdom, who showed great tenacity in the definition and extension of their rights. The master of the crossbowmen, on the other hand, declined in prominence as a result of tactical changes. His responsibilities had already passed back to the marshals by the beginning of the fifteenth century. He was increasingly outshone by the developing powers of the master of the artillery, a post always assigned to nobles after 1470.[42]

The marshals' responsibilities in the organisation of war, their personal experience in command and the fact they could be replaced in office steadily made them the king's leading counsellors on military matters. In the years preceding and during the war between Burgundians and Armagnacs, the key role they had acquired was evident from the way each party had its own candidates for the post. In practice the division of responsibility between the two marshals permitted the development of an equilibrium between opposing occupants, who could each aspire to control the military machine. In the second half of the fifteenth century, the frequent vacancy in the constableship made the office of marshal

---

[40] Contamine in *Lexikon des Mittelalters* 3 (1986), pp. 138–40.
[41] Contamine in *Lexikon des Mittelalters* 6 (1993), pp. 230–1.
[42] Mollat du Jourdin in *Lexikon des Mittelalters* 1 (1980), pp. 535–6.

pre-eminent. This coincided with the developing needs of the monarchy: to secure professional and dependable advice, planning, administration and information, to draw into the king's service the highest number of men possible at the requisite times, and to devise practical measures to maximise the value of the monarchy's military rights and resources.

In England command of individual armies, when not undertaken by the king or one of his sons, brothers, or uncles, was generally entrusted to a senior nobleman. Long series of campaigns in the fourteenth century and again in the fifteenth led to the rise of men of comparatively humble origins such as Sir Robert Knolles and Sir John Fastolf to senior command, but in general the advantages of appointing to leadership those who were used to exercising social dominance outside war outweighed meritocracy. The hereditary great offices of constable and marshal lost any military role they might once have had early in our period, amongst the confrontations between Edward I and his earls. The admirals were more important. In the fourteenth century they were often knights appointed to command a particular fleet for a particular campaign, but from 1408 there was a permanent admiral of England, generally a great nobleman with military experience. He commanded the fleet at sea only sometimes, but he always profited from the jurisdiction of his admiralty courts over wrecks, privateering prizes and other maritime issues. In the fifteenth century the admirals' supervision of the administrators who looked after the king's ships was intermittent, but as the navy, its budget and its bureaucracy expanded in the sixteenth century so the admiral became a powerful noble officer of state. The increasing importance of artillery brought the rise of a second military officer, the master of the ordnance, who presided over the ordnance office, based at the Tower of London and was responsible for the procurement, maintenance and storage of cannon, smaller weapons and stores. By the mid sixteenth century the mastership had become an important office for military-minded noblemen such as Thomas, Lord Seymour of Sudeley and Ambrose Dudley, earl of Warwick.[43]

While England lagged behind France in the creation of military offices, it led the way in the royal patronage of the national community of honour through military orders. The sovereigns and members of the Order of the Garter, founded by Edward III, took its responsibilities as a focus of martial honour seriously. Those elected, while often men of political standing and influence, were almost always experienced and distinguished soldiers. As an instrument of government it was important as a mark of honour

---

[43] Prestwich (1996), pp. 171–5; Rodger (1997), pp. 134–6, 149, 158, 504–7; Gunn et al. (2007), pp. 23–4.

for powerful men, though it did not function as an organ of counsel and political debate. Kings of France, in contrast, made little use of military orders to cultivate the fidelity of their servants. Certainly the main objective of the Order of the Star, founded in 1352 by John the Good, was the revival of a chivalrous spirit to face the English; and indeed, at Poitiers, the members honoured with their death the oath they had taken never to retreat before the enemy. But French kings seem not to have given priority to this method of marking out a chivalrous elite, unlike the princes, such as the duke of Burgundy with his Golden Fleece, or even their own officers, such as Marshal Boucicaut, who founded the order of the *Dame blanche à l'écu vert*. Louis XI did found an order dedicated to Saint Michael in 1469, but clearly did so to stir up national chivalrous excitement in opposition to the orders of the Garter and of the Golden Fleece.[44]

On either side of the Channel, the development of the military aspects of the royal household was a more numerically important feature of the militarisation of the royal entourage. In France after 1450, membership of the military side of the *Maison du roi* was no longer merely a matter of participation in the guard duties and pomp of an increasingly complex ceremonial life. The number of soldiers marked out by wearing the royal livery – men-at-arms, archers or crossbowmen equipped to the highest standards – grew significantly. The members of the king's household – military professionals, sometimes foreigners or younger sons of the established native nobility – took an active part in battles such as that of Saint-Aubin-du-Cormier. At the start of the sixteenth century the military household of the king of France constituted a strong force of more than a thousand combatants. In wartime it was supplemented by a variable number of *pensionnaires*, mostly noble volunteers, French and foreign, which turned it into a small army. The military household included every type of combatant, mounted and on foot, and was alert to innovations in weaponry.[45] It aspired to be a condensed model of the king's military power, a head that ruled the other military organs.

In England all those lords, knights and lesser men attached to the king by household service might be temporarily mobilised with their own retinues to provide the core of large expeditionary forces. The military role of the household in a broad sense was then merely an extension of its role as the focal point of personal loyalty to the king amongst the political nation. Companies of royal bodyguards permanently maintained at court, on the other hand, were comparatively small. Richard II

[44] Boulton d'Arcy (2000); Collins (2000).
[45] Contamine in Contamine (1997), pp. 219–20.

briefly defended himself with an unpopular company of some 300 archers from Cheshire, but the experiment was not repeated until Henry VII founded a rather smaller guard of yeomen archers, probably in imitation of the French court at which he had stayed in exile, an institution which has survived to the present day. Henry VIII tried to go further in imitating French and Burgundian models with successive companies of mounted men-at-arms at court, but financial constraints limited him to fifty gentlemen pensioners funded from the dissolution of the monasteries.[46]

To develop their power further the kings of England and France drew into their service fighting men who owed them nothing by birth. In the ideology of the just war a sovereign could not depend merely upon his vassals to bring about his objectives; he had to surround himself with his peers, who would line up alongside him almost without inducement to sustain the justice of his cause.[47] More prosaically, kings sought to secure by treaty not just bilateral defensive alliances, but the active service of foreign princes. Great imperial feudatories, such as the counts of Savoy who particularly distinguished themselves in the fourteenth century in the service of the kings of France,[48] quite frequently engaged themselves to lead contingents of specified size in the king's wars by means of a political contract which included a *condotta* precisely fixing the terms of their service.

The French monarchy developed a wide variety of forms of recruitment. Philip the Fair gained the loyalty of a significant number of imperial feudatories by granting them fief-rents, simultaneously extending his military power and his political influence in the Empire.[49] The recruitment of significant groups of combatants outside the kingdom was more often designed to remedy a technical deficit identified by strategists than merely to expand the king's already large forces. In the fourteenth century Genoa in particular, but also Provence and Tuscany, furnished the king with thousands of crossbowmen, the first victims of Philip VI's successive defeats. In the fifteenth century, the monarch continued to recruit soldiers from regions bordering the kingdom, from the margins of the king of England's zone of influence – Wales and Scotland – and from Spain, Italy and the Empire. It was a special feature of the years 1410–30, linked to the collapse of military structures and the low prestige of the monarchy, that the number of foreigners was particularly high among those categories of fighting men that had once been the flower of the king's army: Spaniards, Italians and Scots furnished a third or

---

[46] Prestwich (1996), pp. 38–41; Given-Wilson (1986); Gunn et al. (2007), p. 21.
[47] Contamine (1980), pp. 446–62.   [48] Cordey (1911).   [49] Hélary (2012), p. 160.

even a half of the field forces at the king's disposal.[50] In the sixteenth century, the reduction in variety of forms of military service and the need to strengthen expeditionary forces sent to Italy while still providing for the defence of the realm led the king to recruit various regiments in Switzerland and Germany, where Francis I, for example, raised 23,000 *landsknechts*, among them the famous Black Band of Guelders.[51]

This recourse to foreign contingents offered those who led them the opportunity for integration into the kingdom, sometimes on a lasting basis. In the later thirteenth and earlier fourteenth centuries, some members of great Genoese families, such as the Spinola, Doria and Grimaldi, played an essential part in the hiring and then in the command of contingents of crossbowmen and of naval squadrons recruited and equipped in Liguria. These captains then made careers in the king's service, sometimes leading to high office as master of the crossbowmen or admiral. The men-at-arms recruited in large numbers in the first half of the fifteenth century were integrated into units commanded by native captains, but certain groups sometimes kept their identity within more or less unusual units. In this way the Valperga from Italy, or the Stuarts, elevated to be counts of Aubigny, made careers in the *gendarmerie*.[52] The long conflict with the Habsburgs in the sixteenth century led the monarchy to search out the alliance of Italian princes, lords and captains with the influence needed to reinforce the king's military and political position in the peninsula, such as the Gonzaga. As the epicentre of the conflict shifted to the north and east of France from 1536, the monarchy developed its already long-standing relationships with nearby families of imperial vassals: Luxembourg, Cleves and La Marck. This policy, which worked in favour of their integration into the kingdom, enabled certain family networks, such as that led by the Lorraine-Guise, to take at length a decisive influence in the political life of the kingdom.[53]

English armies too were often afforced by foreign mercenaries, men-at-arms and gunners from the Low Countries and later German pikemen or Italian and Spanish arquebusiers. On Edward III's expensive campaigns of 1339–40 these made up perhaps half his forces, on Henry VIII's expeditions of 1513 and 1544 nearly a quarter, but in between they did not form a significant proportion of most English armies. Foreigners' service to the English king rarely drew them far into the English political system. A few, such as the Hainaulters Sanchet d'Auberchicourt and Jean Robessart and the Dane Sir Andrew Ogard, managed to establish landed families in England, but none exercised significant authority there. The

---

[50] Contamine (1972), p. 253ff.   [51] Knecht (1998), p. 80.
[52] Contamine (1972), pp. 419–20.   [53] Baier (2004).

Navarrese captain Janico Dartasso distinguished himself in the service of Richard II and Henry IV, but could find a secure place only on the fringes of English power, in Ireland.[54]

The exclusivity of the English political community tightened as time went by, especially as the loss of lands in France destroyed the relationship between the king of England and the Gascon lords who had served him loyally as duke of Aquitaine. Philibert de Chandée was created earl of Bath for leading Henry VII's French troops at Bosworth; German, Spanish and Italian mercenary captains were knighted and pensioned under Henry VIII and Edward VI; but none of them settled in England. Throughout the period non-Englishmen were elected to the Garter, but among them foreign princes chosen as a diplomatic gesture steadily replaced consistent servants of the English kings such as the three lords from the Gascon family of Grailly elected between 1348 and 1446. When sixteenth-century noblemen from the Low Countries led troops in cooperation with English armies or even as auxiliaries in English pay they cultivated the friendship of the English king, but they did so clearly as subjects of their own Habsburg rulers, just as English lords at war or on embassy gained the confidence of Charles V or Francis I without compromising their allegiance to the Tudors.[55]

War was also a matter of royal image. In France the king was represented, paradoxically, both as a wise prince, devoted to justice and peace, and at the same time as a warrior, endowed with the manly virtues necessary for participation in prolonged and painful knightly combat. While the defeats of Crécy and Poitiers and the military incapacity of monarchs from Charles V to Charles VII put a certain distance between king and army, this was not irreversible. The physical presence of the king in the midst of his troops was a necessity, and with the expansion in the number of commoners needed to contribute to the strength of armies, the monarch's attentiveness extended to visiting his infantry. Parades and military camps became under Louis XI symbolically loaded occasions where the king's power and the devotion of those who served him interacted to magnify one another. In July 1535 at Amiens, Francis I mingled in his doublet with the 6,000 legionaries of Picardy, temporarily took command of them and then tested their steadiness with a feint attack by his cavalry.[56] The staging of the king's *virtus* was a personal speciality of Francis, the Gallic Hercules, thoroughly imbued with classicising Italian models of heroic self-fashioning. Thus the military camp, designed to

---

[54] Prestwich (1996), pp. 154–5; Morgan (1990); Millar (1980); Walker (1999).
[55] Collins (2000), pp. 53–62, 155–85; Gunn et al. (2007), pp. 169–72.
[56] Contamine in Contamine (1997), p. 252.

celebrate the king's energy and authority, was pressed into the service of diplomacy at the Field of Cloth of Gold. If France was at the beginning of the sixteenth century a 'military state',[57] then its king incontestably embodied its values. In England, in contrast, the king's image as a warrior appears to have become less important over time. Though present on one side of the Great Seal, it was always balanced by iconography related to justice, its use on coins was rare and in the sixteenth century Henry VIII's identity as a godly monarch was more insistently presented than that as a continental conqueror, important though it was to him personally to emulate Henry V and well though he could play the part of the conqueror riding into a humbled Tournai or Boulogne.[58]

4.   Political careers, offices and military values

For much of the later Middle Ages, military recruitment and service and local political organisation were less closely linked than historians of England, at least, used to think. But they were not entirely disconnected from each other, as consideration of both England and France suggests. The skills necessary for effective military command largely coincided with those required for effective local direction: decisiveness, sound judgement, the ability to organise, to lead, to consult, to delegate, to inspire, to be respected and obeyed, to use violence in measured but forceful ways. When too strongly flavoured with self-assertive aggression, these qualities produced noblemen who could easily be sent to face the enemy, but who were better kept out of local politics, where they were too disruptive for comfort: that seems to have been equally the case for Bertrand du Guesclin and the young John Talbot, first earl of Shrewsbury. When kept within bounds, however, these qualities seem to have equipped lords such as Jacques de Bourbon, count of La Marche, in the mid fourteenth century, Richard Beauchamp, earl of Warwick in the early fifteenth century, or John de Vere, earl of Oxford in the late fifteenth and early sixteenth century, to be both successful generals and able local rulers, functions which reinforced one another as honour gained in war inspired respect for local lordship.

Yet even Richard Beauchamp found that long absences in France weakened his grip on Warwickshire politics. In England those noblemen best able to combine military leadership with local power were those whose estates lay near the vulnerable borders of the realm, the Percies, the Nevilles and the Dacres in the north and, from the fifteenth century, the Fitzgerald earls of Kildare in Ireland. It was here on the borders

---

[57] Contamine (2002).   [58] Gunn et al. (2007), pp. 250–2.

that peers were created and endowed to fill specific military roles, from Andrew Harclay, Edward II's earl of Carlisle, to Thomas, Lord Wharton, captain of both Carlisle and Berwick in the 1550s. The fees paid to the northern or Anglo-Irish lords as wardens of the marches or deputies or lieutenants of Ireland and their considerable landed revenues enabled them to spend heavily on retaining the followers they needed to mount effective defence of the borders: eighty-four lords, knights and esquires in the extreme case of Henry Percy, fourth earl of Northumberland, in the 1480s. Such payment interacted with feudal lordship, the tenure of offices in seigneurial estate administration and castle captaincies, family traditions of service and repeated warfare against the Scots or Gaels to produce the most coherent and militarily effective affinities in the later medieval English realms. Even the choice of tenants was subordinated to military considerations, Lord Dacre telling his officials in 1536 to give preference to good archers in letting his lands even if they paid lower entry fines. No wonder Percy and Neville troops did much of the most significant fighting of the Wars of the Roses. Richard, duke of Gloucester's usurpation in 1483 was made possible by the strong following he had built up during his years as a northern magnate, leader in the Scottish war and political legatee of his Neville father-in-law. So strong was the Fitzgerald following that mid-sixteenth-century English regimes found that, following the family's revolt in 1534, they could barely govern Ireland without it. Yet the attempt to do so was symptomatic of the growing suspicion of such unfettered noble power at court. The 1530s introduced a period of experimentation in the government of Ireland and northern England designed to increase control from London and lessen the freedom of action of local noblemen. These aims were to some degree achieved, but the cost in the short term was that defending the borders became much harder.[59]

Away from the borders, military service might modify political structures more subtly by its role in careerism and social mobility. Influential offices in central or provincial government might be gained by those who demonstrated competence in wartime leadership. In England, this was particularly true of offices with heavy military responsibility, such as the lieutenancy of Ireland or the county lieutenancies introduced in 1550 to command the county militia and exercise some oversight over local administration, but it also applied to posts in the royal household. At the local level military men might be endowed with a significant estate and a peerage title by royal grant, or be given important offices in the management of the king's landed interest. In France exceptional military abilities

---

[59] Carpenter (1992), pp. 347–98; Ellis (1995).

might win extraordinary promotion, Gaston de Foix becoming general commander-in-chief of the French army and governor of the duchy of Milan in 1511, at the age of just 21 years. More generally there was a strong correlation in the later fifteenth century between captains in the *ordonnance* and holders of the local and regional offices of *bailli*, *sénéchal* and *gouverneur*. This regional concentration of powers, concealing a real subjection of provincial government to military priorities, developed further during the Italian wars.

Yet the relationship between promotion and military service was rarely straightforward. The role of courts as the centres of distribution of military command meant that those close to the king won command as they won influence and reward of other kinds. This left it unclear whether it was chiefly military success or royal intimacy that underpinned their rise. Sir Thomas Erpingham, commander of the archers at Agincourt, was influential in Norfolk through his leadership of the political connection based around the duchy of Lancaster estates there, but had won this power through his close association with Henry IV and Henry V, both of whom he served as steward of the household, long before 1415. Charles Brandon was created duke of Suffolk following his part in Henry VIII's capture of Tournai, but he was already the king's favourite courtier when he was appointed marshal of his army. The rise of Anne de Montmorency, who became *maréchal de France* at the age of 30 years in 1523, was easily justifiable by his military career in the Italian Wars, but was founded above all on the relationship he had built up since the age of 10 with King Francis I, who was not very much younger than him.[60] The supreme example of the interplay between intimacy and military office was kinship with the king, for example in the case of the *lieutenant général du roi*. This office was created in the last decades of the thirteenth century to strengthen royal administration in the French provinces,[61] played a significant role in the following centuries and finally gave birth to the *gouvernements*, yet at least until the fifteenth century it was only given out within the narrow circle of the blood royal.

Lesser captains might be granted offices, pensions or land leases as rewards for military service and returning soldiers might invest their profits in land and the influence that came with it. Examples of both can be found, especially in areas where the dominant lord was the king or a royal prince. But in most English counties soldiers made much less impact on the land market and the turnover of gentry families than lawyers, courtiers or noble household servants. At a time when the land market was not as fluid as it would become at the dissolution of the

---

[60] Knecht (1998), p. 18.   [61] Hélary (2005), pp. 169–90.

monasteries in the 1530s, most soldiers probably did not have the access to information, professional contacts and ability to wait until the right moment to buy that made lawyers such effective competitors for the land that was for sale. It took very large profits and great skill in investing them to turn military success into landed wealth at home, as Sir John Fastolf or Bertrand du Guesclin did; and even Fastolf seems not to have been able to play a significant role in Norfolk politics on his retirement from France. Military careerism may have played a more significant role in the life of nobles from the periphery of the two kingdoms: Bretons, Burgundians and Gascons in France, or the Welsh gentry. The latter's opportunities in local government and land acquisition were restricted by the Edwardian conquest and the aftermath of the Glyndŵr rebellion and some made up for it in war, but even in Wales the rising families were not necessarily those with the most active military records. All in all it is no surprise that captains such as Sir Robert Knolles and Sir Hugh Calveley found it easier to collect castles and estates in Brittany and in Valencia than in England.[62]

Military mentalities shaped politics in another way by creating political networks that were very real to contemporaries, but are now hard for us to recover. The formal relationship of brotherhood-in-arms may have been difficult to translate from the battlefield to the world of government, though it has been claimed that it was the bond tying Edward II to his greatest favourite Piers Gaveston. The looser connection between a knight and the man who knighted him seems to have been sufficiently strong in constituting or confirming allegiances that commanders from Richard, duke of Gloucester in the 1480s to Charles Brandon, duke of Suffolk in the 1520s and beyond were eager to knight their followers, or those they hoped would become their followers, on campaign. The connection between those who had fought together in a great battle such as Crécy, Verneuil or Marignano was powerful and durable enough to colour the personal relationships between great men which were central to peacetime politics and government.

Whether any more specific political views were associated with men of war – a belligerent attitude to diplomatic problems, say, or a ruthlessness in extracting the resources needed for war whatever the constitutional niceties – is much harder to say. But we should not dismiss the possibility that thinking about and practising war made men approach politics in certain characteristic ways, albeit ways less systematically expressed than those of lawyers or clerical intellectuals. Some men of war certainly developed distinctive conceptions of their place in society, though it is

---

[62] Morgan (1987) pp. 49–56, 174–8; Payling (1991), pp. 31–43; Davies (1995), pp. 52–7, 309–13; Fowler (2001), pp. 253–8.

hard to know how typical they were. For the knight Guillaume de La Penne, writing in 1378, a professional soldier who fought in the first rank in the company of Sylvestre Budes, the practice of arms made the warrior a superior being and it was the duty of civilians to serve him in the accomplishment of his mission. The captain whose deeds he related was supposed to have told his troops as they marched against rebels 'take no account of these false, tyrannous villains; they are worse than infidels'; these political opponents were to be denied all human mercy, banished from the bounds of Christendom, justly treated with the most extreme violence.[63]

The attitudes of men-at-arms at war also depended upon whom or what men thought they were serving when they fought. The concept of the fatherland does not seem to have been very well developed in fourteenth-century France. Geoffroy de Charny, the inspiration behind the Order of the Star, distinguished in his *Livre de chevalerie* between those who fought out of duty towards their lord, their kin or their lands and those who fought in distant lands for various reasons, and it was the latter who, he thought, should be more highly esteemed. His advice was thus more fit to win renown for those who followed it than to direct the efforts of the chivalrous classes towards the defence of the realm.[64] In the same way, the biography of Jacques de Lalaing used his remarkable career to glorify the greatness and beauty of Philip the Good's rule more than the duty of Burgundian knights born within the kingdom of France towards that kingdom's king.[65] The standard idea in England, meanwhile, was that those who fought were serving the king, in what they almost universally called 'the king's wars' when writing their wills before going on campaign or making entries for military expenditure in accounts. The realities of recruitment must have meant that many of them were also serving their landlord, household employer or political patron, a duality visually represented by the way in which Percy troops in 1523, for example, wore the king's badge on their jackets but the Percy badge just below it.

In France after Agincourt the king began to be seen as the natural defender of a fatherland, though its shape was still very vague. The change went both with the new intellectual discourse on war of Alain Chartier, secretary to Charles VII, and with a new emphasis on personal sacrifice that elevated those who died in combat to the rank of martyrs, as in the mass for those fallen at Verneuil.[66] However, we should remember

[63] Jamme (1996), p. 162: 'ne faitez compte De ses villains, faux et tirans; Ilz sont pirez que mescreans'.

[64] Contamine (2005), pp. 171–84.   [65] Small (1997).

[66] Contamine (1986); Jones (2002).

that the war-cry of the royal army became 'France' only during the Italian wars and thus outside the context of any notion of defence of the native land. It was in practice only in the sixteenth century that the idea of the fatherland really expanded. By 1550, under classical impetus, some Englishmen were also coming to think that they were serving some more impersonal political entity: the epitaph that Charles Blount, Lord Mountjoy prescribed for his tomb in his will when he went to war in 1544 included the couplet 'Discharged I am of that I ought / To my country by honest wound'.[67]

In France this long absence of a patriotic point of reference left plenty of room for individual hero-worship. In the later medieval centuries chivalrous society generated many biographical narratives and each social layer of men-at-arms had its torch-bearer, whether prince or duke – Louis I of Bourbon, John IV of Brittany, Arthur de Richemont, Gaston IV of Foix – or a humbler knight – du Guesclin, Boucicaut, Lalaing. The social and political circumstances of the later Middle Ages doubtless explain the remarkable prominence of a literary current that held up as models the most gifted representatives of a nobility determined to defend its prerogatives. But these works were not just a vehicle for courtiers' justification of their role in society. The clear-eyed realism of Jean de Bueil in *Le Jouvencel* and the cool claims to class supremacy of Guillaume de La Penne attest to the variety of ways, some of them almost unthinking, in which the case for traditional privileges was expressed. It remains the case that the historical foundation of these biographies, more or less embellished for narrative purposes, conferred a tangible character on the heroes thus marked out. They were not the swan song of outdated values, more or less successfully performed, for they transmitted usable models for action. The legend of the knightly hero Bayard, elaborated in the decades after his death on the basis of Symphorien Champier's biography, set forth an ideal that was still familiar, making service to the prince in his war a sort of blossoming of the personality: Brantôme recommended it as reading for young nobles.[68] Though there were celebrated lives of William the Marshal and the Black Prince, England had a much weaker tradition of chivalric biography than France. That did not mean, though, that it had no heroes: as John Coke wrote in 1550 of Sir Edward Poynings, if the French had had 'suche a noble knight they wold have made of his actes a great boke'.[69]

In France the legend of Bayard also came to meet new historical conditions. Military service to the king had changed considerably. The

---

[67] *Testamenta Vetusta*, ed. Nicolas (1826), vol. II, p. 721; Stow (1971), vol. I, p. 253.
[68] Lazard (1995), n. 943.   [69] Coke (1550), G vii r.

increased technical complexity of war and the near-permanent state of conflict from 1494 had favoured the birth of a distinctive culture which found its identity in war. Blaise de Monluc was among those who best deployed the richness of a specialised and highly coloured language, one inflected with humour and with a sharp sense of mockery, featuring expressions still used today: 'faire une couyonnade' (to make a bad manoeuvre), 'mettre les armes au dessus du fogon' (to ready arms), 'sonner' or 'battre la chamade' (to surrender), 'serrer les fesses' (to clench one's buttocks [in fear]) . . . The Italian Wars played a decisive role in the formation and adoption of a new military vocabulary. It included words for weapons (*canon, mousquet*), ranks (*soldat, sentinelle, caporal, colonel*) and tactical units (*infanterie, cavalerie, bataillon, patrouille*). It included words for actions and operations, *escarmouche* for a skirmish and many more that provided for the precise description of the infinite variety of manoeuvres and tactical situations a conflict might produce by translation of the Italian suffix -ata: *embuscade, arquebusade, cannonade, retirade* and so on.[70] A large proportion of the military terms in use in France up to the eighteenth century were of Italian origin, a side-effect of the French conquest of Italy which certainly did not only touch the language of war but indisputably found there its first victim. This change in vocabulary was one of the main signs of the growing distance between the values of the court nobility and those of the lesser and middling military nobility. In England, in contrast, there was little sign of the emergence of a specialised military nobility before the mid sixteenth century. Only then did the development of court-based clienteles led by militarily active noblemen find a special place for experts in the use of firearms and the defence of modern fortifications, just as the captaincy of artillery forts and naval bases around the English coast and garrison posts in Ireland became part of a new military *cursus honorum*.

Conclusion

The development of the military systems of France and England displays many common features and yet resulted in ultimate divergence. This is best explained by the interaction of a complex series of forces which took effect at different times and in different combinations to produce sometimes similar and sometimes contrasting developments in the two polities.

The first such force was the personality and the political vision of individual kings. Military leadership was a fundamental aspect of kingship

[70] Potter (1992), pp. 352–7.

and military service was above all service to the king. Systemic change originated of necessity with him. The king's initiative negotiated with the interest of his subjects in the construction of the fiscal basis of military power. It is clear that the permanent military institutions of France depended upon the regularity of French taxation, whether the *aides* and *fouages* of Charles V or the *aide* and *taille* of Charles VII. In England, in contrast, the contingency of taxation on parliamentary grant matched the raising of new forces for each campaign. Domestic politics were also important in the sense that military policy formed a central part of the king's relationship with the nobility in both countries. In France, the entrenchment of the standing army was assured by its colonisation by the nobility. In England, foreign war was a joint enterprise of mutual benefit to king and nobles alike.

Tactical and technological changes made certain military formats suddenly more effective or desirable at particular times. The perfection of English archery tactics in the Scottish wars of Edward III shaped English armies and strategies for more than a century thereafter. The rise of Swiss-style infantry armed with pike and arquebuses similarly reshaped the French army from Louis XI's time. The increased effectiveness of artillery in siege and battle gave it a special prominence in French strategy from the re-conquest of Normandy to the Italian Wars. The new navies of the sixteenth century exploited the capabilities of larger cannon firing through gunports and better trimmed ships. Some historians would also link developments in military systems to social and economic change. After the Black Death, it may have been easier for the English to raise small mobile forces suitable for *chevauchées* than large armies of foot-soldiers, as they drew less labour out of the agricultural economy. In a French countryside ravaged by war, payments from the king in return for defending their province probably helped to compensate French noblemen for their losses in estate income.

Clearly, the intense competition between the French and English monarchies did much to shape their respective military arrangements as each sought to respond to the other's strategies. French naval policy in the Channel repeatedly aimed to contest English control. The permanent companies of Charles V were designed to counter English *chevauchées*. But French developments were also determined by a wider range of geopolitical factors. From the 1450s it was confrontation with Burgundy, Brittany and later with the Italian powers and Spain that drove the monarchy to develop ever-stronger armed forces. From these complex processes England emerged unable for a century or more to compete with her continental neighbours in warfare on land, but with the foundations of a formidable power at sea. France was established as one of the most powerful military states in Europe, demonstratively so on land and with ambitions to be so at sea. Yet the Wars of Religion were to show that the monarchy's strength in international conflicts did not correspond to its ability to compel the obedience of its subjects.

BIBLIOGRAPHY

1. INTRODUCTION

Allmand, C. T., 1988. *The Hundred Years War. England and France at War 1300–1450*, Cambridge (revised edn 2001).
Bell, A. R., Curry, A., King, A. and Simpkin, D., 2013. *The Soldier in Later Medieval England*, Oxford.
Contamine, P., 1980. *La guerre au Moyen Âge*, Paris (new edn) 2010; trans. M. Jones, 1984. *War in the Middle Ages*, Oxford.
(ed.), 1992. *Histoire militaire de la France, vol. I. Des origines à 1715*, Paris (2nd edn 1997).

2. SOURCES CITED

Coke, John, *The Debate betwene the Heraldes of Englande and Fraunce*, London, 1550.
Construire l'armée française. Textes fondateurs des institutions militaires, ed. V. Bessey, vol. I, *De la France des Valois à la fin du règne de François Ier*, Turnhout, 2006.
Pizan, Christine de, *Livre de la Paix*, ed. C. C. Willard, La Haye, 1958.
Livre des faits et bonnes mœurs du roi Charles V, ed. S. Solente, SHF, Geneva, 1977.
Stow, J., *A Survey of London*, ed. C. L. Kingsford, Oxford, 1971.
Sur Charles VIII et l'Italie, Livres VII et VIII, ed. and trans. Fr. J. Dufournet, Paris, 2002.
Testamenta Vetusta, ed. N. H. Nicolas, 2 vols., London, 1826.

3. FURTHER READING

Allmand, C. T., 1999. 'Entre honneur et bien commun: le témoignage du Jouvencel au xve siècle', *Revue historique*, 123, 463–82.
Ayton, A. and Preston, P., 2005. *The Battle of Crécy, 1346*, Woodbridge.
Baier, R., 2004. 'Guise, französisches Herzogsgeschlecht', *Biographisch-bibliographisches Kirchenlexikon*, 23, 568–93.
Bean, J. M. W., 1989. *From Lord to Patron: Lordship in Late Medieval England*, Manchester.
Boulton d'Arcy, J. D., 2000. *The Knights of the Crown: the Monarchical Orders of Knighthood in Later Medieval Europe 1325–1520*, Woodbridge (2nd edn).
Bourquin, L., 1994. *Noblesse seconde et pouvoir en Champagne*, Paris.
Boutoulle, F. and Pépin, G., forthcoming. *Routiers et mercenaires dans les conflits de la guerre de Cent Ans. Études offertes à J. Sumption*, Bordeaux.

Brown, E. A. R., 1981. 'Reform and Resistance to Royal Authority in Fourteenth-Century France: The Leagues of 1314–1315', *Parliaments, Estates and Representation*, I, 109–137.

Butaud, G., 2012. *Les compagnies de routiers en France (1357–1393)*, Clermond-Ferrand.

Carpenter, C., 1992. *Locality and Polity: A Study of Warwickshire Landed Society 1401–1499*, Cambridge.

Collins, H. E. L., 2000. *The Order of the Garter, 1348–1461: Chivalry and Politics in Late Medieval England*, Oxford.

Contamine, P., 1972. *Guerre, Etat et société à la fin du Moyen Âge. Etudes sur les armées des rois de France 1337–1494*, Paris-La Haye (new edn 2003, Paris).

1981. *La France aux xive et xve siècles: hommes, mentalités, guerre et paix*, London.

1986. 'Mourir pour la patrie', in P. Nora, ed., *Les lieux de mémoire II La Nation*, Paris, pp. 11–43.

1987. 'Structures militaires de la France et de l'Angleterre au milieu du xve siècle', in R. Schneider (ed.), *Das spätmittelalterliche Königtum im europäischen Vergleich*, Sigmaringen, pp. 319–34.

1997a. 'Le Jouvencel de Jean de Bueil. Une expérience romancée et personnelle de la guerre au xve siècle', *Revue d'histoire de la Société des amis du musée de l'armée*, 114, 42–54.

1997b. *La noblesse au royaume de France, de Philippe le Bel à Louis XI*, Paris.

2002. 'Deux Etats militaires vers 1500: le royaume de France et l'empire ottoman. Une mise en parallèle', *Cahiers du CEHD*, 18, 69–85.

2005. *Pages d'histoire militaire médiévale, xive–xve siècle*, Paris.

(ed.), 1989. *L'Etat et les aristocraties (xiie–xviie siècle). France, Angleterre, Ecosse*, Paris.

(ed.), 1992. *Histoire militaire de la France, vol. I. Des origines à 1715*, Paris (2nd edn 1997).

(ed.), 1998. *Guerre et concurrence entre États européens du xive au xviiie siècle*, Paris (trans. 2000, *War and Competition between States*, Oxford).

Contamine, P., Bouzy, O. and Hélary, X., 2012. *Jeanne d'Arc. Histoire et dictionnaire*, Paris.

Contamine, P., Giry-Deloison, C. and Keen, M. H. (eds.), 1991. *Guerre et société en France, en Angleterre et en Bourgogne, xive–xve siècle*, Villeneuve-d'Ascq.

Cordey, J., 1911. *Les comtes de Savoie et les rois de France pendant la guerre de Cent ans (1329–1391)*, Paris.

Crouzet, D., 2003. *Charles de Bourbon, connétable de France*, Paris.

Curry, A. E., 2005. *Agincourt. A New History*, London.

Davies, M. B., 1944. 'Suffolk's Expedition to Montdidier in 1523', *Fouad I University, Bulletin of the Faculty of Arts*, 7, 33–43.

Davies, R. R., 1995. *The Revolt of Owain Glyn Dŵr*, Oxford.

De Medeiros, M. T., 1998. 'Défense et illustration de la guerre. Le Jouvencel de Jean de Bueil', *Cahiers de recherches médiévales*, 5, 139–52.

Dubost, J.-F., 1997. *La France italienne xvie–xviie siècle*, Paris.

Dunham, W. H., 1955. *Lord Hastings' Indentured Retainers 1461–1483*, New Haven.

Ellis, S. G., 1995. *Tudor Frontiers and Noble Power: The Making of the British State*, Oxford.

Finer, S. E., 1975. 'State- and Nation-building in Europe: The Role of the Military', in C. Tilly (ed.), *The Formation of National States in Western Europe*, Princeton, pp. 84–163.

La France anglaise au Moyen Âge, 111e congrès des Sociétés Savantes, Paris, 1986.

Fowler, K., 2001. *Medieval Mercenaries, Volume 1: The Great Companies*, Oxford.

Gaucher, E., 1994. *La biographie chevaleresque. Typologie d'un genre (XIIIe–XVe siècle)*, Paris.

Given-Wilson, C., 1986. *The Royal Household and the King's Affinity: Service, Politics and Finance in England 1360–1413*, New Haven and London.

Goodman, A., 1981a. *The Wars of the Roses: Military Activity and English Society, 1452–97*, London.

1981b. 'Responses to Requests in Yorkshire for Military Service under Henry V', *Northern History*, 17, 240–52.

Goring, J. J., 1975. 'Social Change and Military Decline in Mid-Tudor England', *History*, 60, 185–97.

Green, D. S., 2000. 'The Later Retinue of Edward the Black Prince', *Nottingham Mediaeval Studies*, 44, 141–51.

Gunn, S. J., 1998. 'Sir Thomas Lovell (c.1449–1524): A New Man in a New Monarchy?', in J. L. Watts (ed.), *The End of the Middle Ages? England in the Fifteenth and Sixteenth Centuries*, Stroud.

, Grummitt, D. and Cools, H., 2007. *War, State and Society in England and the Netherlands, 1477–1559*, Oxford.

Hélary, X., 2005. 'Délégation du pouvoir et contrôle des officiers. Les lieutenants du roi sous Philippe III et Philippe IV', in L. Feller (ed.), *Les agents du pouvoir*, Limoges, pp. 169–90.

2012. *L'armée du roi de France. La guerre de Saint-Louis à Philippe le Bel*, Paris.

Hewitt, H. J., 1966. *The Organization of War under Edward III 1338–1362*, Manchester.

James, M. E., 1986. *Society, Politics and Culture: Studies in Early Modern England*, Cambridge.

Jamme, A., 1996. 'Les soudoyers pontificaux d'Outremont et leurs violences en Italie (1372–1398)', in P. Contamine and O. Guyotjeannin (eds.) *La guerre, la violence et les gens au Moyen Âge, I, Guerre et violence*, Paris, pp. 151–68.

Jones, M. C. E. (ed.), 2004. *Letters, Orders and Musters of Bertrand du Guesclin, 1357–1380*, Woodbridge.

Jones, M. K., 2002. 'The Battle of Verneuil (17 August 1424): Towards a History of Courage', *War in History*, 9, 375–411.

Keen, M., 2002. *Origins of the English Gentleman: Heraldry, Chivalry and Gentilityin Medieval England, c.1300–c.1500*, Stroud.

Kerhervé, J., 1999. 'Une existence en perpétuel mouvement. Arthur de Richemont, connétable de France et duc de Bretagne (1393–1458)', in J. A. García de Cortázar (ed.), *Viajeros, peregrinos, mercaderes en el Occidente medieval*, Pamplona, pp. 69–114.

Knecht, R. J., 1994. *Renaissance Warrior and Patron: The Reign of Francis I*, Cambridge (tr. Fr., 1998. *Un prince de la Renaissance. François Ier et son royaume*, Paris).

Lainé, F. and Given-Wilson, C., 2002. *Les prisonniers de la bataille de Poitiers*, Paris.

Lalande, D., 1988. *Jean II Le Meingre, dit Boucicaut (1366–1421). Etude d'une biographie héroïque*, Geneva.

Lassalmonie, J.-F., 2001. 'L'abbé Le Grand et le compte du trésorier des guerres pour 1464: les compagnies d'ordonnance à la veille du bien public', *Journal des Savants*, 43–92.

Lazard, M., 1995. *Pierre de Bourdeille, seigneur de Brantôme*, Paris.

Le Saux, F., 2004. 'War and Knighthood in Christine de Pizan's *Livre des faits d'armes et de chevallerie*', in C. Saunders, F. Le Saux and N. Thomas (eds.) *Writing War. Medieval Literary Responses to Warfare*, Cambridge, pp. 93–105.

Meek, E. L., 2001. 'The Career of Sir Thomas Everingham, "Knight of the North", in the Service of Maximilian, Duke of Austria, 1477–81', *Historical Research*, 74, 238–48.

Merlin-Chazelas, A., 1977–8. *Documents relatifs au Clos des Galées de Rouen et aux armées de mer du roi de France de 1293 à 1418*, 2 vols., Paris.

Michaud, H., 1977. 'Les institutions militaires des guerres d'Italie aux guerres de religion', *Revue historique*, 523, 29–43.

Millar, G. J., 1980. *Tudor Mercenaries and Auxiliaries 1485–1547*, Charlottesville.

Morgan, D. A. L., 1990. 'From a Death to a View: Louis Robessart, Johan Huizinga, and the Political Significance of Chivalry', in S. Anglo (ed.), *Chivalry in the Renaissance*, Woodbridge, pp. 93–106.

Morgan, P., 1987. *War and Society in Medieval Cheshire*, Chetham Society 3rd Series, 34.

Norris, M. M., 1995. 'The 2nd Earl of Rutland's Band of Men-at-arms, 1551–2', *Historical Research*, 68, 110–16.

Payling, S. J., 1991. *Political Society in Lancastrian England: The Greater Gentry of Nottinghamshire*, Oxford.

Pépin, G., 2006. 'Towards a New Assessment of the Black Prince's Principality of Aquitaine: A Study of the Last Years (1369–1372)', *Nottingham Medieval Studies*, 50, 59–114.

Pérouse, G.-A. Thierry, A. and Tournon, A., 1992. *L'homme de guerre au xvie siècle*, Limonest.

Pollard, A. J., 1983. *John Talbot and the War in France, 1427–1453*, London.

Potter, D. 1993. *War and Government in the French Provinces. Picardy 1470–1560*, Cambridge.

     2001. *Un homme de guerre au temps de la Renaissance : la vie et les lettres d'Oudart du Biez, maréchal de France, gouverneur de Boulogne et de Picardie (vers 1475–1553)*, Arras.

Prestwich, M., 1996. *Armies and Warfare in the Middle Ages: The English Experience*, New Haven and London.

Rodger, N. A. M., 1997. *The Safeguard of the Sea: A Naval History of Britain, Volume One, 660–1649*, London.

Schnerb, B., 1997. *Enguerrand de Bournonville et les siens. Un lignage noble du Boulonnais aux xive et xve siècles*, Paris.

Serdon, V., 2005. *Armes du diable. Arcs et arbalètes au Moyen Âge*, Rennes.

Small, G., 1997. *George Chastelain and the Shaping of Valois Burgundy. Political and Historical Culture at Court in the Fifteenth Century*, Woodbridge.

Vale, M. G. A., 1990. *The Angevin Legacy and the Hundred Years War 1250–1340*, Oxford.

Verrier, F., 1997. *Les armes de Minerve. L'humanisme militaire dans l'Italie du xvie siècle*, Paris.

Walker, S. K., 1990. *The Lancastrian Affinity 1361–1399*, Oxford.

1999. 'Janico Dartasso: Chivalry, Nationality and the Man-at-arms', *History*, 84, 31–51.

4 Offices and officers

Christine Carpenter and Olivier Mattéoni

Bureaucrats cannot be divorced from the administrations that they ran and so this chapter will inevitably also include some account of the governments of these two countries in this period. It is in fact the development of the respective governments that immediately highlights a major difference between the two and in many respects explains the ways in which their servants and the aspirations and career patterns of these men diverged. To put it simply, England developed as a state some time before France did. Recent work on 'state formation' across Europe, notably that sponsored by the CNRS, tends to assume that it occurred at roughly the same time, that is from the late thirteenth century. In England, however, because of the considerable growth in central and local government under the Norman and Angevin kings, one may legitimately speak of a state by the early thirteenth century. This state provided kings with money for their wars on the continent and an administration that could function during their absence abroad. However, the most significant development in medieval English state formation was the creation of a legal system, the 'common law', which brought very large numbers of the king's subjects into the purview of an institutionalised system run by the king's officers and directly under the authority of the king. In France, the emergence of the state owed less to the existence of an institutionalised body of law – there was no equivalent to the common law – than to the activities of kings in judicial, legislative and fiscal matters. In this regard, the reigns of Louis IX, who came to be regarded as the source of all justice, and of Philip the Fair, who was the first king to tax his subjects, are crucial. As the Crown secured more control over the kingdom, its needs changed, and the royal administration developed rapidly at the end of the thirteenth century in both scope and specialisation.

It is not only the history but also the historiography of the two countries which is different, however. Because England was already a highly centralised and much governed country well before 1300, and even more so by 1400, accounts of the development of government in England have not elided medieval growth with the so-called growth of the 'renaissance state' which has been such a feature of continental historiography. Late medieval English government and bureaucrats therefore have a historiography which is much more distinct from the early modern one than one finds in many other countries, including France. England also has a far larger archive of records of the central government, some of which stretch back in almost unbroken series to the mid thirteenth century, and correspondingly much smaller noble administrative archives. The only exceptions here are those which prove the rule : the duchy of Lancaster, which came to the Crown in 1399, and the earldom of Chester, which was Crown property throughout this period. These two, almost uniquely, had their own administrative, legal and estate offices and law, modelled on those of the central government, if on a much smaller scale, and, because they were owned by the kings, their archives have been well preserved with the national records.[1] Otherwise, the historian of England's bureaucrats from c.1250 to 1500 deals almost exclusively with the central government, which was already departmentalised and becoming more so, in some cases with departments which already had a considerable history and powerful culture. In France, the situation is quite different. First of all, the archival situation is much less satisfactory. Many documents, including complete series, have disappeared: most notably the Crown's financial records, which were affected especially badly by the fire which struck the *Chambre des comptes* in 1737 – scarcely a single general account of the receivers has come down to us, for example. But similar gaps exist for the chancery and the *Châtelet*, not to mention the archives of the *bailliages*, which, in many districts, have suffered total destruction. A second difference concerns the administrative development of territorial principalities or *états princiers*. These principalities acquired substantial and specialised administrations, often on the royal model, and, in some cases (Burgundy, Brittany), became innovative centres for the emergence of a bureaucratic culture. Their archives have often survived rather well, those of Burgundy, in particular, offering a real 'embarrassment of riches': the accounts of the ducal receiver-general are more or less complete from 1387 to 1477, and the same is true for the accounts of several Burgundian *châtellenies* in the fifteenth century.[2]

---

[1] The other exception was the palatinate of Durham but, as the preserve of the bishops of Durham, this was non-hereditary and, as a major defensive bulwark in the north, was usually given to men who were close to the king.

[2] Paravicini (1996).

1.   Types of officer

We shall begin by defining the type of officer we intend to discuss. In both countries, there were four main types. First, there were the officers of the central government. In England, these initially travelled with the king as part of his household but increasingly became settled at Westminster, as this became the locus of government in the twelfth to fourteenth centuries. They ranged from the lowliest clerk to the great officers of state, the treasurer and chancellor, who, during the course of the fourteenth century, were joined, as the third great officer, by the keeper of the privy seal. These three officers almost invariably sat on the king's council. There were also the administrative officers of the king's household, among them those who served in the wardrobe, a key agency of royal finance in wartime from the late thirteenth century, and the chamber, which became the centre of the king's finances in the late fifteenth and early sixteenth centuries. The signet office, another part of the household, emerged as a significant body with its own clerks under Richard II and became more fully established in the following century. For most of this period the administrative staff of all these departments were indeed clerks in both senses of the word, though, as we shall see, there were changes later.

In France, the officers of the central government were the heads of its principal departments which were also its sovereign courts – the *Parlement* and the *Chambre des comptes* – which became established in the second half of the thirteenth century with the break-up of the *curia regis*, together with the officers of the royal chancery. A clear separation of personal service to the prince from service to the state meant that the royal household, or more precisely the king's chamber, never had the significance in financial administration that the wardrobe and chamber periodically assumed in England. Rather, as royal fiscality grew, other institutions developed to manage it: notably the *Chambre des Monnaies* (1348), *Cour des aides* (1389) and the *Chambre du Trésor* (1390), all of which dealt with financial disputes. At the same time, certain officers of the royal household may be regarded as ministers of state: this is especially true of the great officers of the Crown – the chancellor for example – whose functions evolved along with those of the monarchy. The *maîtres des requêtes*, often jurists, whose professional world was not limited solely to the household, played an important role in decision-making. Similarly, the treasurers of France, having been one of the essential cogs in the household, experienced an enlargement of their function under Philip the Fair: they organised transfers of funds and rendered their accounts before the *Chambre des comptes*.

Until the reforms of the 1440s, the treasurers were a single body; there-after, each had their own specific jurisdiction.

The officers of the French central administration often played a role on the king's council on account of their specific expertise and responsi-bilities. This is very clear in the case of the chancellor – a highly political officer, who, in theory, presided over the council in the absence of the king – but it applies equally to the members of the *grandes cours*. At the time when the officers were chosen by election (1370–1415), members of the *Parlement* and officers of the *Chambre des comptes* participated in the election procedure which took place in the context of the king's council. The king could also designate his central officers as commissioners or *enquêteurs*: jurists were among the *enquêteurs-réformateurs* appointed by Philip the Fair and his sons, for instance.

In the principalities too, central administrations developed and admin-istrative elites emerged. If not all the principalities had a *Parlement* – many instead held *Grands Jours*, an outgrowth of the council, which acted as a court of appeal – all of them had a *Chambre des comptes*, which often emerged as the sole permanently constituted part of their administra-tion. But there is a significant chronological difference between the royal and the princely administrations: the creation of a central administration occurred later in the princely territories than in the royal government. Thus, the *Chambre des comptes* of Brittany, Berry, the Bourbonnais and Anjou did not appear until the second half of the fourteenth century, only those of Forez (1317), the Beaujolais and the Dauphiné (both in the 1340s) coming earlier.

The second group in England comprises the men who were great about the king and also important local officers. They are found at the beginning and end of the period and their existence reflects political structures which favoured the king's direct rule of the localities. Indeed, by about 1250, this type of officer was already much less integral to royal government. They tended to be very close to the king and thus to be members of his household. Under Henry II and his sons, they were usu-ally military commanders of household forces and often acted as sheriffs, placing the shires under an almost military occupation, especially under John, when some of the most hated figures were men of this kind: for example, William Brewer and Philip Mark. They were therefore usually laymen. From the 1230s, once changes to the shrievalty had made it no longer financially attractive to these great curialists, and royal govern-ment itself was forced to become less predatory, this type of officer began to disappear, although, in the following century, as Richard Partington's contribution to this volume shows, Edward III was still making extensive use, on judicial and military commissions, of men who were close to him.[3] It was under Henry VII that they began to reappear, if in a different guise. Again, they were often members of the king's household and, with few exceptions, laymen, but they were expert administrators, often qualified lawyers, or at least recipients of a legal training. They advised and worked for the king at the centre, often through membership of his council, which was now becoming a complex administrative operation, and acted for him in a variety of capacities in the localities, either in directly mandated commissions and enquiries or by filling the important local offices.

The French equivalent of this group were the *baillis* and *sénéchaux* who played an essential role for the kings, being the interface between the central and local governments and linking the prince to his subjects. These were, at first, temporary royal commissioners sent into the royal *domaine* at the end of the twelfth century, but they became settled in their localities from the 1220s, and this eventually gave rise to the administrative districts which emerged in the second half of the thirteenth century. The number of *bailliages* and *sénéchaussées* rose from twenty-three in *c.*1285 to twenty-eight in 1328, rising to seventy-five under Louis XI and about eighty at the end of the fifteenth century. Between the end of the thirteenth century and the end of the fifteenth, the type of man appointed *bailli* changed. If, at the start of the reign of Philip the Fair, the *baillis*, like Philippe de Beaumanoir for example, were mostly noble, from the small or middling *noblesse* – landowners, lawyers, even jurists (some of them finished their careers in the *Parlement*) – in the second half of the fourteenth century, the military side of their duties was accentuated with the coming of the Hundred Years War. Thus, they often combined their office with the captaincy of a fortification and a military company. Above all, from the 1380s, their responsibilities became politicised, when princely rivalries erupted in Charles VI's entourage. From being the king's representatives, many mutated into agents of the Armagnac and Burgundian parties. It is therefore unsurprising that their fortunes rose and fell with the changes of regime that punctuated the civil war (1408, 1413, 1418); many, moreover, fell at Agincourt. The military character of these offices persisted under Charles VII, who appointed many of his most loyal captains as *baillis* and *sénéchaux*, some of them former *écorcheurs* (such as Robert de Floques, or La Hire). These developments had two consequences. First, the *baillis* and the *sénéchaux* were increasingly recruited from the core of the ancient nobility, where the military tradition was generally strong. Secondly, from the fourteenth century, the *bailli* was assisted by auxiliaries: a general deputy (*lieutenant-général*) or, in the *sénéchaussées*,

---

[3] Carpenter (1976); Painter (1949).

a *juge-mage*, a man of law capable of presiding over the assizes, together with a receiver for financial business, a *procureur*, various captains, and a number of locally recruited clerks. Despite all these changes, the *bailli* remained the fundamental local officer of the Crown, even in the second half of the fifteenth century, when it was challenged by the office of governor: for it was the *bailli* who disseminated royal ordinances and, in this capacity, was charged with the enforcement of royal commands and expectations.

In England, the third group are what is often thought of as the quintessential type of English local officer from the late Middle Ages until well into the nineteenth century.[4] This is the 'gentleman amateur', the local landowner acting as the Crown's local agent. Increasingly from the 1230s, beginning with the sheriff, such offices were filled by local men, and the office of justice of the peace, which emerged during the fourteenth century, was very much a position for local gentry, specifically designed to be a permanent royal presence in the shires as the king's government extended ever deeper into society. In fact, these offices all demanded a measure of administrative expertise and some knowledge of the law, and it was probably not until the end of the fourteenth century or early in the fifteenth that there were enough gentry with these qualifications for such offices to be widely distributed among local landowners. It seems indeed that, for much of the later thirteenth and fourteenth centuries, they were held by rather small groups of local men, who therefore served sufficiently frequently to be seen as semi-professional officers. To their number should be added the merchants who acted as customs officials in the ports in the later Middle Ages. Finally, there were the men who serviced the local officers, acting as clerks and bailiffs – and these are the fourth group. At the start of the period, they were more likely to be clerics, especially the clerks, but by the end they would be laymen, often lawyers, or at least men with some legal training, of rather lowly standing.

In France, there was a similar group of local officers, but their judicial position was far from being the equivalent of that of the English 'gentleman amateurs'. These were the officers of the *châtellenies*, the principal units of administration at the end of the Middle Ages. If the castellan dominates this group, he was far from alone: a whole administrative personnel assisted him, from the captain to the sergeant, the lieutenant to the receiver, the *procureur* to the *prévôt*. The castellans themselves were certainly not a homogeneous group: if, in certain principalities, they were

---

[4] Urban officials of non-seigneurial towns have been excluded since they were, in immediate terms, more answerable to the town than to the king.

military officers, in other places they confined themselves to the tasks of estate management and exercise of lordship. On the royal *domaine*, their judicial function was often given precedence but that was by no means an absolute. While castellans were traditionally nobles *d'épée*, much of the work of the office was typically shouldered by deputies. In fact the job of castellan was not in any way the preserve of the *noblesse*. Although there were nobles among them, and continued to be throughout our period, merchants and lawyers did not spurn this office. More generally, jurists found places for themselves in the offices of princely *châtellenies*. Whatever their origins, in the local hierarchy, castellans were major figures in political society, at the same time as they contributed to fashioning and legitimising the regional elites. They controlled all the officers of the castellanship, some of whom were directly appointed by them. At the same time, because of the military power that was entrusted to them, they were responsible for the military levy within their area of authority. They therefore had authority over local *seigneurs*.

One group that cannot be classified as officers in this period is the English nobility. By the middle of the twelfth century they had ceased to hold the great local offices and, once the central government began to expand, under Henry I (1100–35), the major officers in the central government, apart from a small number who held hereditary positions, were normally careerist professionals and usually clerics. Nobles might offer advice to the king in parliament and council when called upon or, in the later Middle Ages, sometimes act as senior members of royal commissions or normally be named JP in the counties where they held their main estates, but, although they might sometimes be active, their role was more to add their political weight to these offices than to do the day-to-day work. Nobles in the royal household, or those who rose to nobility through the household and court nexus, were, with a few exceptions, less administrative servants than self-advancers who wormed their way into royal favour and attracted opprobrium thereby, for example under Henry III[5] or in the first decade of Richard II's reign. The exceptions were the men like Walter Hungerford, servant to all three Lancastrian Henries, who reached nobility via a career in the royal administration, combined sometimes with service in war.[6] In France, as on the other side of the Channel, the equivalent of the English nobility – that is, the great nobles and the barons – cannot be seen as a distinct class of officers. Certainly, these great nobles played a role in the government of both the realm and the royal household in the twelfth century and throughout the thirteenth. Conscious of this tradition, at the end of the Middle Ages they claimed

---

[5] Carpenter, D. A. (1985).   [6] *Oxford DNB* sub nom.

a place about the king more strongly than ever, considering themselves – like their English counterparts – to be his 'natural counsellors'. This claim did not result in a demand for particular offices, although, as in England, certain heritable positions among the great domestic offices in the household were reserved to them: this was the case with the office of *chambrier*, consistently given to the dukes of Bourbon from the beginning of the fourteenth century, or that of constable, which was nearly always reserved for counts or dukes. Equally, lieutenancies-general were sought by the greatest nobles, because they were very lucrative – the example of the duke of Berry in Languedoc between 1370 and 1380 is particularly well known. But it was above all the royal council, the place where political decisions were made, royal officers nominated and royal money could be seized, that French princes wished to control. This did not happen without some tension. The influence of the great nobles, contested by clerics, jurists and other specialists whom the king had bound to himself, fluctuated during the course of the period and ultimately reflected the condition of their relations with the sovereign himself. At the time of the madness of Charles VI, the council became one of the major players in the civil war: anyone who could control it could control the state for partisan ends.

Another potential group is largely excluded from this discussion: lawyers. This is partly because they are covered elsewhere but also because, when acting in their professional capacity, pleaders in the royal courts, as well as attorneys and other legal advisers in England, and advocates in the royal judicial tribunals in France, were not employed by the Crown. In England, apart from a small number of officers in the common-law courts at Westminster, the only lawyers employed full-time by the Crown, as lawyers rather than as all-purpose administrators with a legal training, were the justices of the common-law courts. Once professional justices had emerged, in the early fourteenth century, it began to be felt that they should serve neither private people, to whom they had sometimes acted as consultants, nor the king, but only the law. It thus became unacceptable for them either to take private clients or to deploy the law as the king willed.[7] While, under Henry VII and his successors, justices played a significant role in promoting royal authority, they remained at least as much servants of the courts as of the king. In France, men with legal training enjoyed a different relationship with the king: for them, royal or princely administration was only one of their possible career paths. And, even if they were able to act as royal judges, lieutenants or *procureurs* in a *bailliage* or *châtellenie*, nothing prevented

---

[7] Maddicott (1978).

them, even in the fifteenth century, from giving part of their time to private legal practice for particular institutions (monasteries, cathedral chapters, hospitals) or for lay administrations. Among the latter, urban authorities, rising in power from the end of the thirteenth century, made great use of lawyers, to whom they awarded annuities. In several towns (Saint-Flour, Dijon, Lyon), the *jurisperiti* and graduates in law retained as legal advisers by the corporation were often royal servants. This situation could lead to problems when conflict and confrontation broke out between their respective employers.[8]

2.   The scale of office-holding

For highly governed countries, the two realms had fairly small bureaucracies. It is always difficult to estimate numbers: even when we know the number of clerks in England (as we do for chancery clerks, thanks to the ordinance of 1388–9), we have to guess at the size of their secretarial staff – who were probably usually apprentice clerks. In the shires, for most of this period, the officers were not professional bureaucrats, but they were supported by a small staff of hundred-based and itinerant bailiffs and clerks (for the sheriff) and a clerk of the peace (for the JPs) in each county. Using the numbers of clerks and similar officers identified for the various offices in the late fourteenth to mid fifteenth centuries, and estimating perhaps one apprentice per clerk (which may be a little conservative), we might guess at a central bureaucracy, including the bureaucrats within the royal household and excluding the earldom of Chester and duchy of Lancaster and the justices and officials of the central courts, of about 340.[9] Figures in the shires are more of a moving target because the commission of the peace grew throughout the period, especially during the fifteenth century, and the number of shrievalties changed a little, but, if we take an average of fifteen for the size of the commission of the peace in the middle decades of the fifteenth century, in forty commissions, and then add twenty-six sheriffs and their staff of perhaps four bailiffs itinerant and two clerks, and twenty-three escheators (the officer responsible for the king's feudal revenues) plus, say, a clerk each, the total is 776.[10] To these we need to add the customs officials:

---

[8] Rigaudière (1984).

[9] An estimate of *c.*600 for Elizabeth I's reign, by which time there had been considerable expansion, with another 600 for the administrators of the Crown's lands, gives some credibility to this figure: Williams (1979), p. 107.

[10] Bailiffs of hundreds are excluded from this figure because the number of hundreds varied from county to county, some of them were privately owned (this was not significant for the king's powers by this time but was chiefly a source of money) and bailiffs of

five senior officials in each of fifteen customs ports by the early fifteenth century, producing a grand total of around 850.[11] Recent estimates of the global population in England are roughly 4 to 4.5 million *c.*1300 when it may have been at its height, shrinking to 2.25 to 2.5 million *c.*1375; and there may well have been some further shrinkage thereafter.[12] None of these figures, especially those for population, is particularly reliable but, even if we were to increase the estimated number of officers and add in those from the palatinate counties, they would show very clearly that England was not in any sense overrun by government officers in this period. This is all the more the case when we consider that, in the counties, only the clerical support staff and possibly some of the bailiffs could be counted as professionals and most of these would have had other legal or administrative employment.

In France, despite the difficulties in reaching a precise figure for the site of the royal bureaucracy, historians are agreed that there was an increase in the number of officers during the first half of the fourteenth century, a period termed by Bernard Guenée one of 'galloping' bureaucratisation.[13] Confining herself to the central institutions alone – and excluding the royal household – Françoise Autrand has estimated the number of officers in the middle of the fourteenth century at about 200, of whom about a hundred worked for the *Parlement,* forty for the chancery and more than twenty for the *Chambre des comptes.*[14] Towards 1450, the size of the bureaucracy had not changed, even if we add the personnel in charge of taxation, henceforth permanent and constituting a separate administration. With Louis XI, the tendency to expand began again, a good example being the numbers in the *Chambre des comptes,* which doubled during his reign. It was the reorganisation of the royal administration after the Hundred Years War and the absorption of the principalities into the *domaine* (Anjou, Brittany, the duchy of Burgundy) that accounts for this increase, which was often merely a question of transferring princely officers to Crown employment. Even so, the new *parlements* (Dijon, Rouen, Aix) and the new *cours des aides* (Montpellier, Rouen, Dijon, Grenoble) created in the second half of the fifteenth century, as well as the existing princely *chambres des comptes* taken over by the Crown (Dijon after 1477, Aix from 1481, Vannes in 1492, Blois in 1498), reflect a movement towards

---

hundreds often doubled up, while bailiffs itinerant sometimes acted as hundred bailiffs. Also excluded from this count are the holders of temporary and ad hoc commissions and the officers attached to the palatinates of Chester, Lancaster and Durham. Note that not every shire had its own sheriff.

[11] Kowaleski (2000), p. 472. There were also several lesser officials and clerks.

[12] Campbell (2000), p. 402.   [13] Guenée (1971), p. 403.

[14] Autrand (1974), pp. 13–14.

administrative decentralisation, as the Crown reduced the size of the sovereign courts in Paris and moved the appeal tribunals closer to their users. It has been estimated that the total number of royal agents at the beginning of the sixteenth century – central and local – was somewhere between seven and eight thousand, allowing for clerks and commissioners who do not appear formally in the sources,[15] and twelve thousand, of whom about five hundred were in the king's immediate administration.[16] This number is small by comparison with the size of the country – one civil servant for forty to sixty square kilometres – and the dimensions of the population – probably fifteen million at the beginning of the sixteenth century – even though we must not forget the support that urban administrations gave to the Crown. We are in any case a long way from the common image of a 'flesh-eating' officer corps that consumed the king's budget, stigmatised throughout the period by reformers and opponents of the government. It was even said in the middle of the fifteenth century that in France there were 64,000 royal officers![17] Faced down by its critics, however, the Crown was obliged on several occasions (1360, 1389, 1413) to reduce the number of its agents.

3.   The provenance, recruitment and appointment of officers

Since England, in contrast to France, did not possess princely courts and administrations, those who wished to advance far as civil servants were really obliged to make their way in the king's service, even though it was not uncommon for men to start in the estate administration of a nobleman and be recommended by his master to the royal service. Both these points must of course immediately be qualified by reference to Chester and Lancaster once they belonged to the Crown and there was, throughout the period, movement in and out of the royal administration and the administration of the palatinates, earldom and duchy. For example, John de Macclesfield went from service to the Black Prince and Richard II in Chester to a career in the privy seal and the wardrobe, and Walter Hungerford pursued a career as a servant of both the Crown and the duchy of Lancaster.[18] Moreover, once the Crown lands became such a central part of the king's income and his political power, under the Yorkists and, especially, under Henry VII, it became common for officers to move from the Chester or Lancaster administration, or that of

---

[15] Chaunu (1977), p. 37.   [16] Demurger (1990), p. 147.
[17] Contamine (1992), p. 135.
[18] Bennett (1983), pp. 150–2; for Hungerford, see above, n. 6.

noble lands that had come more recently to the king, to the exchequer or to the chamber, the household agency which was taking over much of the exchequer's financial work. In this period, the higher reaches of the palatinate and estate bureaucracies of Chester, Lancaster and the Crown were especially closely linked in terms of personnel: examples are John Say and Richard Fowler, under Edward IV, and Reginald Bray and Richard Empson under Henry VII.

In France, the development of the principalities at the beginning of the second half of the fourteenth century was, more than in England, a factor in officers' ability to change employer, and movement between princely and royal administrations was far from unusual, though in France it occurred in both directions. As Contamine puts it, 'la France des principautés' was in great part 'une affaire de familles' and the development of administrations in the apanages and great fiefs can be seen as a form of dissemination of the principles and forms of royal government.[19] Thus, the establishment of certain types of administrative machinery in the princely territories, such as the *Chambres des comptes* in the years 1360–80, was only possible because of the arrival of experienced royal officers. For example, the Parisian *maître* Jean Creté, having reformed the *Chambre des comptes* of the Dauphiné, was sent to Dijon and to Lille in 1386, with a view to organising the two *Chambres des comptes* which Philip the Bold had just set up. In the fifteenth century, several notaries and secretaries of the king found that their multiple expertise earned them employment from a number of princes (Berry, Bourbon, Burgundy) in the areas of finance or justice, without their having to abandon the royal service. But the reverse movement, of officers who had learned their trade in a prince's service joining the royal administration, is also characteristic of the period: a good example is that of Pierre de Giac, a nobleman from the Auvergne, who, having been chancellor to Louis II of Bourbon in the 1360s, then chancellor to Jean de Berry in the 1370s, ended his career as Chancellor of France in 1383. The princes had everything to gain by filling the royal administration with followers who would defend their interests and it is worth noting that, during the reign of Charles VI, princely influence on the royal administration was particularly strong, notably in the financial offices and among the *baillis* and *sénéchaux*. However, beyond the political interest of the princes in taking control of these offices, the movement of officers from one bureaucratic sphere to another was also driven by an awareness on the authorities' part of the importance of experience in making appointments to responsible posts. In this regard, moving from a prince's administration to the royal service was at

---

[19] Contamine, 'Introduction' to Contamine and Mattéoni (1996), p. xxxiv.

the same time a social and professional promotion and a contribution to the diffusion of administrative practice.

How were the officers of the central bureaucracy recruited? In England, for much of our period, they were what would now be called school-leavers, who arrived with the ability to read and write, and well versed in Latin, and were then trained on the job. In both exchequer and chancery, the oldest and best-established of the government departments, men served for lengthy periods: for example, under Henry VI, the average period of service in chancery for those who became senior clerks was thirty years, while one served for over sixty years. Many men remained in chancery for their entire careers and the same was true of the privy seal clerks, when their office became a more or less independent department during the fourteenth century: some served for thirty years and more. In both departments men were promoted from within for example John Thoresby, who eventually rose to be keeper of the privy seal and subsequently chancellor, as well as archbishop of York, had entered chancery as a young clerk. For much of the period, there was a lot of movement between the exchequer and the wardrobe, which administered the finances of the king's household. The main reason for this was the need for cooperation between the two departments in financing the king's wars, for the wardrobe was the key financial agency when the king himself led the expedition. Thus, under Edward III, when wars were large and expensive and, after a false start, extremely well organised, it became not unusual for exchequer men to move into the wardrobe. While the treasurer, chancellor and keeper of the privy seal did not always rise from within their own departments, most of the king's great officers came from the ranks of government-trained clerks until the fifteenth century.

In France, as in England, ability was a factor in recruitment and career advancement, more so than political manoeuvres. In the great central institutions of the *Parlement* or the *Chambre des comptes*, where stability of employment is evident early on, the length of a career could be very great: thus, between 1380 and 1413, the proportion of officers of the *Parlement* who spent more than twenty years there increased from 8% to almost 40% and, of this last group, 11% had more than thirty years of service. During the period 1350–1450 nearly 60% of the counsellors of the Paris *Parlement* died in office.[20] It goes without saying that a number of them had passed their entire career within this institution and had worked their way up through the entire hierarchy (*avocat*, *conseiller* in the *Chambre des enquêtes*, *conseiller* in the *Chambre des requêtes*, *conseiller* in the *Grand' Chambre*, and then, at the end of their career, for the

---

[20] Autrand (1981), pp. 411–12, 417.

most gifted, the best placed or the luckiest, a presidency). Similarly, the chancery offers numerous examples of long careers, even if the notaries and secretaries were less exclusive in their specialisation: some of them were officers of the *Parlement*, others of the *Chambre des comptes*, others in the financial offices. This link between the writing offices and the great financial offices is found also in princely administrations: in Brittany, the Bourbonnais and Burgundy many of the treasurers had formerly been ducal secretaries, who, having worked in financial departments, sometimes for a long time (ten to twenty years), ended their careers as *maîtres des comptes*. At the heart of the central administrations developed by the princes, long careers were similarly not uncommon and doubtless this is why recruitment was drawn from a narrower pool than it was for the royal service. Thus in the *Chambre des comptes* at Vannes in 1468, the officers had on average been in post for fifteen years, but the president, Maurice de Kerloegen, was in his thirty-eighth year and the auditors, Pierre de Bonabry and Jean de Vay, were respectively in their twenty-fifth and sixteenth years of activity.[21]

In a society where education to the required level remained a relative rarity, it was necessary to know where to go to find young men of the right calibre. This was the reason for the emergence of recruitment networks. In England, the best known of these was based in the north midlands and the north, and it provided numbers of recruits for chancery. To a large extent, it worked through the interconnection of bureaucratic family clans and much of its force has been attributed to Archbishop Melton of York, who was treasurer in 1325–6. For example, it was probably Melton who recruited Thorseby to the chancery, while Thorseby's brother, another royal clerk, rose to become keeper of the hanaper in chancery. In the exchequer, as in chancery, there were bureaucratic dynasties, and here, going to known sources of capable new staff was made all the easier by the fact that so many offices were in the treasurer's own gift. The northern connection in chancery began to weaken in the first decades of the fifteenth century and the arrival of clerks from a wider geographical range may indicate that across the country the level of literacy and provision of formal education had now reached a point which meant it was no longer necessary to look for new staff from a single known source. Thus, it is important for the modern scholar, familiar with open competition for jobs among a large number of suitably qualified candidates, to remember that there were good reasons for what would now be perceived as nepotism.

---

[21] Kerhervé (1987), p. 792.

Similar considerations need to be brought to bear when considering the role of the nobility in placing men in government positions in England. Again, it was a way of finding suitable candidates: young men who had been recommended to a nobleman who had a good idea of what kind of qualities were required in the royal government and might put them forward for the king's service. They were recommended perhaps because they belonged to a family which worked in the nobleman's own administration, and sometimes certainly because they themselves were employed by the nobleman himself. There was also the other side of the equation: that it was part of a great man's duty to help provide for his followers and their families, however lowly they were. The northern connection of the fourteenth century owed something to northern lords, notably the earls and dukes of Lancaster, and, for obvious reasons, the Lancastrian connection with chancery became stronger in the first decades of the fifteenth century, especially under Henry V, the kind of king who is likely to have been on the sharp look-out for talent that he could see at first-hand. Such access to office through noble patrons has been taken by some to have been a noble ploy to obtain powerful influence within government departments.[22] However, while it might be possible, up to a point, to get a chancellor, treasurer or keeper of the privy seal to bend the administration on behalf of a magnate, the ordinary bureaucratic processes within these departments were so hierarchical and regulated that it is difficult to see what great benefits could have been derived from influence over even a senior clerk. It is more than probable that a nobleman could persuade an employee whose appointment he had arranged to deal with minor matters, like searching the records more expeditiously and without a fee, but most unlikely that that was the reason for placing him in post. Improper pressure is more likely to have come from lesser people and on only a minor scale. It was indeed recognised that favours might be done, but clerks were expected to ask permission of senior colleagues first. A nobleman who really wanted to influence what the government did on his own behalf was going to find it much easier to act through direct speech with the king.[23] Moreover, some royal servants who had moved from noble service can be shown to have been conspicuously loyal to their new master, even when he came into conflict with their former employer.[24]

In France, the existence of recruitment networks is similarly well attested in this period. While access to royal office was unusually politicised in the period of competition between the Armagnacs and Burgundians at the start of the fifteenth century (notably in the purges of 1413

[22] E.g. Wilkinson (1929).   [23] Watts (1996), p. 79.
[24] E.g. John Brome: Carpenter (1992).

and 1418), it was typical at other times for particular factions to establish
a hold over appointments: one thinks of the house of Melun at the end
of John the Good's reign, for example; of the Dormans and the Marmousets, political heirs of the network of Cardinal Guy de Boulogne,
at the time of Charles V; or of the Angevin faction in the entourage of
Charles VII before and after his coronation. But this tendency did not
mean that recruitment was completely closed. On the contrary, political
society in the fourteenth and fifteenth centuries remained an open one,
in which new men might emerge. It is true that, as in England a little
earlier, the great central institutions, like the *Parlement* and the *Chambre
des comptes*, permitted bureaucratic dynasties to establish themselves from
the second half of the fourteenth century (and the point applies equally to
the *chambres des comptes* of princes in the fifteenth century), but this gave
these institutions a strength and coherence which helped the emergence
of an *esprit de corps*. At the time of the civil war, it was this factor – due,
in the case of the *Parlement*, to the fact that the dynasties of counsellors
were often related to both sides – that allowed royal justice to retain its
impartial character and ensured the survival of the state. Whether there
were recruitment networks or not, we can establish that the majority
of the officers of the central administration who worked in Paris came
from northern France – from Paris itself, from the Île-de-France and
from Champagne – and then, to a lesser extent, from the regions of the
Loire, Burgundy and central France. By contrast, southerners were in
the minority in the *Parlement*, the chancery and the *Chambre des comptes*,
and this state of affairs was as much to do with the distance of Languedoc from the capital as with the language of the south, which the royal
chancery did not use. The central administration became more accessible to men from the south at the time of Charles VII, as a result of the
establishment of the royal administration at Bourges and Poitiers in the
1420s. At the end of his reign and during that of Louis XI, the role of
men from the Loire grew at the heart of the administration, especially in
the financial offices.

4.   Appointment, venality, laicisation

In France there were various terms on which offices might be held. If
tenure in fee and at farm were possibilities, custodial tenure tended to
become the predominant mode in the course of the period, as criticisms
of the practice of farming, both older objections and newer ones that
continued to appear throughout the period, led at the very end of the fifteenth century to the farm being more or less abandoned, at least for the
prévôtés. While in the custodial system nomination was formally a matter
for the king alone, it often allowed for the intervention of a third party in

obtaining the office. We must remember that royal letters of appointment were issued in response to requests. Someone wanting an office might well need help to get his petition put before the king and council, and this opened the way for the operation of influence and networks. This means of appointment did not guarantee objectivity and quality, leaving 'une large place au désordre et à la faveur'.[25] These abuses provoked criticism, which – heavily influenced by Aristotelianism – contributed to the adoption of the elective principle for important offices in the reigns of Charles V and Charles VI. For its supporters, election was the only means of guaranteeing the competence of officers. Between 1370 and 1415, the main offices of the central administration and the offices of the *baillis* were bestowed in this way. But the practice of election disappeared with the disasters affecting the Crown after 1415. The ordinance of 1454 made renewed reference to it, but Louis XI did not apply it, since he wished to be able to appoint to posts in the great offices himself. As election receded and scheming over appointments resumed, the delegation of public responsibility became a more and more venal matter. Thus, the possibility of resigning an office in favour of a third party – the procedure known as *resignatio in favorem* – was often merely a cover for financial transactions. Meanwhile, in certain places, offices were handed out to guarantee a loan or to pay a debt, as in the Dauphiné or in Burgundy, where the *mutua super officiis* became a heading in the accounts of treasurers and castellans from the second half of the fourteenth century. Certain offices, such as those attached to *châtellenies*, were routinely treated as pledges given to lenders while they awaited repayment, and the prince could even go as far as granting out the *châtellenie* itself and the revenues attached to it. In the royal administration, the sale of office is evident for certain offices from the second half of the fourteenth century. During the following century it was extended to the most important offices. At this stage, offices were sold only on a private basis – public sales only made their appearance with Francis I in 1521. Nevertheless, wherever one looks, money seems to be at the heart of the distribution of office and venality was certainly more common than the more recent historiography has acknowledged.

Money, networks, the use of recommendation and influence: it is clear that obtaining an office brought into play many of these criteria. Even so, the Crown had ways of maintaining the sense that office involved public duty. In particular, the procedures for registering and investing new officers emphasised the demands attached to their offices, while the rituals involved in taking up office contributed an atmosphere of sacrality. All letters of appointment for an important office had to be registered by the competent authority: *Chambre des comptes* and *Parlement* for the offices of the central administration and for the *baillis*; *baillis* and *sénéchaux* for local offices. Above all, investiture with an office meant taking an oath, a real 'rite d'institution', which can be analysed as an 'acte de magie sociale qui crée une différence' (Bourdieu). In this, the oath contributed to distinguishing the officer and conferring upon him a little of the charisma of the prince. In sum, the oath endowed the officer with a solemn power – a share in public power – which bound him in two ways: certainly in relation to the king, but also in relation to himself, for on his own success depended the possibility of promotion. This is the reason why office should not be analysed solely in bureaucratic terms. The importance of faith and loyalty in writings on office, the fact that an office was often asked for by means of a petition, the further fact that petitioners, at the same time as they urged their desire to serve the prince faithfully if he gave them the anticipated office, promised to pray for him and his family, all show that the relationship created by the grant of an office was not one of simple subordination.

Purchase of offices in the central government was alien to England in this period and only developed in the following century. However, something akin to purchase began to appear in the exchequer during the fifteenth century. Under Henry VI, men began to be appointed to exchequer office because they were in a position to make loans to a Crown that was in an increasingly financially beleaguered state. They were of course unlikely to do so unless they received some return on their investment. But this development is part of a wider change in the pattern of recruitment during this century: the advance of laymen in central government. Justices had long been lay, and the financial officers of the royal household were usually laymen from the early fifteenth century, but it was only later in the century that these developments began to affect the older writing offices, the chancery and privy seal, and the newer one, the signet office, as well as the exchequer. In general terms of course, this change reflects the rise of the fully literate layman. However, in the writing offices, it was less a question of recruitment of laymen than of the usual type of entrant electing to marry and thus not to follow the usual career path of reward by way of promotion to a church office, a change which, in turn, may reflect the great competition for the wealthier benefices. But, in the exchequer, the new type of recruit was indubitably a layman and, as we have just seen, was often acceptable precisely because he already had a successful career as a businessman. The arrival of laity in the exchequer was also due to the laicisation of the head of the department: under Henry IV, a majority of the treasurers were lay, and thereafter nearly all of them were. With the number of exchequer offices in the treasurer's gift, it was likely that, with a lay treasurer, laymen would be appointed to some of these and this was increasingly the case from the 1420s. Some of the appointees under Henry VI undoubtedly owed their places to acts of patronage rather than to being highly rated as potential exchequer employees. Moreover, laicisation also introduced another element which was eventually to lead to purchase. This was the gift of offices in heredity, a practice that had long been essentially defunct in England outside a small number of great ceremonial offices. It has been rightly described as 'the conception of offices as a form of property'.[26] The first grant of an exchequer office for life was made in 1411, and in 1447 the first reversionary grant. Paradoxically, when the Crown was able to take back the exchequer offices in the treasurer's gift in the late fifteenth and early sixteenth centuries, this kind of privatisation began to extend almost throughout the exchequer. The change from clerics to laymen in the king's household was noted above, with respect to its principal financial officers. It was, however, from the 1460s, when extensive Crown lands, administered through the chamber, became such a central part of the king's finances, that large numbers of laymen were employed by the chamber, in the management and oversight of these properties and in the rapidly growing chamber financial administration. Eventually, this was to bring into being the official dynasties of the Tudor period, most of them in the lowlier posts but some, notably the Cecils, at the very top.

The same phenomenon of laicisation is visible in France. Certainly, clerics did not disappear entirely from the royal administration, if only because of the internal structure of certain institutions which reserved a portion of their offices for them. Thus, in the *Parlement*, there was a double hierarchy of lay and clerical counsellors. This practice, confirmed with some force in the ordinances of 1345, was maintained through-out the period (fifty-one clerics to forty-one laymen in 1345; thirty-six clerics and thirty-six laymen in 1454). For the *Chambre des comptes*, the Ordinance of Vivier-en-Brie provided for a clerical president and a lay president, each of them having authority over eight ordinary masters (four clerics and four laymen). Nevertheless, in the second half of the fifteenth century, the majority of the clerical masters' offices were given to laymen, despite Charles VIII's order of 1485 that each clerk should be succeeded in office by another clerk. The same pattern is found in other institutions, both royal and princely: although they were in the majority at the time of Philip the Fair, clerics comprised only 8 per cent of notaries and royal secretaries during the reigns of Louis XI, Charles VIII and Louis XII.

---

[26] Williams (1979), p. 107.

In the financial offices, where clerics were already few in number in the fourteenth century, they shrank to a very small minority in the fifteenth century, even if they did not completely disappear. Yet the numerical decline of clerics in the administrative hierarchy does not in any way indicate their political eclipse, for we must take into account the calibre of the offices they still held on to. Thus, in the office of chancellor, clerical dominance remained strong until the beginning of the fifteenth century. Of the twenty chancellors who succeeded one another between 1316 and 1413, fourteen were clerics and, among them, eight were bishops (among these was Pierre Roger, the future Pope Clement VI, in 1334). By contrast, of the seven chancellors of Charles VII, Louis XI and Charles VIII, only three were prelates. But these were not ordinary prelates: Martin Gouge, bishop of Clermont (1421–5), Regnault de Chartres, archbishop of Rheims (1425–45), Robert de Briçonnet, archbishop of Rheims and former president of the *Chambre des comptes* (1495–70). All three in their time played a political role of the first order.

5.   The rewards of office

The laicisation of office had considerable implications for the officers' remuneration, the subject to which we shall now turn. In England, although the members of the king's central bureaucracy were in some cases paid directly by the Crown and, especially at the lower end, could command fees for their services, the real paymaster of the Crown's officers for most of this period was the church. Lesser men would hope for a reasonable competence; an indication of what they might expect is the annuity of £20, described as 'unusually large', given in the later fourteenth century to Walter Maupas, later a senior chancery clerk, at an early stage in his career, to tide him over until he obtained a suitable benefice.[27] This would equate, in lay terms, to an income for a substantial gentleman or a fairly minor esquire in the first half of the fifteenth century. But the men at or near the top of the pile would expect more from the church: Maupas himself was to acquire much more and Richard Andrew, secretary to Henry VI in the 1440s, accumulated benefices worth about £200 a year – a large knightly income – while a bishopric, or even an archbishopric, would be the reward for the greatest officers. On the basis of such incomes, the senior officers who had a mind to make money on their own account were very well placed to do so, with their ready access to the London money markets and to possible money-spinners

[27] Richardson (1999), p. 42.

like wardships. Adam of Stratton, who was brought down in the bureau-cratic scandal of 1289–90 under Edward I, lent money on one occasion at 900 per cent interest on any arrears and, on his arrest, had £12,000 in cash in his house, but even Edward's exemplary chancellor, Robert Burnell, died in possession of eighty-two manors.[28] But the expense of all this fell not on the king but on the church, or on the king's subjects.

Once lay officers became the norm, costs fell much more heavily on the Crown. At the lower end of the scale, although the cumulative effect of paying numbers of officers should not be ignored, ambitions were quite lowly. For example, an exchequer auditor in the fifteenth century received a fee of £10 a year, while Thomas Hoccleve, poet and privy seal clerk, was able to marry in the early fifteenth century on the strength of his Crown annuity being raised to twenty marks. But the reference to marriage reflects the higher income that any lay clerk, no longer able to share lodgings with his fellow clerks, as had been the norm, and with a wife and possibly children to support, would require. It was, however, those with greater aspirations who could really put pressure on the royal purse, for not only would they require a sizeable income but they would want this income to be taken from a sizeable estate, since founding a lineage was even more important than making a lot of money, and estates were both expensive and difficult to come by in the fifteenth century. Beyond the cost to the Crown of giving them its own lands and/or money – for example the £400 a year in fees paid by Henry VII to Thomas Lovell – there was a danger they would defraud either the king or his subjects. Ralph, Lord Cromwell built a grand castle in the latest style at Tattershall while he was treasurer to Henry VI, decorating it with the emblem of his office, and, while he was a very conscientious treasurer, one cannot help wondering whether the king's money contributed to the cost. Henry VII's closest servants became notorious for extracting money and lands from their fellow subjects, on their own behalf as well as on the king's. Reynold Bray, one of his most intimate, starting his career with a very small income, was able to invest over £10,000 in land between 1485 and his death in 1503. Moreover, it was potentially more dangerous for the king to bring down great laymen who abused their office or disobeyed the king, with their large personal estates and the wealth and military power that these brought. By contrast, clerical officers, even the greatest and most powerful princes of the church, owed their position, and much or all of their income, to a combination of royal and clerical office and, like Stratton, could easily be dismissed and their ill-gotten gains confiscated.

---

[28] See also *Oxford DNB*, sub nom.

In France, meanwhile, wages were almost universal, and no doubt this was a motivation for a number of people who sought office. In this respect, as in England, laicisation had the effect of forcing royal and princely budgets to support the full weight of the bureaucracy. In fact, it was this development that lay behind the concern of princes to have favour with the king and good representation in his council, so that they could get access to the royal pensions and gifts that they needed, to provide for their own budgets. The cost of maintaining officers was not negligible for either the king or the princes. Difficult though it is to calculate, it is clear that it accounted for part of the growth in the financial needs of the Crown. While taxation was justified by war, it can be explained also by the growth in the number of officers, notably during the first half of the fourteenth century – though kings scarcely attempted to use this unpopular argument. In the same way, the vertiginous growth in expenses under Louis XI was caused in part by the wages and pensions that the 'universal spider' paid out, notably to his own officers – 40 per cent of tax income went on this one area of expenditure. The remuneration that royal officers might obtain from their service could amount to some very attractive sums, especially in the central hierarchy: 2,500 *livres tournois* (*l. t.*) for the chancellor; 1,250 for the first president of the *Chambre des comptes*; between 350 and 700 for a *bailli* (but, from this sum, he had to pay his deputies); 100 for the *élus*. At the local level, the size of remuneration depended on one's place in the hierarchy. Nevertheless, the wages that were paid out, which barely increased during the period, did not always match the size of the responsibilities. This is particularly true of the lieutenants and the *juges-mages* in the *bailliages* and the *sénéchaussées* (ranging from 100 to 160 *l. t.* in the time of both Philip IV and Philip VI). Strayer has cited this as one of the reasons for the relative brevity of the careers of jurists and other doctors of law as royal justices in the south, suggesting that they preferred to work as teachers of the law and legal counsel, since these posts were much more lucrative. In general terms, service to the king was more profitable than service to a prince. Wages were lower in the principalities, except perhaps in Burgundy, where the level of pay gave officers no cause for envy of what they might obtain in the royal administration.

But the pecuniary advantages of office were not limited to wages. Pensions, 'customary payments', grants of money and in kind, presents, princely favours – right down to the help given to aged or sick officers who could fall back on a hospital specially founded to take them in, like the one Louis II of Bourbon founded at Moulins – not to mention the possibilities of accumulating wealth within or outside the administration, all added to the attractions of a career as an officer. The most important officers, those most visible, or those whose loyalty was most vital – one thinks of the Burgundian turncoats – were at the heart of the economy of favour which Louis XI raised to a level never seen before. Service to a prince could therefore take men to extraordinary heights, as is attested, for example, by the career in Burgundy of Nicholas Rolin, the celebrated chancellor and patron, of whom Georges Chastellain wrote, 'there was not an office, nor a benefice, in town or in country, throughout the land, nor a grant, nor a loan that was given unless he made and arranged it'.[29] Or there was Pierre de Landais in Brittany, the power of whose network came from the considerable wealth he had accumulated in more than twenty-five years in the financial service of the dukes,[30] or Jean de Montaigu, whose residence of almost princely grandeur, which he had built at Marcoussis, spoke eloquently, in its luxury, of his accumulated riches. But the punishment that he suffered in 1409, just like the end of Pierre de Landais, the fall of Jacques Coeur or the death of Olivier Le Daim, and before them of d'Enguerran de Marigny, show how far social climbing, transgressing the traditional hierarchies, could generate resentment and hatred among a ruler's subjects. Public opinion was all too ready to assume that official malpractice lay behind such mould-breaking careers, and, to respond to criticism, the prince had sometimes to protect his own image and power by sacrificing the vilified officer. But perhaps this was the price that had to be paid to persuade people to accept bureaucratisation and the state's constraining power.[31]

6.   The education of officers

Laicisation was not the only change in the royal bureaucracy in the fifteenth century. The other major novelty was the arrival in greater numbers of university graduates, especially graduates in civil law. This phenomenon can be seen in both countries. In England, from the 1340s, an increasing number of chancellors had been men of this type, usually qualified in one or both of canon or civil law, often of both, and from about the same time the keepers of the privy seal were also often civil lawyers. It was under Henry VI that graduates began to dominate both offices, and ten of the sixteen appointees were civilians. Probably under the influence of chancellors with this background, the number of civilians among the senior clerks of chancery began to grow. Indeed, curiously for

---

[29] Cited by Cockshaw (1982), p. 1.

[30] In 1480, his acquisitions amounted to no less than two *châtellenies*, three *seigneuries*, twelve *domaines* and three town palaces on an annual wage of 500 livres: Kerhervé (1987), vol. II, p. 904.

[31] Gauvard (1985), esp. pp. 365–6.

such an ineffective king, Henry had an extraordinarily learned group of
men at the heart of his administration, many of them participants in the
humanist 'new learning'. As the equitable Court of Chancery grew apace
towards the end of the century, it became normal for the chancellor to be
a civilian or a canon lawyer and at this point the necessary expansion in
the court's secretariat led to the recruitment of graduates in civil law for
these positions. The readiness of some of the senior graduate officers to
replicate themselves, by investing wealth garnered during their careers in
the foundation of colleges at Oxford and Cambridge, produced a growing pool of graduates available for employment in all parts of the central
government. At this time, civil lawyers and indeed most graduates of any
sort, were of course still in most cases clerics but, when it became customary for young men of good family to go to Oxford or Cambridge, there
was going to be an increasing army of university-trained men, among
younger sons and the eldest sons of the less well-off families, looking for
work in the royal government and adding to its laicisation. Until then,
as we have seen, training was usually done within the department. It
is highly probable that the all-important training in writs for chancery
clerks was given them by the senior clerks, since, during the fourteenth
century, this instruction became formalised in the Inns of Chancery run
by senior clerks. In fact, despite the graduate recruitment to chancery's
writing office, non-graduates, internally trained, and promotion within
the department were still the norm at the end of the fifteenth century,
among the clerks of both chancery and the privy seal.

In France, the account given earlier of the different types of office has
already shown that men trained in the learned law occupied an important
place at all levels of the government apparatus. Certainly, it was initially
with the king, in the central administration, but also in his household,
with the *maîtres des requêtes*, that university graduates found themselves in
the majority. Moreover, it was not just in the *Parlement*, the key judicial
institution, that the role of jurists was significant from the beginning.
The chancellor was often juristically trained – although this was not an
absolute rule – as were certain royal notaries and secretaries. In the Paris
Chambre des comptes, by contrast, just 15 per cent of the institution's
membership was certified as having a degree during the fourteenth century. But the proportion grew during the following century. At the local
level, if law graduates were not entirely absent from the administration,
they were few in number until towards the middle of the fifteenth century. It was not until later, in the period of reconstruction, that their
numbers increased in any significant way. Without doubt, there was a
distinction between the north of the realm and the south, where, because
of the 'Romanist' tradition, doctors of law and other qualified lawyers

were already more numerous at the heart of the royal administration at the beginning of the fourteenth century. Some of these (William de Nogaret, William de Plaisians) also made a career at Paris, in the entourage of the king, and the presence of these famous legists shaped the ideological profile of the reign of Philip the Fair.

Similar points can be made about the princely administrations. Here also, men with juristic training were increasingly integrated into the bureaucracy. In the lands of the dukes of Bourbon for example, the role of law graduates was important in the *Chambre des comptes* of Moulins (a third of the officers between 1450 and 1520). It was yet more pronounced among the justices and the officers of the judicial system, among whom nearly 50 per cent were graduates in law between 1400 and 1520. This concern for greater expertise in the theory of law, acquired in the schools or universities, explains the vogue for the foundation of colleges at Paris during the fourteenth century and of universities in the realm as a whole in the fifteenth. Founding universities was exclusively a royal or princely project in France (Caen and Bordeaux by the Plantagenet king, Poitiers and Bourges by the Valois one, Valence by the Dauphin, Nantes by the duke of Brittany, with still others established by the dukes of Burgundy outside the realm). In these new centres, it was instruction in the learned law, in particular Roman law, which was given precedence. That was where the demand was. This was all the more so because in France there was no equivalent of the English inns of court where instruction in the law as it was actually practised could be given. Those intending a career in legal practice in central and southern France had first to study the learned law and then to train among the advocates and judges of the region's *bailliages*.

7.   Probity, ability, adaptability

What was the quality of the officers who staffed the king's central bureaucracy before these changes? In France, despite the criticisms to which officers were regularly subjected from the thirteenth century onwards concerning their competence, their cupidity and their excessive number, it is clear that administrative practices, in both the financial and judicial spheres, testify, as in England, to a bureaucratic culture of high quality, especially in the central institutions of the administration. The royal government, just like princely governments, encouraged competence, as we can see from the letters of appointment. In the fourteenth century these gave priority to two main qualities: morality and loyalty. From the 1380s, the letters emanating from the royal chancery become more precise on the subject of the technical expertise of officers, stating that they were henceforth to be 'idoines [fitting] et suffisants', 'experts et convenables', 'bons et bien instruits'. In the course of the fifteenth century, the number of desired qualities increased further, an indication of greater demands. In the chancery of the dukes of Bourbon after 1450, for example, letters of appointment listed five to eight qualities which, depending on the type of office, included probity, industry, authority, knowledge and expertise. Theoretical understanding, practical competence, experience and virtuous comportment: these were the kind of qualities on which the authorities placed ever greater emphasis, and we should not fail to note the same qualities were presented in mirrors for princes as models for officers to follow. More particularly, the exercise of justice, because it was a sacred charge, was the focus of attention on all sides. In 1408, an ordinance of Charles VI specified that men should be recruited to the *Parlement* 'who know the customs and are expert in these'.[32] Nearly a century later, in 1499, Louis XII demanded that anyone who took up a position in the *Parlement* should have his legal knowledge tested.

In England, it is easy to dismiss the officers either as self-advancers, interested only in making as much as they could out of the king and his subjects, whether they were notoriously venal great officers like Adam of Stratton, or humble clerks who squeezed the maximum number of words into a writ because they were paid by the line, or mindless pen-pushers, wedded to a meaningless routine. And it is not difficult to find criticisms aimed either at individual officers who were deemed to be especially self-serving, such as William of Wykeham, or at whole classes of officials, for example the late fourteenth-century clerks, who were said to be 'over fatt, both in boddie and purse, and over well furred in ther benefices '.[33] If these men were not somewhat full of themselves and reluctant to change established systems, they would have been a most unusual civil service. But this is a very superficial view of the king's servants. On closer perusal, a very powerful bureaucratic culture emerges, notably in the older departments. Certainly, much of this was related to routine, but the routine itself is as impressive as anything. In the exchequer, for example, the ability to keep track of even the smallest debts owed to the Crown was the result of a carefully regulated procedure for entering debts and following them through from year to year, and, in chancery, copies of all the non-judicial writs and grants were kept in the patent, close and fine rolls. In both chancery and the exchequer, careful archiving made it possible to check on the progress of payments and on the accuracy of returns to enquiries, and also for both officers and outsiders to search

---

[32] Cited by Demurger (1990), p. 153.   [33] Richardson (1999), p. 38.

their records for information. For example, a search of records as far back as John's reign is recorded in the fifteenth-century exchequer.

Nevertheless, these were not just pen-pushers stuck in a never-changing routine. What makes their bureaucratic culture so particularly impressive is their ability to adapt routine to meet new needs, and much of this ability came precisely from that expertise and sense of departmental pride which arose from the clerks' lifetimes of training, working, and often living, together in a single department. Take, for example, record-keeping in the exchequer. Here, a system designed to deal with the financial obligations of tenants-in-chiefs and sheriffs found itself, from the late twelfth century, coping with hundreds and then thousands of debts, many of them exceedingly small, as the royal government expanded and the number of both local officials and, above all, subjects directly answerable to royal government increased exponentially. The exchequer quickly responded with a series of reforms, which became particularly intensive between 1270 and the 1320s. By an elaborate system, in which new records subordinated to the pipe rolls were created and then keyed into the pipe rolls by the use of symbols, it was possible to streamline the rolls while not losing track of even the least debt owed to the Crown. If this seems a trifle ludicrous, given that the king was now beginning to derive the really large sums needed for war from national taxation, it is still indicative of enormous departmental cohesion and bureaucratic imagination.

Almost more impressive is that, in the reforms of the 1320s, there was an archival spring-cleaning in the exchequer. The office had grown so early, from the early twelfth century, and, latterly, so fast that its records were less than tidily stored. Accordingly, in what must have been a massive enterprise, they were taken out of their home in the Palace of Westminster to the Tower, sorted, tidied up and taken back to Westminster. From the middle of the fourteenth century, the exchequer was producing periodic budgets of the king's income and expenditure, to help in financing wars while avoiding gross indebtedness. Not only does this demonstrate expertise and ambition of a high order but it would not have been possible without the organising of the departmental archive which made it possible to search numbers of different financial records. Chancery and the privy seal office, although their processes have been less intensively studied than those of the exchequer, seem to have been similarly adaptable and, even in the fifteenth century, a time when the older departments have often been judged to be ossified and ready to be bypassed by the household government of the last decades, they were still able to make improvements and meet new demands. Despite the strong departmental cultures that made all this possible, there was also cross-departmental cooperation, notably that which brought together the financial offices or the writing offices. It is this 'collegiality' under Edward III which Ormrod has cited as a major cause of the cohesion between the king's government abroad – the household offices of wardrobe and privy seal – and, at home, the exchequer and chancery. This finally resolved the problems of absentee rule and overextending the king's finances which had surfaced when the wars with Scotland and France began under Edward I. Movement of some of the senior officers between the financial or the secretarial departments helped in ensuring this kind of cooperation, both under Edward and in other reigns. For example, in the fifteenth century, under Henry IV, Thomas Langley was in turn secretary (keeper of the signet), keeper of the privy seal and chancellor,[34] and it was close cooperation among Henry V's senior officials that made that king's triumphs possible.

In France, as in England, the establishment and then reinforcement of developed structures of government that were both hierarchical and specialised were accompanied by a rationalisation of the work of the bureaucracy. Officers, whether working in the finances, or as secretaries in the chancery, lieutenants of a *bailliage*, or *maîtres des comptes*, had to follow administrative procedures according to set norms. These norms were defined in royal or princely ordinances, of which certain celebrated examples – the Ordinance of Vivier-en-Brie on the structure of the *Chambre des comptes* (1320), the ordinances organising the chancery (1321) and the *Parlement* (1345) – were in effect administrative codes. From the second half of the fourteenth century, princely administrations, often following the example of royal administrative practice, were also places where a bureaucratic culture was forged. As in England, financial preoccupations were one of the earliest spurs to administrative creativity. Already in the course of the thirteenth century, the increase in the king's financial needs had necessitated some improvements in the accounting procedures of the *baillis* and the *prévôts*, and these became the basis for new norms. Thus, the accounts of the *prévôts* and the *baillis* of Ascension 1248, which are presented in a set order (first the balance of receipts and expenditure of the *prévôtés*, then the accounts of the *bailliages* and the *sénéchaussées*, organised on the same principle, with the name of the *bailli* indicated subsequently), would serve for a long time as the model for royal accounts in the regions.[35] Moreover, we should note that, from this time, the finances of the royal household had their own separate account. The auditing procedures that were put in place in the reign of Louis IX and which became the business of *gentes in compotis* in the time of Philip the Fair – the *Chambre des comptes* – assisted the process

---

[34] See *Oxford DNB*, sub nom.   [35] Sivéry (1995), pp. 91–100.

of reaching uniformity in the accounts. Accounts increased in number and became more complex with the arrival of the new tax revenues, at the same time as they necessitated the creation of new tools for checking accounts (journals, *libri memoriales*). The Ordinance of Vivier-en-Brie, apart from setting up organised structures in the *Chambre des comptes*, set out a calendar for the hearing of accounts, with two annual sessions requiring the attendance of accounting officers at Paris, on the model of the English exchequer. In the *Parlement* there was also a calendar for the hearing of appeals: each *bailliage* and each *sénéchaussée* had its particular days during the year. This practice, already mentioned in the ordinance of 1278, was brought to full fruition at the beginning of the fourteenth century, at the time when the institution was becoming more organised: now the *baillis* and the *sénéchaux* were obliged to come to the court on the days assigned to them.

To sum up, the centralised auditing procedures in the *Chambre des comptes* and the assigned days in the *Parlement* helped to establish both a stratified political hierarchy and a vision of the royal *domaine* and realm, organised by a kind of state around the king. The experiences of the administrators gave force to the ideas of the jurists. We should note here a certain simultaneity with the chronology in England: the years 1280–1320 were in France an essential period for the formalisation of the central institutions of the Crown, just as there were years when, in England, an older set of institutions was adapted for new purposes. One particular document symbolises this expansion of the territorial and administrative monarchy: the '*Etat des paroisses et des feux*' of 1328. In this fiscal memorandum, which was drawn up as a result of the war in Flanders, the taxable hearths of the royal domain are listed and grouped by parish, *bailliage* and *sénéchaussée*. The outcome is very detailed and the expertise indicated by its handling of the data impressive: no fewer than 2,469,987 hearths in 32,500 parishes. The capacity to produce a document like this, coming twenty years after a similar piece of administrative prowess on the part of the royal administration – the arrest on a single day (13 October 1307) of all the Templars in France – shows in itself the level of technical expertise and efficiency attained by the royal administration: this was the first time that a general enquiry of this kind had been undertaken in France (long after England's Domesday Book, of course, but over a much larger area and population). To bring it to fruition, the king's agents went into the localities, having first examined the fiscal archives which the officers of the *comptes* kept in their possession at Paris.

Here we touch on another important matter, on which it is worth dwelling since it is such a good vantage point for observing bureaucratic culture in the course of its development: the emergence of a 'science of archives' similar to that in England.[36] The phenomenon is all the more remarkable in that the French royal archives were dispersed in several depositories, each corresponding to one of the great central offices (*Parlement, Chambre des comptes, Trésor des chartes, Châtelet*). In all these places, the urgent necessity of conserving, classing and inventorying documentation that was constantly growing gave free rein to 'creative archiving', in which practical considerations were not always separated from ideological issues. An instance is the *Trésor des chartes* which in the early fourteenth century acquired a general responsibility for archiving royal acts and grants: Pierre d'Etampes, the first head, innovated by arranging the archives in drawers, which he inventoried in the *Quaterni de papiro*. Innovations continued after his time and culminated in the years 1370–80 with Gérard de Montaigu. The work of the latter is impressive: he embarked on a reclassification of the material in the repository which was accompanied by numerical coding, a unique feat for this period; most noticeably, the classification of the registers which he effected enabled the creation of an alphabetical catalogue. This catalogue, decked out in its 1373 edition with a preamble that coupled the glorification of the king with the more mundane concern of ensuring the availability of important records, contained an index of 364 keywords. Montaigu's classification – place-names, royal documents, types of assets, rights etc. – reflects both the territorial power and the governmental determination of the Crown.[37] Similarly, the *Chambre des comptes*, with its central function of protecting the royal domaine, was obliged to register royal acts and quickly found itself having to innovate in order to manage its growing collection of records. This preoccupation with record-keeping was not exclusive to the monarchy: from the 1330s, inventories were set up for the archives of the princes (as in the duchies of Burgundy and Bourbon and in the Dauphiné). While the principles on which these were based always fell short of the innovations put into place for the royal archives, the princes, like the king, knew that their archives were an important foundation of their legitimacy. The 'geste archivistique', by giving an abstract organisation to record series, according to arrangements in chests, sacks or drawers, bestowed coherence on groupings of rights and territories which, on the ground itself, was lacking.

8. Attitudes

It seems that reflections on, and discussions of, office – a 'discourse of office' – were much more developed in France than in England. The campaigns of Louis IX against official abuses helped to encourage literature

---

[36] Potin (2000).   [37] Guyotjeannin (1996), pp. 307–27.

on the qualities needed in an officer. While mirrors for princes, such as the *De Regimine Principum*, written for the education of the future Philip the Fair, focused on the qualities that royal councillors should have – loyalty, love of the public good, a sense of truth – political thinking in the reign of Charles V tackled directly the question of office and the role of officers in the administration of the realm. This thinking was profoundly coloured by Aristotelianism – the *Politics* was translated into French between 1370 and 1374 by Nicole Oresme – and also by the writings of Cicero, which had long been known, but received particular attention from Christine de Pizan. It was accompanied by the development of legal doctrine and of legislation guaranteeing the officer protection in the exercise of his responsibilities. This protection, which was now attached to the status of an officer rather than to his person, is important. Thus, the protection of the officer, under the safeguard of the king, gave rise to the idea that an attack on his person constituted an attack on the king. In the same way, the idea of royal responsibility for official actions meant that the officer should be defended by the *procureur* of the king if he were impleaded in a tribunal for acts related to the exercise of his official function. If we add the permanence of office, officially recognised by the ordinance of 1467, which declared that only treason, resignation or death could deprive an officer of his position, there can be no doubt that all these measures helped to solemnise the role of serving the public power. They contributed also to creating among the officers a 'unique and unified culture',[38] indeed an 'identity' for the holders of the great offices, which the king tended to encourage while demanding their exclusive service.

It is interesting and significant that there was no equivalent in England of the French 'discourse of office', that is, a serious consideration of what it was to be an officer, written for the benefit of those in government. There was plenty of negative comment on royal officers throughout the later Middle Ages. Much of this came from subjects: for example, there were the complaints associated with the so-called Baronial Reform Movement of 1258–65, many of them made to the special commissions of enquiry, and, from the time of Edward II, once the parliamentary records become full, there is scarcely a parliament without complaint from the Commons about officers. Kings were also ready to put their officials on the spot, notably Edward I and III. Justices were frequent targets of complaint, in the period between the mid thirteenth and late fourteenth centuries, when their status as men who should be above the hurly-burly of private advice and high and low politics was finally established. However, although central officials (including justices), were sometimes attacked by kings, either individually or en masse, it was the

---

[38] The formulation of Guido Castelnuovo (1999), p. 188.

local officers, from sheriff down to very minor bailiffs, who were most likely to be condemned by subjects, and indeed, on occasion, by kings, for overuse of their power, on behalf of themselves, or the king, or a great local power, and for anything from pocketing the king's or his subjects' money to manipulation of the law.[39] Although there were early treatises on government and the law, when these institutions were in their infancy in the twelfth and early thirteenth centuries, the idea that office per se was something that was worth consideration really only began to appear towards the end of the fifteenth century, gaining force in the sixteenth, when 'magistracy' became an important subject of consideration. It was at this time that there began to appear the first treatises on the office of Justice of the Peace and works on government by present or former royal servants, such as Sir John Fortescue, the justice in exile with the Lancastrians, and Edmund Dudley, Henry VII's notorious close servant.[40] It was also in the late fifteenth century that serious interest began to be taken in a text that became fundamental in the discussion of the 'magistracy' in the sixteenth century, Cicero's *De Officiis*. We might note, for example, that Bishop Russell, Richard III's chancellor, owned an early printed copy of it.[41] There seem to be two initial reasons for this emergence of positive works on office, both of which are related, significantly, to England coming closer to France. The first is the centralisation of government, politics and political structures on the king and his court. That meant that holding any kind of public office under the king, even the local offices, previously as important in the web of local politics as they were in royal governance, conferred a position in the chain of power and preferment that culminated in the king and encouraged a complacent view of official status.[42] Secondly, the arrival of graduates in the civil service, some of them, and eventually all of them, with a standard 'humanist' education, would be likely to lead to more reflective views on office. Later, of course, the Reformation added the idea of a 'Godly magistracy'.

Conclusion

What can we say, in summing up, of the quality of the bureaucratic elite in the two countries? In England, the question of their susceptibility to

---

[39] Jacob (1925); *Parliament Rolls of Medieval England (PROME)*, ed. C. Given-Wilson et al. (2005); Prestwich (1988), pp. 92–8; Maddicott (1978). Great ministers of the Crown, justices and local officers were all physically attacked, sometimes murderously, in the revolts of 1381 and 1450: Dobson (1983); Harvey (1991).

[40] See also *Dialogus de Scaaccario and Constitutio Domus Regis*, ed. Amt and Church (2007); Mortimer (1994), p. 52; Putnam (1924); for Dudley, *Oxford DNB*, sub nom.

[41] *Oxford DNB*, sub nom.   [42] Carpenter, C. (1997).

influence from private parties has often been raised. That local officers and their offices were a central part of late medieval politics is well known and needs no elaboration here – except to reiterate what has been said many times in recent years: that this should not be seen as a form of corruption, but was simply how local politics worked, although there were circumstances under which it was held to be corrupt. At the centre, however, external influence on officers was a much rarer phenomenon. The fact that the nobility rarely held such office and that it was in the monarch's counsels, the legitimate place for this, that their voice was heard was a significant factor in this. When nobles were deemed to be bringing undue influence via the household, they became a focus for intense criticism. When great ecclesiastical figures who held high office overreached themselves in pushing their own agendas, they were simply cut down by the king. Noble influence over the lesser bureaucrats of central government has already been touched on and discounted. As we have seen, pressure of this sort was more likely to be applied by lesser men and it certainly could be used to benefit parties in disputes that were entangled in local politics. However, it seems that this sort of behaviour was the exception rather than the rule, in a bureaucratic culture where the needs of the king and the department (if not necessarily always in that order) came first. In sum, these men were doubtless as self-satisfied, wedded to routine and ready to look after their own prospects as modern bureaucrats are often alleged to be. However, they were also devoted and meticulous public servants, capable of conceiving and implementing imaginative new ways of doing things, both within departments and between them, and there were sound reasons for their conservatism, which generally served the monarch well.

In the kingdom of France, the rise to power of the institutions of the king and the princes contributed, as we have seen, to the emergence of a genuine bureaucratic culture, whose solid foundations lay in some first-rate administrative achievements. Fortified by belief in their own competence and in the importance of their mission, the king's agents were also given a high worth by some of the writings on politics. However, on the ground and in their daily practice, they were always subject to accusations of inefficiency, abuses and malpractice during the second half of the fifteenth century, a testament to the difficulty facing the authorities in reforming a body of officers that was once again in an expansive phase. Although he was aware of these criticisms, in 1467 Louis XI preferred to exalt the function of his agents in quasi-mystical terms: 'In our officers, under our authority, lies the management of the actions by which the public affairs of our realm are ordered and maintained . . . and from this it follows that they are our indispensable agents, as the limbs of the body of which we are the head.'[43] For the king, his officers occupied a special place in the body politic. They were distinct from the rest of society and a part of the body of the king. From this time, they were to become a new estate within society, 'the fourth estate'. For those in authority, this separation was the recognition that, by their actions, their know-how and their institutional culture, these officers helped in the emergence of 'a renewed conception of the science of government and administration'.[44]

BIBLIOGRAPHY

1. INTRODUCTION

Autrand, Fr., 1974. *Pouvoir et société en France (XIVe–XVe siècle)*, Paris.
Brown, A. L., 1989. *The Governance of Late Medieval England 1272–1461*, London.
Carpenter, C. 2010. 'Henry VI and the Deskilling of the Royal Bureaucracy', in L. Clark (ed.), *The Fifteenth Century IX*, Woodbridge, pp. 1–37.
Collard, Fr., 1999. *Pouvoirs et culture politique dans la France médiévale, Ve–XVe siècle*, Paris.
Gunn, S., 1995. *Early Tudor Government, 1485–1558*, Basingstoke.
Harriss, G. L., 1993. 'Political Society and the Growth of Government in Late Medieval England, *Past and Present*, 138, 28–57.
    2005. *Shaping the Nation: England 1360–1461*, Oxford.
Lachaud, Fr., 2010. *L'Éthique du pouvoir au Moyen Âge. L'office dans la culture politique (Angleterre, vers 1150–vers 1330)*, Paris.
Mattéoni, O., 1998. *Servir le prince. Les officiers des ducs de Bourbon à la fin du Moyen Âge (1356–1523)*, Paris.
Rigaudière, A., 1994. *Pouvoirs et institutions dans la France médiévale. Des temps féodaux aux temps de l'État*, vol. II, Paris.
Tellier, R., 2005. *Per potentiam officii. Les officiers devant la justice dans le royaume de France au xive siècle*, Paris.
Tout, T. F., 1920–33. *Chapters in the Administrative History of Medieval England*, 6 vols., Manchester.
Warren, W. L., 1987. *The Governance of Norman and Angevin England 1086–1272*, London.
Willard, J. F., Morris, W. A., et al. (eds.), 1940–50. *The English Government at Work 1327–1336*, 3 vols., Cambridge , MA.

2. SOURCES CITED

Dialogus de Scaaccario and Constitutio Domus Regis, ed. E. Amt and S. D. Church, Oxford, 2007.
Dobson, R. B., (ed.), *The Peasants' Revolt of 1381*, 2nd edn, London, 1983.
Parliament Rolls of Medieval England, ed. C. Given-Wilson et al., CD-Rom, Leicester, 2005.

---

[43] Cited by Collard (1999), p. 219.   [44] Rigaudière (1994), vol. II, p. 284.

3. FURTHER READING

Autrand, Fr., 1969. 'Offices et officiers royaux en France sous Charles VI', *Revue historique*, 242, 285–338.

1981. *Naissance d'un grand corps de l'État. Les gens du Parlement de Paris, 1345–1454*, Paris.

(ed.), 1984. *Prosopographie et genèse de l'État moderne*, Paris.

Bartier, J., 1955–7. *Légistes et gens de finances au xve siècle. Les conseillers des ducs de Bourgogne Philippe le Bon et Charles le Téméraire*, 2 vols., Brussels.

Bennett, M. J., 1983. *Community, Class and Careerism: Cheshire and Lancashire in the Age of Sir Gawain and the Green Knight*, Cambridge.

Bowers, R. H., 1983. 'From Rolls to Riches: King's Clerks and Money-lending in Thirteenth-century England', *Speculum*, 58, 60–71.

Brand, P., 1992. *Origins of the English Legal Profession*, Oxford.

Brown, A. L., 1971. 'The Privy Seal Clerks in the Early Fifteenth Century', in D. Bullough and R. L. Storey (eds.), *The Study of Medieval Records*, Oxford, pp. 260–81.

Buck, M., 1983. 'The Reform of the Exchequer 1316–26', *English Historical Review*, 98, 241–60.

Burt, C., 2013. *Edward I and the Governance of England, 1272–1307*, Cambridge.

Cam, H. M., 1930. *The Hundred and the Hundred Rolls*, London.

Campbell, B. M. S., 2000. *English Seigniorial Agriculture 1250–1450*, Cambridge.

Carpenter, C., 1992. *Locality and Polity: A Study of Warwickshire Landed Society, 1401–1499*, Cambridge.

1997. *The Wars of the Roses*, Cambridge.

2003. 'General Introduction to the New Series', in K., Parkin (ed.), *Calendar of Inquisitions Post Mortem*, xxii, 1–5 Henry VI, Woodbridge and The National Archives.

2007. 'War, Government and Governance in England in the Later Middle Ages', in L. Clark (ed.), *The Fifteenth Century*, vol. VII, pp. 1–22.

2014. 'Bastard Feudalism in England in the Fourteenth Century', in S. Boardman and J. Goodare (eds.), *Kings, Lords and Men in Scotland and Britain, 1300–1625: Essays in Honour of Jenny Wormald*, Edinburgh.

Carpenter, D. A., 1976. 'The Decline of the Curial Sheriff in England, 1194–1258', *English Historical Review*, 101, 1–32.

1985. 'King, Magnates and Society: The Personal Rule of Henry III', *Speculum*, 60, 39–70.

Castelnuovo, G., 1999. 'Physionomie administrative et statut social des officiers savoyards au bas Moyen Âge: entre le prince, la ville et la seigneurie (xive–xve siècle)', in *Les serviteurs de l'État au Moyen Âge*, Paris, pp. 181–92.

and Mattéoni, O. (eds.), 2006. *De part et d'autre des Alpes. Les châtelains des princes à la fin du Moyen Âge*, Paris.

Catto, J., 1985. 'The King's Servants', in G. L. Harriss (ed.), *Henry V: The Practice of Kingship*, Oxford, pp. 31–51.

Cazelles, R., 1982. *Société politique, noblesse et couronne sous Jean le Bon et Charles V*, Geneva.

Chaunu, P., 1977. 'L'État', in Fernand Braudel and Ernest Labrousse (eds.), *Histoire économique et sociale de la France, Tome I: 1450–1660* (Paris).

Cockshaw, P., 1982. *Le personnel de la chancellerie de Bourgogne–Flandre sous les ducs de Bourgogne de la maison de Valois (1384–1477)*, Kortrijk-Heule.

Condon, M. N., 1978. 'A Wiltshire Sheriff's Notebook', in R. F. Hunnisett and J. B. Post (eds.) *Medieval Legal Records Edited in Memory of C. A. F. Meekings*, London, HMSO, pp. 410–28.

Contamine, P., 1992, *Des pouvoirs en France, 1300–1500*, Paris.

and Matténi, O. (eds.), 1996. *La France des principautés. Les chambres des comptes, XIVe et XVe siècles*, Paris.

Demurger, A., 1978. 'Guerre civile et changements du personnel administratif dans le royaume de France de 1400 à 1418: l'exemple des baillis et des sénéchaux', *Francia*, 6, 151–298.

1990. *Temps de crises, temps d'espoir, XIVe–XVe siècle*, Paris, Seuil.

Fédou, R., 1964. *Les hommes de loi lyonnais à la fin du Moyen Âge. Étude sur les origines de la classe de robe*, Paris.

Gauvard, C., 1980. 'Les officiers royaux et l'opinion publique en France à la fin du Moyen Âge', in W. Paravicini and K. F. Werner (eds.), *Histoire comparée de l'administration (IVe–XVIIIe siècle)*, Munich, pp. 583–93.

1985. 'Le roi de France et l'opinion publique à l'époque de Charles VI', in *Culture et idéologie dans la genèse de l'État moderne*, Rome, pp. 353–66.

Genet, J.-Ph., 2001. 'Les conseillers du prince en Angleterre à la fin du Moyen Âge: sages et prudents?', in R. Stein (ed.), *Powerbrokers in the Late Middle Ages*, Turnhout, pp. 117–51.

Genet, J.-Ph. and Lottes, G. (eds.), 1996. *L'État moderne et les élites, xiie–xviie siècle. Apports et limites de la méthode prosopographique*, Paris.

Given-Wilson. C., 1986. *The Royal Household and the King's Affinity: Service, Politics and Finance in England 1360–1413*, New Haven and London.

Gorski, R., 2003. *The Fourteenth-Century Sheriff: English Local Administration in the Late Middle Ages*, Woodbridge.

Grassi, J. L., 1970. 'Royal Clerks from the Diocese of York in the Fourteenth Century', *Northern History*, 5, 12–33.

Griffiths, R., 1980. 'Public and Private Bureaucracies in England and Wales in the Fifteenth Ccentury', *Transactions of the Royal Historical Society*, 5th Series, 30, 109–30.

Grummitt, D., 2003. 'Public Service, Private Interest and Patronage in the Fifteenth-century Exchequer', in L. Clark (ed.), *The Fifteenth Century*, Woodbridge, vol. III, pp. 149–62.

Guenée, B., 1963. *Tribunaux et gens de justice dans le bailliage de Senlis à la fin du Moyen Âge (vers 1380–vers 1550)*, Paris.

1971. 'Y a-t-il un État des xive et xve siècles?', Annales, *ESC 26*, 399–406.

1991. *L'Occident aux XIVe et XVe siècles. Les États*, 4th edn, Paris.

Gunn, S., 2001. '"New Men" and "New Monarchy" in England, 1485–1524', in R. Stein (ed.), *Powerbrokers in the Late Middle Ages*, Turnhout, pp. 153–63.

Guyotjeannin, O., 1996. 'Les méthodes de travail des archivistes du roi de France (xiiie–début xvie siècle)', *Archiv für Diplomatik*, 42, 297–373.

Harriss, G. L., 1975. *King, Parliament, and Public Finance in Medieval England to 1369*, Oxford.

1985. 'Financial Policy' in G. L. Harriss (ed.), *Henry V: The Practice of Kingship*, Oxford, pp. 159–79.

1986. 'Marmaduke Lumley and the Exchequer Crisis of 1446–9', in J. G. Rowe (ed.), *Aspects of Late Medieval Government and Society*, Toronto, pp. 143–78.

2008. 'Budgeting at the Medieval Exchequer', in C. Given-Wilson, A. Kettle and L. Scales (eds.), *War, Government and Aristocracy in the British Isles, c.1150–1500: Essays in Honour of Michael Prestwich*, Woodbridge, pp. 179–96.

Harvey, I. M. W., 1991. *Jack Cade's Rebellion of 1450*, Oxford.

Jacob, E. F., 1925. *Studies in the Period of Baronial Reform and Rebellion, 1258–1267*, Oxford.

Jobson, A. (ed.), 2004. *English Government in the Thirteenth Century*, Woodbridge and The National Archives.

Jones, M., 1990. 'Le cas des États princiers: la Bretagne au Moyen Âge', in N. Coulet and J.-P. Genet (eds.), *L'État moderne: le droit, l'espace et les formes de l'État* Paris, pp. 129–42.

Kerhervé, J., 1987. *L'État breton aux xive et xve siècles. Les ducs, l'argent et les hommes*, Paris.

Kowaleski, M., 2000. 'Port Towns: England and Wales, 1300–1540' in D. M. Palliser (ed.), *The Cambridge Urban History of Britain, I, 600–1540*, Cambridge, pp. 467–94.

Krynen, J., 1993. *L'Empire du roi. Idées et croyances politiques en France, xiiie–xve siècle*, Paris.

Leguai, A., 1967. 'Les États princiers en France à la fin du Moyen Âge', *Annali della Fondazione italiana per la storia amministrativa*, 4, 133–157 (repr. in A. Leguai, 2005. *Les ducs de Bourbon, le Bourbonnais et le royaume de France à la fin du Moyen Âge*, Yzeure, pp. 23–48).

Lemonde, A., 2002. *Le temps des libertés en Dauphiné. L'intégration d'une principauté à la Couronne de France (1349–1408)*, Grenoble.

Lewis, P. S., 1968. *Later Medieval France*, London.

Lot, F. and Fawtier, R. (eds.), 1957–8. *Histoire des Institutions françaises au Moyen Âge*, 2 vols., Paris.

Lusignan, S., 2004. *La langue des rois au Moyen Âge. Le français en France et en Angleterre*, Paris.

McLane, B. W. (ed.), 1988. *The 1341 Royal Inquest in Lincolnshire*, Lincoln Record Society, 78.

Maddicott, J. R., 1978. 'Law and Lordship: Royal Justices as Retainers in Thirteenth- and Fourteenth-Century England', *Past and Present Supplement* 4.

Mattéoni, O., 2003. '"Plaise au roi". Les requêtes des officiers en France à la fin du Moyen Âge', in H. Millet (ed.), *Requêtes et suppliques. Le gouvernement par la grâce en Occident (xiie–xve siècle)*, Rome, pp. 281–96.

2007. 'Vérifier, corriger, juger. Les Chambres des comptes et le contrôle des officiers en France à la fin du Moyen Âge', *Revue historique*, 641, 31–69.

2010. *Institutions et pouvoirs en France (xive–xve siècles)*, Paris.

Meekings, C. A. F., 1981. 'The Pipe Roll Order of 12 February 1270', in C. A. F. Meekings, *Studies in 13th-Century Justice and Administration*, London.

Mortimer, R., 1994. *Angevin England 1154–1258*, Oxford.

Ormrod, W. M., 1987. 'The *Protecolla* Rolls and English Government Finance, 1313–1364', *English Historical Review*, 102, 622–32.

1997. 'Accountability and Collegiality: The English Royal Secretariat in the Mid-Fourteenth Century', in D. J. Guth and K. Fianu (eds.), *Écrit et Pouvoir dans les chancelleries mediévales: espace français, espace anglais*, Louvain, pp. 55–86.

Otway-Ruthven, J., 1939. *The King's Secretary and the Signet Office in the Fifteenth Century*, Cambridge.

Painter, S., 1949. *The Reign of King John*, Baltimore.

Paravicini, W., 1996. 'L'embarras de richesses: comment rendre accessibles les archives financières de la maison de Bourgogne-Valois', *Académie royale de Belgique. Bulletin de la Classe des Lettres*, Series 6, VII, pp. 21–68.

Pinet, M. (ed.), 1993. *Histoire de la fonction publique en France*, I, *Des origines au XVe siècle*, Paris.

Potin, Y., 2000. 'L'Etat et son trésor. La science des archives à la fin du Moyen Âge', *Sciences de l'Etat: Actes de la Recherche en Sciences Sociales*, 133 (June), 48–52.

Prestwich, M., 1988. *Edward I*, London.

Putnam, B. H., 1924. *Early Treatises on the Practices of the Justices of the Peace in the Fifteenth and Sixteenth Centuries*, Oxford.

Richardson, M., 1999. *The Medieval Chancery under Henry V* (List and Index Society Special Series, 30).

Rigaudière, A., 1984. 'L'essor des conseillers juridiques des villes dans la France du bas Moyen Age', *Revue historique de droit français et étranger*, 62, 361–90.

2003. *Penser et construire l'État dans la France du Moyen Âge (xiiie-xve siècle)*, Paris.

Les serviteurs de l' État au Moyen Age, *Congrès de la SHMES*, 29, Paris.

Sivéry, G., 1995. *Les Capétiens et l'argent au siècle de Saint Louis. Essai sur l'administration et les finances royales au xiiie siècle*, Villeneuve- d'Ascq.

Strayer, J. R., 1970. *Les gens de justice du Languedoc sous Philippe le Bel*, Toulouse.

Tout, T. F. and Johnstone, H. (eds.), 1906. *State Trials of the Reign of Edward I, 1289–93*, Camden Society, 3rd Series, 9.

Walker, S., 1999. 'Between Church and Crown: Master Richard Andrew', *Speculum*, 74, 956–91.

Watts, J. L., 1996. *Henry VI and the Politics of Kingship*, Cambridge.

Wilkinson, B., 1929. *The Chancery under Edward III*, Manchester.

Williams, P., 1979. *The Tudor Regime*, Oxford.

Wolffe, B. P., 1971. *The Royal Demesne in English History*, London.

5   Royal public finance (c. 1290–1523)

David Grummitt and Jean-François Lassalmonie

The development of royal finances is inseparable from the growth of royal government in the final centuries of the Middle Ages. The present chapter considers the institutional, human and political aspects of the system of revenue collection and the redistribution of the wealth of the kingdom put in place by the kings of England and France for their needs and in the name of the common good. It focuses on the collection, management and disbursement of these revenues, putting aside allied functions of these institutions such as the striking of coinage (carried out in England by the Mint in the Tower of London, and in France by between twenty and thirty workshops spread across the kingdom and the Dauphiné); the consideration of litigation, in the English exchequer, for example, or in France in specialised courts with jurisdiction over the collection of revenues, such as the *Chambre du trésor* for the domain and the *Chambre des aides* for the late medieval tax system; or, finally, the oversight of accounting officials, carried out in France by the *Chambre des comptes* for much of the kingdom, and in England by the exchequer at Westminster.

1.   The genesis of modern state finance

How then does the chronology of the development of public finance compare on each side of the Channel? In their beginnings the two systems followed parallel paths, but increasingly went their separate ways from the mid fourteenth century onwards. In England, the period from the end of the thirteenth to the beginning of the sixteenth century saw the evolution, maturity and decline of a fiscal system based upon regular, national taxation. The replacement of the earlier domain-based fiscal system of the Norman and Angevin kings by the tax-based system of the later Plantagenet kings was a direct result of war and the expansion of the Crown's administrative, legal and military ambitions. The origins of this system can be found in the wars of Edward I during the 1290s and it reached its apogee during the middle years of the fourteenth century. As Gerald Harriss has described, by the end of Edward III's reign England had a system of public finance by which, through parliament, kings were, in theory at least, accountable in some way to their subjects for their responsibility to spend according to the common good.[1] The national, public fiscal system became increasingly separated from the private financial affairs of the king and his household (although, at times – for example, during the 1340s and 50s and from the 1470s – public finance was partly administered through the departments of the household). It came under sustained pressure from the military, political and economic crises of the first half of the fifteenth century and underwent significant and permanent change from the 1470s, resulting in an early Tudor tax state that was able to tap its subjects' wealth more effectively than at any time since the beginning of our period. Moreover, the distinctions between the private financial affairs of the king and the Crown's public fiscal responsibility were blurred and, at times, disappeared under the early Tudor kings.[2]

In France, similarly, a fiscal system was first established in its outlines, at least, from the last decade of the thirteenth century by Philip IV and his successors in response to the need to finance the development of royal government and to pay for policies henceforth conceived and directed on a national level. It quickly evolved, however, as a result of the military disasters and the profound political crises which marked the first phase of the Hundred Years War, just at a moment when the English fiscal system reached its classic form: between 1355 and 1360 the Estates General of the Languedoil put in place fiscal and administrative machinery which was very quickly taken over by the Crown. The long persistence of the English threat, followed by the Burgundians from the second half of the fifteenth century, allowed the monarchy to justify the continued application of a modern fiscal system which now provided its principal source of finance. Through the political and military vicissitudes suffered by the French monarchy, the new system remained unchanged in its essentials until the financial reforms of Francis I (1523).

In this way, a modern fiscal system was perfected in both kingdoms as a consequence of growth of royal government and of military needs, the latter coming to the fore with the Hundred Years War. On the other hand, whereas in England this system came into being primarily in order to finance military endeavours abroad, in France the aim was increasingly to provide for the defence of the kingdom on its own ground. This difference had important consequences as much with regards to the motivation of

---

[1] Harriss (1975).   [2] Grummitt (2013), pp. 164–73.

taxpayers as for the destination of funds raised for war. Moreover, it also ensured that the fiscal system in England, its success and failure, depended more heavily on the personal ambitions and capabilities of the monarch.

2.   Revenue

Types of revenue

Historians of both England and France often divide royal revenue into ordinary and extraordinary categories. In England, the former were those types of revenue upon which the 'domain state' of the twelfth and thirteenth centuries had been based: the income from royal lands, the prerogative rights of the king as feudal overlord, fiscal prerogatives (notably seigniorage) and the profits of justice. The latter were the extraordinary taxes raised occasionally and for specific purposes, both direct (parliamentary subsidies, fifteenths and tenths etc.) and indirect (the customs and subsidies on wool, tunnage and poundage etc.). It was these that constituted the great increase in royal income in the first hundred years or so of this period and which allowed the even greater increase in royal expenditure. Nonetheless, a more meaningful division, in the English case (and one also employed by contemporaries) might be that between regular and casual revenue. The increased royal expenditure of the fourteenth century necessitated the making of complex budgets and, in order to manage revenue, the council, parliament and exchequer commonly divided revenue into regular income whose annual yield was fixed (landed income being the most important category) and that which was 'casual', that is, which fluctuated from year to year (profits of justice, feudal rights and, most importantly, indirect taxation). Significantly, after the fixing of the level of the parliamentary subsidy – that is, direct taxation – known as the fifteenth and tenth in 1334, direct taxation was part of the first category. Because of the frequency of parliamentary grants, it had become the foundation of royal finance by the beginning of the fifteenth century.

In France as in England, 'ordinary' receipts came from the royal domain, that is, the king's prerogative rights, either of a seigneurial kind over Crown lands or regalian rights (for example, justice and control of the currency supply) throughout the kingdom. In popular opinion, these ought to have permitted the king to 'live of his own' without taking recourse to the aid of his subjects in normal times, hence they were termed 'ordinary'. The 'extraordinary' revenues arose from the right of the king to levy charges on his subjects in the name of the common good, an attribute of sovereignty rediscovered in Roman law by jurists. It was the exceptional circumstances created by the Hundred Years War which permitted this second kind of levy to be imposed for the defence of the kingdom. These levies were either direct, like the *fouage* under Charles V (1364–80) and the *taille* later on, or indirect. Indirect levies included the taxes on merchandise called *gabelles* in the fourteenth century and *aides* in the fifteenth century, the name '*gabelle*' being reserved for the salt tax only from then on. In practice, just as in England, these became permanent regular sources of income, despite being put into question with varying success and durability in 1380, 1418, 1465 and 1484.

Unlike in England, however (with the exception of specific liberties, such as the earldom of Chester, which were excluded from parliamentary grants) the fiscal system in France differed from region to region. In Normandy and the west of the Massif Central, *aides* were replaced by a direct tax, the *équivalent des aides*. Poitou did not pay the *gabelle* but another tax, the salt quarter (*le quart du sel*). The Languedoc, in particular, enjoyed a quite separate fiscal regime with a direct tax, the *aide*, which was based on property and not on persons as in the north. This represented the contribution of this region to the *taille* of the kingdom. An *équivalent des aides* was raised there under the form of indirect rights which were different from the *aides* elsewhere in the kingdom. The Languedoc also had its own particular form of administrative organisation.

The classic division between ordinary and extraordinary finances is thus to be found on both sides of the Channel, corresponding to the division between old and new revenues, and the growth of royal tax receipts was built on the establishment and development of the latter. Each kingdom nonetheless devised its own specific fiscal system, and adapted its own political and economic realities. The English system was more uniform than the French model, which arguably resulted from its greater territorial heterogeneity, except for those liberties alluded to above, and other parts of the realm, such as the northernmost counties, were periodically exempted from the national system of taxation on the grounds of poverty or the depredations of border warfare. At the same time, export taxes, which were of marginal importance in French royal finances, occupied a central place in those of the English king as a result of the importance of wool exports.

Amount of revenue

Estimates of royal revenue in both England and France during this period are notoriously difficult to make. The situation is the most difficult in the case of the French monarchy, where the sources are simply lacking for most years, reducing the historian to more or less happy approximations.

Even where the documentation exists, in the 1320s or from the end of the fifteenth century, it is biased by innumerable errors of arithmetic made by financial officials handicapped by Roman numerals. The totals for the general review of finances of 1523, for example, which have been preserved, are all incorrect. The reconstitution proposed below, following the calculations of modern scholars or suggestions from the sources, can most often provide no more than an order of magnitude. The annual revenues of the French royal government may have passed from 860,000 *livres tournois* (*l. t.*) between 1295 and 1314, under Philip the Fair, to 884,000 *l. t.* between 1322 and 1330, under Charles IV and Philip VI, 1,600,000 *l. t.* under Charles V, and 2,250,000 *l .t.* around 1390, at the peak reached in the reign of Charles VI. After the collapse at the start of the fifteenth century (to perhaps 674,000 *l. t.* in 1418?) they rose to 1,800,000 *l. t.* at the death of Charles VII (1461), and reached their peak at 4,700,000 *l. t.* at the end of the reign of Louis XI (1483), before being brought down by the Estates General of Tours to 2,350,000 in 1484 and then beginning to grow once more: 3,462,000 in 1497, at the end of Charles VIII's reign; 4,865,000 in 1514, at the end of Louis XII's reign and 5,054,176 after correction in 1523, on the eve of the reforms of Francis I.

In this form, however, these figures are not mutually comparable because of variations in the value of the *livre tournois*. These, above and beyond the serious upsets caused by periods of monetary crisis in the fourteenth century and at the beginning of the fifteenth century, inexorably devalued this currency of account over the long term. The buying price of a silver mark in the royal workshops went up from 2 *l. t.* 18*s.* in 1290 to 13 *l. t.* 5*s.* in 1523, peaking at 90 *l. t.* in 1422 at the worst moment of monetary collapse. One possible solution is to convert these sums into their equivalent weight in fine silver, following the official value of marks bought by the king to strike his coins. Expressed in this way, the annual resources of the French monarchy may have passed from forty-six tonnes of fine silver in 1295–1314 to 50.5 in 1322–30, 71.5 in 1364–80, 88 around 1390, 17 in 1418, 48 in 1461, 110 in 1483, 55 in 1484, 74 in 1497, 104 in 1514 and 89.5 in 1523.

The structure of royal revenues was transformed in the course of this period. The proportion represented by the royal domain became negligible after the establishment of a modern fiscal system in the second half of the fourteenth century. From 30% under Philip the Fair and even 43% in the 1320s, it fell to 11% around 1390 and to less than 2% in 1483, before the effort to improve the revenues of the royal domain raised it back to 7% in 1523. Among so-called 'extraordinary' receipts, the tenth paid by the clergy occupied an important place in the first half of the fourteenth century (21% of total revenue in the 1320s), but this later became an occasional supplement when new taxes transferred the burden onto the towns and peasantry. In the fifteenth century, direct taxation took first place ahead of indirect levies. The former account for the greater part of the increase in royal revenues in the second half of the century. From 67% of total revenue in 1461, the proportion taken up by the *taille* increased to 83% in 1483, went down again to 64% in 1484 and 61% in 1497, before coming back up to 68% in 1514 and to 71% in 1523.[3]

Similar problems face any attempt at measuring revenue in England. The most recent figures show a sharp increase in royal revenue, particularly from direct and indirect taxation, in the period *c.*1290 until 1360. At the beginning of Edward I's reign the ordinary revenues were in the region of £15,000 per annum. It has been estimated that lay and clerical taxation raised as much as £800,000 in Edward I's reign, while the customs yield increased from £8,000 in 1284 to some £116,000 in the three years between 1294 and 1297. This new-found dependence on taxation was the basis of Edward III's fiscal system: in 1340–1 over £200,000 was raised from lay and clerical subsidies, while in the years 1350–70 taxation averaged some £70,000 per annum.[4] In the same period, traditional sources of income, such as the sheriffs' farms, feudal incidents and the profits from the royal mint, declined. The net amount of revenue declined slightly in the second half of the fourteenth century, but then rose again in the 1390s and especially during the wars of Henry V. Under Henry VI, income declined sharply and, coupled with the European-wide economic crisis of the mid fifteenth century, meant that the Crown's revenue had a reached a crisis point by 1450. Under the Yorkist kings and Henry VII revenue slowly rose, aided principally by a reinstatement of the Crown lands as the cornerstone of royal finance. By 1500 royal income stood at roughly £110,000 per annum, the most significant part of this from the royal demesne. This in fact slowed under Henry VIII, but was more than compensated for by a fundamental overhaul of the system of direct taxation between 1515 and 1523. While regular income in the early 1520s may have been some £30,000 per annum less than at the

---

[3] Following Clamageran (1867–8), vol. I, pp. 322–7, 407 and vol. II, p. 98; Henneman (1971), table 2, p. 348; Rey (1965a), tables on pp. 81–90, 97–8, 262; Chaunu (1977), p. 145; Lassalmonie (2002), tables 3 (p. 60), 39 (p. 613); Hamon (1994), p. 77; Doucet (1922), p. 10. The equivalent in fine silver is Lassalmonie's own calculation, the results of which sometimes differ from Chaunu (1977), pp. 134, 145, 147, 150–1, 162.

[4] Prestwich (1972), pp. 128–9, 191, 197; Ormrod (2000), pp. 205–7.

beginning of the century, taxation and loans (never repaid) netted some £550,000 between 1522 and 1527. Converting the revenues of the kings of England into weights of fine silver permits a clearer comparison with those of the king of France: on average the former peaked at about 40 tonnes between 1371 and 1380, came close to 32 tonnes in 1391–1410 and hardly exceeded 17 tonnes in 1462–85.[5]

The total revenues of the king of France were thus greater than those of the king of England, a difference easily explained by the relative size and population of the two kingdoms. It also appears that the evolution of these revenues was not the same in the two kingdoms, each following its own logic, to the rhythm of the weakening and recovery of royal power and the construction, decline and reconstruction of the financial system on either side of the Channel.

The limits of a statistical approach

This statistical approach to medieval financial history cannot be pushed very far. In both England and France, historians are constrained by the nature of the sources. In the latter, the first problem is a simple lack of documentation. Not only do the sources rarely provide global figures, which when they do occur are marred by errors, but even when they are available and can be corrected they are rarely mutually comparable, since they are not of the same nature: sometimes predicted receipts are given, sometimes receipts actually received, sometimes expenditure ordered, sometimes expenditure actually made. Too often the historian is tempted to run together into misleading sequences data of heterogeneous origins in order to give the impression of tracing developments over time. The synthesis put together by Mark Ormrod is thus of necessity only based on the discontinuous series, limited in chronology and exceptional for its preservation, of receipts of the *Trésor* for 1322–5 and 1328–30,[6] and J. F. Lassalmonie's own attempt to reconstitute the king's revenues combines estimates with figures taken from a variety of accounting sources.

Although the English medieval accounting records are on the face of it more abundant, similar traps lie in wait for the researcher. The records of the exchequer do not provide a full picture of the royal finances. The king's own money, kept in his chamber, was free of the public accountability which characterised the exchequer and throughout the period at crucial times – such as the royal ransoms of the 1350s and 60s, Henry V's Norman campaign and the Yorkist and early Tudor innovations in 'Chamber Finance' – there are important gaps in the record.

---

[5] Ormrod (1995), graphs 23 and 25.   [6] Ormrod (1995).

Secondly, the records of the exchequer do not provide 'profit and loss' style accounts, but merely show, at the most basic level, the discharge of accountants' debts to the Crown.[7]

Such source problems are not the only ones associated with a quantitative method, which cannot give a full picture of all the definitions of fiscal pressure. On the one hand, lacking any historical appreciation of the conditions of each period, a statistical method cannot on its own provide a properly contextualised appreciation of the material impact of taxation on late medieval economic structures. In France, the record fiscal pressure of the end of the reign of Louis XI (perhaps 3 per cent of GDP) seems to us derisory. But this must have been much more difficult to support in the state of development of the late medieval economy: contemporary financial techniques only permitted a far slower circulation of the means of payment, a state of affairs further worsened by chronic insufficiency of money supply. Certainly what the state took was re-injected, but in different parts of the economy. As a result, these levies must have disturbed, more than is at first apparent, a pre-industrial economy already undersupplied with currency, especially in the economically depressed context of the years 1350 to 1450. In England, the effects of high taxation are similarly hidden from the record: the decline in the amount of silver coin in circulation, from c.£700,000 in 1351 to c.£150,000 in 1422 must have had an effect on the ability of the Lancastrian regime to collect taxes; similarly, the high taxation of the early sixteenth century had an adverse effect on the velocity of merchant capital.[8]

On the other hand, the quantitative approach is by nature blind to the subjective weight of taxation. It was the perception by contemporaries of the weight of taxation which determined their reactions and their attitudes, and not the objective reality of it, and even less the reconstruction that a modern historian might hope to put together on the basis of sources which hardly permit it. On a larger scale, the psychology of the actors, their conceptions and their mental representations of the world which surrounded them play a significant, if not decisive, role in fiscal and financial history, which even trustworthy statistics could not represent. A perhaps more fruitful approach, then, to understanding the nature of the fiscal system and the importance of financial matters in the making of both polities is to trace the evolution of the discourse on fiscality, in the Crown's response to financial and political crisis and in the kingdom's response to royal policy shown through its willingness to offer

---

[7] See, for example, the problems of archival evidence described in Grummitt (1998), pp. 277–99 and Grummitt (1999), pp. 229–43.

[8] Allen (2001), p. 607; Hoyle (1998), p. 673.

credit and pay taxes. This approach, when accompanied by the study of the material, technical and human structures of the financial system, makes it possible to understand the essence of the 'financial state' and the prevailing national fiscal culture from the twofold perspective of ideas and reality.

3.   The personnel of royal finance

Numbers

In France, the expansion of the royal finances in the last two centuries of the Middle Ages led to an increase in the number of financial officials as new financial institutions developed and spread their influence across the kingdom. This growth was particularly remarkable in the second halves of the fourteenth and fifteenth centuries, either side of the crisis years between 1410 and 1430. Contemporaries had the impression of a ruinous proliferation of financial agents and this was a recurrent target of attacks until the end of the Middle Ages. In England, there was a similar growth in the number of officials, although popular condemnation was more muted than in France. How many financial officials did the king employ? The answer depends on how we define them and varies over time, although the overall trend was upwards in both polities across our period.

At the senior level, the calculation is relatively simple. In England, the Crown maintained only a small number of men in its permanent employ. By the fifteenth century there were forty salaried officers based at the exchequer in Westminster. Headed by the Treasurer of England (who enjoyed the nomination of the majority of the offices), more men were involved in the accounting side of the exchequer (the 'Upper' or 'Exchequer of account') than with the custody of the money (the 'Lower Exchequer' or 'Receipt').[9] As well as those in receipt of regular wages, there was a small army of clerks, some in the pay of the Crown, but most kept as private servants of the salaried officers. In France, there were six senior officials for ordinary finances and a number which grew from ten to thirty over this period for extraordinary finances. There were less than ten principal civil and military payment officers in 1300, but several dozen by 1500. In all, the financial apparatus of the monarchy lay in the hands of perhaps twenty or so men in the time of Philip the Fair, and, although this increased over the period, it was still less than a hundred under Louis XII.

[9] Sainty (1983).

The financial high administration was more decentralised in France than in England, which is explained by the greater extent and territorial variety of the kingdom of the Capetians. Not only did those who directed the financial administration at the top – the *trésoriers de France* for ordinary finances and *généraux* for extraordinary revenues – travel throughout their vast jurisdictions (the *charges* or *généralités*) in tours of inspection (the *chevauchées*), but in every jurisdiction a central accountant for extraordinary finances, the receiver general, and his assistant, the controller general, were permanently installed in its administrative centre.

Things were more complicated at the lower level. In England the Crown's local financial officers were not salaried as such, but the most important of them received some financial reward for their services. Principal among these were the customs collectors, at least two in each of the head ports, as well as controllers, surveyors, searchers and clerks. By the end of the fourteenth century they received regular cash rewards at the exchequer, besides their costs and expenses, when they rendered account. At first a primarily financial official, the sheriff still held important financial responsibility in this period, not least the pursuit of the king's debtors, despite his burgeoning workload as the principal conduit of royal justice in the shires. The sheriff was served by a deputy (the under-sheriff) and a collection of clerks. Like the customs officials, the sheriff, too, could claim his reasonable costs, but by the first half of the fifteenth century he was also in receipt of a cash reward given *ex officio*. By the close of our period the amount was fixed for each county and was, in effect, a salary paid at the end of the shrieval year. The Crown's feudal rights at a local level were surveyed by the escheator.

In France, the situation was somewhat different, with local officials being directly employed and salaried royal officers. The number of *bailliages* and *sénéchaussées* varied according to the size of the royal domain. After the acquisitions of Charles VII and Louis XI there were almost sixty in the kingdom, not including Brittany, the Dauphiné and Provence. Under Charles VI, as later under Charles VIII, there were between eighty-five and ninety districts of extraordinary finances, called *diocèses* in the fourteenth century and *élections* in the fifteenth century, of which twenty-three were in the Languedoc. There were less than one hundred royal salt warehouses (*greniers à sel*) at the end of the fourteenth century, and half as many again under Louis XI. Their number then fell back to some 125 at the start of the sixteenth century. Considering only regional officials specialised in raising and managing the king's money (which excludes *baillis* and *sénéchaux* with broader competences), there were up to sixty receivers in ordinary finances, as many controllers (*contrôleurs*) and, in the fourteenth century, forty or fifty master payers of works (*maîtres payeurs des oeuvres*). In extraordinary finances there were some 130 officers in charge of *diocèses* or *élections* (*élus*), 100 or so receivers and as many *contrôleurs*, 100 to 150 salt warehouse officials (*grenetiers*) and as many controllers. In total, there were perhaps 150 royal financial officials in the regions under Philip the Fair and 700 under Louis XII, of whom more than a hundred were for ordinary finances and about 600 were for extraordinary finances.

Beyond the question of payment, two principal differences characterise the local personnel on each side of the Channel. On the one hand, tax collectors on exports had an importance in England with no equivalent in France, reflecting the different structure of royal revenues in the two kingdoms. On the other hand, unlike the English sheriff, the *bailli* (in the north of France) or the *sénéchal* (in the south) had little to do with finances from the fourteenth century onwards. These officers were first dispossessed of their functions associated with Domain finance by the *receveur ordinaire*, and they were not accorded any authority over extraordinary taxes, whose direction was put in the hands of the *élus* (who, despite their name, were officers named by the king).

The expansion of the fiscal system in this period touched all levels of society. In England, as well as those local officials who had always been involved in the Crown's finances (bailiffs, mayors of towns and cities and episcopal officers to name a few), the growth in direct taxation saw the appointment of temporary, unsalaried, local officials to collect the tax and, at times of innovation particularly in the 1340s, 1371–81 and the later fifteenth century, to assess it. They accomplished their task with the assistance of vill constables, as well as manorial, town and hundred officers. The nature of the fifteenth and tenth, after 1334 the standard direct form of lay taxation assessed on a fraction of the moveable goods of taxpayers, was essentially communal and local. The individual burden of taxation was determined locally, with no intervention by the central government or royally appointed tax collectors and in this important regard royal taxation involved ordinary people at every level in the business of government.[10] Very few aspects of royal finance were alienated from the control of the exchequer. There were the farmers of the alnage in each county (a tax on the domestic sale of cloth) and their clerks, but overall, the fiscal system demonstrated a large degree of central control and supervision in the business of collection was devolved to local, unsalaried officials.

[10] Dyer (1996).

In France also, much of the expansion of royal financial government was carried out by unsalaried local officials. Most indirect rights were farmed out to individuals: by 1300 there were already several hundred such individuals charged to collect domain rights. There were probably several thousand two centuries later, collecting the *aides* or the *imposition foraine*, a tax on goods being brought for sale in places where the *aides* were not levied, either within or outside the kingdom. In fact, there were innumerable farmed-out rights, generally conceded in every subdivision of the *bailliage*, *sénéchaussée* or *élection* for each tax or taxable category of merchandise. In Paris there were sixty-six for the *aides* alone before the simplification of 1465. Even when it is taken into account that it was common for one person to hold several farms, it can be seen that farmers of royal rights make up the greater part of financial officials of this second level, of whom there were several hundred at the start of our period and several thousand at the end. In addition, this reckoning of financial officials does not include all those in the service of the financial administration of the king. When lieutenants, scribes, prosecutors, advocates, sergeants, salt measurers and so forth are considered, the complete personnel of a *bailliage*, *sénéchaussée* or *élection* is counted in tens, whereas that of a salt warehouse comes to perhaps half a dozen. The army of private servants employed by officers, commissioners and farmers to accomplish their public duties must also be taken into account, as must the immense crowd of collectors of the *taille* designated by their fellow citizens in tens of thousands of parishes. The total number of agents of royal finance considered in this way would come to several thousand under Philip the Fair, and several tens of thousands under Louis XII (or still a good ten thousand or so if the parish collectors are excluded).

Finally, despite the decision of the French monarchy to exclude independent individuals from the management of public affairs, after 1380 the royal administration limited itself to assigning to each parish the total amount of the *taille* which was to be paid, leaving the parishioners to divide the tax burden amongst themselves. This formula, identical to the fifteenth and tenth in England, protected the king from a certain kind of recrimination: the taxpayer who felt he was too heavily taxed could only blame the parish assembly which had fixed his contribution.

If we abandon for a moment the prudence that ignorance imposes on the historian, and hazard some figures which can only be a guide, it is possible that the finances of Philip the Fair employed in the broadest sense 3,000 out of 15 million subjects, and those of Louis XII 40,000 out of 12 million: that is to say, one in 5,000 around 1300, and one in 300 around 1500. As for financial officials in the strictest sense – royal officers, king's commissioners and farmers (who are very much in the majority) taking up responsibilities at all levels – their number would pass from less than a thousand at the start of the period to perhaps 3,000 at the end. Thus, in terms of the numbers involved, the fiscal system in France was far more wide-reaching and provided employment for a far greater number of individuals than it did in England.

If we put aside the uncertainty of the figures, it can be seen that the development of royal taxation in both kingdoms led to the involvement of an ever-increasing number of local notables and men of lesser condition who made sure the system worked on the ground, in the service of the king but generally without the status of an officer. It nonetheless seems that there was a tangible difference in the middle ranks of the financial machinery, in that royal officers were used in France, while in England much of the day-to-day business of administration, collection and expenditure of royal revenue was devolved to local elites who were not nominally in receipt of royal fees.

Change and development

The origins of those recruited as financial officials also changed over this period. In France, at the birth of the king's extraordinary finances, the Estates General of the Languedoil – which as we have seen was responsible for setting the system in place – decided that the three estates would collaborate in running the system on an equal footing. At the top, nine superintendents (the future *généraux des finances*) including three clerics, three nobles and three burgesses would direct the new organisation, supported in each diocese by an *élu* from each estate. Already, however, the management of the funds was in the hands of the burgesses: the four receivers general put in place in 1355 for Normandy were all burgesses of Rouen. The monarchy, however, soon asserted its control over extraordinary finances, rapidly putting an end to this theoretical equilibrium, and the three estates were not henceforth equally represented in royal service.

Even after custody of the royal treasury was taken away from the Templars in 1295, churchmen continued for a long time to play a prominent role among the central financial officials of the king. Under Charles V, Cardinal Jean de la Grange was the principal architect of the new fiscal system, and there were many bishops among the *généraux* until the reign of Charles VII. Charles' restoration of royal financial institutions was a turning point in the laicisation of senior personnel: after 1456 there were no churchmen among them. The same evolution is seen at the regional level. Ecclesiastics were quite numerous to begin with among *élus*; Charles VI even put in place one clerical *élu* per diocese in 1383 to supervise his rights over the church, but they disappeared after 1416. The management of royal money was not, on the other hand, considered an appropriate activity for a man of God: the receiver general Guillaume Charrier only became a bishop in 1439 after resigning from his office and the case of churchmen who took the office as receivers of *aides* remained extremely rare.[11]

In England, too, the principal change which occurred in the nature of salaried royal financial officers in this period was their increasing laicisation. Beginning slowly in the second half of the fourteenth century, it gained pace in the 1390s and the first decades of the fifteenth century and by the mid fifteenth century the vast majority of offices in the exchequer were held by laymen. Increasing lay literacy and the declining appeal of a career in the church, as well as the pressures coming from the need to reward royal servants and creditors, all help explain this trend.

The eclipse of the churchmen – which can also be detected in other areas of service to the king – can be found simultaneously in the financial administration of the two kingdoms. Yet if we consider the chronology more closely, this movement is both later and quicker in France: although it only began in the first half of the fifteenth century, it was complete, as in England, by 1460.

One of the most interesting and significant aspects of laicisation in England was the degree to which it was driven by the desire of the Crown and powerful individuals to reward their servants: in other words, to what extent did the fiscal system become prisoner to the demands of patronage? Already by the beginning of the fifteenth century, the use of office in the exchequer to reward good service or ensure political compliance was apparent, but as the system struggled to cope with the financial and political crisis of the first half of Henry VI's reign it became clear that office in the exchequer was increasingly placed in the hands of those who, through their contacts with the London-based merchant community, could mobilise merchant capital to assist the Crown. At times, as in the 1440s, this led to conflict between the 'court', eager to reap the material benefits that office in the exchequer offered, and the 'exchequer', keen to ensure administrative continuity. The recovery of the royal finances under Edward IV and Henry VII allowed an increase in the number of offices used as patronage. Nevertheless, the need for administrative continuity and the desire to maintain public confidence in the fiscal system ensured that there were remarkable continuities in

[11] Dupont-Ferrier (1930–2), vol. I, pp. 68–9, 112, 170, 183, 186, appendix IV, no. 26, pp. 284–5; Rey (1965a), pp. 229–30; Autrand (1994), pp. 693–5; Lassalmonie (2002), p. 42.

personnel throughout the political upheavals of the later fifteenth century. Even the emergence of exchequer dynasties during the sixteenth century should not necessarily be seen as a sign of corruption, but rather as a demonstration of the desire for administrative continuity.[12]

In France, the situation was rather different. The nomination of financial personnel by the king theoretically put his finances in the hands of those faithful to him. In practice, individuals, or rather their families and professional networks, were themselves part of political networks which intervened to facilitate access to office or promotion to a higher level. At the regional level, outside the royal domain, office was filled through the patronage of the great lord, whose protection was indispensable to obtain royal office over his lands. These networks were as numerous as the territorial principalities of the kingdom, but the monarchy tended to take them over when it became strong enough to put royal service before fidelity to the prince. At the top level, during periods of weakened central power, office was distributed within a faction organised around one or several princes with ambitions to involve themselves in government, whether they opposed the king, supported him or held him in tutelage. These factions, which allied the client networks of different princes to the rhythm of their shifting alliances, were particularly concerned to control royal finance. They placed their partisans in the highest offices of the financial administration whenever they gained power, as did the Armagnacs and Burgundians in the civil wars of the beginning of the fifteenth century. Those who ran the royal finances were easy targets for accusations of misappropriation in propaganda attacks. Thus, in 1406, the *Songe véritable*, a pamphlet of pro-Burgundian inspiration, criticised the king's senior financial personnel, dominated by the network of those close to Jean de Montaigu, who was protected by the duke of Berry, but spared the Chanteprime network which Montaigu and his associates had supplanted.[13] The role of these factions declined when the king imposed his authority, as, for example, under Louis XI, and office was then apportioned directly to royal clients.

It thus seems that in France, despite the existence of political networks, the concern to reward personal services was less important for the nomination of financial officials than it was in England, even when a faction had taken control of the government of the kingdom. Rather than merely rewarding loyal servants, interested parties attempted to infiltrate the system by introducing reliable agents, but also competent ones, and this last criteria remained essential to guarantee the correct functioning of the system of tax raising and of revenue distribution in the interests of those in power. In England, however, the pressures of patronage undoubtedly

[12] Grummitt (2003); Carpenter (2010); Alsop (1986).   [13] Autrand (1994).

had a negative impact on the effectiveness of royal administration from the fifteenth century – what Christine Carpenter has called a 'deskilling of the royal bureaucracy'.[14] This had an ultimately disastrous effect in the medium to long term and underpinned the fiscal crises that characterised later Tudor and early Stuart rule.

4.   Fiscal culture: principles and practice

Principles: 'To live upon mine own'

In France, the idea that the king should in normal times finance himself with the resources of the royal domain and not ask for financial aid from his subjects except in exceptional circumstances, remained deeply anchored until the end of the Middle Ages,[15] as the continuing appellation of 'ordinary' and 'extraordinary' finances bears witness. In his coronation oath, the King of France swore to return to the domain those lands which had been removed from it by his predecessors, and every reign opened with an ordinance for the restoration of the domain. The disjuncture with the realities of state finance increased, and the cold clear-sightedness of Louis XI, who distributed to his followers lands whose contribution to royal receipts had become derisory next to the product of the *taille*, shocked contemporary authors, who reproached him for having dissipated his domain when he ought to live from its revenues, whether they opposed the king (like Thomas Basin) or supported him (like Jean de Roye). The idea was all the more deeply rooted on account of the tendency of the French to overestimate the size and wealth of the kingdom, which even literate people with links to the royal government believed to contain 1,700,000 parishes.[16] At the Estates General of 1484 the deputies, confronted for once with royal revenue figures, protested that they were grossly under-estimated.[17]

The English equivalent of this was the theory of the 'fisc', those inalienable resources that belonged to the Crown and were to be employed for the public affairs of the kingdom, rather than the private affairs of the king. This distinction was undoubtedly complicated in the fifteenth century by the accession to the Crown of the duke of Lancaster in 1399 and by the circumstances of the usurpation of Henry IV. It called into question the status of the lands belonging to the Crown as duke of Lancaster, and after 1461 as duke of York; this ambiguity was evident in the debates concerning the enfeoffment of part of the duchy of Lancaster for the performance of Henry V's will after 1422. The conceptual problems

---

[14] Carpenter (2010).   [15] Scordia (2005).
[16] Contamine (1973).   [17] Masselin (1835), pp. 364–7.

begun by Henry III's acquisition of the earldom of Chester in the thirteenth century became more apparent and pressing during the fifteenth
century, but the problem had been prefigured in a sense from 1389 when
Richard II, with the resources of Chester, Cornwall and Wales at his
disposal, had made peace with France. Potentially, with such valuable
private resources at his disposal, the king could formulate policy driven
by his own private ambitions and not govern according to the necessity
of the 'common good'.

Traditionally, the fisc was to be employed to meet the ordinary charges
of the Crown and royal government (most notably the king's household).
When this fell short, extraordinary taxation was used to meet those costs.
Under these circumstances, the Commons began to question whether the
Crown's fiscal policy was being conducted properly and in accordance
with the public good of the realm. From the beginning of the fifteenth
century this questioning manifested itself in the form of demands for the
resumption of those parts of the fisc and royal patrimony that had been
granted away. In other words, during the reign of Henry IV the Commons
demanded resumption on the suspicion that the fisc had been alienated to
support the king's own Lancastrian affinity.[18] Demands for resumption
were also central to the confrontational parliamentary politics of 1449–
55. The later Yorkist acts of resumption in 1465, 1467 and 1473, while
serving to rearrange the distribution of land and power in the localities,
were also passed amidst debates in the Commons which reflected the fiscal rhetoric used by their Lancastrian predecessors. In 1467, Edward IV,
underlining the political community's belief in the notion of the fisc and
its centrality to ideas of effective kingship and commonwealth, told the
Commons that he purposed 'to live upon mine own, and not to charge
my subjects but in great and urgent causes, concerning more the weal of
themselves . . . rather than mine own pleasure'.[19] The conundrum of the
relationship between the Crown's inalienable resources and taxation was
finally addressed towards the end of the fifteenth century by a significant
shift in the Crown's attitude towards its patrimony, the fisc and extraordinary revenues. The early Tudor period saw a significant blurring of the
conceptual and practical differences between the three.

Principles: the legitimacy of taxation

The king's recourse of the private wealth of his subjects raises the question
of the legitimacy of taxation. In the context of the Hundred Years War

---

[18] Wolffe (1971), pp. 52–96.
[19] *Parliament Rolls of Medieval England (PROME)*, ed. Given-Wilson et al. (2005), parliament of 1467, item 7.

and its aftermath, the French, confronted with external invasion, pillage and destruction, did not contest the right of the king to raise tax in the name of the common good (in this instance for the defence of the realm), borrowed from Roman law by jurists at the end of the thirteenth century and affirmed definitively by Charles VII in 1439. In areas covered by estates, such as Normandy and Languedoc, tax was in principle accorded to the king by a representative assembly, but in the second half of the fifteenth century, royal initiative progressed at their expense. The vote tended to become a formality and, even in distant Languedoc, whose fiscal specificity was respected by the monarchy, estates which had still been combative under Charles VII submitted to Louis XI.

The legitimacy of taxation was linked to the uses to which it was put, and so to a hierarchy of expenditure according to their usefulness. In the *état général des finances* of 1470, when the French king's financial officials themselves noted certain charges which they knew to be of higher priority in the eyes of Louis XI, these were military credits and significant payments direct to the king, in particular the funds destined for the households which provided for the upkeep of the royal family but also often the means necessary for the government of the sovereign, such as the horsemen of the stable, who carried his orders. These priorities accorded with the expenses considered to be legitimate by public opinion, as is shown by the debates of the Estates General in 1484: those which permitted the king, the queen and their children to maintain their estate for the honour of the kingdom, and those which assured its defence. The whole question was to evaluate what was necessary to accomplish these objectives: the deputies of 1484 crossed swords with the Constable and Chancellor of France concerning the evaluation of the number of men needed by the royal army.[20] In the same way, the taxpayers judged the financial weight of pensions to be excessive, which the pensioned nobility ranked, on the contrary, among necessary expenditure. In 1465, the programme of the aristocratic revolt of the *Bien Public*, which combined the suppression of tax and the sharing out of military commands and pensions among the conspirators, betrayed the incoherence of a movement caught between its anti-fiscal demagogy and its desire to take a greater part of the redistribution of royal taxes.[21]

Across the Channel, the heart of the theoretical conception of the English 'tax state' of the later Middle Ages was again the notion of extraordinary taxation developed in the first half of the fourteenth century, but the king did not succeed in controlling it to the extent he did in France. It was accepted by the late thirteenth century that parliament,

[20] Masselin (1835), pp. 310–19, 328–37, 368–77.
[21] Lassalmonie (2002), pp. 194–6, 198–200.

representing the community of the realm, should be consulted before the king imposed extraordinary taxes. At first both direct and indirect taxes were included, but during the fifteenth century some trade taxes came to be granted for the life of the monarch. Once the necessity had been explained the Commons could not refuse, but they could put into place measures that ensured the proper collection and spending of tax revenues (as indeed happened in 1371, 1377, 1404 and 1450). This was the defining feature of the English '*dominum politicum et regale*' and, to commentators of the latter part of our period, differentiated England from France.[22]

Thus, in broad outline, the attitude of political society to the king's finances was similar on both sides of the Channel. Nonetheless, the monopoly of tax-raising powers established by the Capetian monarchy created a fundamental difference in the form of political debate about finance. The only equivalent to the regular, national, institutional platform provided in England by the assemblies of the Commons in parliament is to be found in the meetings of the Estates General, which were frequent in times of political crisis (1346–59, 1423–39). The rest of the time, the expression of any debate about the king's finances was divided between rare sessions of the Estates (notably that of 1484, which is exceptionally well documented, and thus priceless to the historian) and the regular, but more restricted, framework provided by regional assemblies. In these conditions, despite the recurrent affirmation of grand principles, the form of political debate was less fully realised in France than in England, and the theories of French political thinkers, such as Jean Juvénal des Ursins, archbishop of Rheims under Charles VII, had little resonance in public opinion. In England, on the other hand, the position expressed by writers such as the author of the poem *Crowned King* in the 1410s, Sir John Fortescue in the 1470s, or even Sir Thomas Smith in the 1560s was testimony to a widely shared, common fiscal culture that persisted across our period and beyond.

Practice: shortage of money supply

In reality, however, the operation of the fiscal system was governed by a series of practical constraints: economic, structural and political. More often than not it was these factors, rather than the theoretical, that determined the nature of fiscal change in the late Middle Ages. In both polities, the principal factor that shaped the dynamics of the fiscal system was

---

[22] Plummer (1885), pp. 111–27.

liquidity – the simple problem of a shortage of bullion to meet the competing demands of royal government. Both kingdoms were affected, and although monetary flows from England to garrisons in France might have attenuated the problem there, the movement was reversed on a number of occasions through the booty of *chevauchées* under Edward III, Henry V and their captains, John II's ransom (from 1360) or the payments negotiated by Louis XI at Picquigny (1475) and Charles VIII at Étaples (1492). In England the situation appears to have worsened considerably in the years after 1420 and must have been related to the economic crisis then apparent. A decline in the volume of the wool trade, upon which the income from indirect taxation principally relied, and the 'bullion famine' of the middle decades of the fifteenth century were important factors in the fiscal crisis of Henry VI's reign.[23] Related to this was the fact that the nature of the Crown's need for money (above all, for war in France) meant that there was a flow of bullion out of England. These very real economic limitations should be kept in perspective. Nonetheless, in the middle of the fifteenth century the same shortage of money supply which contributed to the financial collapse of the Lancastrian monarchy did not prevent the reconstruction of the Valois finances. It seems as if the political dynamics in each kingdom, which worked against Henry VI but favoured Charles VII, were more important than any economic handicap.

Practice: credit

The role of credit in the public finances of these two kingdoms brings to light a number of important contrasts. To raise funds more quickly than the collection of taxes allowed, the French king made use of loans, although these were far less significant than those raised by his English counterpart. They were in theory only an anticipation of fiscal receipts, which should have served to reimburse them, but often became a supplementary source of income whose repayment could be problematic. Raised from bankers, towns, royal servants, merchants, the nobility or senior churchmen, credit was presented as a test of the loyalty of a community or individual to their sovereign more often than taxation was. This simultaneously emotional and political appeal was all the more necessary since, when the will or capacity of the king to repay appeared doubtful, the amount raised was proportional to his effective authority. Under Louis XI the reimbursement of his first great campaign of borrowing (1463) assured the success of the second (1468), but the poor rate of repayment for this one led to strong resistance to the third (1471);

---

[23] Hatcher (1996); Nightingale (1997).

all the same, in the last decade of his reign the king, having vanquished his enemies, was in a position to transform the raising of a loan into a veritable tax in all but name, for it became annual and was not reimbursed any more.[24] It is necessary to consider, moreover, that advances from accountable officials to the treasury were another form, invisible but permanent, of credit to the king in the absence of a state bank or public working capital.

Credit was incomparably more important for the English royal finances, with profound consequences for the relationship between the sovereign and political society. During this period, the fiscal system came to rely more and more on public credit. War, the royal household and the defence of the realm increasingly relied upon a system of assignment whereby income was anticipated and spent before it was collected. As early as the reigns of Edward I and Edward III, the king's wars were funded by credit. By 1307, Edward I's debts stood at £200,000 and by 1339 a debt of £300,000 threatened the collapse of Edward III's foreign ambitions. The crucial difference, however, was that from the 1360s onwards the Crown's policies (especially war) were funded by loans not from foreign bankers but made by its own subjects. In the fifteenth century it was English mercantile capital, dependent on the fortunes of the wool trade, rather than the loans of the great southern European banking houses, that maintained the Lancastrian Crown. When the treasurer, Ralph, Lord Cromwell made a declaration of the Crown's financial position in 1433, debt stood at £168,000; by 1450 this had risen to £372,000.[25] The effectiveness of Lancastrian government was judged, in part, by its ability to manage this debt and repay its domestic creditors.

Credit from one's own subjects, of course, had an entirely different political significance than loans from abroad. It was not possible for the Crown to renege upon its debts to its own subjects and still retain the political support of the community of the realm. This was manifested in the Commons' criticism of royal fiscal policy, especially during the reigns of Henry IV and Henry VI. The willingness to offer the Crown credit was a barometer of political confidence, most apparent in the decision of the London mercantile community to support the rebel Yorkist lords in 1459–60. The ability of Edward IV after 1471, and especially the early Tudors, to free themselves from the constraints on royal policy imposed by a reliance on domestic credit allowed these kings to pursue more ambitious and radical policies both at home and abroad. By the early sixteenth century the dynamic in the relationship between the Crown and its domestic creditors had changed fundamentally. Between 1522

---

[24] Lassalmonie (2002), pp. 320, 482–5.   [25] Ormrod (1999a), pp. 37–8.

and 1523, Henry VIII collected loans totalling more than £211,000. In 1528, parliament wrote off these loans, a measure of the Crown's strength and skill at managing parliamentary affairs, but also of the support and political capital the Henrician regime enjoyed in the country.[26]

In France, as in England, Italian bankers played a role of first importance at the end of the thirteenth century and in the first decades of the next century, although they seem to have disappeared earlier in Paris. Thereafter, although the French king made use of credit, the very nature of his fiscal system, resting entirely on his ability to raise tax from his subjects, meant that he was less dependent on internal credit than the King of England, at least from the middle of the fourteenth century onwards. As a result, his position was in principle more secure with regards to balancing the support of political society.

Practice: where was the money kept?

On both sides of the Channel, the material context for the administration of the royal finances remained largely private. In France under Charles VI, as under Francis I, the offices and clerks of the senior financial officers were located in their private residence, their town house in the regional centre of their jurisdiction (Paris, Tours, Rouen and Montpellier) rather than in their country manor houses. Subsequently their professional archives (notably the copies of their accounts submitted to the *Chambre des Comptes*) were also kept at home, but retained a semi-public status. Conserved by their heirs they remained at the disposition of the king; the most useful papers were, moreover, given by the departing office-holder to his successor.[27] For example, amongst the servants of Louis XI, those of Jean Bourré are now in the Bibliothèque Nationale, while those of Jean de Reilhac were still in the hands of his descendants at the start of the eighteenth century. In England, although the treasurer and other officials regularly conducted business from their private residences, the records they produced were, in a sense, public and were kept at the exchequer.

Where the king's money was kept varied depending on the size of the funds in question and the seniority of the officials responsible for it. In both England and France, state treasuries and the king's private residences were used to store cash. In England, the Exchequer of Receipt at Westminster functioned as the main treasury, although cash was also stored at the Tower of London, while the king's personal money (that accounted for in his chamber) was stored in royal palaces or deposited

---

[26] Hoyle (1995).   [27] Rey (1965a), p. 212; Hamon (1999), p. 78.

with the church. With the development of chamber finance under the Yorkists and early Tudors, these distinctions were eroded, and by the 1520s it seems likely that the king's palaces at Whitehall and Greenwich, as well as the Tower, were the most important treasuries. In France, throughout the period, at the highest level the largest sums were deposited primarily in royal fortresses. The Louvre took over this role after the transfer of the royal treasury from the Temple in 1295 and was still serving this function under Francis I, as did a number of other châteaux: Vincennes and Melun under Charles V and Charles VI, Blois under Francis I. Secondarily, money was deposited in royal urban residences such as the Hôtel Saint-Pol in Paris under Charles V. At a lower level, the accountable official kept them at home: funds earmarked to pay for men-at-arms were stolen from the house of the *clerc des guerres* François Raudin in Paris in 1491.[28]

Practice: how well informed was the king about his financial situation?

To master the management of royal finances, rulers needed to be able to evaluate the state they were in. It is clear that in England the government regularly prepared budgetary statements under the authority of the treasurer and, at least until the reign of Henry VI, these were presented to parliament as a means of influencing the grant of taxation.[29] These appear to have been made less systematically prepared under the Yorkist and early Tudor kings. The so-called 'Declaration of the State of the Treasury' (first introduced in 1505) was an internal exchequer development for the king and council and not designed to 'declare' the state of the royal finances to parliament or the wider public.[30] In France the preparation of budgetary statements seems to have been more standardised, although they were prepared solely for the king and his financial officials. To understand the state of his finances, the King of France had at his disposition, at least since Charles V, a summary of his receipts and his charges, the *état général des finances*, prepared each year by his officials. Although it comes close to it, this document is not, however, the state 'budget' in the sense that we would understand, since it does not cover the entirety of revenues and expenditure. On the one hand, receipts granted out by the king were not taken into account, since the monarchy was no longer the beneficiary of them, even if his appointees

[28] Autrand (1994), pp. 675, 685; Rey (1965b), pp. 446–8, 473–8, 481; Hamon (1994), pp. 272–4; *Lettres de Charles VII*, ed. Pélicier (1902), vol. III, pp. 219–21.
[29] Harriss (2008); Grummitt (2013), pp. 167–70.   [30] Alsop (1986), pp. 190–2.

still took care of its collection. On the other hand, 'ordinary' charges on the revenues of the royal domain were not recorded among expenses in the *état général* but figure in the accounts of the particular receipts of the domain, after local ordinary revenues. These expenses included the wages of local domain officers, the fiefs and *aumônes* – that is, the rents assigned to vassals and religious establishments respectively – the cost of works and repairs, in short the expense of maintaining the infrastructure of the domain. Thus, only the estimated net product of the domain, with alienations and ordinary charges already deducted, is taken into account in the *état général des finances*, whereas a whole raft of state expenses – the most traditional ones – are excluded, the result in a certain fashion, along with pre-assigned receipts, of a decentralised budget. All this escapes us then, but it represents a smaller and smaller part of the total budget of the state. In a similar fashion, the *état général* left out the reserve infantry of free archers created in 1448, whose upkeep was directly assigned to parishes and did not enter into royal finances in times of peace.

Practice: the structural weakness and inertia of the system

On both sides of the Channel, governments attempted to make improvements in the fiscal and financial system in order to improve efficiency and the level of receipts, but this produced results which differed as a result of both economic realities and the reactions of different actors.

In France, once the institutions of royal taxation and financial administration had finally emerged, by about 1360, after a long period of experimentation begun under Philip the Fair, they showed some shortcomings. This could be seen, for example, with regards to the difficulty of getting a complete picture of what could be taxed and of actually collecting taxes from these potential sources, or in the frustrating slowness of collection and of payment which often clashed with the urgency of the king's needs. Nevertheless, over the long term, these deficiencies did not prevent the system from functioning, or even from adapting to changing circumstances. This can be seen in the successful reforms of Charles V, Charles VII and also Louis XI, and although the latter did have to abandon his more adventurous reforms after the experiences of the beginning of his reign, he was able both to refine the powerful fiscal tool of direct taxation and to rationalise indirect taxation by refocusing it on articles where it was most productive, in particular wine and salt.[31]

In England, on the other hand, successive kings found the Commons reluctant to fundamentally reform the system of direct taxation, based

---

[31] Lassalmonie (2002), pp. 674–7.

on a fraction of taxpayers' moveable goods, established in the early four-teenth century. The period after 1334 saw important changes to the sys-tem of indirect taxation, notably in the development of the wool subsidy and tunnage and poundage. Yet despite numerous attempts at innova-tion, the Crown and the Commons failed to fundamentally alter the system of direct taxation between 1334 and 1523. The ninth and tax on wool of 1340, the parish tax of 1370, the disastrous poll taxes of 1377–80 and the experimental taxes on income and lands under Henry IV and Henry VI all failed to generate significantly more income than the fifteenth and tenth, or provoked widespread and, at times, violent oppo-sition. This was a symptom of the mistrust between the two sides of the fiscal equation, but it was also perhaps indicative of administrative inertia and a reluctance on the part of the Commons to discuss innovation. This persisted into the later fifteenth century and Edward IV's Benevolence of 1481, and Henry VII's subsidy of 1497 also saw serious opposition in both parliament and the localities and failed to significantly increase the amount of revenue collected.[32] Equally, despite Richard II's exper-iments with tunnage and poundage, the failure to shift the burden of indirect taxation from the export of raw wool to finished cloth was a sign of both reluctance on the part of the merchants to part with more of their profits and of the Crown's inability (or unwillingness) to impose change upon the fiscal system.[33] Similarly, the various acts of resumption of the fifteenth century were hampered in their effectiveness by the numerous exemptions which were the price of political support for the Lancastrian and Yorkist kings. Once again, it was not until 1523 that a significant and long-lasting innovation was made. Henry VIII's lay subsidy of that year, collected over four annual instalments, raised over £150,000 while the clerical subsidy probably raised a similar sum. Moreover, the Crown secured the return of records of individual wealth into the exchequer to form the basis of future assessments. The subsidy introduced in 1523, a directly assessed tax on personal wealth, would remain the standard form of lay taxation (in conjunction with the ancient fifteenth and tenth) until the 1620s.

Consequently, the ability of royal finances to adapt to changing circum-stances depended less on internal structural considerations than on the capacity of the monarchy to have these innovations accepted by political society, whether by force, by negotiation or even by voluntary conces-sion. Here, too, the essential factor was political. The financial apparatus fell apart when political power lost its way, whether at the end of the reign of Charles VI of France or under Henry VI of England, whilst the

[32] Jurkowski (1999); Jurkowski et al. (1998), pp. 278–89.   [33] Ormrod (1999b).

restoration of political authority was accompanied by (and drew strength from) financial recovery, in the second half of Charles VII's reign, under Edward IV or the first Tudors.

5.   Politics, political culture and finance

On both sides of the Channel, once the king began to ask his subjects to provide the money necessary for the functioning of the royal government, the organisation and control of finances became a key element in the relationship between the monarchy and political society.

In France, while in the first half of the fourteenth century fiscal experiments were driven by royal power, the birth and rise of a modern fiscal system in the century and a half that followed were the object of competition between representative assemblies and the monarchy to control the new system. It was the Estates General of the Languedoil who implemented it from 1355 onwards, but after 1358 the future Charles V managed to take control from them. Estates assemblies took their revenge in the 1420s after the collapse of the Capetian state, but Charles VII regained the upper hand after 1439. Under Louis XI, the aristocratic revolt of the *Bien Public* failed in 1465. Louis' death allowed the Estates General of 1484 to mount a final counter-offensive, quickly countered by the regency of Anne and Pierre de Beaujeu. Except in the first half of the reign of Charles VII, the authoritarian model imposed around 1360 by Charles V, which separated social elites from the direction of royal finances to the benefit of the monarchy and its servants, won in the long term. Even the regional assemblies which voted taxes were not informed of the state of royal finances, a veritable state secret which was only revealed once, at the Estates General of 1484. From this date the king at least informed his subjects how much the *taille* raised each year, which had not been the case before. The consequence of this was the absence of a culture of public management in the elites of French society and their incapacity to take part in the management of royal finances when the opportunity was offered them, after one century had already elapsed. The fiscal reforms of the beginning of the reign of Louis XI, in Normandy and Languedoc, failed in part because the Estates assembly in the first case and the merchant class in the second case proved to be unable to take on the financial responsibilities which the king had wanted to delegate to them.[34]

In these conditions, civil society only participated in the functioning of the system inasmuch as certain milieus furnished the royal financial

---

[34] Lassalmonie (2002), pp. 129–37.

administration with their qualified personnel, men of law to run the system and money men to keep the accounts. The status of royal officer, which was generally conferred to them, made them servants of the state, whose private network (business relations, domestic establishment) was then put at the service of royal power and its attempts at fiscal assessment of the population. Elites also provided the lenders whom the king needed, but in the absence of any control over royal finances they remained dependent on the good will of the government to get their money back. The king and society (or certain elements of it) did enter into a mutually profitable cooperation, but on a far less equal footing than across the Channel.

In the end, the game of tax and redistribution orchestrated by a financial apparatus entirely in the hands of royal power (whether that be exercised by the sovereign himself or by aristocratic factions) profited the state first of all, which found in it a means to finance itself, then the elites, whose consensus was necessary for the establishment and maintenance of the system. Such was the case for the nobility and the clergy. They were exempt for the most part from taxes and were paid for service to the king in his armies, his tribunals and his offices. They benefited from pensions and gifts to retain their loyalty, including pious liberality to churches. Certain burgesses also profited, whether the minority of the great merchants who supplied the court and the army, or the more numerous technicians who put their skills in law and money management at the service of the king. Unsurprisingly, the greatest losers were the peasantry, who paid and who received in return for their investment in the state almost nothing but harassment by local officials and the brutality of an irregularly paid soldiery. Although they formed the overwhelming majority of the population, they had no weight in political society and paid the expenses of a consensus of elites on which the monarchy built its financial support.

The following chronology can be outlined for France:

- ***c*. 1290–1355:** from Philip IV the Fair to John II the Good, the last Capetians of the senior line and the first Valois tried out various formulae to finance the expansion of royal government and the first episodes of the Hundred Years War.

- **1355–1418:** the political and financial crisis caused by the military defeats of this period and by the capture of John II (1356) led on to the creation of a modern fiscal system and a financial administration (1355–60) which the regent, the future Charles V, placed under royal control (1358–60) and developed further (1369). At his death a brief abolition of taxation (1380–2) only served to demonstrate its necessity for the royal government. Once the system had been quickly re-established it began to grow once more, up until the collapse of royal authority at the end of the reign of Charles VI, amidst civil wars and the English invasion (1418).

- **1418–39:** in a country broken between Capetian and Anglo-Burgundian obedience, each camp tried out new financial formulae in which representative assemblies regained their right to raise taxation.
- **1439–1523:** Charles VII made ready for the reconquest with great reforms (1439–45) which re-established, with certain modifications, the fiscal and administrative model in place under Charles V and Charles VI. The ill-fated innovations of the beginning of Louis XI's reign (1461–4) were quickly abandoned, the system thus restored stayed in force without great change until the remodelling of the financial administration by Francis I (1523).

The kingdom of France was larger and more populated than the kingdom of England and so with an equal degree of efficiency the French fiscal system would have brought more money to the king than the English system. From the middle of the fifteenth century, the French system became genuinely more efficient than the English system for a political reason: while the King of England had to secure the vote of parliament, Charles VII succeeded in securing for himself the right to raise taxation without recourse to the estates. Although Charles V had already done as much in the middle of the fourteenth century, the conditions were not yet brought together which would make it possible to take full advantage of this. The slow progress of reconquest from the English between 1369 and 1380 did not offer the same prestige to the king. In addition, the king's financial and fiscal organisation was still recent. It was necessary not only for taxpayers to get used to it, but also for the rulers themselves, who may not have been ready, mentally and morally, to take on its consequences, as was shown by Charles V's scruples: he abolished the *fouage* on his death bed (1380). In the 1440s, after decades of painful development and in the face of the necessity for the political and military reconstruction of the state, the decisive stage was reached and the victorious campaigns of 1449 to 1453, at the same time as they legitimated the effort imposed by Charles VII on his subjects, strengthened royal authority enough to maintain its momentum. From then on, not only could the French king collect funds more quickly, but he himself determined the level of taxation, whereas across the Channel his rival had to submit to the goodwill of parliament. Louis XI, above all, would make the most of this state of affairs, going too far in the last years of his reign, and provoking after his death a reaction which spectacularly reduced fiscal pressure while leaving intact the foundations of the system.

In England, the question of the relationship between the king, society and the apparatus of royal government has been much debated. Was the

Crown able to tap effectively its subjects' wealth and employ it to realise its ambitions at home and overseas? Or did the community of the realm seek to limit the fiscal and political ambitions of the Crown, anxious to ensure that the realm of England remained a *dominium politicum et regale* in opposition to its French counterpart? Alternatively, it is possible that the fiscal system was developed to meet the needs of both the Crown and its subjects and that conflict was atypical, occasioned only by economic and political crises. These debates characterise the historiography: an older generation of scholars wrote about the 'Lancastrian constitutional experiment' and the lapse into 'Tudor despotism' as part of a teleology that ended with the mature, liberal parliamentary democracy of the nineteenth century. More recent scholarship has stressed the consensus between the Crown and subject, the common political culture which underscored the discourse between the two and downplayed the differences between the medieval and early Tudor conceptions of kingship and government. It has to be noted, too, that since the dialogue between the king and the political community was at the heart of the system of public finance in England, the concept of political culture, and especially of fiscal culture, is particularly important in understanding the nature of this system, although they have only secondary significance in the authoritarian French model which left a limited space for discussion of taxation.

In summary, the fiscal history of England in the later Middle Ages can be divided into the following loose periods:

- *c.* **1290–1340/1:** these years saw the emergence of the Commons as a political force and the negotiation of the fundamental features of the system of public finance between king, Lords and Commons. Despite a common political language and culture, the period saw the alliance of the Lords and Commons against the Crown in 1297, 1311 and 1340–1. What emerged from it, however, was an advanced notion of public finance in which the Lords and Commons agreed to assist the Crown through regular taxation, but in return the Crown agreed to rule by the accepted principles of politic government.
- **1340/1–76:** the Black Death saw the mutual aspirations of the Crown and the political classes reinforced, thanks notably to their common interest in retaining control over the cost of labour, and this was to be seen in the apparent consensus which characterised fiscal policy up to 1376. It was also made easier by the bonus of significant royal ransoms after 1346 and the sharp increase in customs revenue from a buoyant wool trade.
- **1376–99:** the crisis of 1376–81 was, however, as much fiscal as political, and the ability of the Commons in 1376 to withhold taxation

as part of their demand for political reform was a reminder of the potentially fraught nature of the fiscal discourse and of the ability of royal weakness to destabilise the system. This was also apparent in the failure of the Crown to secure adequate tax grants throughout the 1380s. Related to this failure was Richard II's fiscal policy during the 1390s, the abandonment of fiscal innovation based on direct taxation and such potentially tyrannical steps as the appropriation of the wool subsidy for life in 1398. Moreover, his failed attempt to renegotiate the basis of indirect taxation points to a breakdown in the consensus which had characterised the third quarter of the fourteenth century.

- **1399–*c*.1450:** the Lancastrian period witnessed the disintegration of the system of public finance established under the later Plantagenets. Conflict in parliament, the failure of fiscal innovation in the first half of Henry IV's reign and the Commons' unquiet at the demands of Henry V's Norman campaigns all pointed to long-term structural tensions. As it had done in the late 1370s and 80s, a sustained crisis of kingship further exacerbated the problem and combined with economic and military crises to bring the fiscal system to the point of collapse by the late 1440s.

- **1450–71:** the period of civil war in the middle of the fifteenth century saw a variety of improvised methods of fiscal management, but the most significant development was a rise in importance of the private resources of the Crown as kept in and administered through the chamber (the most personal of the departments of the king's household). This had been important, for example, during the reigns of Edward II, Henry V and Richard II, but during the late 1450s it emerged as the means by which the Lancastrians maintained their political position and supported their military efforts against the rebel Yorkist lords, while during the 1460s Edward IV increasingly used the royal patrimony to augment his authority alongside the public revenue from direct and indirect taxation.

- **1471–1523:** during the 1470s and 80s the chamber took over from the exchequer as the principal fiscal institution and income from the Crown lands superseded indirect taxation as the most important source of royal revenue. This was not a return to a domain-based fiscal system and it did not mark a retreat in the political ambitions of the Yorkist and early Tudor monarchy. Rather, it marked a renegotiation of the fiscal and political culture of England to one in which the Crown was also to derive political, as well as financial, capital from its new emphasis on the importance of the royal patrimony and, through Henry VII's enforcement of his judicial and feudal rights, the fisc. In turn, this greater political power, partly a result of financial strength, allowed, in the first fifteen years or so of Henry VIII's reign, the Crown to introduce innovations in direct taxation which made the early Tudors at least as effective as Edward I and Edward III had been in using their subjects' wealth for their increased ambitions both at home and abroad.

The comparison between the chronology of developments in England and France illustrates well how in each country the evolution of the financial apparatus followed its own rhythm, determined by the internal political life of the kingdom. The Hundred Years War did not synchronise the two systems: events had different effects on the internal situation of each kingdom, effects which could be reversed over the short or medium term. Thus victory reinforced the authority of the king with regards to his subjects in the short term (as in the case of Henry V after Agincourt) whereas a defeat weakened him (after Crécy, Philip VI met with sharp criticism in the Estates General of 1347); but in the medium term, success could be followed by a loss of enthusiasm on the part of taxpayers as the costs of occupation began to grow, while a defeat could plunge a kingdom into a political crisis which finally brought fruitful reforms (the capture of John II at Poitiers ultimately led to the birth of the modern fiscal system in France). In England, defeat in the Hundred Years War did not lead to immediate root and branch fiscal reform. Yet the extended period of civil unrest and civil war from 1455 until 1487 (which had its origins in the domestic political crisis occasioned by the loss of Normandy and Gascony) led to a gradual transformation of the dominant fiscal culture.

Beyond institutional differences, contrasting local traditions and chronological variations between the two kingdoms, the royal finances in England and France seem to rest on a common basis (arguably similar to that present throughout Western Europe): a *modus vivendi* between the monarchy and the dominant parts of political society. That said, this arrangement took very different forms in the two kingdoms: in England the elites took part in the system as autonomous actors, whilst in France the monarchy tried to establish its own monopoly on the right to raise taxation, and to restrict national and local elites to the role of qualified agents working in the king's service. Nonetheless, it was still the case in both kingdoms that the game of tax raising, redistribution and the mobilisation of greater and greater resources, in the name of the common good, under the guidance of the royal government emerges as an eminently 'political' phenomenon at the end of the Middle Ages. It was 'political' because royal finances were now at the heart of power relations, determined more by the political context than by the economic situation.

Conclusion

The new English model which emerged in the second half of the fifteenth century was closer than the one that preceded it to its French contemporary. Yet significant differences remained: the English parliament retained control of part of royal revenue; domain finances and loans continued to carry a weight without equivalent in France, while the marginal financial role of the chamber of the French king, which remained no more than a simple household department, does not bear comparison with the primacy won by its English counterpart. In contrast to the duke of Burgundy and other territorial princes in the Valois kingdom, Edward IV and his successors never tried to draw inspiration from the French royal model. The tyranny denounced by Fortescue made this system in all regards absolutely unacceptable to English public opinion, which was as hostile to the French as it was proud of its liberties. It is a telling observation of the changes introduced by Henry VII to the English fiscal system that, in 1498, the Spanish ambassador observed that the king wished to govern in the 'French fashion but he cannot'.

BIBLIOGRAPHY

1. INTRODUCTION

Chaunu, P., 1977. 'L'État de finance' in F. Braudel and E. Labrousse (eds.), *Histoire économique et sociale de la France*, tome I, vol. I, Paris, pp. 129–91.

Clamageran, J.-J., 1867-8. *Histoire de l'impôt en France*, vols. I and II, Paris.

Dupont-Ferrier, G., 1930-2. *Études sur les institutions financières de la France à la fin du Moyen Âge*, 2 vols., Paris.

Jurkowski, M., Smith, C. and Crook, D., 1998. *Lay Taxes in England and Wales, 1188–1688*, Kew.

Ormrod, W. M., 1990. *The Reign of Edward III: Crown and Political Society in England, 1327-1377*. London.

1995. 'The West European Monarchies in the Later Middle Ages', in R. Bonney (ed.), *Economic Systems and State Finance*, Oxford, pp. 123–60.

1999a. 'England in the Middle Ages', in R. Bonney (ed.), *The Rise of the Fiscal State in Europe, c.1200–1815*, Oxford, pp. 19–52.

2. SOURCES CITED

Fortescue, Sir John, *The Governance of England*, ed. Charles Plummer, Oxford, 1885.

Lettres de Charles VIII, roi de France, ed. P. Pélicier, vol. III, Paris, 1902.

Masselin, Jehan, *Journal des états généraux de France tenus à Tours en 1484, sous le règne de Charles VIII*, ed. A. Bernier, Paris, 1835.

Parliament Rolls of Medieval England (*PROME*), ed. C. Given-Wilson et al., CD-Rom, Leicester, 2005.

3. FURTHER READING

Allen, M. R., 2001. 'The Volume of the English Currency 1158–1470', *Economic History Review*, 2nd Series, 54, 595–611.

2012. *Mints and Money in Medieval England*, Cambridge.

Alsop, J. D., 1986. 'The Exchequer in Late Medieval Government, *c*.1485–1530', in J. G. Rowe (ed.), *Aspects of Late Medieval Government and Society*, Toronto, pp. 179–212.

Autrand, F., 1994. *Charles V le Sage*, Paris.

1999. 'La guerre des gens de finance en 1406 d'après le Songe véritable', in J. Kerhervé and A. Rigaudière (eds.), *Finances, pouvoirs et mémoire, hommages à Jean Favier*, Paris, pp. 292–301.

Carpenter, C., 2010. 'Henry VI and the Deskilling of the Royal Bureaucracy', in L. Clark (ed.), *The Fifteenth Century IX: English and Continental Perspectives*,Woodbridge, pp. 1–37.

Contamine, P., 1973. 'Contribution à l'histoire d'un mythe: les 1 700 000 clochers du royaume de France', in *Économies et sociétés au Moyen Âge. Mélanges offerts à Édouard Perroy*, Paris, pp. 414–27.

Doucet, R., 1922. 'L'état des finances de 1523', *Bulletin philologique et historique (jusqu'en 1715) du Comité des Travaux historiques et scientifiques, année 1920*, 5–143.

Dyer, C., 1996. 'Taxation and Communities in Late Medieval England', in R. Britnell and J. Hatcher (eds.), *Progress and Problems in Medieval England*, Cambridge, pp. 168–90.

Grummitt, D., 1998. 'The Financial Administration of Calais during the Reign of Henry IV', *English Historical Review*, 113, 277–99.

1999. 'Henry VII, Chamber Finance and the "New Monarchy"', *Historical Research*, 72, 229–43.

2003. 'Public Service, Private Interest and Patronage in the Fifteenth-Century Exchequer', in L. Clark (ed.), *The Fifteenth Century III: Authority and Subversion*, Woodbridge, pp. 149–62.

2013. *A Short History of the Wars of the Roses*, London.

Hamon, P., 1994. *L'argent du roi. Les finances sous François Ier*, Paris.

1999. *'Messieurs des finances.' Les grands officiers de finance dans la France de la Renaissance*, Paris.

Harriss, G. L., 1975. *King, Parliament and Public Finance in Medieval England to 1369*, Oxford.

1985. 'Financial Policy', in G. L. Harriss (ed.), *Henry V: The Practice of Kingship*, Oxford, pp. 159–79.

2008. 'Budgeting at the Late Medieval Exchequer', in C. Given-Wilson, A. Kettle and L. Scales (eds.), *War, Government and Aristocracy in the British Isles, c.1150–1500: Essays in Honour of Michael Prestwich*, Woodbridge, pp. 179–96.

Hatcher, J., 1996. 'The Great Slump of the Mid-Fifteenth Century', in R. Britnell and J. Hatcher (eds.), *Progress and Problems in Medieval England*, Cambridge, pp. 237–72.

Henneman, J. B., 1971. *Royal Taxation in Fourteenth-Century France. The Development of War Financing, 1322–1356*, Princeton.

Hoyle, R. W., 1995. 'War and Public Finance', in D. MacCulloch (ed.), *The Reign of Henry VIII: Politics, Policy and Piety*, Basingstoke, pp. 75–99.

1998. 'Taxation and the Mid-Tudor Crisis', *Economic History Review*, 2nd Series, 51, 649–75.

Jack, S. M., 1998. 'Henry VIII's Attitude Towards Royal Finance: Penny Wise and Pound Foolish', in C. Giry-Deloison (ed.), *Francois Ier et Henri VIII: deux princes de la Renaissance (1515–1547)*, Lille, pp. 145–55.

Jurkowski, M., 1999. 'Parliamentary and Prerogative Taxation in the Reign of Edward IV', *Parliamentary History*, 18, 271–90.

Lassalmonie, J.-F., 2002. *La boîte à l'enchanteur. Politique financière de Louis XI*, Paris.

Nightingale, P., 1997. 'England and the European Depression of the Mid-Fifteenth Century', *Journal of European Economic History*, 26, 631–56.

Ormrod, W. M., 1999b. 'Finance and Trade under Richard II', in A. Goodman and J. L. Gillespie (eds.), *Richard II: The Art of Kingship*, Oxford, pp. 155–86.

2008. 'Poverty and Privilege: The Fiscal Burden in England (14th–15th Centuries)', in S. Cavachiocchi (ed.), *Fiscal Systems in the European Economy from the 13th to the 18th Centuries*, Florence, pp. 637–56.

Plummer C. (ed.), 1885. *The Governance of England: Otherwise Called the Difference between an Absolute and a Limited Monarchy*, Oxford.

Prestwich, Michael, 1972. *War, Politics and Finance under Edward I*, Oxford.

Rey, M., 1965a. *Le Domaine du roi et les finances extraordinaires sous Charles VI, 1388–1413*, Paris.

1965b. *Les finances royales sous Charles VI. Les causes du déficit, 1388–1413*, Paris.

Sainty, J. C., 1983. *Officers of the Exchequer*, London.

Schofield, R., 2004. *Taxation under the Early Tudors, 1485–1547*, Oxford.

Scordia, Lydwine, 2005. *'Le roi doit vivre du sien.' La théorie de l'impôt en France, XIIIe – XVe siècle*, Paris.

Wolffe, B. P., 1971. *The Royal Demesne in English History: The Crown Estate and the Governance of the Realm from the Conquest to 1509*, London.

6 Justice, law and lawyers

Michelle Bubenicek and Richard Partington

Law and justice were crucial to the exercise of royal government in both England and France in the later Middle Ages, but political and legal differences between the two realms make comparison problematic. The emergence of a single, royal common law in England in the second half of the twelfth century made the king's rule more direct and effective in the localities, whereas in France royal justices had to contend with different systems of law – Roman law, canon law and customary law, as well as precedent and royal ordinances – even though a single *coutume générale* of the kingdom of France and a *droit commun du royaume* progressively emerged during the period. From the twelfth century, the general eyre and other common-law mechanisms allowed the English king's subjects to gain access to his law locally, whereas in France locals depended substantially upon private, seigneurial justice for dispute settlement – although, from the second half of the thirteenth century, the institution of *baillis* and *seneschaux*, and the possibility of appeal to the *Parlement* at Paris represented an advance in kingly authority expressed through royal justice. This difference was heightened by the fact that the English king's writ ran in virtually all of his English lands, while direct rule in France was restricted to the *domaine,* large parts of the kingdom lying outside his immediate authority. In these areas, French royal judicial involvement depended on the mechanism of appeal, a crucial tool for the assertion of the king's authority and control, especially in border areas. As law grew in importance and scale in both kingdoms, lawyers, legal training and expertise became more and more vital. In England, as in France, a profession emerged, based around training (in the inns of court and universities), although in France professional solidarity was reinforced by family networks, as dynasties of lawyers – a *noblesse de robe* or 'fourth estate' – came to dominate judicial office, especially in the *Parlement.*

The difficulty of comparison is exacerbated by significant differences in the historiography of the later medieval legal system in the two countries.

English historians, substantially because of the early emergence of the common law, have focused extensively on structures, and the political implications of the role played in staffing those structures by nobles, gentry and lawyers. French historians, in contrast, have been most interested in how royal law worked to define and extend monarchical authority.

Accordingly, this essay will consider separately, though in parallel, the form and development of the legal systems of later medieval England and France, the personnel who staffed them and how these men were perceived by political society. We will draw conclusions about justice, law and lawyers in each country before assessing the similarities that existed between the two systems – despite their obvious structural differences.

1.   The law and royal government

England: the legal system and its development

The king's law or common law was carried to, and enforced in, the localities of England by a combination of public authority, represented and created by royal office, and private power, a matter of force and influence. Both were enacted principally via networks. But at the same time, the common law reinforced public authority because law was, by now, the medium through which that authority was principally expressed, and it secured private power by underpinning the landholding on which power was based. So, although considerations of personnel are essential to any proper assessment of late medieval English justice, the legal system itself is the best place to start.

Not all the English king's subjects had access to royal justice and, even for the great majority who did, resolving disputes frequently involved non-royal, or non-common-law courts or mechanisms. Manorial courts provided the most immediate local justice to free tenants and were the only judicial refuge of the unfree. Church courts regulated moral behaviour and also dealt with some civil cases. We now know, thanks to the work of Edward Powell and others,[1] that arbitration was central to dispute resolution and the maintenance of order, and a good deal of legal action was probably intended to force resort to it. Equity – the exercise of the king's authority to provide 'natural' justice, via the council, the chancery and the chamber, where normal legal mechanisms could not –

---

[1] Powell (1983).

was increasingly important. But the common law – the engine that so frequently drove non-common-law settlement – undoubtedly dominated.

By the later thirteenth century the common law – a combination of near-universal royal law and a legal system to enact it – was well established. In 1166 Henry II had, through the Assize of Clarendon, supplemented the royal justice hitherto available to all freemen from the king's court at the centre by creating royal legal structures for the localities. The 'instrument *par excellence*' (in the words of Powell)[2] of this Angevin legal system was the general eyre, whereby itinerant justices, predominantly drawn from the permanent judicial staff at the centre, were despatched to shire after shire to hear and try all manner of pleas, both civil and criminal, and especially those concerning the Crown. This provision apparently imposed from above was seized upon hungrily from below, and the system developed with a rapidity that now seems startling. This rapid development came in part because the eyre, despite its radicalism, was unwieldy and slow – visiting each shire only once every few years. So, almost from the beginning, certain of its functions were devolved to specially created subsidiary mechanisms. These, like the eyre, were itinerant in the counties.

The most important were the commissions of assize and of gaol delivery. Assize, by the fourteenth century, dealt overwhelmingly with the so-called 'petty assize' of *novel disseisin*, through which civil property disputes could be settled. Gaol delivery became, and effectively remained for most of our period, the principal means by which everyday criminal cases – that is, murder, rape, assault, arson, robbery and serious theft – were dealt with. It is striking that these amplified functions – the settling of routine property disputes and dealing with the run-of-the-mill criminality that necessarily afflicts every society – were precisely those of the most common utility to the king's subjects. The usefulness of assize and gaol delivery was mirrored by their accessibility. To bring a plea of assize of *novel disseisin* one had to purchase a writ, but this was relatively affordable: in the surviving assize rolls, actions brought or defended by landholders of mean estate predominate. Initiating a prosecution via gaol delivery was perhaps even more straightforward. It simply involved persuading a regular tribunal of local men – typically the hundred court presided over by the sheriff – that one was the victim of a crime and that a named person (or named persons) could reasonably be suspected of having committed it. If one's opponent was politically powerful or well connected this might pose problems, but few criminals were. During the later thirteenth and early fourteenth centuries assize and gaol delivery,

---

[2] Powell (1989), p. 10.

originally ad hoc provisions, were first regularised and then coordinated with one another. In the first half of the fourteenth century – before they were combined with the new peace commission – they were probably the Crown's most widely used, though not of course its supreme, judicial mechanism in the shires.

By the beginning of the fourteenth century the eyre, which had given them life, had vanished, not quite completely, but to all intents and purposes. In 1294 it had been suspended on the outbreak of war with France and was never revisited on a national scale. Why it was not is uncertain. Edward I certainly envisaged restarting it and this was attempted, abortively, under both Edward II and Edward III. Failure in England did not preclude success in other royal jurisdictions – it was visited upon the Black Prince's liberties of Wales and Chester in the late 1340s and 1350s to great effect – and it remained a potent symbol of the king's judicial might. But fail in England it did. Alan Harding argued that it collapsed under the weight of its own success,[3] overwhelmed by a 'flood' of plaints after 1278, when it began to hear informal pleas of trespass brought against royal officials and others. Caroline Burt has shown that, while the business of the eyre did increase, the increase did not come from plaints against officials, and was in any case only moderate.[4] One might still argue that the eyre had become too unwieldy; its perambulation of the shires of England had indeed become slower and slower; in the end, a county might typically expect an eyre visitation only once every seven years. But Burt's demonstration that the eyre did not reach a critically overburdened state and then 'collapse' suggests that the needs of justice simply moved beyond it. This may partly have been about extraordinary crisis in politics and order, deriving primarily from a pernicious and comprehensive failure of kingship under Edward II and demanding very particular judicial responses that the eyre could not make. It may partly have been because the common law and those serving it evolved as rapidly in the fourteenth century as they had in the thirteenth, leaving the cumbersome eyre behind.[5]

The historiographical implications of justice moving beyond the eyre are great, because our understanding of the remainder of the legal system in the localities – besides assize and gaol delivery – has until very recently rested on the assumption that the 'collapse' of the eyre left a gaping judicial void that had to be filled. It is a commonplace that this 'hole' was eventually plugged by the justices of the peace (JPs). The JPs

---

[3] Harding (1978).   [4] Burt (2005).
[5] For the rapid expansion of royal justice in the fourteenth century, see Musson and Ormrod (1998) and Palmer (1993).

definitively emerged in 1350, but before this there was, according to the traditional view first delineated by Bertha Putnam,[6] a protracted struggle for local judicial control between the peace commission and 'rival' agencies: the justices of special and of general oyer and terminer; the justices of trailbaston; the 'keepers of the counties' (in the 1330s); the so-called 'superior' eyre – the central court of King's Bench itinerating in the localities as a court of first instance. The triumph of the JPs has been seen as a victory of local and knightly interest over the central and kingly concerns represented by the competing judicial mechanisms just listed.[7] The perceived political implication of this is immense: that Edward I and Edward III, under pressure of war with the Scots and French, gradually surrendered judicial control of the localities to the gentry in return for their military support, expressed principally through unprecedented grants of taxation made to the Crown by the gentry's representatives, the Commons in parliament. The consequences of this surrender for the integrity of justice, it is said, were grave: the local hijacking of the judicial system by nobles and gentry produced vast corruption.[8] (Both the relationship between king and judges, and alleged judicial corruption are matters to which we shall presently return.)

This view rests upon erroneous assumptions. Some of these relate to questions of staffing, which will be addressed later, when we consider legal personnel. Others concern the purposes of the peace commission and its 'rivals'. Historians have assumed they were the same; in fact they were not, and, if their functions were different, how could they 'compete'? What we must ask here is what did the peace commission actually do; what was its utility in governance? A comparison with assize and gaol delivery is instructive. The surviving records indicate that, in practice, the peace commission in the fourteenth century performed a very similar function to gaol delivery: it dealt with everyday disorder – murder, assault and theft – on a routine basis, in every county, periodically throughout each year. It differed more fundamentally from assize, which focused entirely upon disputes over property ownership, but both mechanisms relied, like all common-law courts, upon adjudication by local juries.[9] That assize, gaol delivery and the peace commission were essentially variations on a theme is shown by their effective merger in the 1360s, when their sessions were combined and their key personnel

---

[6] Putnam (1929).

[7] The debate is summarised in Musson and Ormrod (1998), chs. 3–4.

[8] Maddicott (1978).

[9] See, for instance, records of assize, gaol delivery and the peace commission from fourteenth-century Essex: The National Archives (TNA), JUST1/1412 (assize); JUST 3/129 (gaol delivery); JUST1/268 (peace).

shared (as will be discussed below). It is true that the peace commission had purposes essentially unconnected with assize and gaol delivery – it provided economic regulation, for instance, enforcing the labouring legislation introduced after the first outbreak of the Black Death and checking on weights and measures – but these, too, were largely matters of routine, and this is the key point.

It is key because the peace commission's supposed 'rivals' in the struggle to fill the void apparently left by the eyre did not, for the most part, engage in the ordinary and everyday business of providing redress and maintaining order; instead, they concerned themselves with exceptional and extraordinary disorder – in particular, with what we might term 'political' crime: rebellion, conspiracy, corruption and tax evasion. These extraordinary commissions had their origins in the thirteenth century, in another arguable offshoot of the eyre: ad hoc commissions of inquiry sent into the localities to investigate both infringements of royal rights and official corruption. Such investigations had advanced dramatically under Edward I, with the Hundred Roll inquiries, 'state trials' and trail-baston commissions.[10] Because they required a strong and effective king to drive them, they fell largely into abeyance under Edward II, but under Edward III they seem to have reached their height, particularly in the 1340s and 1350s when the 'new' or 'great' inquiries, the 'superior' eyre and a plethora of other ad hoc judicial commissions pursued, imprisoned and massively fined allegedly corrupt officials, knights and nobles on a grand scale.[11] They flourished finally and dramatically under Henry V (another warrior king, we should note) in the early fifteenth century.[12]

In the late thirteenth, fourteenth and early fifteenth centuries, then, common-law courts in the localities provided governance in two fundamental ways. First, they provided routine tribunals to deal with the everyday property disputes and commonplace crimes that would always constitute a threat to the king's free subjects and to justice and order. This provision increased significantly during the fourteenth century, with the regularisation of assize and gaol delivery, the rise of the peace commission and, finally, the effective merger of the three. Secondly, they provided the Crown with a means – again, increasing during the fourteenth century – aggressively to pursue organised crime, and corrupt or rogue elements among what we might term the 'political' classes: the officials and lords. Perhaps these extraordinary tribunals could only be properly conducted

[10] Burt (2012), pp. 238–41.
[11] Jones (1973); McLane (1988); Booth (1976); Maddicott (1978); Partington (2001), pp. 99–103; TNA, JUST1/258, /266, /267.
[12] Powell (1985).

by powerful, even warlike, kings, but they did enable Edward I, Edward III and Henry V legitimately to use the common law as an interventionist weapon in the localities. The extent of their intervention was, at times, breathtaking. Neither the routine nor the extraordinary elements in this judicial system were replacements for the vanished eyre. More flexible and immediate, and therefore more capable than their predecessor, they reflected the continued success and growth of the common law in the fourteenth and early fifteenth centuries.

How did the legal system change in the localities thereafter? Critically, Henry V was the last king to deploy the grand mechanisms for extraordinary judicial intervention developed by Edward I and Edward III – 'great' inquiries and the 'superior' eyre. As has been argued, it seems their effective deployment required kingship of a particular potency or quality; if they were not weapons of warrior kings (it is notable that Edward II, Richard II and Henry IV had all failed to utilise them properly), then they were certainly weapons of active, determined rulers, whose great vitality was shown in foreign, as in domestic, policy. So the obvious reason for their demise in the fifteenth century is the enduring inanity of Henry VI, immediately followed by the compromised first reign of Edward IV. After Henry V's death, therefore, fifty years elapsed before a king was again strong enough to deploy them, by which time they had atrophied. Alternatively, perhaps even their utilisation by Henry V was backward-looking; perhaps they were, by 1414, already a mechanism essentially of the past – of the 'good old law' before 1377. Whatever the case, by the mid fifteenth century the peace commission – which had already essentially absorbed gaol delivery and, to a lesser extent, assize – was the principal means by which the common law was administered in the shires. In the mid fourteenth century a typical bench of JPs had consisted of three or four central and local lawyers, from time to time led by a noble president; all these men regularly sat. Now 'interest' was emphatically represented among the justices of the peace; as many as twenty or more substantial landed figures in each shire might be appointed; a core of 'working' professional or semi-professional justices – the fifteenth-century equivalents of the fourteenth-century JPs – conducted the bulk of the business, but the other justices, appointees whose judicial office may seem at first glance purely honorific, sat when their interests, or those of their followers, required it. Thus a shift to self-regulation occurred. While the Crown – with neither local police force nor standing army at its disposal – had always relied, latently at least, upon landed, private power to enforce the public authority that the common law expressed, in the second half of our period its capacity actively to intervene notwithstanding local interest apparently declined. Locals were increasingly able to settle their own

differences while wearing royal judicial clothes, but it was now harder
for the Crown directly to intervene if they could not. In this way, the
bipartite judicial system that we saw in the localities in the fourteenth
century became essentially unitary in the fifteenth.[13]

Two further points should be made about the peace commission. The
first is that, by the sixteenth century, with the decay of manorial and
church courts, to the JPs' brief was added social, as well as criminal
and economic, regulation. The second takes us back to the political
centre, to which, with the growth of literacy and the legal profession, and
the consequent ready availability of legal expertise and advice, landholders in general, and nobles and gentry in particular, increasingly looked.
They sometimes petitioned for special oyer and terminer commissions
to be sent to the shires to deal with their plaints, but more commonly
used the peace commission as a conduit to the *rex* side of King's Bench.
King's Bench could also be approached directly, as could the other great
common-law court at Westminster, Common Pleas. King's Bench dealt
with pleas touching the Crown, but wealthier landholders could prosecute their enemies there too, usually for criminal trespass. Its distance
from most localities made it difficult to access, and therefore slow and
expensive. Depending upon one's purpose, this could be a dreadful hindrance or a boon; if one wanted, as a defendant, to kick the judicial
ball into the long grass, or, as a plaintiff, to exert great pressure upon
one's opponents, it was almost the perfect place; this is why wealthier
litigants came to favour its use in their disputes in the fifteenth century. Common Pleas dealt primarily with cases of debt – and on a vast
scale. (Debts of less than 40 shillings were usually dealt with locally by
the non-common-law county court.) The rising primacy of Westminster
for landed disputants was intensified and underlined by the other great
development that this later period saw, a vital one, but not of the common law. This was the ascent of equitable jurisdiction (as mentioned in
the opening of this section), exercised principally by the king's council,
the chancellor, the chancery and the chamber. These agencies provided
practical and flexible solutions to disputes that the increasingly complex,
and at times unwieldy common law could not. Edward IV and Henry VII
employed the courts of equity as they sought to impose their rule on the
kingdom. The rule of the former, especially, saw political centralisation
characterised by the creation of a vast royal affinity; this chimed with
legal change as the polity looked to the royal court (in all senses) at the
centre.[14]

[13] Carpenter (1997), chs. 2–3 and 12.   [14] Carpenter (1997), chs. 9–12.

France: the law as a tool of royal power

The study of the development of royal government in France in the last three centuries of the Middle Ages can hardly neglect the activity of the men of law who, from the famous 'legists' (*légistes*) to the 'men of justice' (*gens de justice*), came together to reinforce the authority of the sovereign in their specific area of activity. This is because the progressive establishment of what might be considered to be the earliest form of French monarchical absolutism owed much to the use of legal learning by the governmental elite and, more precisely, to 'the eruption of Roman law into the political field'.[15] Furthermore, the ever-expanding use of sovereign justice, as a guarantee of order in society, became more than ever the principal foundation of a reinforced monarchical authority. Theoreticians and practitioners, judges and jurists thus perfected new working methods, based on practical effectiveness and on experience, but also on the use of texts.

In the later Middle Ages, indeed, it was realised that directing the royal government was an art, an art which could be greatly improved through the knowledge and practice of law, which generated both professionalism and technical competence. It was thus that a whole army of *administratores* and *judices*, often trained in the law, were commissioned to act in the name of the prince. The term *officium* (office) was employed from the beginning to designate the role filled by these royal agents, although usually as the office *of* something, *officium judicis* (the office of a judge) for example, or *officium bajuli* (the office of a *bailli*). The fact of being paid seems to be the criteria which defined *officium publicis* (public office): an office is public from the moment that its holder receives payment from the state.[16] And amongst these royal agents, the lawyer (the *juriste*) is everywhere.[17] Nonetheless, this lawyer was more often a man of practice than a man of theory: he was to be found in the king's central government, that is, in his inner council and in the chancery; he was also to be found in the *Parlement*, doing justice in the name of the sovereign; finally, we come across him in local administration, where he helped to give structure to the cogs of an ever-more-complex machine, as judge, as prosecutor or as an attorney. It is true that historians traditionally make a distinction between 'political lawyers', those who were the closest to power – and naturally one thinks of the most famous of them, the counsellors of Philip the Fair[18] – and other lawyers: we can either refer to all these men of law with a training in Roman law as 'legists', following medieval tradition,

---

[15] Krynen (1992), p. 280.   [16] Rigaudière (1992), pp. 196–7.
[17] Giordanengo (1987), p. 20.   [18] Favier (1969), pp. 97–9.

or as 'jurists', to give them a more modern title which also makes it possible to include, beyond those influential counsellors in the royal entourage, the men of the *Parlement* (advocates, councillors, presidents) and, more generally, the 'judges'.

It remains the case that those who were the most influential on a political level, the 'political lawyers' (chancellors and members of the council), a minority within the profession, were the exception amongst royal counsellors.[19] We should thus certainly not neglect the fundamental role of the king's judges, whether by this we mean the men of the *Parlement* or the personnel of royal tribunals on a local level. We might think, for example, of the activity of the redoubtable Jean de Terrevermeille as the king's advocate in the Languedoc: all of them contributed efficiently to the construction of a royal law which magnified the person of the sovereign, an indispensable service for a monarchy which took the very essence of its legitimacy from the exercise of justice. More than ever, indeed, all justice came from the king, the supreme judge. From the thirteenth and fourteenth centuries the importance, as well as the volume, of litigation caused new institutions to develop, which rapidly asserted their primacy over competing forms of justice, ecclesiastical or seigneurial. There was the *Parlement* of Paris, an ordinary court, but also a court of appeal, and later the provincial *parlements* created in the fifteenth century. There were the *assises* of the *bailliages* and the *sénéchaussées*, courts which were initially presided over by the king's *bailli* or *sénéchal*, his principal officials in his domain, but which were increasingly taken over by professional auxiliary judges, such as the *lieutenants de bailliage*, who were in turn attended on by a staff of notaries, sergeants and clerks. Finally, from the fourteenth century, there were the specialised administrative courts: dealing with accounts (*cour des comptes*), with coinage (*cour des monnaies*), with taxation (*cour des aides*).

Nevertheless, if jurists were undoubtedly ubiquitous within royal institutions, whether these were central or local, they were also to be found, although in a smaller proportion, amongst the 'men of justice' of seigneurial tribunals and the courts of urban communities: it is true that prosecutors and sergeants were rarely trained jurists, but the same cannot be said of advocates. Up until the end of the fifteenth century at least, no formal qualifications were officially necessary to exercise the profession of advocate and many practitioners would only have attended a simple grammar school in the *bailliage*. With the passage of time, however, a specific university education, at the faculty of arts, and then in law, became increasingly necessary. At the level of the *bailliage*, the most sought-after

---

[19] Giordanengo (1992), p. 212.

practitioners generally had at the very most a bachelor's degree in civil law – in the provinces, a doctorate seldom fed its holder – sometimes rounded off with a diploma in canon law,[20] a qualification which could sometimes open the way to more prestigious local offices, in the service of the Crown: *bailli*, lieutenant to the *bailli*, advocate or king's prosecutor.

In any event, whether they were members of the monarchy's central institutions, or whether they represented the interests of the Crown at a local level, royal jurists were often much more intransigent, more unyielding when it came to the rights of their sovereign, in a word 'more royalist' than the king himself: the affirmation of the supreme authority of the prince was, for example, always on the lips of royal advocates,[21] and it was they who went so far as to formulate, in the *Parlement*, the principle according to which resistance to royal authority constituted the 'crime of *lèse-majesté*'.[22]

Indeed, although the omnipresence of jurists, in the government or in the courts of justice, can be explained by their mastery of sophisticated legal argument and by the well-known progress of royal justice, which subordinated competing modes of justice, it is probably even more closely related to the exceptional place taken by the law in the practice and exercise of power. This was because the law, notably Roman law, became the preferred instrument of the construction of the authority of the prince,[23] at the same time as it provided, for all who held power, *the* indispensible method of government.

Although the role of law and jurists in the expansion of royal power in France in the last three centuries of the Middle Ages is widely acknowledged, this recognition has paradoxically not produced as much investigation as one might have expected, such that the introduction to a relatively recent volume still remarks that 'although everyone agrees that the "renaissance" of Roman law in the twelfth century was immediately put to the service of political interests, [and] that the centralisation of the government of the church by means of canon law served as a model for the monarchical state, all in all, legal historians have not hurried to explore these decisive questions, even though some [of their] predecessors strongly advised them to do so'.[24] One first fundamental question to consider is that of the growth of monarchical states which, from the thirteenth century on, manifested itself by the revival of effective legislation, insofar as the re-establishment of the pre-eminence of royal power was assuredly enabled by a model of Roman *majestas* and its corollary,

[20] Guenée (1963), pp. 186–202.   [21] Krynen (1992), pp. 279–80.
[22] Lewis (1977), pp. 141, 221–6.   [23] Krynen (1992), pp. 279–80.
[24] Krynen (1992), p. 10.

the law or, at least, by the legitimate ambition of a free power to define the norm. However, it is incontestably true that we have to wait until the end of the thirteenth century and even more the fourteenth century before we start to see appearing under the pens of jurists like Bartole or Balde a more sophisticated conception of the state. From the thirteenth century, jurists substituted 'for a Roman model in which the law was the source of authority. . . a Romano-canonical model sensitive to feudal political reality in which the authority of the prince was the source of law'.[25] Drawing in his own time on the *Code*, John of Salisbury, in his *Policraticus*, already advocated the coming of a form of royalty founded on the 'law'. By the end of the Middle Ages this had come to pass. For many writers, prominent amongst whom figures the jurist and Archbishop of Rheims, Jean Juvénal des Ursins, in an address to the king of 1452, it seemed obvious that it was by promulgating new ordinances that a monarch re-established his authority over his kingdom: after his decisive victories over the English, Charles VII was exhorted to manifest his 'royal majesty' by fully assuming his role as the *conditor legis*.[26]

Nonetheless, it is also true that the affirmation of the absolute authority of the king over all his subjects was enabled by the efficient delivery of justice, whether at the level of the *bailliages* or, at a central level, in the *curia regis* which had become the *Parlement*, a body which, from the moment of its creation, included, besides the still-important presence of the magnates, a good number of members who were products of the juridical *studia*, and prominently amongst these the *studium* of Orléans.[27] It is this same competent justice which, by means of appeal, fashioned little by little a common law for the kingdom,[28] which lay behind the customary law compilations of the fifteenth, and above all, of the sixteenth, centuries.

2.   Personnel

England: justices and the king

As Paul Brand has shown,[29] an identifiable legal profession, consisting of sergeants or pleaders (the medieval equivalent of barristers) and attorneys (solicitors), existed by the beginning of the fourteenth century. They constituted a profession, first, in that they derived all, or a substantial part, of their income from pleading before the courts or providing

---

25   Mayali (1992), pp. 131, 136.   26   Krynen (1999), pp. 96–9.
27   Giordanengo (1999), p. 220.   28   Hilaire (2000), pp. 151–60.
29   Brand (1992a) and Brand (1992b).

legal advice, and, secondly, in that they were bound by rules governing their professional behaviour. From among the sergeants practising in the central courts were drawn the royal judges, the highest lawyers in the land: the chief justices of King's Bench and Common Pleas, the other justices of those courts – usually termed the 'puisne' justices – and the 'barons' of the exchequer. The cleverest and most influential of these, men such as Geoffrey le Scrope and William Shareshull, helped define the law by their judgments and in their debates with one another, and drove, or at least formulated, Crown judicial policy.[30] The central-court justices and sergeants, relatively limited in number and based in Westminster and London (where, by the end of the fourteenth century, 'inns' for the provision of legal training were fully established), constitute the group most readily identifiable as full-time professionals within the legal system. While the chief justices, and 'barons' in particular, were certainly politically engaged, and all justices from time to time directly appealed to by the Crown (usually via privy seal writs), they were expected to be politically independent. This is clearly shown both by the murder in 1326 of Chief Baron Roger Bellars, for his complicity in the tyranny of Edward II and the Despensers, and, finally and definitively, by the events leading up to the Merciless Parliament of 1388. The Appellants savagely punished former Chief Justice Robert Tresilian for the judiciary's apparent willingness, in the previous year, to support Richard II's attempts to characterise as treason any attempt to force him to act against his will.[31] Separating the attorneys, especially those in the localities, from the wider political world is much more difficult, however. Low politics was all about noble and gentry networks, and most attorneys were middle- and lower-ranking gentry in the shires.

Why does this matter? It matters because of the great question that has for so long – and especially since the work of Putnam – dominated the historiography of English internal rule: was the realm governed by the centre or the locality, by professionals or amateurs? Putnam's theory that the rise of the justices of the peace produced devolution to the gentry in the localities depended upon a crude social categorisation of those appointed to the peace commission. She judged the JPs either 'lawyers' – by which she meant men who could be identified as senior legal professionals within the central courts – or 'gentry'.[32] This, of course, ignored the reality that central lawyers, like John Stonor, set about making themselves into local lords – through the purchase of land or advantageous

[30] Putnam (1950), pp. 20, 51–110.   [31] Harriss (2005), pp. 462–5.
[32] *Proceedings Before the Justices of the Peace in the Fourteenth and Fifteenth Centuries*, ed. Putnam (1938), 'Introduction'.

marriage – as soon as they possibly could. More importantly, it over-looked the truth that many of the 'gentry', the apparent amateurs who, with one or two justices of the central courts, staffed the peace com-mission in each shire in the fourteenth century, were almost certainly lawyers, or at the very least, knowledgeable in the law. As soon as one begins a prosopographical investigation of such men, one uncovers the difficulty of classifying them as central or local, professional or amateur.

John Delves, justice of the peace for Shropshire in the 1350s, is a case in point. Delves' popular claim to fame lies in his identification as one of the valiant esquires of the English war hero, Sir James Audley, at Poitiers in 1356. At Crécy a decade earlier, the records tell us, he had served in the retinue of the earl of Arundel; much later, on his death, he chose to be memorialised in martial splendour. A soldier, then, whose social position produced his appointment as a JP? Not quite. He first appears in the records acting as an attorney in the late 1330s. By the late 1340s he was Arundel's steward, or chief judicial officer, in the Welsh Marcher lordship of Clun and Oswestry. At the end of the 1340s he moved into the service of the Black Prince, in a deal brokered by Edward III for the reorganisation of rule in North Wales. Thereafter, he became the Prince's maid-of-all-work in his liberties of Wales and Chester, making extents, auditing accounts, presiding over trials – doing all manner of judicial, financial and other administrative business. When Edward of Woodstock was made Prince of Aquitaine in the 1360s, Delves was sud-denly appointed as a justice of Common Pleas. Overnight, the Shropshire knight, soldier and JP had become a royal judge. What are we to make of this? It is hard to imagine that Delves might have acted as steward and justice in private service to Arundel and the Black Prince had he not possessed substantial legal expertise, but without two obscure references to his acting as an attorney, we would have no indisputable evidence of his status as a legal professional – until his sudden appointment to Com-mon Pleas in the twilight of his career.[33] How many other members of the gentry, to whom power was supposedly devolved, had legal training or knowledge of which no firm record survives? In the fifteenth century, for example, Richard Armburgh was apparently a lord, not a practising

[33] JP: Calendar of Patent Rolls (CPR), 1350–4, pp. 284, 449; CPR 1354–8, p. 388. Military service with Arundel: *Crécy and Calais from the Public Records,* ed. Wrottesley (1898), pp. 34, 114, 246. Attorney in 1339 and 1347: TNA, JUST 1/1406, p. 21; The Black Prince's Register (BPR), I, p. 139. Arundel's steward in 1348–9: Shrewsbury Borough Library, Do 7308; Shropshire Record Office, 1093/1; The National Library of Wales, Aston Hall, 942. Entering the Black Prince's service: CPR, 1350–4, pp. 220–1; BPR, III, p. 52. Service with the Black Prince: e.g. BPR, III, pp. 50, 88, 125, 141, 151, 216–19, 276, 370, 397, 399, 410, 452, 479.

lawyer, but his letters show that he provided his tenants with the most expert legal advice. So many men acted as stewards, financial agents, auditors and witnesses in their shires, and were so regularly appointed by the king as justices – of oyer and terminer as well as of the peace – that it is difficult to imagine that they were not legally expert. Yet most are recorded nowhere as attorneys. Nor are such confusions restricted to the gentry. Nicholas, Lord Cantelupe was one of the greatest land-holders in the North Midlands in the 1320s, 1330s, 1340s and 1350s. He was a soldier, a diplomat, and a friend and adviser to the king; and from the mid 1330s he was commissioned as a justice in the Midlands and the north with such regularity and consistency that his appointment was effectively permanent. Like many great lords so appointed in the fourteenth century, he actually acted; his position was not honorific. In the 1340s, John Winwick was simultaneously an attorney, a royal clerk, a clergyman, a justice of oyer and terminer, a king's sergeant-at-arms and deputy-constable of the Tower of London.[34]

Throughout our period, such men were as a matter of course appointed as justices in the shires alongside the senior legal professionals of the central courts: Delves, for instance, usually served with the central justices William Shareshull or Hugh Aston. This process was formalised within the peace commission by the delineation, effectively from 1344, of a *quorum* of central justices without whom the other appointees could not fully act. Edward Powell and Simon Walker have shown how this practice – later made a mechanism – tied county commissions staffed by local men to the king's justices at the judicial centre, and how those among the local men who in practice did the bulk of the work – and who were probably trained lawyers – developed independent relationships with the centre.[35]

All this strongly suggests that the apparent 'locals' or 'amateurs' to whom judicial power was arguably devolved during the fourteenth century (and certainly granted in the fifteenth) were often anything but amateur. They were indeed local, in the sense that they usually held lands locally and were involved in local society. But we should not assume that this necessitated their championing of local interests against the centre. Clearly, they represented the centre, as well as the locality. In a sense, they inevitably did so as soon as they accepted the king's commission, and there is evidence that royal officials in the shires forsook their local ties when the king demanded that they choose between the two.[36] For

---

[34] *Calendar of Close Rolls, 1333–7*, pp. 338, 729; CPR, 1338–40, p. 216; CPR, 1340–3, pp. 566–7; CPR, 1343–5, pp. 26, 95, 100, 124, 275, 280.

[35] Powell (1989), pp. 56–60; Walker (1993), pp. 290–1, 310–11.

[36] TNA, JUST 1/258, p. 3; C49/46/13; KB27/365, cr 101, rex 19d, 38–38d, /366, rex 35.

instance, in Essex in 1351–2, Sir John Coggeshall played a key role, both as sheriff and as leader of the JPs, in the judicial pursuit, prosecution and punishment of John Lord Fitzwalter, despite the fact that Fitzwalter had previously used his influence with Edward III on Coggeshall's behalf to arrange that the latter be tried before the council, not an oyer and terminer commission, for official abuses he had allegedly committed. Indeed, it may have been precisely their dual relationship with centre and locality that made the king's justices effective agents of governance – they were both representative of public authority and impartiality, and acceptable and responsive to local interest. It seems right that we should think of them primarily as local agents of governance, enactors and enforcers representing Crown and locality and perhaps, by their very presence, performing vital mediation between the two. Maybe we should conceptualise them as professionals in rule, with central expertise and objectivity, and local knowledge and connection. Delves, Cantelupe and Winwick, in their various ways, and even Chief Justice William Shareshull, seem to fit into this categorisation – more useful, surely, than the discreteness of professional and amateur, centrist and local man.

What of others who periodically acted as the king's justices on local common law commissions – the great lords, for instance, who were not, so far as we can tell, especially knowledgeable in the law? What function did they serve, and did their appointment represent devolution? In answering this, we return to considerations of structure and of kingship. If we exclude those nobles in whom the king placed special administrative trust – men like Nicholas Cantelupe – we find great lords in the fourteenth century being characteristically appointed to local office in time of marked disorder; the noble 'keepers of the counties' in the 1330s, for example, were appointed because the peace commissioners had apparently been unable to deal effectively with the crime and unrest they faced. Occasionally, we see the most explicit enlistment of noble power to enforce judicial action: in 1331, for instance, the earl of Arundel's men in the marches of Wales were among those appointed to attach (that is, arrest) John Lord Charlton, whose immense power as Lord of Powys had been allowing him blithely to ignore the justices of the peace, before whom he had been indicted.[37] Put crudely, great lords provided muscle. They surely did so, in the most general, latent sense, even when they held no royal appointment. This was a matter of sustaining the established social order. Their connections with local royal officials, who so often acted as their stewards, witnesses and attorneys, must have made the latter harder – at least potentially – for disputants or criminals to

---

[37] TNA, JUST 1/1432, 83d.

resist. It is a mistake to believe that the king did not have the power (as opposed to the authority) to intervene without local noble support; the central administration and royal household – in the form of the sergeants-at-arms, for instance – provided sufficient men to take on even the most powerful locals. But it is the case that, without a salaried bureaucracy in the shires, a police force or standing army, the monarch relied on the nobility for everyday, universal enforcement. In the late thirteenth and fourteenth centuries, when kings dealt directly with 'political' crimes via powerful ad hoc judicial commissions, the granting of judicial office – especially the peace commission – to locals probably had only a limited devolutionary effect; as we have seen, the JPs were at this time dealing predominantly with the routine administration of justice. Although a really detailed examination of local social and political networks in the fourteenth century might reveal the system being manipulated for lordly gain, it seems likely (as has been argued above) that it was in the fifteenth century, with the retreat of the Crown from full-scale, extraordinary intervention, that devolution really occurred.

France: judges and legal dynasties – a 'fourth estate'?

In late medieval France, there was hardly any remaining concrete administrative or political problem for which there was no legal solution, and this was clear not only to the king, but also to princes and to lords, to religious and urban communities. From the first years of the fourteenth century, it is thus possible to discern the appearance, and then the growth in number, within local administration, of technicians, and more specifically jurists, who were often also in clerical orders.[38] Dukes and counts, in particular, no longer thought twice about retaining lawyers, sometimes borrowed from the towns,[39] or from neighbouring lords; and it was not unusual for the most competent amongst them to catch the eye of the king or of another personage more powerful than their initial master, and so to pass into his service. Indeed, one of the merits of a prosopographical approach is that it makes it possible to distinguish the personalities of jurists and, by comparing their different trajectories, to reconstitute careers composed of often contrasting episodes. What comes to the fore here are the networks and the career streams through which recruitment took place. Particularly instructive in this regard is the example of the doctor *in utroque* Jean Canard, who was the councillor and advocate of the countess of Bar and lady of Cassel, Yolande

---

[38] Gilissen (1947), p. 137; Bubenicek (1996), pp. 339–76.
[39] Rigaudière (1964), p. 362.

of Flanders, before passing into the service of the duke of Burgundy, Philip the Bold, and finally becoming the chancellor of Burgundy.[40] One could also cite, once again linked to Yolande of Flanders, the jurist Jean de Villeaminon, who after having led the team of advocates charged to defend her interests in the Paris *Parlement*, left her service in 1390 to become 'councillor and *maître des requêtes* of the household' to Charles VI. In general, movement between the service of the great and that of the king was common; one might even say that there was a high level of fluidity, an ease of movement from one to the other, with entrance into royal institutions doubtless being considered as the crowning moment of a career, for, from the fourteenth to the sixteenth century, there is no doubt that the great, the judges and indeed pleaders believed that the best 'counsel' was to be found in the capital, whether in the *Parlement*, in the *requêtes* of the household, or indeed in the *Châtelet*.

Recruited in this way for their legal training and for their experience, often acquired in the context of local administration, whether royal or seigneurial, these jurists were nonetheless not always employed in specifically legal or political tasks. Rather, they were entrusted with jobs of surprising diversity, ranging from scribal duties – essential in a society where the role of writing was becoming ever-more important, insofar as it permitted the authority of the king along with that of towns and princes to control, in certain regards, the actions of their subjects – to advocacy in the *Parlement*, through diplomacy and accounting.[41] Specifically in the king's service, however, they perfected a new method of government – very widely criticised, as we shall see – which was based on the strict application of law, the *jus strictum*, and, notably, on the literal and most absolute interpretation possible of maxims drawn from Roman law.

Chosen by the king according to new criteria which marked a division with earlier practice – election, imposed, from Charles V onwards, for the nomination of the presidents of the *Parlement*, and from 1389 for all councillors[42] – they rapidly became, in any case, a body of 'civil servants' assigned a particular status which could be considered to be the first precursor of the modern French *'fonction publique d'État'*.[43] Heavily inspired by canon law, this status put in place strict rules of recruitment and duties designed to prevent favouritism, such as compulsory geographical mobility, exclusivity of service and obedience to the hierarchy,

---

[40] Bubenicek (2002), pp. 361–2.

[41] Lot and Fawtier (1958), p. 88; Renardy (1979), p. 307; Bubenicek (1996), p. 370.

[42] Autrand (1981), p. 22.

[43] That is to say, a status which binds the individual and the state, distinguishing the former from the rest of society to a greater extent than is clear in casual usage of the English expression 'civil servant', even if it remains present in its etymology.

with the aim of creating a true civil-service ethic capable of overruling private interests. Traditionally, this new service ethic is illustrated by the well-known example of the *marmousets*, totally devoted to the Crown. Yet is this the same as saying that personal interests were put aside? Today we would rather say that, if we consider the effectiveness of royal service from the point of view of pragmatic realism, the most zealous royal officers were incontestably those who, looking after their own interests first, found undeniable advantages in service to the king, and jurists were no exception to this rule.

For social advancement soon followed professional success. At first drawn from a broad range of backgrounds, most royal agents finally came to constitute, by the very end of our period, a new privileged body, the start of what would become the *noblesse de robe*.

In the first half of the fourteenth century, jurists and notably the famous 'legists' were in the main isolated individuals who did not necessarily found dynasties of royal servants: they formed an efficient group of servants around a prince or the Valois king and were recruited from a patronage network or a region. Their descendants, such as Simon de Bucy, turned by preference towards the church or a military career. After this period came the jurists of Charles V and the first dynasties of the men of the *Parlement* – such as the Dormans or the Jouvenels (or Juvénals) – which were established the better to resist a variety of pressures and to be more effective, insofar as family networks took the place of administrative hierarchy, which was as yet insufficiently developed.[44] Non-noble jurists or new nobles forged by recent successful careers, notably in the *Parlement*, wove around themselves tight family networks, mostly through marriage, by marrying their daughters or their nieces to their colleagues, to such an extent that, by the end of the fourteenth century, it had become impossible for those who did not possess a kernel of active relatives in the *Parlement* to reach its highest ranks.

From the reign of Charles V to that of Charles VII, these very strong familial loyalties nevertheless made it possible to resist external pressures effectively, notably the pressure of princely patronage in the period 1380 to 1436. Whilst it is undeniable that in the very disturbed context of the conflict between Armagnacs and Burgundians, the princes tried hard to pack central institutions, notably the council and the *Parlement*, with clients of their choice and their allegiance, in the final analysis it can be observed that, with one or two exceptions, the world of the jurists did not adhere to either of the parties of the period, and tended, despite everything, to bring about the triumph of a certain conception of the

[44] Autrand (1981), p. 101.

state. So, although it was not rare, early on, to be simultaneously in the service of a prince and in that of the king – and indeed exchanges of personnel remained a common practice – from Charles V onwards, the idea won the day that royal service ought to be exclusive. It was the jurist, above all, who was concerned by this development: only the advocates of the *Parlement* succeeded in resisting this tendency and keeping one or several masters.

From then on, the royal jurists, and especially those of the *Parlement*, thus formed an established social group, that of the *robe*, which was identifiable in processions, notably in royal entries, by their livery – the lay members of the *Parlement*, for example, wore a long vermillion robe. It was a social group which, from the second half of the fifteenth century, took over a number of functions offered by the central government or by the institution of the *Parlement*, notably by means of resignation in favour of a selected successor, a procedure which lay behind the development of the hereditability of office.[45]

Very quickly, this new social group, closely united and mutually supportive, rose to nobility. Becoming noble was, after all, the dream of every lawyer. For if the members of the old nobility became, with the passage of time, less numerous amongst the jurists in royal service,[46] the percentage of nobles did not decrease, since they were replaced by new nobles, loyal servants raised to nobility by means of royal ennoblements. Charles V is doubtless in this regard the monarch who ennobled his lawyers most. This was the period of the 'letters of state of ennoblement' (*lettres d'estat de nobilitation*)[47] or letters of nobility obtained from the *maîtres des requêtes* of the king's household. The example of the knighthoods given, at Christmas 1373, to Pierre d'Orgemont and to Arnaud de Corbie, president of the *Parlement*, can be found in every monograph, but it does indeed seem that this tendency towards social progression was not limited to the servants of the king. In imitation of the sovereign, the great nobles were also preoccupied with the elevation of certain of their ministers, such as Yolande of Flanders, who in 1375 assisted the entry into nobility of her chancellor and 'prime minister', the jurist Thibaut de Bourmont, by giving him the lands of Manicamp and Saulx,[48] since the possession of noble land often provided the basis for a future ennoblement. From the middle of the fifteenth century, however, renown seems to have sufficed to obtain noble status, even if ennoblement by royal letters still remained possible; it is nonetheless clear that being a member of a family of *Parlement*

---

[45] Autrand (1981), Chapter 2.
[46] Renardy (1979), pp. 156–8; Verger (1976), pp. 289–313.
[47] Bloch (1934), p. 29.   [48] Bubenicek (1996), p. 375.

men automatically led to noble status. Civilian service to the prince was henceforth equivalent to military service. Every lineage of the *robe* was, following the example of seigneurial lineages, conscious of its grandeur and its exceptional status. Still, we should note that the idea was already widespread in the fourteenth century that advanced legal studies and the possession of a royal office were equivalent to nobility,[49] and there were many who, from one day to the next, in the *Parlement* in particular, began to style themselves as *messire*, passing from the status of lawyer to that of 'nobleman'.[50] For certain jurists, it even seems that there was, from the end of Charles V's reign, a call for a 'right to nobility', as the contents of Chapter 148 of the *Songe du Vergier* bear witness: the knight who discusses the carrying of armorial bearings and other distinctive signs of appurtenance to a particular social category, and the necessity of punishing those who contravene acceptable practice, mentions in this context the 'gilded spurs' (*esperons dorez*) normally worn by 'doctors in law' (*docteurs en loix*) and which could be scandalously worn by others.[51] Here we certainly find proof of the extreme confidence and the accumulated pretensions of royal jurists, faced with which society inevitably reacted.

The development of the 'men of justice' (*gens de justice*) in the *bailliages* was, however, perceptibly different. Up until the beginning of the fifteenth century, the office of judge, which was almost always inaccessible to advocates and prosecutors, lay in the hands of the traditional nobility or those of the great families of the merchant bourgeoisie. Justice was not only the business of professionals. All the same, the most widely renowned advocates were able to build a fortune through their professional competences which allowed them quickly to join the bourgeois elite of the town, but rarely the nobility, or to aspire to fulfil the same offices as them. After the middle of the fifteenth century, on the other hand, 'professionals' alone staffed the tribunals, where jurist-advocates were able to live the high life, acquiring fiefs without too much trouble. The time of reconstruction was for them assuredly the 'time of active lives and brilliant careers'.[52] But their success stopped there, for, in the provinces, the only kind of nobility was the nobility of the sword and only the holder of high office could hope to attain nobility. Although the great social rise which made it possible to reach nobility was therefore possible in the provinces, we would have to admit that it remains the exception. From what we can tell, the most brilliant careers took place close to the king, in the central institutions of the monarchy. And it is these, of course, which provoked the most lively criticism.

---

[49] Cazelles (1982), pp. 82–3.   [50] Autrand (1981), p. 185.
[51] *Songe du Vergier*, ed. Schnerb-Lièvre (1982), p. 83.
[52] Guenée (1963), p. 398: le 'temps des vies actives et des belles carrières'.

3.   **Lawyers and political society**

England

Since, as has been argued above, justice was not devolved to the localities of England until the fifteenth century, it is striking – given the theory among some historians that noble and gentry control over local judicial processes necessarily led to 'bastard–feudal' corruption – that malevolent officialdom apparently reached its height in the late thirteenth and fourteenth centuries. Under these circumstances, it may seem perverse to deny the argument that there was, in fact, an earlier transfer of control to local hands. But, without this earlier transfer, the proliferation of corruption cases against royal officials, great lords and their officials in the early period is still readily explicable. In short, these cases were a product partly of the birth-pangs of the legal profession and partly of the paranoia and might of Edward I and Edward III.

To take the kings first, it is no coincidence that formal corruption charges were brought, almost universally, by the ad hoc, extraordinary judicial commissions that Edward I and Edward III developed, partly for political reasons. The Crown's willingness ruthlessly to pursue its own officials through the royal courts for alleged offences 'against the king and people' reflected heightened interest among kings in their rights, and was echoed by the similar judicial pursuit of certain great lords (such as John Molyns, John Fitzwalter and James Audley of Heighley in the 1340s and 1350s), by the development of legislation concerning treason and conspiracy, and by increasingly rights-focused international relations. In other words, allegations of official corruption came with the growth of the state under masterful kingship. A detailed examination of the accusations contained in the 'state trials' of 1289–93, the 'new' or 'great' inquiries of 1340–4, and the eyres and 'superior' eyres of the late 1340s and 1350s reveals, first, the targeting or even victimisation of the accused, for instance, justice Richard Willoughby in 1340–1, and, secondly, the broken-backed nature of many of the charges brought. The latter is perhaps further indicated by the notably high acquittal rate observable in the records of 1340–4, an acquittal rate scarcely reflected in the massive fines nonetheless extracted from his hapless officials by a penurious and incandescent Edward III, quite wrongly convinced his foreign ambitions had been undone by corruption at home. It is upon the accusations brought in 1289–93 and especially in 1341 – so uncannily similar across shire boundaries and, indeed, the length and breadth of the realm – that the evil historical reputations of justices Ralph Hengham, Thomas Weyland, Willoughby, Robert Scarborough and John Inge, as well as those of sheriffs John Oxford, Gilbert Ledred and John Coggeshall, are based. There is, of course, something in the theory that there is no smoke without fire, but the severity of the fire here has been seriously overestimated. Among those accused in the early 1340s were justices Stonor and Shareshull, men of conspicuous intelligence, probity and dedication to duty.[53]

Was there fire at all? It would be extraordinary if there had not been. Justices Thomas Brompton in the 'state trials' and Henry Green in 1365 certainly appear to have been guilty of corruption, and doubtless there were others who sailed close to the wind: Chief Justice Hengham, despite his famously spirited denials, seems to have been one. But a *cordon sanitaire* between judicial judgment and private connection was established only progressively during the course of the late thirteenth and fourteenth centuries. The rapid expansion of royal justice was justified on the grounds that the king's courts were the most effective and impartial. At the same time, as the common law expanded and became more complex, lay and ecclesiastical lords, and urban corporations increasingly sought to retain the services of the realm's most expert lawyers, the king's justices. It was only with the emergence of an identifiable legal profession and with the concomitant working out of an effective code of ethics for lawyers that the closest ties between royal judges and the wider social and political world were undone. While they remained, accusations of 'maintenance' – the corruption of justice – were likely, even where judges had essentially clean hands. Developing ideas first enacted in the Statute of Westminster of 1275, the Ordinance of Justices of 1346 required all justices to take no fees except from the king. Although this did not eradicate maintenance, its restatement in 1384, together with the murder of the allegedly corrupt Chief Justice John Cavendish during the Peasants' Revolt and the (above-mentioned) execution by the Appellants of former Chief Justice Tresilian, contributed to a sharp decline in the retaining of justices in the 1390s. In the fifteenth century, widely held suspicions as to the corruptibility of justice – witness the *London Lickpenny*[54] – remained, but it is notable that there were no further substantial attacks, whether legal or physical, on royal judges.

France

In a society so attached to tradition, the arrival of jurists in high office and their claim to be an integral part of the social elite constituted novelties which were not always well received, giving rise to the most severe

---

[53] See above, n. 11; Burt (2012), p. 152; Putnam (1950), p. 20 and *passim*.
[54] Recent edition in *Medieval English Political Writings*, ed. Dean (1996).

criticisms: for these two reasons in particular, the French jurist at the end of the Middle Ages was not generally liked.

From the moment when lawyers were both efficient agents of the government and had reached a certain 'governmental visibility', they became the target of very virulent criticism. In the last two centuries of the Middle Ages there was indeed, in France, a strong current of criticism aimed at jurists which coincided with the increasing influence of these men, either in the royal central government (politically active lawyers being heavily involved in the debates of the Hundred Years War and those linked to the Schism), or in the judicial apparatus. Thanks to the *Parlement* and the hierarchised network of local royal tribunals, a royal legal system was established little by little, which tried to regulate violence and to impose its own vision of the law on the various elements of society. One might even say that diatribes against jurists are a constant in the political literature of the era. Generally speaking, contemporary society showed itself very hostile to the 'men of justice', whether this meant sergeants, advocates or judges, who were all attacked with greater or lesser intensity for their cupidity, their duplicity and their real or supposed incompetence, criticisms which become veritable commonplaces.[55] Yet, paradoxically, these complaints can also be seen as measures of the importance now assumed by judges and jurists in society, and, paradoxically, of the extent of the expectations of the subjects of the royal judicial system, disappointed not to have had what they wanted from the king's direct justice.

What, though, more precisely, were the criticisms made of political jurists, of legists, in the context of political writings on the 'body of policy' at the end of the Middle Ages? On a strictly governmental level, the legists are first of all typically accused of leading the French monarchy towards tyranny and despotism. One can cite, in this context, Sir John Fortescue's well-known analysis of around 1470,[56] or, earlier, those of Nicole Oresme or of Jean Juvénal des Ursins. With one voice, these authors attack the king's lawyers for making an excessive and simplistic use of Roman law, in particular for making use of the literal sense of isolated maxims taken out of context – such as the famous *Quod principi placuit legis habet vigorem* or *Princeps legibus solutus est* – and applying them to the political circumstances of the time with the sole aim of promoting at any price the reinforced authority of the king. It was, indeed, often by transposing the political or administrative mechanisms of antiquity on to present-day circumstances that royal legists justified, not without disturbing results, the growing 'interventionism' of royal power: the royal

[55] Guenée (1963), pp. 4–6.   [56] Genet (1973).

right to raise taxes,[57] the principle of the sovereignty of the king in the legal domain or even the principle of political justice – thanks to the rediscovered concept of *lèse-majesté* – which prefigured the absolutism of the modern period. Authoritarian, intolerant of criticism (in the words of Nicole Oresme to Charles V: 'I have seen some of them so determined in their opinion that they could not hear the contrary'),[58] imbued with Roman law, but more attached to the letter than to the law, jurists were held to have hardened royal authority, risking tyranny: in the judicial domain alone, the danger was thus that the merciful 'good justice' (*bonne justice*) of the sovereign would be replaced by the 'rigour of justice' (*rigueur de justice*) alone.

Although these critiques were certainly well founded, an attentive examination of the approach, of the 'method' of royal jurists, inasmuch as it is possible to perceive it, sometimes shows, however, an altogether more sophisticated attitude, since the use of Roman law, although it undeniably contributed to the reinforcement of the state, did not necessarily lead to its absolutism, since reflection based on legal theory could lead them, in certain cases, 'to limit royal law by reconsidering its conditions and its domain of application.'[59] Beyond Roman law, moreover, jurists also knew how to invoke and to use custom and canon law, if necessary, or even history, religion or philosophy.[60] Far from piling up citations, the more the better and without nuance, the jurist was, on the contrary, he who knew how to make an arrow out of any wood and to make the law serve his purposes, sometimes going so far as to use the same reference to defend contradictory positions.[61] Indeed, although this mindset particularly characterised the pleading of advocates devoted to the royal cause, it could also, where necessary, do good service for great nobles.[62] It is true that in the latter case this sometimes involved a rather superficial use of the sources, but it at least had the merit of a certain effectiveness.

More generally, jurists in royal service were attacked for their excessively close family relationships with one another: in the *Parlement*, for example, they were said to be too young, too ignorant, owing their position to favour alone.[63] There was implicit criticism, too, of the riches they had obtained in the service of the state. Around 1370, Bertrand du Guesclin could thus counsel the king to raise a forced loan from his judges in the *Parlement*: since their fortune came from the king, it was

---

[57] Krynen (1992), p. 286.
[58] Krynen (1992), p. 291: 'Je les ay veu aucuns si affichiés a leur opinion que il ne povoient oïr le contraire.'
[59] Weidenfeld (1999), p. 472: '. . . limiter le droit royal en s'interrogeant sur ses conditions et son domaine d'application'.
[60] Krynen (1992), pp. 283–4.   [61] Leca (1999), p. 107.
[62] Bubenicek (1999), pp. 421–39.   [63] Autrand (1981), p. 43.

only justice that it should come back to him in case of necessity.[64] The exemption from taxation (specifically, the *taille*) which the members of the *Parlement* enjoyed naturally produced criticism and jealousy. It was held to be a corrupt milieu, more concerned with preserving its own ill-gotten gains through favouritism than with protecting the public good. It was thus a milieu which was the first target for political purges, whether at the moment of the Parisian revolts after the Battle of Poitiers or during the civil war under Charles VI.

These varied criticisms are, in truth, very instructive in the way that they reveal the expectations and malaise of a political society undergoing profound changes. Indeed, every attack on lawyers reveals something about how the evolution of governmental practice was perceived by all or part of political society.

To begin with, the allegation of an excessive use of family links might seem surprising in a period when it was common practice for royal servants to be supported by their own people, and the same criticism could easily be made against the clergy or the nobility. But what was really disturbing in this case for contemporary political society was the appearance of a social milieu which was frightening in its 'novelty' in a society which was quintessentially hostile to innovations. We should keep in mind the image of a political society with defined contours, a 'body of policy' where everyone was assigned a place according to his social rank, and which the supreme court of justice – the *Parlement* – ought to reflect. For the new milieu of the men of law and the jurists did not fit into the accustomed framework of society of three *ordines*. Although it tried to link itself to nobility, it escaped from all earlier social classifications. The critiques formulated against the occasionally brutal methods of government of the jurists went in a similar direction: by excessively flattering the absolute power of the king, they ran the risk of breaking the organic unity of the kingdom. As much from a political point of view as from a social point of view, the jurists put in peril the established order.

Nobles of ancient lineage, whether they were clerics or laymen, soon became conscious of the emergence of a group of competitors who were dangerous as much from a political point of view as from a social one: other men than they would now have access to 'the king's ear' and would, by consequence, be able to influence him.[65] We should note, moreover, that from the beginning of the fifteenth century, the jurists, with the members of the *Parlement* at the forefront, had begun to construct and impose by their own decrees a new definition of nobility, one certainly threatening for the traditional nobility, by means of the concept of 'notability'. From now on a noble would be more a 'notable' than a combatant,

---

[64] Autrand (1981), p. 228.   [65] Bartier (1955), pp. 6–7.

distinguishing himself by service to the king and by his style of life. The old nobility tried in vain to react, to limit, for example, the recruitment of councillors and presidents of the *Parlement* to men of ancient lineage. The recurrent demands of the noble leagues for the dismissal of 'evil counsellors' are well known. All that remained for members of the nobility who wanted to continue to be part of the inner circle of the powerful was to study law, their knowledge of the law becoming the means to guarantee the maintenance of their monopoly of power.

The same problem of lawyers trespassing on areas previously reserved to other groups is to be found in the case of theologians, who were loath to tolerate the appearance on the political scene of another form of intellectual training which led to different methods of government and which proposed new models of collective life and of the social order. Roman law succeeded, indeed, in destroying the hitherto uncontested supremacy of theology, beginning in the domain of education. At the end of the Middle Ages, apart from Paris and Montpellier, provincial universities were dominated by the faculties of law and, amongst the creations of the fifteenth century, many of them, such as the University of Caen, at first taught only law. For Peter Lewis, the most remarkable thing was the growing importance of legal studies for offices held by all three estates,[66] so much did the competition of law with theology advance in the area of counsel to princes and of governmental responsibilities, which were rapidly taken over by the jurists. In accordance with the spirit of the age and the evolution of political practice, Evrard de Trémaugon, the author of the *Songe du Vergier*, could thus declare that 'the first concern and study of a king' should be 'to well rule his people by the counsel of the wise . . . principally the Jurists'.[67]

Thus the criticisms levelled at lawyers have much to say about the psychological reflexes of a society faithful to tradition and generally hostile to any innovative tendency perceived as disruptive, a society which was very attached to its caste privileges and most unwilling to share them.

Yet the reaction of political society to the emergence of the jurists' milieu was probably all the more lively because they were themselves so uninhibited with regards to their competitors. Indeed, rather than inhibitions, if the psychological metaphor might be continued, we might say that jurists suffered from something more like a 'superiority complex', so much did numerous specialists in law consider that 'everything is in

[66] Lewis (1968), p. 141.
[67] *Songe du Vergier*, ed. Schnerb-Lièvre (1982), p. 410: 'le principal propos et estude d'un roi . . . bien gouverner son pueple et par le conseil dez sages, . . . principaulment, lez Juristes'.

the *Corpus*' (a significant response of Accursius to the question of knowing whether it was appropriate for a jurist to read theology)[68] and that the law, the science of good government, could, as much as, and perhaps more than, theology, lead to eternal salvation. The words of the jurist Jean de Montreuil with regards to the role of his peers in society are extremely revealing of the assurance of an elite which already thought of itself as such: government, he says, ought to pertain to 'good men' (*boni viri*) who possess moral qualities and knowledge, but knowledge mixed with experience, since theoretical knowledge is nothing without practice. Only practice provides, as it were, active knowledge, political wisdom. What remained to be seen, however, was who exactly was included in this description: for Jean de Montreuil, there was no doubt that this meant neither clerks without any practical experience,[69] nor uncultured nobles,[70] nor the incompetent royal councillors,[71] nor, finally, the courtiers, in whom not a single fault was lacking,[72] but the men of the *Parlement* and the jurists of king's chancery.

Conclusions

How did English kings in the late thirteenth, fourteenth and fifteenth centuries use the common law and judicial offices to govern the realm internally, and what role did networks play in this? First, the common law had, since its creation in the second half of the twelfth century, expanded to carry royal rule directly to all of the king's free subjects. It was now the Crown's principal instrument of local control and the chief manifestation of its public authority. Its expansion had created an ever-growing corps of actual and potential local administrators: the professional lawyers. This was one network that the government employed to provide law and order. On a day-to-day basis, however, in engaging with routine crime and in dispute resolution, it depended upon the private power, whether active or latent, of great lords to enforce its judicial will in the localities; this involved another series of networks. At the same time, lords needed the king's law and public authority if order were properly to be maintained – and, whatever their private ambitions, this was ultimately in the interests of them all. This necessary marriage of centre and locality for the common good was witnessed time and again by judicial appointment, where the justices of King's Bench and Common Pleas or other central officials were commissioned side-by-side with local

---

[68] Krynen (1992), p. 283.   [69] Montreuil (1962–86), p. 349.
[70] *Ibid.*, l. 184, p. 274.   [71] *Ibid.*, l. 38, p. 60.   [72] *Ibid.*, l. 37–8, pp. 52–63.

knights. It reached its ultimate and most effective expression when centre and locality were joined within, rather than among, individuals; when public authority was harnessed to local power through the appointment of a key member of a local network to royal office. Sometimes, as we have seen with Nicholas Cantelupe, the appointee was in fact the head of the network. It was then that royal appointment must have been at its most potent. The very act of appointment brought the appointee into the orbit of royal rule, and, when repeated and multiplied, created a new, super-network of professionals in rule, simultaneously public and private, central and local, which carried governance from the king to the locality and vital information back again. It was the maintenance of this super-network of rule that was arguably the Crown's most critical internal function. It had to monitor the effectiveness of its officers and their relationship with the all-important local networks. It had to ensure that its business was properly done in the face of local particularism, but that, at the same time, the locality was not abused or alienated. Rogue elements had to be kept under control. The great warrior kings seem to have done this, at least in part, through dramatic intervention, which must have dislocated connection and required that it be rebuilt. For Edward I, Edward III and Henry V, though, there were obvious compensations for this trouble – political, military and financial. Later, the absence of such intervention arguably contributed to lords principally accessing royal justice directly at Westminster; advancing literacy and legal expertise were probably factors here, too. It also meant that regulating problematic individuals or rivalries increasingly fell to local networks. Since this was done substantially via an expanded peace commission, the common law remained all-important, and so networks continued to rely upon the Crown to match appointment to the realities of local power. This is how England was ruled.

In France, meanwhile, in a state where the function of judging remained the first mission of public power, the jurists, and particularly the judges, thought of themselves, at the end of the Middle Ages, as the principal 'members' of the body politic whose 'head' was the king, a position which was hardly contested until the sixteenth century.[73] Imitating theological language in a society where this idiom remained fundamental, they did not hesitate to present themselves as the 'priests'[74] of the public good charged to make the king's peace reign, in particular through justice. What is more, this opinion came finally to be shared by a fair number of their contemporaries, such that a papal legate could go so far as to apply to them a scriptural text: 'you are the royal priesthood'.[75]

---

[73] Renoux-Zagamé (1999), p. 157.   [74] Krynen (1992), p. 283.
[75] Autrand (1981), p. 17. Cf. Peter I, 2:9 and Exodus 19:6.

The ideological and political exploitation of *lèse-majesté*, already clearly perceptible under Charles V and reinforced under Charles VII, can certainly be explained partly by this: this ultimate crime was dominant from then on as the lay expression of political sacrilege. The government had become a religion of the state, a religion whose high priests were the jurists.

The legal systems of later medieval England and France display significant similarities, despite their fundamental differences. Although the English legal system was based on a universal royal common law, in contrast with a French legal system which was based primarily on Roman and customary law, despite the emergence of a royal common law in the later part of our period, there existed in both countries a discernible 'super-network' of public authority and office backed by private power and connection that had to be managed by the Crown if order was properly to be maintained – even if the intensity of royal management, or even concern about order, in the localities differed. It mattered for the governed, as well as the government. Dispute settlement was frequently a private affair impelled by the threat of legal action through the royal judicial system. Despite the differences in the terminology that we apply to lawyers and non-lawyer justices in the two countries, the career-paths of lawyers were strikingly similar. In England, as well as in France, demand for the services of such men who possessed great expertise through formal training mounted as the law became increasingly technical. They were equally required in private as well as public service, often building careers as the attorneys or judicial officers of great lords before advancing to royal service, for instance as justices of the peace or of oyer and terminer in England, or *baillis*, lieutenants to the *bailli* or commissioners of inquiry in France, and in both countries it was this that created the crucial web of public and private, central and local, connection that, as we have argued, carried governance from the king to the locality and information vital to both ruler and ruled back again.

BIBLIOGRAPHY

1. INTRODUCTION

Baker, J. H., 1990. *An Introduction to English Legal History*, 3rd edn, London.
Brand, P., 1992a. *The Origins of the English Legal Profession*, Oxford.
    1992b. *The Making of the Common Law*, London.
Carpenter, C., 1997. *The Wars of the Roses*, Cambridge.
Cazelles, R., 1982. *Société politique, noblesse et couronne sous Jean le Bon et Charles V*, Mémoires et documents de l'Ecole des chartes, 28, Paris.
Gauvard, Cl., 1991. *'De grace especial'. Crime, État et société en France à la fin du Moyen Age*, 2 vols., Paris.
Harding, A., 1973. *The Law Courts of Medieval England*, London.

Harriss, G. L., 2005. *Shaping the Nation,* Oxford.

Lewis, P. S., 1968. *Later Medieval France. The Polity,* London (tr. Fr. 1977. *La France à la fin du Moyen Age,* Paris).

Lot, F. and Fawtier, R., 1958. *Histoire des institutions françaises. II. Institutions royales,* Paris.

Musson, A. and Ormrod, W. M., 1998. *The Evolution of English Justice: Law, Politics and Society in the Fourteenth Century,* Basingstoke.

Powell, E., 1989. *Kingship, Law and Society: Criminal Justice in the Reign of Henry V,* Oxford.

Prestwich, M., 2005. *Plantagenet England,* Oxford.

2. SOURCES CITED

The 1341 Royal Inquest in Lincolnshire, ed. B. W. McLane, Publications of the Lincoln Record Society 78, Woodbridge, 1988.

Medieval English Political Writings, ed. J. M. Dean, Kalamazoo, 1996.

Montreuil, Jean de, *Opera,* ed. E. Ornato, G. Ouy and N. Pons, 4 vols., Turin and Paris, 1963–86.

Proceedings Before the Justices of the Peace in the Fourteenth and Fifteenth Centuries, ed. B. H. Putnam, London, 1938.

Songe du Vergier, ed. M. Schnerb-Lièvre, Paris, 1982.

Crécy and Calais from the Public Records, ed. G. Wrottesley, London, 1898.

3. FURTHER READING AND SOURCES

Autrand, Fr., 1981. *Naissance d'un grand corps de l'État: les gens du parlement de Paris, 1354–1454,* Paris.

Bartier, J., 1955. *Légistes et gens de finances au xve siècle: les conseillers des ducs de Bourgogne Philippe le Bon et Charles le Téméraire,* Brussels.

Bellamy, J. G., 1970. *The Law of Treason in England in the Later Middle Ages,* Cambridge.

Bloch, J., 1934. *L'anoblissement en France au temps de François 1er,* Paris.

Booth, P. H. W., 1976. 'Taxation and Public Order: Cheshire in 1353', *Northern History,* 12, 16–31.

Bubenicek, M., 1996. 'Au "conseil madame". Les équipes de pouvoir d'une dame de haut lignage, Yolande de Flandre, comtesse de Bar et dame de Cassel', *Journal des savants* (July–December), 339–76.

—— 1999. 'Droit romain et pratique. Le droit romain dans une affaire de "bail" d'enfants mineurs, en Parlement, au xive siècle', in J. Krynen (ed.), *Droit romain, jus civile et droit français,* Toulouse, pp. 421–39.

—— 2002. *Quand les femmes gouvernent. Droit et politique au xive siècle: Yolande de Flandre,* Mémoires et documents de l'Ecole des chartes, 64, Paris.

Burt, C., 2005. 'The Demise of the General Eyre in the Reign of Edward I', *English Historical Review,* 120, 1–14.

—— 2012. *Edward I and the Governance of England, 1272–1307,* Cambridge.

Carpenter, C., 1983. 'Law, Justice and Landowners in Late Medieval England', *Law and History Review,* 1, 205–37.

1992. *Locality and Polity: A Study of Warwickshire Landed Society, 1401–1499*, Cambridge.

Castor, H., 2000. *The King, the Crown, and the Duchy of Lancaster: Public Authority and Private Power, 1399–1461*, Oxford.

Favier, J., 1969. 'Les légistes et le gouvernement de Philippe le Bel', *Journal des savants*, 97–9.

Genet, J.-Ph., 1973. 'Les idées sociales de Sir John Fortescue', in *Economies et sociétés au Moyen Age: Mélanges offerts à Édouard Perroy*, Paris, pp. 446–61.

Gilissen, J., 1947. 'Les légistes en Flandre au xiiie et xive siècles', in *Bulletin de la commission royale des anciennes lois et ordonnances de Belgique*, vol. 15, fasc. 3, 117–231.

Gilli, P., 2003. *La noblesse du droit. Débats et controverses sur la culture juridique et le rôle des juristes dans l'Italie médiévale (xiie–xes)*, Paris.

Giordanengo, G., 1987. 'Du droit civil au pouvoir royal: un renversement (xiie–xve siècles)', *Politiques et management public*, 5:1 (March), 9–25.

1992. 'De la faculté de décrêt aux *negocia regis*: une répétition d'Evrard de Trémaugon (Paris, 1371)', in J. Krynen and A. Rigaudière, *Droits savant et pratiques françaises du pouvoir (XIe–XVe siècles)*, Bordeaux, pp. 211–52.

1999. 'Jus commune et "droit romain" en France du xiiie au xve siècle', in J. Krynen (ed.), *Droit romain, jus civile et droit français*, Toulouse, pp. 219–47.

Guenée, B., 1963. *Tribunaux et gens de justice dans le bailliage de Senlis à la fin du Moyen Age (vers 1380–vers 1550)*, Strasbourg.

Harding, A., 1978. 'Early Trailbaston Proceedings from the Lincoln Roll of 1305', in R. F. Hunnisett and J. B. Post (eds.), *Medieval Legal Documents*, London.

Harriss, G. L.,1975. *King, Parliament and Public Finance in Medieval England to 1369*, Oxford.

Hilaire, J., 1992. 'La procédure civile et l'influence de l'État autour de l'appel', in J. Krynen and A. Rigaudière (eds.), *Droits savant et pratiques françaises du pouvoir (XIe–XVe siècles)*, Bordeaux, pp. 151–60.

2000. *Science des notaires: une longue histoire*, Paris.

Jones, W. R., 1973. '*Rex et Ministri*: English Local Government and the Crisis of 1341', *Journal of British Studies*, 13, 1–20.

Krynen, J., 1992. 'Les légistes "tyrans de la France"?' in J. Krynen and A. Rigaudière (eds.), *Droits savants et pratiques françaises du pouvoir (XIe–XVe siècles)*, Bordeaux, pp. 279–99.

1999. 'Princeps pugnat pro legibus: un aspect du Policraticus' in J. Krynen and A. Rigaudière (eds.), *Droit romain, jus civile et droit français*, Toulouse, pp. 89–99.

ed., 1999. *Droit romain, jus civile et droit français*, Toulouse.

Krynen, J. and Rigaudière, A. (eds.), 1992. *Droits savants et pratiques françaises du pouvoir (XIe–XVe siècles)*, Bordeaux.

Leca, A., 1999. 'Le droit romain dans le Songe du Vergier' in J. Krynen and A. Rigaudière (eds.), *Droit romain, jus civile et droit français*, Toulouse, pp. 101–24.

Maddicott, J. R., 1978a. 'Law and Lordship: Royal Justices as Retainers in Thirteenth and Fourteenth Century England', *Past and Present Supplement*, 4.

1978b. 'The Birth and Settings of the Ballads of Robin Hood', *English Historical Review*, 93, 276–99.

Mayali, L., 1992. 'De la juris auctoritas à la legis potestas: aux origines de l'État de droit dans la science juridique médiévale', in J. Krynen and A. Rigaudière (eds.), *Droits savants et pratiques françaises du pouvoir (XIe–XVe siècles)*, Bordeaux, pp. 129–49.

Palmer, R. C., 1993. *English Law in the Age of the Black Death, 1348–1381: A Transformation of Governance and Law*, Chapel Hill and London.

Partington, R., 2001. 'Edward III's Enforcers', in J. Bothwell (ed.), *The Age of Edward III*, Woodbridge.

Powell, E., 1983. 'Arbitration and the Law in England in the Late Middle Ages', *Transactions of the Royal Historical Society*, 5th Series, 33, 49–67.

1985. 'The Restoration of Law and Order', in G. L. Harriss (ed.), *Henry V: The Practice of Kingship*, Oxford.

Putnam, B. H., 1929. 'The Transformation of the Keepers of the Peace into the Justices of the Peace, 1327–1380', *Transactions of the Royal Historical Society*, 4th Series, 12, 19–48.

1950. *The Place in Legal History of Sir William Shareshull*, Cambridge.

Renardy, C., 1979. *Le monde des maîtres universitaires du diocèse de Liège (1140–1350): recherches sur sa composition et ses activités*, Paris.

Renoux-Zagamé, M.-Fr., 1999. 'Et a le roi plus d'autorité en son royaume que l'empereur en son empire . . . ': droit romain et naissance de l'État moderne selon la doctrine et la pratique du palais', in J. Krynen and A. Rigaudière (eds.), *Droit romain, jus civile et droit français*, Toulouse, pp. 155–86.

Rigaudière, A., 1964. 'L'essor des conseillers juridiques des villes dans la France du bas Moyen Age', *Revue d'histoire du droit*, 62, 361–90.

1992. 'État, pouvoir et administration dans la Practica aurea libellorum de Pierre Jacobi (vers 1311)', in J. Krynen and A. Rigaudière (eds.), *Droits savants et pratiques françaises du pouvoir (xie–xve siècles)*, Bordeaux, 161–210.

Verduyn, A. J., 1993. 'The Politics of Law and Order during the Early Years of Edward III', *English Historical Review*, 108, 842–67.

Verger, J., 1976. 'Noblesse et savoir: étudiants nobles aux universités d'Avignon, Cahors, Montpellier et Toulouse (fin xive siècle)' in Ph. Contamine, *La noblesse au Moyen Age. Essais à la mémoire de Robert Boutruche*, Paris, pp. 289–313.

Walker, S. K., 1993. 'Yorkshire Justices of the Peace, 1389–1413', *English Historical Review*, 108, 281–313.

Weidenfeld, K., 1999. 'Les privilèges du fisc et les avocats du parlement de Paris: quelques exemples de l'influence du droit savant sur les praticiens à la fin du Moyen Age', in J. Krynen and A. Rigaudière (eds.), *Droit romain, jus civile et droit français*, Toulouse, pp. 441–72.

7 Church and state, clerks and graduates

Benjamin Thompson and Jacques Verger

It is difficult to imagine a medieval form of government, except perhaps the Italian city states or the free towns of the Empire, in which the church did not play an important role, and this was certainly true of the kingdoms of England and France. The purpose of this chapter will thus be to focus on the participation of the church in political power in these two kingdoms, in the fourteenth and fifteenth centuries.

We will first attempt to identify where clergy and graduates were to be found in the circles of political power, which in this case means primarily royal central and local government, although princely and even noble administrations will not be ignored, especially for France. Who these men were and how they had been trained will also be addressed, alongside the question of their clerical identity, and the changes wrought by the 'laicisation' of government in our period. Secondly, this chapter will assess the role of the church as a whole in the process of governance and in political culture. It will examine in particular how kings and princes deployed the church's material and ideological resources in pursuit of their objectives. This raises a third issue, that of the relationship of the Crown to the church more broadly, especially from the church's point of view: why did clergy serve the king, and why did the church need him? This will be placed in the context of late medieval developments to assess the tensions and paradoxes involved in the church's participation in governance, and in the development of these patterns into the sixteenth century.

This theme is not as straightforward as it might seem, since the church was, according to high medieval reforming theory, a body separate from secular authority, subject to a higher calling and a different master. Yet in practice, its contribution to royal governance was essential and multifaceted, as well as evolving. This tension between the theory of ecclesiastical separateness and the practice of the church's involvement forms part of the background to our story of its participation in political power and, in its resolution, is itself part of that story. Indeed, the fact that the 'church' was a far more diverse and multifarious institution than the unity of clergy under the pope claimed by reforming theory (and reiterated early in our period Boniface VIII's *Unam Sanctam*)[1] is another tension which also helps to explain the complex patterns which we will address.

We propose therefore to investigate this question as much in terms of the practicalities of people and institutions as of doctrine and theory. Without repeating what is said in the chapters of this book dedicated to officers, lawyers and those involved in the royal financial administration, we have tried to define the place within the political society of this period of the 'men of the church'. Even this concept is a complex one, however. As we shall see, those who can be clearly identified as members of the clergy by their personal status, the vows they had taken or the sacred orders they had received, are not the only individuals at issue here. It seems to us that, within the larger field of the medieval clericature, it is important to include the *gens de savoir* or 'men of learning', those who, having passed through the schools or the university, institutions which were almost always controlled by the church, retained a certain ecclesiastical character, as much social as cultural, even though they had ultimately returned to a lay or quasi-lay state.[2]

1.   'The debate between the clerk and the knight'

The Gospel put forward the principle of a clear separation between the temporal and spiritual spheres ('Render therefore unto Caesar the things which are Caesar's, and unto God the things which are God's' – Matt. 22:21) and medieval societies were based on a strict division between clergy and laity, which could be expressed in terms of a radical opposition: 'History tells us that laymen have always been the enemies of clerics', Pope Boniface VIII stated baldly in the bull *Clericis laicos* of 25 February 1296.[3] Indeed, the clergy's pretentions to a superior position, marked out from the laity, and exercising a sort of moral and religious tutelage over them, all whilst themselves rendering account only to God and their superiors, inevitably provoked the suspicions of rulers. The latter thus seemed to have every interest in seeking support from other 'natural' auxiliaries – their relatives, their vassals, their barons, their knights, or in other words their nobility[4] – and keeping far from power the men of the church whose loyalty was always conditional. One might have thought that this tendency towards division between state and church,

---

[1] *Registres de Boniface VIII*, ed. Digard et al. (1907–21), III, no. 5382, col. 888–90.
[2] For the notion of *gens de savoir* or 'men of learning' see Verger (1997).
[3] *Registres de Boniface VIII*, ed. Digard et al. (1907–21), vol. I, no. 1567, col. 584–5: 'Clericis laicos infestos oppido tradit antiquitas...'
[4] Contamine (1997), pp. 316–26.

even towards mutual antagonism, would have become stronger at the end of the Middle Ages, with the progressive 'laicisation' of the expanding royal government and its ever-greater claims to absolute sovereignty over temporal affairs.[5]

In France, from Philip IV to Charles V, the 'Debate between the Clerk and the Knight', and also that between the theologian and the lawyer, came to appear the classic expression of this political rivalry, for example the *Disputatio inter militem et clericum*,[6] written around 1297 in the context of the first quarrel between Philip the Fair and Boniface VIII, and the *Songe du Verger*, composed in 1378 by Évrard de Trémaugon in the form of a debate between 'the knight' and 'the clerk'.[7] This debate, when it was written by royal propagandists, usually ended with the victory of the 'knight', who was also the faithful spokesman of the ambitions of the king and therefore, one might imagine, the most obvious candidate for the various tasks and missions which the service of the state and the greatness of the prince might require.

The challenge posed to kings by the church originally stemmed from the reformed papacy of the eleventh and twelfth centuries. This offered an alternative source of authority to the secular powers, who therefore had to perform the complex trick of procuring the maximum participation of the church in government while preventing the papacy and the clergy infringing on secular power. While there were parallel tensions between church and state in both realms, notably over investiture at the beginning of the twelfth century, the greater precocity of English government meant that such tensions ran deeper and came to a head earlier. At a time when French kings were playing up their ideal role of crusader, England witnessed both the iconic set piece between Henry II and Becket – which remained an enduring image of the hostility between princes and clerks – and the interdict imposed on King John's England by Innocent III. The 1290s witnessed another bout of confrontation in parallel with France, as Archbishop Robert Winchelsey led resistance to Edward I's taxation. But this was the last defence of the liberty of the *ecclesia Anglicana* on a heroic scale. Thereafter, as we shall see, anti-clericalism in England was more commonly anti-papalism, which probably provided the context for John Trevisa's translation of the *Disputatio*.[8] Until the sixteenth century there was only occasional hostility in England to the clergy's role in government, and this was at moments of political tension occasioned by poor performance in the war when clerical ministers were temporarily replaced by laymen. And on their side there was little

[5] Krynen (1988).   [6] *Disputatio*, ed. Erickson (1967), pp. 288–309.
[7] Songe du vergier, ed. Schnerb-Lièvre (1982).   [8] Trevisa, *Dialogus*, ed. Perry (1925).

resistance to royal demands by the English clergy, which in fact welcomed the king's protection against the pope.

Thus, paradoxically, even if it is not impossible to detect here and there some traces of a political 'anti-clericalism' in both kingdoms – noted, for example, in France by the 'monk of Saint-Denis', Michel Pintoin, in the case of the *prévôt* of Paris, Hugues Aubriot, who allegedly 'nurtured an unforgiving hatred for all men of the church, infringing their privileges whenever he could'[9] – the expanding claims of royal government, increasingly sovereign in England as much as in France, did in fact make large and extensive use of the services of clerics and *gens de savoir*, to the detriment – and often the indignation – of the 'knights', readily suspected of restiveness or incompetence. In his *Chronique métrique* (*c.* 1316), for example, Geoffroy de Paris, although a clerk himself, gives voice to the complaints of the French barons against upstart men of the church: 'villeins and converts... become masters at court' (*vilains et convers... à cour maîtres devenus.*).[10] For their part, clerks and *gens de savoir* (or at least some of them) willingly replied to the call to serve, in the face of religious and moral literature which continued to recommend the contempt of the world and of the court, mock the futility of the *curiales*, and praise the contemplative life and the *otium* of the humanists.[11] They were apparently unmoved by the call to leave aside worldly and political commitments, even as others were inspired by the reformist movements of the time, from mysticism and the *devotio moderna*, to pastoral renewal and 'strict' regular observances.

It is thus to the different aspects of this paradox in these two kingdoms that the next section of this chapter will turn. What was the importance and the role of what were, in the French case, new servants of the state? What skills did they bring with them? What did the prince hope to gain from them? What advantages did churchmen and *gens de savoir* derive in return for devoting at least some of their existence to the service of the public good?

2.   An expanding group?

Although it would be impossible to compile a complete statistical table, a large number of studies in social and administrative history, making use more or less systematically of the methods of prosopography, have demonstrated how, in England and in France, from the twelfth to the

---

[9] *Chronique du Religieux de Saint-Denys*, ed. Bellaguet (1839), vol. I, p. 104.
[10] Geoffroi de Paris, *Chronique métrique*, ed. Diverrès (1956), pp. 211–12.
[11] See the texts discussed in Autrand (1989).

fifteenth century, the prince made more and more use of clerks and graduates.

English government was highly literate well before our period, after the Anglo-Saxon use of written instruments had been taken up by the Normans and reshaped by the Angevins to create the bureaucratic machine of the thirteenth century. The royal finances were accounted for on parchment from the beginning of the twelfth century; the king not only made grants but also gave orders in written form; and the systematisation of royal law in the second half of the twelfth century both increased exponentially the need for written instruments, and created the 'literate mentality' which encouraged the king's subjects to trust them and need them.[12] Moreover, the keeping of enrolled copies in the royal archives, especially from the reign of King John, more than doubled the need for clerical skills, and created a massive database for reference. By the beginning of our period there was therefore an army of clerks in the royal bureaucracy, which continued to grow and develop.

The head of this administration, the chancellor, was nearly always a bishop, or a clerk who would become one. Exceptions occurred in periods of specific political tensions, such as during the war in the early 1340s and 1370s, and in the crisis of the mid 1450s. But from 1455 he was always a bishop, and from 1486 until 1529 always an archbishop (Morton, Warham and Wolsey). Except in the 1370s, the keeper of the privy seal was also always a high-ranking cleric who was increasingly likely to attain a bishopric then or later. It is, of course, significant that the clerical headship of these two departments came to an abrupt end in 1529–30. The Treasurership was similarly clerical in the fourteenth century, but gave way to laity in Henry IV's reign, the last episcopal treasurer being Marmaduke Lumley, 1446–9. The tiers of officials beneath these great officers, such as the barons of the exchequer and (in the royal household) the Keeper of the Wardrobe, and the clerks who staffed the many sub-departments throughout the system, as well as the courts, were generally clergy, or at least aspirants to benefices, until the end of the fourteenth century, although this was to change in the fifteenth.

Bishops and other clerics also kept the wheels of government turning by attending the council, whether it was a routine bureaucratic meeting coordinating the work of government, or a body providing political leadership, as in minorities and political crises, and indeed in Henry VI's majority. Bishops were more likely to attend routine meetings than their lay counterparts, often functioning as heads of the civil service more than political players. The twenty-one bishops, along with twenty-seven major

---

[12] Clanchy (2013).

heads of religious houses, were summoned to parliament to sit with the Lords, giving them an overtly political role in advising the king and representing the realm to him. Few of the abbots, whose numbers had been whittled down by the mid fourteenth century from an earlier list of about fifty, attended in person, most sending proctors, often royal clerks. The lower clergy continued to be summoned through the bishops to parliament, but from the 1330s their proctors ceased to attend, as taxation of the clergy was negotiated separately in provincial councils, although these often took place concurrently with parliament.

There were more specifically ecclesiastical and religious functions to be performed by clergy within the structures of the English government, notably the king's chaplains and confessors in the household, the originals of the royal bureaucracy in the king's chapel. Their counterparts outside the household were the clergy of the important royal churches, such as the monks of Westminster and the canons of Windsor, and perhaps the fellows of colleges such as King's Hall and King's College, Cambridge. Indeed, all the clergy were obliged to pray for the king and for the welfare of the realm, but we must limit at some point our category of royally employed clergy.

The most significant additions to the places where clergy were to be found in central government concern the need for the specific skills of the highly educated, especially university-educated civil lawyers. From the mid fourteenth century, civilians were regularly employed as diplomats, their knowledge of international law having become essential in making the royal argument and conducting negotiations during the war; Henry V's episcopal promotions all came from such doctors. Moreover, the expertise of university-trained lawyers was essential to royal intervention in the Great Schism and the councils of the early fifteenth century. Civilians were also required to practise in the new courts based on the civil rather than common law, above all chancery in the fifteenth century. Another new position of government was that of king's secretary in the late fourteenth century, invariably occupied by a cleric of increasingly advanced education; he was rewarded with benefices and other offices, and, from the mid fifteenth century, a bishopric.

Some churches had a long-established role in local government as holders of delegated royal powers, from the bishop of Durham's palatinate, through liberties of significant portions of counties, such as those of Ely and Bury St Edmunds in East Anglia, to the tenure of individual hundreds, as well as the usual perquisites of manorial lordship. Dating from the Anglo-Saxon and Conquest periods, these gave particular bishops or religious houses a routine stake in the exercise of local power which was elsewhere performed by lay royal officials. As local government came increasingly to be conducted by royal commissions to the shires, some clergy were deployed on these bodies; bishops and abbots headed many of the county panels to prevent further outbreaks of rebellion in 1382. In 1424, the bishops were systematically added to the commissions of the peace, where they remained until the 1530s, a few heads of a religious house joining them. This was a recognition of the local lordship they exercised through their tenure of property, but also perhaps a reflection of new chancellor Henry Beaufort's conception of the public responsibilities of bishops.

In some ways, the clergy acquired a wider local role in later medieval England, as part of a system which was increasingly using local resources in the process of royal governance. The clergy's role in collecting their own taxes for the king stemmed from their own insistence, recognised by the 1300s, on keeping clerical taxation separate from lay, and on granting it in provincial councils rather than parliaments. Collection was therefore delegated to the bishops, who generally appointed one or two religious houses to collect the tenths on each occasion; some abbots and priors became almost permanent collectors, whereas in some dioceses the duty was rotated in order to lighten the burden.

The local organisation of defence and military recruitment also involved the clergy. Some prominent ecclesiastics were responsible for the defence of their regions, most obviously the bishop of Durham in the north, although it was Archbishop Zouche of York who won the Battle of Neville's Cross against the invading Scots in 1346. Commissions of array might include local clergy to raise local forces, and the clergy themselves were sometimes arrayed to play their part in defence. Indeed, clergy are found on the many other sorts of commission used by the king in the late-medieval locality: clergy, usually bishops and religious, raised loans (not least from themselves), were given responsibility for dykes and ditches, received oaths to keep the peace, investigated the abuses of officials, resolved disputes, requisitioned workers for royal building works, surveyed royal castles and parks, investigated enclosures and performed other miscellaneous duties, including judicial ones. Their presence was only a small contribution to the overall burden of such commissions on the nobility and gentry; nevertheless, the use of clergy in these ways was largely new in the fifteenth century, and may not be unrelated to the growing perception that the fifteenth-century clergy were becoming more secularised. These activities manifested a feeling, expressed in parliamentary debates over taxation, that the clergy were subjects of the king whose resources, as much as those of the laity, must be put at the disposal of the community.

Because the kingdom of France was larger and more varied locally, it is more difficult to give an overall analysis of the roles of churchmen and *gens de savoir* in the service of the royal government. It is not enough to

trace the general evolution in the number of officers, since many of these –
nobles chosen for their practical, administrative or military abilities; tax
collectors; sergeants; the simple executors of the decisions of justice – who
are considered elsewhere in this volume, were predominantly laymen.[13]
From the point of view of the present chapter, it does, however, seem to be
proven that, in France, until the middle of the thirteenth century, with the
exception of chapel clerks and some bishops or religious who enjoyed the
personal confidence of the king, churchmen and men of letters were not
numerous around the Capetian king, nor in his service.[14] This situation
began to change in the reign of Louis IX. Not only did he make room in
his entourage for mendicant friars and bishops, but also for jurists trained
in Roman law at the universities of Bologna or Orléans, and often also
for clerics, who now made a notable appearance amongst the counsellors
of the king.[15] This tendency was only confirmed under his immediate
successors, Philip III and Philip IV. Amongst known officers in the reign
of the latter, 15 per cent were also canons,[16] to which we should add
some bishops and religious on the one hand, and some lay jurists on
the other, which begins to give an idea of the role, a minority but not
negligible one, of clerks and men of letters amongst the servants of the
king. Even though we do not have the same series of precise figures for
the fourteenth century, it is probable that this proportion continued to
increase.

The presence of these men was felt especially at the level of central
institutions, which took on a stable and autonomous form from the first
half of the century. The chancery, the *Parlement*, the *Chambre des comptes*
and the *Chambre des aides* were now filled with graduates, most often
in law. A significant proportion of the notaries and secretaries of the
chancery, half at least of the councillors of the *Parlement* and a good
proportion of those of the *Chambre des comptes* and the *Chambre des aides*,
apart from the chancellor himself and many of the presidents of the
Chambres, were clerks, bishops, or at least canons.[17] Some of these men
sometimes sat on the council too, even if the most important places were
still reserved for the princes of the blood, military leaders, or nobles:
Pierre-Roger Gaussin has thus calculated that out of the 283 counsellors
of Charles VII for whom he has information, 20% came from the higher
nobility, 31% from the middle or lesser nobility, 21% were prelates,
23% were officers, and 5% were of undetermined status.[18] With some

---

[13] Guenée (1991), pp. 276–84.   [14] Cf. Baldwin (1976) and Verger (2011).
[15] Rigaudière (1988).   [16] Lalou (1992).
[17] See the bibliographical references and numerous examples in Gazzaniga (1992).
[18] Gaussin (1982).

fluctuations, this situation continued until the end of the Middle Ages. The 'early Gallicanism' of the fifteenth century, which, under the regime of the Pragmatic Sanction (1438), enabled the king to control election to the episcopal sees and great abbeys of the kingdom more and more easily, and so to install in these benefices a growing number of loyal individuals, must also have resulted in the greater presence of bishops and abbots in the central institutions of the royal government. In fact, the situation is a complicated one, and a complete survey of the fifteenth-century French episcopate has yet to be undertaken. In a study of the crucial date of 1438 (the year of the Pragmatic Sanction), Vincent Tabbagh has estimated that about 50 per cent of French bishops owed their nomination to the support of the king or a territorial prince.[19]

The question of the involvement of churchmen and graduates in the workings of the royal administration at a local level in France is more complex. At the beginning of our period, it was certainly very limited. The majority of clerics still preferred to pursue a purely ecclesiastical career. In the fourteenth century, especially in the south, the Avignon papacy offered them particularly rich possibilities.[20] And even lay graduates often found it more advantageous to find service with a lord or a commune, or to live from private practice, rather than by seeking royal office, something which has been thoroughly demonstrated for the Languedoc at the start of the fourteenth century.[21]

But little by little, things changed. A royal administration growing ever-larger and more cumbersome required competent lawyers and secretaries capable of keeping records, and its needs were largely met by a society which readily responded to this demand with increased supply. The appearance and expansion of provincial universities multiplied the number of graduates, particularly in law, and on a larger scale the general strengthening of the network of educational institutions put onto the market an increasing number of clerks able to fulfil administrative and scribal functions. At the same time, the crisis of ecclesiastical revenues and, at least in the case of the south of France, the permanent return of the papacy to Rome at the beginning of the fifteenth century, forced many clerks and graduates to go to princes for the chance of advancement which the church no longer offered them.[22]

At the highest level, that of doctors and graduates in law, it was of course the creation of provincial *Parlements* which offered the best career opportunities, starting with that founded in Toulouse in 1443.[23] Many studies have nonetheless shown that at a more modest level, that of the

---

[19] Tabbagh (2006).   [20] Verger (1990).   [21] Strayer (1970).
[22] Gazzaniga (1976).   [23] Viala (1953), vol. I, pp. 169–74.

jurisdiction of the king's *baillis* and *sénéchaux*, there was a similar increase in the number of posts which clerks or graduates could occupy.[24] What was true of the royal demesne could also be said of the great principalities in the same period – in the lands of the duke of Burgundy or the duchy of Brittany, for example – as much at a central level as at a local one.[25]

It is true that the growth and the increased cultivation of the world of officers did not necessarily lend it a genuinely clerical character. It is probably possible to consider this as a progressive laicisation; the way of life of many subaltern officers with modest cultural achievements and a practical education, or indeed, even numerous graduates drawn from the 'university clergy', was altogether that of laymen, not least because alongside their public functions they often also pursued economic activities and municipal roles which would have been difficult to reconcile with the clerical estate. But this evolution did not prevent churchmen and educated men who resembled them from taking up positions in the service of the prince which were sufficiently numerous and 'visible' that contemporaries became aware of them, with consequences both for the nature of political power and of the institution of the church.

We can thus say that, in this regard at least, the situation at the end of the Middle Ages was comparable, although with some important differences, in France and in England.

3.   Unity and diversity of the 'clergy'

Even if we put to one side the mass of lay officers, as we have done in this article, the world of the medieval 'clergy' in the service of the prince was very varied. This diversity is linked as much to the different educational routes followed – given that the possession of certain intellectual competences was one element which defined what contemporaries called *clergie* – as to status in the sense of belonging more or less directly to the church or to its immediate spheres of influence. This can be seen in both France and England, even if the contours and internal divisions of this group were not exactly the same.

Classification of the clergy deserves closer scrutiny, especially our overlapping but distinguishable categories of 'clerk', 'clergy' or 'cleric', and 'graduate'. How these terms were used, as well as the identities they denoted, needs to be understood more clearly, as do their shifting meanings in our period. Although *clericus* and *literatus* were thought of as equivalent in the late twelfth century, even by a century later the term

---

[24] Shown in the case of Senlis by Guenée (1966), pp. 383–92.
[25] See Bartier (1955–7) for the dukes of Burgundy and Kerhevé (1987) for Brittany.

'clerk' did not necessarily denote a man in holy orders. It was already in use to mean someone with literate and administrative skills, who might well make a living from such work, such as the clerks of Norwich who formed a professional cadre of lawyers and administrators in the town.[26] It was therefore not necessary to secure ecclesiastical preferment rather than marry. Even those who did take orders usually only did so once appointed to a benefice. Indeed, in principle one had to have such a post before ordination was possible. Many clerks in royal and other bureaucracies, therefore, were not ordained, and even delayed ordination when they started to enjoy the fruits of a benefice.

It was not only the level of formal education which determined career paths. Birth, membership of a network of patronage and practical experience were all important too, although it still needs to be said, in the French case for example, that there was a world of difference in terms of competence as much as notoriety between the graduates and doctors of medicine, law and theology from the great universities (Paris and Orléans, but also Angers, Toulouse or Montpellier) and those who held inferior qualifications (such as the *baccalauréat*), a simple Master of Arts, or other diploma from the provincial universities which multiplied and spread locally in France in the fifteenth century.[27] Students who left university without any degree must have had even less prestige, as must those who simply passed through urban grammar schools, or clerks who acquired their training by apprenticeship with a local practitioner or in a local jurisdiction.[28]

To the variety of the qualifications obtained should be added that of the subjects studied. It might be thought that given the often rather theoretical and abstract nature of the teaching, especially medieval university teaching (which left no place, for example, either for the vernacular or for customary law), the passage through school or university led less to the acquisition of particular skills and more to a certain *forma mentis* and the acquisition of common areas of basic knowledge (Latin, some of the canonical references in history and religious writing, the fundamental concepts of logic and Aristotelian philosophy, etc.) which were shared, although at greatly varying levels, by all churchmen and *gens de savoir*.[29] It does seem, however, that disciplinary distinctions were not only real, but were often observed by contemporaries and maintained, at the court as much as in the schools, by corporate rivalries. Chroniclers, scribes and chancery clerks, jurists, the theologians who, in the *Songe du Vergier*,

---

[26] Rutledge (2005).   [27] Verger (1998).   [28] Verger (1997), pp. 49–84.
[29] This idea of a kind of basic body of university learning emerges quite well from Piltz (1981).

label their colleagues from the faculty of law as 'political idiots', even doctors and astrologists were all convinced of the excellence of their own discipline and its high importance for the common good.[30]

Formally trained jurists in civil law, canon law or *utriusque juris* might have seemed the best-placed to occupy royal offices, notably in the *Parlements* and in the courts of the *bailliages* and the *sénéchausées*, but Charles V liked to surround himself with astrologers, philosophers and theologians like Nicole Oresme,[31] and Louis XI promoted his doctors to important political and ecclesiastical offices, for example Guillaume Brun, Jacques Coictier and Angelo Cato.[32]

The issue of the range of skills, abilities and education overlaps with that of the varied statuses of churchmen. Even without taking into account classic divisions linked to social or geographical origin (nobles or non-nobles, native or foreign) or to appurtenance to a particular network defined by partisan loyalty (divisions from which they were not excluded) the *clercs*, as they were often referred to in generic terms, who served in the royal government did not all have the same status with regards to the church.

Certainly, during their studies, all the *scolares* belonged, it seems, to a kind of vast clerical order of the schools and universities which, in return for certain disciplinary demands (tonsure, long clothing, celibacy) took them under the wing of ecclesiastical privilege and, if they had at least taken minor orders, allowed them to take up benefices.[33] But once they had left school or university, this common affiliation shattered into varied statuses. Religious, monks, canons and mendicants, and also those who had received major orders, especially if they held a higher qualification, normally in theology or canon law, could have an excellent ecclesiastical career all whilst exercising various princely and royal offices. These men were incontestably regarded as churchmen, by the king who made use of their services, and by their colleagues and contemporaries. But what about all those who, renouncing clerical orders and, where relevant, any benefices they might hold, returned to the world and devoted themselves to the sole service of the king, all whilst getting married and founding a family? Some of them, as we have said, were now pure laymen, with nothing in common with the personnel of the church. But it is legitimate to imagine that *viri litterati* who became laymen and married most often still bore the mark of their initial status as university clergy, not only in the form of judicial and fiscal privileges, but also in their

---

[30] Krynen (1991).   [31] Autrand (1994), pp. 728–47.
[32] Gaussin (1976), pp. 145–6.
[33] On the complex question of the university 'clergy', see Ridder-Symoens (2007).

cultural accomplishments and assumptions, their way of life and their mental attitudes.[34] In other words, might one suggest that the world of officers in France at the end of the Middle Ages tended to remain a 'clerical' universe in which true men of the church rubbed shoulders with a new type of austere, pious layman – naturally inclined, all whilst serving the prince, to defend Christian values and to pay close attention to ecclesiastical affairs?

In England, as in France, the prerequisite of clerical status was a level of literacy, which was originally acquired informally through a local priest or household chaplain, or in a prelate's household. After the establishment of cathedral schools in the twelfth century, more formal schooling was emerging in the course of our period, with the establishment of song schools and elementary schools, the almonry schools of monasteries, and above all endowed grammar schools and subsidised town schools. There remained more informal methods of acquiring literacy, through the local parish or chantry priest, or through a master setting up on his own to attract pupils. But the increasing availability of education equally meant that many of those who acquired some form of literacy did not go on to become clergy. Although the ability to read was useful in proving clerical status before the common-law courts, it was used by a much wider spectrum of society than ordained clergy.

Administrative skills were learnt on the job, essentially by apprentice-ship. Clerks in a bishop's household learnt the basics of ecclesiastical administration, just as royal clerks learnt their trade by immersion in the details of civil-service routine. The key issue was entry into this system, which was by networks of locality, kinship and patronage, not to men-tion commercial exchange. This was even true of the endowed grammar schools such as Winchester, although their fuller geographical coverage presumably gave greater scope to an element of meritocracy, by which promising boys could gain entry into the system.

University education (obtainable in England only at Oxford or Cam-bridge), was also increasingly important in England in the later Middle Ages. Possession of a degree was more and more necessary for promo-tion in the church, and by the mid fifteenth century bishops were almost all graduates. Being a graduate did not necessarily make one a cleric, however, despite the fact that, as in France, students were in theory regarded as clergy and required to have the first tonsure. In practice, not all did, and at least 5 per cent of graduates pursued lay careers, alongside

---

[34] The libraries of officers of the Parisian Parlement in the fourteenth century still retained a very 'clerical' appearance: canon law, pious works, and the absence of vernacular literature. See Autrand (1973).

perhaps many of the 40 per cent whose careers are unidentified, as well as many of those who did not get as far as taking a degree. Nevertheless, graduates were more likely than not to take up clergy (over 50 per cent did have recorded clerical careers) because they had a good chance of acquiring a benefice, and the more highly educated they were, the truer this was.[35]

In the thirteenth and fourteenth centuries the church's revenues were used fully by the Crown to fund its administration; the chancellor disposed of all benefices in royal patronage worth less than 20 marks as a way of providing stipends for his clerks and those in other departments. Ecclesiastical benefices were the natural reward of service in royal administration. Hence the political tension over the issues of pluralism, non-residence and jurisdiction over royal chapels, especially in Edward I's reign: then, the last two archbishops in the high-medieval reforming mould, Pecham and Winchelsey, unsuccessfully attempted to exercise jurisdiction over the king's clerks to claim them as more officers of the church than of the Crown.[36] The most successful royal clerks went on to secure bishoprics; many continued in government service thereafter, although some devoted themselves after promotion largely to their dioceses (and their souls), which they were more likely to do the longer they continued to live.

These arrangements changed from the later fourteenth century to the early sixteenth century, with the increasing laicisation of government service.[37] An example had already been set by the common lawyers; judges in the thirteenth century might still have ecclesiastical benefices and thus be ordained, but professionalisation into the fourteenth century had involved a wholesale laicisation. At the top of royal administration, there were lay treasurers and chancellors in the 1340s and 1370s; but whereas lay chancellors proved to be only occasional until 1529, in the fifteenth century most treasurers were laymen. Latterly, under the Tudors royal councillors were less likely to be bishops than common lawyers, and there were no clerical ministers on the council in the 1530s. These trends were mirrored lower down the system from the late fourteenth century. Increasingly, royal clerks were laymen rather than beneficed clergy: whereas William of Wykeham had had charge of the king's building works in the 1350s and went to take his reward in the form of plural benefices and then the see of Winchester, in 1389–91 the clerk of the king's works

---

[35] Catto and Evans (1992), p. 520.
[36] Douie (1952), chapters III–IV; Denton (1980), Chapter 6.
[37] Storey (1982) for this paragraph; there are lists in Fryde (1996); see also Tout (1920–33).

was none other than Geoffrey Chaucer, who remained firmly a layman.[38] The process was seen first in the treasury, and last in chancery, where the last six clerks were allowed to marry in 1523; it became particularly noticeable in the second quarter of the fifteenth century. Laicisation did not involve a change in the kind of person becoming a royal clerk, but rather the adoption of a different path by the existing royal clerks, who chose now to marry and to seek remuneration in secular offices and grants – alongside the money-lending and work as attorneys they had long undertaken – rather than in ecclesiastical benefices. In other words, it was literate and administrative skills which the Crown needed, not clerical status, and at this period the former was increasingly separated from the latter, allowing 'clerks' to adopt a different, secular, identity from the 'clergy'.

These trends – the laicisation of the civil service and the increasing importance of graduates at the top of the church – combined to produce perhaps paradoxical results. Laicisation meant that there was less pressure on benefices from the Crown, allowing them to be used for the church, including for graduates. Appropriation of the greater part of benefices to corporate churches, and the falling value of benefices, also made them of less interest to outsiders. While the church was less represented in the rank-and-file of government service, there were some graduates in the system, including a few lay ones who would become more numerous in the sixteenth century. But the civil service was headed by graduate bishops who had therefore come from outside the system after a long time in education, rather than learning their trade entirely on the job. This was a fortiori true of those who had spent longer at university earning the higher degrees in the laws or theology, who came to dominate the episcopate, especially those trained in civil law.

One might expect this to have introduced a more ecclesiastical and slightly less royally focused ethos to government; many fifteenth-century administrator-bishops were lawyers who had made their name practising in the ecclesiastical courts, like Henry Chichele and John Kemp. But it is hard to detect the signs of these changes. The Crown's secure control over the church, especially under Henry V and then the Yorkists and Tudors, perpetuated the earlier tradition of bishops serving the king as administrators, perhaps seen most vividly in the archiepiscopal monopoly on the chancellorship, whose last exponent, Wolsey, was a cardinal. It seems that the professional ethos of graduates was one of service which was just as likely to produce commitment to the Crown as was the in-house production of royal clerks. Indeed it might equally have been that

[38] Davis (2007).

the presence of civilians reinforced high royalist claims to the supremacy of the prince. Edmund Stafford, Doctor of Civil Law at Oxford, was the chancellor who opened parliament at the moment of Richard II's triumph over his enemies in September 1397 with a sermon on the text 'Rex unus erit omnibus', emphasising the subject's duty of obedience to the king and submission to the law.[39] Royal title-inflation may owe something to closer awareness of Roman law. But under the Tudors, common lawyers proved equally capable of exalting the Crown, and the case for strong civilian influence here seems unproven.[40]

In England, as in France, it was probably more the honed intellectual capacities of graduates rather than the substance of their learning which made them valuable to government, except in those specialist areas where specific knowledge was essential, notably the civil law in chancery, admiralty and chivalry courts. The introduction of humanist Latin into the king's letters by royal secretaries, notably Thomas Beckington (1437–43), was a change in the medium more than the message; rhetoric belonged to the Arts, which comprised the tools of thought, communication and administration. Amongst fifteenth-century royal bishops, theologians took their place alongside lawyers, especially in mid-century, when they secured a greater number of dioceses. While this may have helped in principle to make the king conscious of his duties to the church and his subjects' souls, in practice the benefit seems to have gone the other way, putting the professional abilities of graduate-clergy at the disposal of the Crown, in line with their developing ethic of service.

4.   From the use of skills to the sacralisation of power

What did the prince want from these men of learning, in particular those who were also men of the church? The contribution of the church to government was not just a question of the role played by individual clerics. At least as significant, and perhaps more so with the passage of time and the reduction of the presence of actual clergy, was the way in which the king used the church to participate in the processes of governance more generally through its own institutional structures and functions.

The simplest reason why the prince employed such men in both these kingdoms was because they possessed some of the skills needed to fulfil

---

[39] *Parliament Rolls of Medieval England (PROME)*, ed. Given-Wilson et al. (2005), Sept. 1397, no. 1. Discussion in Walker (1995) and Saul (1995).

[40] Dodd (2007), pp. 287–8; Gunn (1995), pp. 163–6.

the growing ambitions of the emergent 'modern state' and the ever-more-complex tasks which the good government of the kingdom required. Their training in the schools and universities and their experience within the church guaranteed that they would, it seemed, possess the knowledge necessary for the correct operation of the state and of society: the mastery of writing and of record-keeping, and so of memory, a reasonably clear perception of the goals which needed to be pursued in a long-term political vision.

Moreover, another advantage of using this kind of political personnel was that they were not too expensive in a time both of recurrent financial difficulties and of the repeated denunciation of allegedly cash-hungry officials, since these men drew significant revenues from their ecclesiastical benefices, making it possible to pay them thriftily and to dispose of them without fuss. To cite Bernard Guenée: 'If bureaucratisation was able to progress so much up to the middle of the fourteenth century, it was in part because God had provided.'[41]

The political interest of kings and princes in the education of clerks and men of letters was manifested at the end of the Middle Ages by concrete measures (the foundation of colleges, universities, libraries) which were in the end quite modest and inexpensive. Consider, for example, in the case of Paris, the Collège de Navarre, founded in 1305 by the then queen, Joan of Navarre, the Collège de Bourgogne, founded again by the queen, this time Joan of Burgundy, in 1332, and the Collèges de Laon (1314), du Plessis (1322), de Hubant (1336), de Mignon (c. 1350), de Dormans-Beauvais (1370), de Maître-Gervais (1370), founded by the counsellors or officers of the king.[42] Provincial universities in France were more often princely foundations, for example Aix-en-Province (1409), Dôle (1422), Valence (1452) or Nantes (1460), or at least partially municipal, as in the case of Poitiers (1431) or Bordeaux (1441). Only the universities of Caen (founded in 1437 by Henry VI of England and 'refounded' in 1450–2 by Charles VII after the reconquest of Normandy) and Bourges (1464) can be considered to be true royal foundations.[43] The stated motivations were clear, for example in the foundation of the University of Valence in the Dauphiné by the Dauphin Louis (the future Louis XI) on 26 July 1452: 'We judge it necessary and convenient to establish in our country, in the lands subject to us, a university where theology, canon law, civil

[41] Guenée (1991), p. 279.
[42] Rashdall (1936), vol. I, pp. 536–9; for the colleges of Navarre, Laon and Dormans-Beauvais, see more precisely Gorochov (1997), pp. 125–82, Fabris (2005), pp. 29–52 and Kouamé (2005), pp. 1–155.
[43] Rashdall (1936), vol. II, pp. 186–206; for the University of Caen, see Roy (2006), pp. 11–53.

law, medicine and the liberal arts will be taught; there is indeed hardly a prince who has not founded a university in his dominions; and yet there is none in ours; this is why we, who in truth love wisdom (*la science*), have decided to found in the lands subject to us a university where those who are capable might be instructed, so that once they have been educated, they will shine in all our country "like the brightness of the firmament... like the stars for ever and ever" (Daniel 12:3)... Wishing to provide for our own utility, for that of the public weal as much as that of our subjects, we have thus established and founded by our wisdom (*notre certaine science*) and plenitude of power a university in our aforementioned city of Valence'.[44] But in reality the effort involved remained limited and there was never any question in this period of putting schools or universities under the tutelage of public authority to the detriment of the church which traditionally filled this role.

Ultimately, it is possible to talk of the sharing of responsibilities, since this is indeed what we are talking about in the final analysis. In other words, it was not only specific knowledge and technical abilities that clerks and graduates brought to the service of the prince, but also the moral and religious demands and the social practices inherent to their estate. Just as the nobility, always present amongst the political collaborators of the king, were supposed to ornament monarchical power with chivalric virtues such as courage, honour and largesse, so churchmen and men of learning, merely by their participation in government, transferred in some regards some of the values traditionally attached to *studium* and *sacerdotium* to the *regnum*. Their rhetorical, philosophical, juridical and philosophical training and, where they possessed them, their holy orders naturally equipped them for certain roles: as men of justice, their substantial presence in the royal courts was supposed to guarantee 'good and prompt justice'; as men of peace, bishops and doctors staffed the embassies which provided arbitration or negotiated truces and peace treaties; as men of faith, they gave valuable counsel to the prince, now that the emancipation of post-conciliar 'national churches' necessitated his more direct and regular intervention in ecclesiastical institutions and ecclesiastical discipline.[45]

This cooperation between monarchical power and the church was particularly visible at the level of the higher circles of power, that of the counsellors and confidants of the prince (whether this be the king or

---

[44] *Statuts et privilèges des universités françaises*, ed. Fournier (1890–4), vol. III, no. 1785, p. 362.

[45] On the religious dimension of the political role of churchmen, see Gazzaniga (1992), pp. 262–6.

the territorial princes), the great officers and the sovereign courts. It can also be seen, although in a less developed form, within local institutions. At this level, it was not only apparent in the actual exercise of office, but also in more diffuse and multiform ways. We need to ask what role was played by lesser literate men in towns or villages, graduates or not – local prosecutors, scribes, clerks or notaries – and even more, the parish clergy. Although these men might take part in popular revolts in exceptional circumstances at the end of the Middle Ages,[46] they are more often to be found acting as the official purveyors of royal propaganda, or of the social and political order which the prince desired: public prayers, sermons and processions staged by the church were no doubt effective means for maintaining patriotic sentiment and the 'royal religion'.[47]

In England as in France, the church provided support for the Crown at an ideological level. Monarchy functioned in a religious framework: the king was crowned and anointed by the archbishop of Canterbury, and the coronation oath he took made him accountable to God for his rule. This was difficult to enforce at a human level, especially as, despite the theoretical possibility of using spiritual sanctions against violators of the liberties in the charters, excommunicating the king was not a practical option. Rather, the church offered excommunication as a sanction against those who resisted royal rights, disturbed the peace, and broke laws (as in 1434, for instance). Such sanctions might have a dynastic edge: Henry VII persuaded Innocent VIII to excommunicate rebels against the new regime and its heirs under the new settlement.

The church was intrinsically obliged to pray for the welfare of king and the realm, as habitual requests from royal representatives at Convocation illustrate. In 1455, Archbishop Bourchier expounded in his summons to Convocation that nothing was more efficacious when facing enemies than prayer to invoke divine aid.[48] Special prayers were also requested on particular occasions, especially for the success of military expeditions (against the French or the infidel), both prospectively and retrospectively, as well as for peace, the king's health, the arrival of a new queen (in 1444–5), good weather for the harvest, or warding off pestilence.[49] These requests often involved special processions and litanies on several days of the week, as well as regular suffrages. Henry VII institutionalised these practices, along lines laid down in the tenth-century *Regularis Concordia*; he asked all cathedrals, religious houses and collegiate churches to grant

---

[46] S.K. Cohn estimates that, for the whole of Europe, less than 1 per cent of popular revolts were led by clerics. See Cohn (2006), pp. 111–112.
[47] See for example, on prayers and processions for peace, Offenstadt (2007), pp. 165–76.
[48] *Registran Thome Bourgchier*, ed. Du Boulay (1957), p. 7.
[49] For these prayers and for this paragraph in general, Thompson (2004), esp. pp. 78–9.

him confraternity and to say unceasing prayers and suffrages for his health and prosperity and for the succession.[50] The English church was the official prayer-house of the realm, obliged to pray for its safety and well-being and for that of its head. Prayers and processions advertised the objects for which they interceded, and were themselves forms of proclamation and propaganda. More specifically, the church's resources were deployed to publicise the king's argument, to inspire unity behind the king's projects, and equally to procure tangible support in the form of taxation and military service; the king's case was to be affixed to church doors, or actively promulgated in sermons to the people. While the shire and hundred courts constituted one network through which the king could get his message to his subjects, the pulpit was potentially far more effective in reaching every locality and every settlement, because of the dense coverage of the parochial system in England.

In thus spreading the royal word, the church gave constant support to the notion of the realm as a single community headed by the king, just as much as it had when it had opposed Edward I in the name of the common profit of the community. It might thus qualify its support for a particular king in the name of the community, but it thereby promulgated the blessings of kingship as a whole and the virtues required of kings in particular. While English kingship may have benefited from the exalted notions of princely rule inherent in Roman law, more significant was the insular heritage of the king as guarantor and enforcer of the law, in which the church was inextricably involved and which it proclaimed.

Religious practice and culture were also deployed in support of the monarchy, especially through the cult of saints. Royal saints were invaluable symbols, and Edward the Confessor was promoted not only by unsuccessful kings such as Edward II and Richard II, but also by Henry V. The latter initiated the enlargement of the feast of St George as a national saint, as well as English saints such as Chad and John of Beverley. Henry VII's exploitation of the cult of Henry VI as part of his attempt to entrench his own dynasty point towards the importance of church buildings in the cult of monarchy; the new Lady Chapel of Westminster Abbey was to be the last resting place of the saint-king, as well as of Henry VII himself, and the chapel was decorated in stone and glass with Tudor dynastic imagery. Indeed, the devotion of the lower-storey glazing of the chapel exclusively to dynastic badges was unprecedented in a church. Similarly, new royal churches, such as St George's, Windsor, founded by Edward III and rebuilt by Edward IV, and Eton and King's Colleges, founded under Henry VI, the latter finally completed under Henry VII and VIII,

---

[50] *Concilia*, ed. Wilkins (1737), vol. III, p. 649; *Calendar of Close Rolls, 1500–9*, p. 246.

arose from the needs of new dynasties to identify themselves with the historic monarchy and proclaim their arrival.[51]

These royal churches also embodied the aspirations of monarchy more generally. In England, there were no new universities in the later Middle Ages, but many new colleges at Oxford and Cambridge.[52] In addition to Henry VI's King's College, Cambridge, Edwards II and III founded King's Hall and Henry VIII refounded Christ Church after taking it over from Wolsey. Other collegiate foundations involved queens, in particular Jesus and St John's at Cambridge and the eponymous Queens' Colleges at both universities. While many of the other colleges were founded by bishops, some of these were leaders of royal governance, from Walter Stapledon at Exeter, through William of Wykeham, to Wolsey. Kings explicitly gave their support to most of these foundations, with Chichele acknowledging at All Souls, Oxford, that making the king co-founder was a deliberate move to secure the college's future.[53] The rhetoric of the foundation documents of these institutions is illuminating: they were to increase the supply of clerks suitable to take part in public business in serving the state, providing the learning necessary to conducting the law and other business of the realm; and they were to provide more learned clergy able to preach the orthodox faith, to instruct people by word and example, to increase divine observance, strengthen the vigour and fervour of the Christian faith, and to counteract heresy. These benefits were seen as the common concern of the Crown and leading clergy (and some laity). Edward III held educated clergy to be the chief support of religion and good government, and in 1442 Henry VI's government confirmed the foundation of the University of Caen, for the glory of God, the orthodox faith, and the 'utility and support of the state committed to us by God'.[54] Both the business of the *res publica* and the care for the faith and for virtue and learning were royal concerns, just as the church's spiritual care came to be seen as part of the business of government. These institutions were therefore joint projects by an establishment seeking to underpin the foundations of both monarchy and church through learning.

In this way the church made a contribution to governance through its own structures and functions. Late-medieval sermons, especially those aimed at parishes, are heavily moralistic in content; they suggest that the clergy envisaged their function as constant exhortation to shape

---

[51] See in general, Colvin (1963–82), vol. III.

[52] Convenient summaries are in *Victoria County History, Oxford*, ed. Salter and Lobel (1954), vol. III, and *Victoria County History, Cambridge*, ed. Roach (1959), vol. III.

[53] *Statutes of the Colleges of Oxford* (1853), pp. [7], 11–12.

[54] *Concilia*, ed. Wilkins (1737), vol. III, p. 33; Bekynton *Correspondence*, ed. Williams (1872), vol. I, p. 123.

behaviour according to the various schemes developed by the church, the ten commandments and two of the new law, the seven vices and the seven cardinal virtues, the seven spiritual works of mercy and seven corporal. How effective this was is impossible to say, but it is clear that the church's role was conceived as part of social regulation, and to that extent part of the enterprise of governance. The connection is evident in attitudes to heresy: it has become clear that trawls for heretics and the encouragement to communities to denounce suspects picked up oddballs and non-conformists, as well as those actively committed to heterodox belief and practice, and also overlapped with the regulation of other social sins such as defamation and lechery.[55] Royal concern with heresy and the close connection of heresy with treason (seen in the alleged aims of the Old-castle plot of 1414, and the punishment of more of the rebels for the latter than the former), emphasise the impossibility of drawing a strict line between rebellion against secular power and rejection of ecclesiastical authority, between social non-conformity and spiritual error, between crime and sin.

The church thus acted as an agency of social regulation under the aegis of the Crown. The same was true of the ecclesiastical courts more generally. They continued to exercise jurisdiction in certain spheres because they continued to be used as useful mechanisms for the conduct of business and the solving of disputes in these areas. As well as the bedrock matters of marriage and testaments, they dealt in principle with spiritual matters, which could extend widely: breach of faith was used as a way of disputing debt and contract, and it was often preferable to pursue it in a church court because penance could involve restitution. Moreover, these procedures allowed for negotiation and compromise, often used in preference to the blunter methods of secular courts until the early sixteenth century. Even sexual and moral regulation by ecclesiastical authorities might in fact stem from presentations by neighbours attempting to rein in unacceptable behaviour in the community. Defamation was similarly used as a way of airing a quarrel, without significant consequences for either party and with arbitration always a possibility. The fact that the Crown could prohibit business in the ecclesiastical courts when it chose, or when it was applied to, shows that the courts functioned with royal consent and under royal control, an element in the social regulation which was a part of governance. This is a tangible instance of the way in which the late medieval church was coming to be seen as an arm of royal government, separate from secular power, but under the authority

---

[55] Thomson (1989); Forrest (2005).

of the king whose purposes the clergy promoted, albeit in different ways, as much as the laity.

Thus in many different ways, the presence in the king's entourage and in his service of numerous churchmen and men of learning contributed to the evolution – and, at least in England, the reinforcement – of the nature of royal power at the end of the Middle Ages. They helped not only to affirm the king's sovereignty, but also his majesty and even his sacrality, by granting him the characteristics of a 'wise' (*sage*) and, in France explicitly, 'most Christian' ruler, inspired both by reason and by Truth, friend of wisdom and close to the church.

5.   Serving two masters

Both the clergy as individuals and the church as a whole were therefore fundamental to late medieval government, even if the former may have been becoming less numerous in the corridors of power. The issue therefore arises of what it was that prompted the church to serve the king. What, moreover, was the role of the king in the church? The symbiotic relationship between church and Crown must be more fully probed in order to bring out the full implications of the features so far described, the changes in our period and the differences between England and France.

There is no need to insist on the importance of tradition. Since the early Middle Ages, there had always been churchmen in the entourage and in the service of kings. Yet it is perhaps more pertinent to stress that the first reason why clergy served princes was individual and family interest: material gain, access to the corridors of power and social mobility. Clergymen and graduates did not escape loyalties of family and affinity. It was because they belonged to families which were anyway ensconced at court, familiar with offices and public burdens, that they themselves naturally turned to those functions for which their ecclesiastical status and intellectual training gave them an extra qualification. Many ecclesiastical servants of the kings of France were members or protégés of noble families themselves close to the sovereign, such as the Juvénal des Ursins, the Espinay, the Pompadour, and the d'Amboise.[56] In England between 1350 and 1480 there were around twenty bishops of noble stock, many of them at the forefront of church and government such as Courtenay, Bourchier and Neville. These families secured an additional presence in the counsels of the realm in a different dimension, sometimes with spectacular political effect, as in the cases of Thomas Arundel's opposition to

---

[56] Gazzaniga (1992), pp. 266–72.

Richard II and support for the Lancastrians, and Beaufort's promotion of his family within Henry VI's regime.

Yet in England, perhaps because of a more restricted higher nobility and greater intellectual demands, the aristocratic nature of the episcopacy at the end of the Middle Ages was less marked than it was in France; most bishops were of humbler origin – gentry, yeomen, or even below. For these classes the church offered the quickest available route to power and wealth, in a few cases involving a spectacular rise from an agricultural or artisan family to a bishopric and power at the heart of government: Wolsey is the obvious example. Of course, they only had life-tenure of their bishoprics or benefices, and no legitimate heirs: thus the most they could hope to do for the future was to establish their families as minor gentry on the basis of property acquired for themselves. Here again, in England the common law offered an increasingly significant challenge, because lawyers could found dynasties, as the Pastons did, even if it took many generations to get from husbandman to nobility. It is not surprising to find sixteenth-century English graduates becoming common lawyers rather than clergy, whereas in France, service through university and the church continued to provide an important route to political power.

The desire for material advancement was accentuated by the economic and social difficulties of the late Middle Ages. For new men in search of resources and respectability, as much as for groups threatened in their traditional position, service to the prince was a tempting remedy, even an indispensable one. The impoverishment of benefices provided an obvious motivation to seek alternative sources of wealth. This was especially true in France, where there were more noble bishops, from old families struggling with the crisis of seigneurial revenues. Moreover, as we have seen, the end of the Avignon papacy left a void in the material rewards available to French clergy. Such material motives evidently opened the door to the 'abuses' to which the sources did not fail to draw attention when they attacked the behaviour of officers and judges. Beyond individual excesses, can we talk, without anachronism, of a *trahison des clercs* at the end of the Middle Ages? The doctor or the prelate became courtiers, no longer knowing any rule but political conformity and obedience to an almost-deified royal power, thus becoming the inventors of absolutism; this accusation, probably excessive, was at least suggested in France.[57] Yet this was less true in England, where the prospects for advancement in the church through service to the Crown were to diminish.

At the other end of the spectrum of interest, the church served the king because it was an engrained obligation, part of the ideological context of

---

[57] Krynen (1992) and Krynen (1993), esp. pp. 339–455.

governance already noted. It was the clergy's duty to pray for the king and the whole realm unceasingly. And their duty to support defence with subsidies was emphasised at every request for aid. Moreover, prelates were obliged to counsel the king because of their wisdom and experience, qualities which were emphasised in letters to popes recommending individuals for bishoprics. These qualities were engrained by the practice of episcopal attendance at council and, in England, at parliament, and by the emergence of many bishops from service to the Crown. More generally, their ecclesiastical status and education had familiarised churchmen and *gens de savoir* in the prince's service with concepts such as 'the common good of the public weal', the defence of the Christian faith and the reform of the church. In an era marked by the crisis of the 'feudal' structure of society and by the faltering of the central institutions of the church, with the decline of the papacy and the failure of the councils, it could be tempting to seek for the means to implement the potential *utilitas* of the knowledge to which medieval scholars had always been attached, but in alliance with the prince, rather than independently through the church, and so to contribute to the religious and moral regulation of society.

The church also served the king because it needed his support. As we have seen, their relationship was based on mutual advantage, in that the Crown secured the service of churchmen and graduates to run its growing administration, and the church secured royal support and investment, as the foundations of royal churches and colleges demonstrate. Indeed, these neatly demonstrate the symbiotic nature of the relationship: whether the initiative in any particular case came from Crown or church, these are best conceived as joint foundations designed to perpetuate the kind of episcopal civil servants who founded them, and perhaps also to deploy royal resources to maintain the place of the elite clergy in the counsels of the realm. When the Crown negotiated with the church, it was often represented by clergymen who were thus in dialogue with their colleagues: when royal envoys came to Convocation to ask for a subsidy in 1417, they were led by the chancellor, Thomas Langley, bishop of Durham. His colleague Archbishop Chichele responded that the whole clergy were obliged to pray for the king, in return for the innumerable benefits he brought them.[58]

He might have added that Henry V had appointed both him and Langley for their service to him. For this example also shows the balance of power shifting towards firmer royal control. This process took

---

[58] *Register of Henry Chichele*, ed. Jacob (1937–47), vol. III, p. 40.

different paths in France and England, where royal control was well-established earlier; but the fact that the conflicts of the 1290s and 1300s in both countries witnessed the last ecclesiastical attempts to stand up for the high-medieval conception of autonomy and liberty at a national or supra-national level is in itself significant. It is not that there were no subsequent tensions or negotiations, notably and endemically over taxation and jurisdiction; but in both these spheres the ultimate sovereignty of the king was increasingly accepted, as we have seen with the cooperation of the English clergy in taxing themselves for the king. The writ of prohibition had always given a strong tool to those wishing to avoid or limit the church courts in England. *Praemunire* now added a stronger measure, and it was increasingly in use from the mid fifteenth century until it took a leading role against the clergy as a whole at the Reformation.

The moment of division is less easily identified in France, but it can be seen here, too. The *Parlement*, half of whose membership had always been made up of 'clerical counsellors' who could judge according to canon law, took over a growing number of cases at the end of the Middle Ages which had previously fallen under the jurisdiction of ecclesiastical courts.[59] Many procedural principles which derived from a broad conception of royal sovereignty – 'privileged cases' (*cas privilégiés*), that is, cases reserved to the competence of royal judges; or 'appeals as abuse' (*appels comme d'abus*) for cases where ecclesiastical justice did not seem to satisfy the demands of public order – made it possible to transfer out of church courts – as well as out of seigneurial courts – matters which they would traditionally have judged. The 'Gallicanism' of the fifteenth century, which began with the brief 'withdrawal of obedience' of 1398–1403 and 1408–9 and was systematised with the Pragmatic Sanction of Bourges (1438),[60] even if the latter was only partly applied before the concordat of Bologna (1516), also reduced appeals to Rome, and royal courts now regularly intervened in litigation over benefices.[61]

Royal control was manifested above all in the sphere of appointments. In England the king had long controlled episcopal appointments by instructing chapters who to elect; from the mid fourteenth century he instead told the pope who to provide, a procedure in which his arm was strengthened by anti-clerical pressure from parliament which led to the Statute of Provisors, enacted in 1351 on the basis of a 1307 petition and again in the 1360s and 1390s. By the latter decade, the Schism had also strengthened the arm of kings against popes who desperately needed their support. Richard II was able to exploit the Schism to secure from Boniface IX not only an end to provisions but also a recognition

---

[59] Royer (1969).   [60] Valois (1906).   [61] Gazzaniga (1976).

of the king's complete control over episcopal appointments, a concordat nullified in the event by the king's deposition.[62] The post-Schism papacy was equally unable to reassert papal authority in the matter of provisions, Martin V failing to make headway against either the firm government of Henry V or the minority council of his son.

In the kingdom of France, in the fourteenth century, the Avignon popes largely controlled the major benefices, even if the king often had his say in favour of his protégés, especially in the case of 'royal bishoprics' and 'royal abbeys'. As in England, it was the Great Schism which brought matters to a head, at least from 1398 onwards, by promoting the slide towards a truly national church, an *Ecclesia Gallicana*, headed by the king, at least in temporal matters. In any event, fifteenth-century France, in contrast to England, did not experience any great heretical movement which might have worried the powers that be and inspired their direct intervention in spiritual matters. Theoretically, under the Gallican regime, canons and monks recovered their liberty to elect bishops and abbots and still in 1438, the Pragmatic Sanction officially confirmed the return to the 'liberties of the Gallican Church'. In practice, however, and especially as the victorious outcome of the Hundred Years War reinforced his authority and prestige, the king involved himself more and more in episcopal and abbatial elections, with the dual aim of placing his close counsellors (or their relatives) and of ensuring the political docility of the high clergy. Most often, the king succeeded in imposing his candidate on the electors, although when the latter showed too much ill-will he might even prefer, in spite of his own ordinances, to negotiate the appointment of loyal prelates with popes weakened by the conciliar crisis and its aftermath.[63]

The very negotiations between different parties during the Schism and councils highlight the problem of diversity in the church, with its many different orders and interests pulling in different directions and often involved in disputes over property or jurisdiction. In principle, it was the pope who had the ultimate authority to resolve these tensions; but the king was increasingly fulfilling this role not only in practice – as the only ruler with the actual power to solve disputes – but also in theory. This is also seen in the increasing assumption of responsibility by kings for ecclesiastical reform (which was partly a matter of adjudicating between different ideas and interests within the church), both in their response to the Schism and councils, and in taking initiatives locally. French kings, notably Louis XI, sponsored religious houses of observant orders,[64] while Henry V summoned the Benedictines to a reform council in an attempt

---

[62] Perroy (1933).   [63] For numerous examples, see Julerot (2006).
[64] Le Gall (2001).

to return them to their fundamental function of providing constant prayer for king and realm. Henry VII followed up his example, taking an interest in monastic reform in general and the Observant Franciscans in particular. Church leaders were only able to attempt reform when they held both ecclesiastical and royal authority, as did, for example, Morton and Wolsey as both archbishop or legate and chancellor. Yet the irony is that neither made much headway with reform because they were too busy running government; and in Wolsey's case, he fell when royal support was withdrawn, before he could put his reforming schemes into practice.

The extent of royal control was such, therefore, that the church needed royal cooperation and support in order to function at all. Both Edward I and Philip IV had demonstrated where the clergy stood without the benefits of royal rule and law, and occasional further demonstrations of royal power were a reminder of the king's temporal control (such as in England in 1372 when Edward III seized bishops' temporalities to force them to disgorge taxation). More positively, the clergy repeatedly emphasised that the king was protector of the church, not least against its enemies. These might range from excommunicates whose cooperation in legal procedures the church needed royal officers to enforce, to the pope himself, whose demands for benefices or taxation could be fended off by appealing to the king (as the English convocation successfully did in 1464). The king was also the church's champion against heretics, who appeared in England for the first time in the 1370s in the form of Wyclif and his followers. The secular arm was deployed in opposition to them, above all in the statute *De heretico comburendo* of 1401 and in putting down the 1414 rebellion. It was said to be the role of Christian princes to care for the unity and prosperity of the church, and to defend the faith.[65] Once again, as in the matter of reform, we see the king's control over the church extending to its core spiritual function. Ultimately, the clergy served the king because their churches were inextricably and increasingly entwined with royal power, to the extent that they were beginning to be understood not as a separate order of society, but as arms of royal governance.

We might therefore speak legitimately of a reflex of service to the state amongst these churchmen and *gens de savoir*, but only if we are careful about what we mean by this: service to the prince to serve truth and justice; service to the prince to serve God; service to the prince to restore the church to her former liberty and dignity. The example of Jean Jouvenal des Ursins (1388–1473), archbishop of Rheims, brother of the Chancellor of France, himself a counsellor of King Charles VII at the same time as he was a passionate advocate of the 'liberties of the

---

[65] Bekynton (1872), vol. I, p. 135, vol. II, pp. 43–4, 56, 79, 84–5, 88, 93, 95, 96–7, 101.

Gallican Church',[66] shows how some sincere prelates were able, despite the Gospel precept, to agree to 'serve two masters' without a betrayal of their religious vocation. Similarly, the chancellor–archbishops under the early Tudors in England served the king while also upholding the rights and liberties of the church. More broadly, there is no doubt that this convergence of ideals was fundamental to the late medieval development of the 'modern state' and its governmental practices at the end of the Middle Ages.

Conclusions

In assessing the contribution of clerks, clergy, the church and graduates to governance in late medieval France and England, one is first struck by the kaleidoscopic and unstable nature of these terms and the identities which they denoted, which makes it difficult to judge with any assurance some of the developments under review, or to be confident in comparisons between the two realms. Nevertheless, some of these developments and contrasts do stand out, beyond the obvious ones of circumstance which run through this volume, such as the different experiences of the Hundred Years War, the disruptions of the Wars of the Roses in England, and the presence of the common law there. That, before this period, England both established a literate governmental culture and subjected the church to royal control earlier is partly an index of the greater power of the English Crown over its realm. Thus the civil-servant bishop, appointed to his diocese as a reward for royal service and in expectation of more, was a standard figure in fourteenth-century England before that was true in France, whilst on the other hand, churchmen of noble extraction always occupied fewer episcopal sees in England, although this may be partly a function of the different definition of nobility on either side of the Channel. That England added no new universities to Oxford and Cambridge to match their princely proliferation in France, but only colleges to perpetuate this type of clerical servant, further attests to comparative centralisation. Nevertheless, the fact that by the later fifteenth century both educational systems were producing graduates to serve the king or a royally controlled church indicates that France had caught up, with its establishment of a powerful monarchy in the wake of the Schism and councils and of the war.

Both realms witnessed the same apparently contradictory developments, albeit with local nuances. On the one hand, the king's control of the church was increasingly firm, even if Gallicanism in France was

---

[66] *Écrits politiques*, ed. Lewis, vol. III (1992), pp. 133–52.

newer than the unbroken English tradition going back to the period of papal reform itself. Concomitantly the ethos of ecclesiastical autonomy gave way to an ethic of service[67] which not only made a virtue of service to government (royal as well as non-royal), but also began to understand the church's core spiritual function as part of the work of regulating society which was par excellence the role of the prince, just as the king's role extended to aiding clerics with their responsibility for souls. On the other hand, while the king continued to use graduates in ever-greater numbers, the process of laicisation by which clerks and even graduates could increasingly choose to remain laymen meant that he did not have to rely so fully on churchmen for his clerical staff, with a potential loss of the church's influence in government. While in France this pattern evolved gradually towards the formation of the early modern absolutist state, in England there was a more abrupt end to a process which had been going on at lower levels for a century and a half with the replacement of clerical ministers by common lawyers in the 1530s. Perhaps paradoxically, this exclusion might have enabled the church to revert to a more separate, spiritual function and identity, funded by benefices no longer in so much demand from royal servants. Instead of being an essential resource of administrative skill to the state, the clergy might have been able to resume a more high-medieval notion of autonomy, a possibility suggested by the increasing clamour for clerical reform in terms of disentanglement from secular mores and public office.

The resolution of this paradox lies in the perception of the church's functions as part of the work of governance, albeit a separate part. Royal control could not be undone, even if anyone had wanted to do so; the process of nationalisation of churches had proceeded too far by the early sixteenth century. So the church increasingly performed its duties under royal aegis, but with a changing relationship to the secular structures of power. The paths of graduates and clergy thus began to diverge, with educated graduates serving the king increasingly as laymen (and even in England common lawyers started to have degrees as well as their non-university legal training), and the clergy doing so by fulfilling their ecclesiastical functions. Yet both made their contribution to the growing power, even absolutism, of the early modern state. The apparently dramatic divergence of the 1530s does in part signal a difference in structures between the two kingdoms, in that the availability of common lawyers provided an alternative source of expertise in England (just as the common law was to provide the brake on English absolutism). Yet France experienced in practice much of what was made explicit in England: the

---

[67] On this notion see, for example, Lachaud (2010); Thompson (2004).

formal subjection of the church to royal headship, the conception of its spiritual function as part of the work of governance and the deployment of concepts developed by clergy and graduates in the exaltation of the state and the prince.

BIBLIOGRAPHY

1. INTRODUCTION

Autrand, F., 1994. *Charles V le Sage,* Paris.

Bernard, G. W., 2012. *The Late Medieval English Church: Vitality and Vulnerability before the Break with Rome,* New Haven and London.

Gunn, S. J., 1995. *Early Tudor Government, 1485–1558,* Basingstoke.

Harper-Bill, C., 1989. *The Pre-Reformation Church in England, 1400–1530,* Harlow.

Heath, P., 1988. *Church and Realm, 1272–1461: Conflict and Collaboration in an Age of Crises,* London.

Krynen, J., 1993. *L'empire du roi. Idées et croyances politiques en France, xiiie–xve siècle,* Paris.

Lachaud, F., 2010. *L'Éthique du pouvoir au Moyen Âge. L'office dans la culture politique (Angleterre, vers 1150–vers 1350),* Paris.

Swanson, R. N., 1989. *Church and Society in Late Medieval England,* Oxford.

Thompson, Benjamin, 2004. 'Prelates and Politics from Winchelsey to Warham', in L. Clark and C. Carpenter (eds.), *The Fifteenth Century, IV, Political Culture in Late Medieval Britain,* Woodbridge, pp. 69–95.

Tout, T. F., 1920–33. *Chapters in the Administrative History of Medieval England,* 6 vols., Manchester.

Verger, J., 1997. *Les gens de savoir en Europe à la fin du Moyen Âge,* Paris.

2. SOURCES CITED

Bekynton, Thomas, *Official Correspondence,* ed. G. Williams. 2 vols., Rolls Series, London, 1872.

Calendar of Close Rolls, 1500–1509, ed. R. A. Latham, London, 1963.

Chronique du Religieux de Saint-Denys contenant le règne de Charles VI de 1380 à 1422, ed. and trans. L. Bellaguet, 6 vols., Paris, 1839 (repr. Paris, 1994).

Concilia Magnae Britanniae et Hiberniae, a Synodo Verolamiensi A.D. CCCC XLVI. ad Londinensem A.D. M DCCXVII, ed. D. Wilkins, 6 vols., London, 1737.

Disputatio inter militem et clericum, ed. N. N. Erickson in *Proceedings of the American Philosophical Society,* 111, 1967, 288–309.

Écrits politiques de Jean Juvénal des Ursins, ed. P. S. Lewis, 3 vols., Paris, 1978–92.

de Paris, Geoffroy, *Chronique métrique,* ed. A. Diverrès, Strasbourg, 1956.

The Parliament Rolls of Medieval England (PROME) ed. C. Given-Wilson et al., CD-Rom, Leicester, 2005.

Register of Henry Chichele, Archbishop of Canterbury, 1414–1443, ed. E. F. Jacob, 4 vols., Oxford, 1937–47.

Registres de Boniface VIII, ed. G. Digard, M. Faucon and A. Thomas, 4 vols., Paris, 1907–21.

Registrum Thome Bourgchier, Cantuariensis Archiepiscopi, A.D. 1454–1486, ed. F. R. H. Du Boulay, Canterbury and York Society, 54, Oxford, 1957.

Le Songe du Vergier, ed. M. Schnerb-Lièvre, 2 vols., Paris, 1982.

Statutes of the Colleges of Oxford, 3 vols., Oxford, 1853.

Statuts et privilèges des universités françaises depuis leur fondation jusqu'en 1789, ed. M. Fournier, 4 vols., Paris, 1890–4.

Trevisa, John, *Dialogus inter Militem et Clericum*, ed. A. J. Perry, Early English Text Society, old series 167, London, 1925.

3. FURTHER READING

Autrand, F., 1973. 'Culture et mentalité. Les librairies des gens du Parlement au temps de Charles VI', *Annales ESC*, 28, 1219–44.

1989. 'De l'Enfer au Purgatoire: la cour à travers quelques textes français du milieu du xive à la fin du xve siècle', in P. Contamine (ed.), *L'État et les aristocraties (France, Angleterre, Écosse), xiie–xviie siècles*, Paris, pp. 51–78.

Baldwin, J. W., 1976. 'Studium et Regnum. The Penetration of University Personnel into French and English Administration at the Turn of the Twelfth and Thirteenth Centuries', *Revue des études islamiques*, 44, 199–215.

Bartier, J., 1955–7. *Légistes et gens de finances au xve siècle. Les conseillers des ducs de Bourgogne sous Philippe le Bon et Charles le Téméraire*. 2 vols., Bruxelles.

Catto, J. I., 1985. 'Religious Change under Henry V', in G. L. Harriss (ed.), *Henry V: The Practice of Kingship*, Oxford, pp. 97–115.

2000. 'Masters, Patrons and the Careers of Graduates in Fifteenth-Century England', in A. Curry & E. Matthew (eds.), *Concepts and Patterns of Service in the Later Middle Ages*, Woodbridge, pp. 52–63.

(ed.), 1984. *History of the University of Oxford: I: The Early Oxford Schools*, Oxford.

Catto, J. I. and Evans, R. (eds.), 1992. *History of the University of Oxford: II: Late Medieval Oxford*, Oxford.

Clanchy, Michael, 2013. *From Memory to Written Record*, 3rd edn, Oxford.

Cohn, S. K., 2006. *Lust for Liberty. The Politics of Social Revolts in Medieval Europe, 1200–1450*, Cambridge, MA and London.

Colvin, H. M. (ed.), 1963–82. *The History of the King's Works*, 5 vols., London.

Contamine, P., 1997. *La noblesse au royaume de France de Philippe le Bel à Louis XII. Essai de synthèse*, Paris.

Davis, V., 2007. *William Wykeham*, London.

Denton, J. H., 1980. *Robert Winchelsey and the Crown, 1294–1313: a Study in the Defence of Ecclesiastical Liberty*, Cambridge.

Dodd, G., 2007. *Justice and Grace: Private Petitioning and the English Parliament in the Late Middle Ages*, Oxford.

Douie, D. L., 1952. *Archbishop Pecham*, Oxford.

Fabris, C., 2005. *Étudier et vivre à Paris au Moyen Âge. le collège de Laon (xive–xve siècles)*, Paris.

Forrest, I., 2005. *The Detection of Heresy in Late Medieval England*, Oxford.

Fryde, E. B. (ed.), 1996. *Handbook of British Chronology*, 3rd edn, London.

Gaussin, P.-R., 1976. *Louis XI. Un roi entre deux mondes*, Paris.

1982. 'Les conseillers de Charles VII (1418–1461). Essai de politologie historique', *Francia*, 10, 67–130.

Gazzaniga, J.-L., 1976. *L'Église du Midi à la fin du règne de Charles VII (1444–1461) d'après la jurisprudence du Parlement de Toulouse*, Paris.

1992. 'Les clercs au service de l'État dans la France du xve siècle à la lecture de travaux récents', in J. Krynen and A. Rigaudière (eds.), *Droits savants et pratiques françaises du pouvoir (xie–xve siècles)*, Bordeaux, pp. 253–78.

Gorochov, N., 1997. *Le collège de Navarre de sa fondation (1305) au début du xve siècle (1418). Histoire de l'institution, de sa vie intellectuelle et de son recrutement*, Paris.

Guenée, B., 1966. *Tribunaux et gens de justice dans le bailliage de Senlis à la fin du Moyen Âge (vers 1380–vers 1550)*, Strasbourg.

1991. *L'Occident aux xive et xve siècles. Les États*, Paris.

Julerot, V., 2006. *'Y a ung grant desordre'. Élections épiscopales et schismes diocésains en France sous Charles VIII*, Paris.

Kerhervé, J., 1987. *L'État breton aux xive et xve siècles. Les ducs, l'argent et les hommes*, 2 vols., Paris.

Kouamé, T., 2005. *Le collège de Dormans-Beauvais à la fin du Moyen Âge. Stratégies politiques et parcours individuels à l'Université de Paris (1370–1458)*, Leiden and Boston.

Krynen, J., 1988. '"De nostre certaine science . . . ". Remarques sur l'absolutisme législatif de la monarchie médiévale française', in A. Gouron and A. Rigaudière (eds.), *Renaissance du pouvoir législatif et genèse de l'État*, Montpellier, pp. 131–44.

1991. 'Les légistes, "idiots politiques". Sur l'hostilité des théologiens à l'égard des juristes en France, au temps de Charles V', in *Théologie et droit dans la science politique de l'État moderne: actes de la table ronde organisée par l'École française de Rome avec le concours du CNRS, Rome le 12–14 novembre 1987*, Rome, pp. 171–98.

1992. 'Les légistes, "tyrans de la France"? Le témoignage de Jean Juvénal des Ursins, docteur *in utroque*', in J. Krynen and A. Rigaudière (eds.), *Droits savants et pratiques françaises du pouvoir (xie–xve siècles)*, Bordeaux, pp. 279–99.

Lalou, E. 1992. 'Les chanoines au service de Philippe le Bel, 1285–1314', in H. Millet, (ed.), *I canonici al servizio dello Stato in Europa, secoli xiii–xvi / Les chanoines au service de l'État en Europe du xiiie au xvie siècle*, Modène-Ferrare, pp. 219–30.

Le Gall, J.-M., 2001. *Les moines au temps des réformes, France, 1450–1560*, Seyssel.

Offenstadt, N., 2007. *Faire la paix au Moyen Âge. Discours et gestes de paix pendant la guerre de Cent Ans*, Paris.

Perroy, E., 1933. *L'Angleterre et le Grand Schisme d'Occident: étude sur la politique religieuse de l'Angleterre*, Paris.

Piltz, A., 1981. *The World of Medieval Learning* (Engl. trans.), Oxford.

Rashdall, H., 1936. *The Universities of Europe in the Middle Ages*, new edn F. M. Powicke and A. B. Emden, 3 vols., London.

Ridder-Symoens, H. de, 2007. 'Les matricules universitaires et le statut des clercs à l'université médiévale et seiziémiste', in *Université, Église, Culture. L'université catholique au Moyen Âge*, Paris, pp. 321–43.

Rigaudière, A., 1988. 'Législation royale et construction de l'État dans la France du xiiie siècle', in A. Gouron and A. Rigaudière (eds.), *Renaissance du pouvoir législatif et genèse de l'État*, Montpellier, pp. 203–36.

Roach, J. P. C. ed., *Victoria County History, Cambridge*, vol. III, London, 1959.

Roy, L., 2006. *L'université de Caen aux xve et xvie siècles. Identité et représentations*, Leiden and Boston.

Royer, J.-P., 1969. *Paris, L'Église et le royaume de France au xive siècle, d'après le 'Songe du Vergier' et la jurisprudence du Parlement*, Paris.

Rutledge, E., 2005. 'Lawyers and Administrators: The Clerks of Late Thirteenth-Century Norwich', in C. Harper-Bill (ed.), *Medieval East Anglia*, Woodbridge, pp. 83–98.

Salter, H. E. and Lobel, M. D., eds., *Victoria County History, Oxford*, vol. III, London, 1959.

Saul, N., 1995. 'Richard II's Vocabulary of Kingship', *English Historical Review*, 110, 854–77.

Storey, R. L., 1982. 'Gentleman-Bureaucrats', in C. H. Clough (ed.), *Profession, Vocation, and Culture in Later Medieval England*, Liverpool, 97–109.

Strayer, J. R., 1970. *Les gens de justice de Languedoc sous Philippe le Bel*, Toulouse.

Tabbagh, V., 2006. 'Les évêques du royaume de France en 1438', in V. Tabbagh, (ed.), *Gens d'Église, gens de pouvoir (France, XIIIe–XVe siècle)*, Dijon, pp. 87–186.

Thomson, J. A. F., 1989. 'Orthodox Religion and the Origins of Lollardy', *History*, 74, 39–55.

Valois N., 1906. *Histoire de la Pragmatique Sanction de Bourges sous Charles VII*, Paris.

Verger, J., 1990. 'Études et culture universitaires du personnel de la curie avignonnaise', in *Aux origines de l'État moderne. Le fonctionnement administratif de la papauté d'Avignon*, Rome, pp. 61–78.

1997. *Les gens de savoir en Europe à la fin du Moyen Âge*, Paris.

1998. 'Les universités françaises de la fin du Moyen Âge ont-elles été des "petites universités"?', in G. P. Brizzi and J. Verger (eds.), *Le Università minori in Europa (secoli xv–xix)*, Soveria Manelli, pp. 13–28.

2011. 'Les serviteurs de l'État au début du xiiie siècle (France et royaumes voisins): gens de savoir ou hommes d'expérience ?', in *1212–1214: El trienio que hizo a Europa. XXXVII Semana de estudios medievales, Estella, 19 a 23 de Julio de 2010*, Pamplona, pp. 389–402.

Viala, A., 1953. *Le Parlement de Toulouse et l'administration royale laïque, 1420–1525 environ*, 2 vols., Albi.

Walker, S., 1995. 'Richard II's Views on Kingship', in R. E. Archer and S. Walker (eds.), *Rulers and Ruled in Late Medieval England: Essays Presented to Gerald Harriss*, London and Rio Grande, pp. 49–63.

8   Political representation

Christopher Fletcher

Any discussion of political representation in late medieval Europe must contend with the many different ways in which rulers interacted with a variety of overlapping social structures to exercise power on the ground level of politics.[1] It would be wrong to focus exclusively on those institutions which present a reassuring formality when analysing the multiple dialogues in multiple spheres which historians now consider to be part of late medieval political culture. As a result, any discussion focused on formal mechanisms of political representation, despite renewed interest in these matters in recent years, still risks seeming rather dated.[2] Much of the rest of the present volume is made up of studies which consider modes of ruling and being ruled beyond those embodied in late medieval representative institutions which could nonetheless be thought of as modes of representation. The process of petitioning, for example, both enabled the ruled to impress their desires on the centre and to mobilise its authority,

This article emerges from an ongoing collaboration with Neithard Bulst which had initially been intended to produce a collaborative article. Unfortunately, administrative and other commitments finally made such an enterprise impossible. I remain in debt to the remarks of Professor Bulst on earlier drafts of this paper, and for the opportunity to present it at Bielefeld in 2005.

[1] For a survey, see Watts (2009).

[2] The present article was developed between 2003 and 2007. During this time the study of the English parliament enjoyed a remarkable renaissance. This was thanks in part to the completion of archival projects, notably the new electronic edition of the Rolls of Parliament and the cataloguing of the Ancient Petitions class (SC 8) in The National Archive (TNA). On these developments, see Clark 2004; *Parliament Rolls of Medieval England* (*PROME*), ed. Given-Wilson et al. (2005); Dodd 2007; Ormrod, Dodd and Musson (2009). A more literary approach to parliamentary forms also flourished in this period, for which see Scace (2007); Giancarlo (2007); Oliver (2010). More recently still, renewed interest has been focused on estates mechanisms within France (see e.g. Hébert (2014)). As a result, it now seems all the more useful to present a series of reflections which were formed independently of these developments, and which consider the specific role of representation in England and France in its late medieval social and political context, aside from the question of the origins of later institutions.

just as it allowed the centre to inform itself and to ensure the more efficient exercise of that authority. Everything from royal office-holding, to legal mechanisms to the use of loyal language by communities in revolt, to the noble affinity are all, in their way, forms of political representation. They provided a zone in which common ground and common goods were negotiated between central authority and local power. The present article will nonetheless focus on formal modes of representation current in England and France between the late thirteenth and the early sixteenth centuries, to ask what there was about these forms of interaction between ruler and ruled which distinguished them from other modes of governing and being governed. In the process it will try out once again an exercise popular between the mid nineteenth and mid twentieth century, although somewhat fallen out of fashion in recent times.[3] It will compare the representative institutions of these two kingdoms and consider whether there was already something which set them apart from one another in the fourteenth and fifteenth centuries which would become clearer in the sixteenth and seventeenth centuries. It is hoped that, aided by the researches of historians undertaken since this exercise fell into desuetude, it will be possible to bring about a slightly different outcome from earlier essays on the subject.

1.   Historiography

When English and French modes of political representation were contrasted in the fifties and early sixties by writers such as R. Fawtier (1953) and A. R. Myers (1961), it was the Estates General which presented itself for study as a kind of parliament *manqué*, an institution which somehow, unaware of its destiny, failed to develop along the same lines as English parliamentary institutions. Reasons had to be found for the failure to produce a single institution which united representatives from across the country to negotiate with the king over taxation, to submit their common grievances against the royal government, and to petition the king's officers to legislate binding solutions to these problems. Objections were soon raised to this mode of proceeding. For Peter Lewis (1962), it was by no means clear that the towns and localities of late medieval France had any interest in bowing to the king's demands to organise themselves into readily consultable bodies, the better to be taxed. Informal means of approach, the use of paid agents, or the procurement of the favours of

---

[3] Maddicott (2010), Chapter 7 is concerned with demonstrating the unusualness of English mechanisms, especially with regards to France, which is a different exercise from comparing their role in politics and government in these two kingdoms.

those with access to court, provided a much more promising means for the *bonnes villes* of France to get their way, as the work not only of Lewis (e.g. 1981, 1995) but also of Bernard Chevalier (e.g. 1984) and, more recently, Graeme Small (2000) has shown. Why focus on institutions just because they looked like the English example? French communities had other ways of representing themselves to the king, and the king of representing himself to them.

Around the same time as these criticisms were made, further reasons to reconsider the traditional contrast between these two kingdoms were emerging from a renewed questioning of the nature of the English parliament. The nature of the 'representation' of the Commons in parliament had seemed clear to nineteenth-century writers: the Commons were the people, the third estate, standing in their name against the encroachments of royal authority. In the mid twentieth century, this view took a battering from the work of those who styled themselves as the debunkers of Whiggish myths. For H. G. Richardson and G. O. Sayles,[4] who concentrated on the development of the judicial role of parliament, the Commons were of little importance, and certainly of no 'political' significance. The focus of attention on their 'representative' role was misleading, the consequence of the nineteenth-century regurgitation of seventeenth-century controversies. What was important was the influence of the lords and the authority of the king.

Yet still, even after the work of Richardson and Sayles, it remained clear that there was something special about certain institutions which set them apart from other mechanisms of political representation. Between the thirteenth and the sixteenth centuries, across Europe, experiments were made with a number of more or less successful institutions which were 'representative' in a more overt way; that is, they enabled political activity by crediting a few with the right to 'represent', like a modern advocate in court, certain far larger groups. The legal underpinning of these developments had been considered in detail by Gaynes Post (1964), their deeper roots in medieval ways of thinking about kings and communities were now investigated by Susan Reynolds (1984). Writers with their eye on early modern developments, such as H. G. Koenigsburger (1977) or more recently Neithard Bulst (1996), still asked themselves whether there was something in late medieval institutional forms which finally enabled some representative bodies to abolish their monarch, whilst elsewhere kings and princes could safely ignore them.

---

[4] Richardson and Sayles (1927–8), (1928–9), (1930–1), (1931–2); Richardson (1946); Sayles (1975).

Even as Richardson and Sayles applied themselves with enthusiasm to the destruction of older models, other writers concerned with the English case produced contradictory arguments and evidence which they never fully addressed. The work of K. B. McFarlane (1944) and J. S. Roskell (e.g. 1951, 1964, 1965) drew attention to the importance of individual members of the Commons in local society. Since then, the continuing researches of the History of Parliament[5] have shown how, collectively and individually, the Commons undoubtedly carried weight as prominent members of county communities, experienced soldiers, royal and seigniorial officials, and urban oligarchs. Knights of the shire had often served in county office as sheriffs, escheators, justices of the peace or tax collectors.[6] Nearly half those present in the parliament of 1422 had served in France under Henry V.[7] It would be wrong to overstress the importance of the links between the Commons and the lords evidenced by retaining or office-holding. Their independent standing in county communities made the Commons quite capable of acting independently, both as individuals and collectively. Until 1421, at least, professional lawyers amongst the Commons, although a significant presence, were far from numerically dominant.[8] As royal and seigniorial officials, local gentry carried the weight of that class of men in collectively considering abuses by those who held similar positions in local society across the kingdom without becoming a subservient caste of royal or baronial *cadres*.

In the same year that G. O. Sayles argued that the Commons were no more than a conduit for petitions to the king, G. L. Harriss published his magisterial study of the development of the Commons' role in public finance up to 1369, how under Edward I, II and III it was established that the knights and burgesses, had to be consulted for grants of exceptional taxation.[9] In later years, the desire to diminish the significance of the Commons in parliament ran up against growing evidence of the importance of 'county communities' and the values of the locality in the government of the realm.[10] The gentry of the shires, from whose ranks the knights of the shire (and increasingly those of the boroughs) were taken, were also the foremost 'representatives' of the king in the localities, in their capacity as royal office-holders. As the king's men in the counties, they stood to gain by seeing the royal will put into action with themselves as its agents. As landowners, they had an overriding interest in the good operation of royal justice. It has become difficult to believe

---

[5] See Roskell (1993).   [6] See for example Brown (1981), p. 119.
[7] Roskell (1954), p. 94.   [8] Clark (1993).   [9] Harriss (1975).
[10] Discussed by Maddicott (1978).

that they were as irrelevant to politics at the centre as Richardson and Sayles suggested. Few would now see the knights and burgesses in the English parliament as fledgling democrats. Certainly, they had interests in common with the king, and certainly they had multiple relationships with the lords of mutual advantage and reciprocal influence. But was there perhaps still some value in seeing negotiations over taxation and legislation as a struggle between the Commons and the king?

The tension between 'Whig' and 'Tory' interpretations of late medieval political representation has taken a less violent form in post-war writing on medieval France. Perhaps the nature of the evidence encouraged a more gradual shift as research, into both representative institutions per se and the development of taxation in general, began to fill in the gaps in the complex picture of French medieval representation. The work of Joseph Strayer, Charles Taylor and Elizabeth Brown traced out the outlines of early experiments with representative assemblies under Philip IV and his sons. The monographs of J. B. Henneman illuminated their revival in the 1340s and 1350s during the first crisis of the Hundred Years War. That of Maurice Rey drew the story on to the second major crisis of the early fifteenth century, whilst Russell Major made use of his own and earlier French research to strike his way through the multiplicity of representative institutions which characterised the reigns of Charles VII and Louis XI, and on into the sixteenth century. More recently, Neithard Bulst (1984), (1988) has built on this work by approaching the Estates General of 1468 and 1484 through a prosopographical method similar to those working on English institutions. The reasons why French representative institutions have proved so difficult to handle have emerged more clearly from the labours of historians, which have underlined both their multiplicity of form and their concentration in certain limited periods. Perhaps most importantly, it remains clear that an exclusive focus on 'Estates General', that is to say estates bringing together the entire kingdom, would be misguided, since such gatherings were rare next to assemblies of, say, parts of the Languedoïl, or of the Languedoc, Burgundy, Brittany or the Dauphiné, or even in smaller regions.[11] A fuller story has to be told of multiple representative institutions with which the king and other princes consulted in order to raise tax, and to gain support for his policies.

With this material to hand, it would now be possible to undertake a more precise comparison of English and French representative institutions than was possible fifty years ago. In the present article, however, I do not propose to attempt a point-by-point comparison of what are

---

[11] Considered recently in Hébert (2014).

anyway multiple and changing institutions. Instead, I would like to focus on one central problem: namely the senses in which these institutions might be thought to be 'representative'. To do so, it is important to work out precisely what it is that we are interested in, since 'representation' is one of those terms of multiple meanings whose relationship to one another is not always clear. We might choose to define representation as something along the lines of: 'the matter of speaking for and/or standing in for others within the political process'.[12] It can be seen that this definition of representation already contains two things at once. Speaking for somebody, like a modern advocate in court, is not necessarily the same as standing in for somebody, or doing what you would imagine they would do in similar circumstances, like a proxy vote in a modern election. Jeannine Quillet (1988), speaking of the development of the political theory of medieval representation makes a further useful refinement which in some ways corresponds to this initial distinction. On the one hand she identifies a majoritarian form of representation, in which a represented group is taken as an organic body having a single will, which can then be passed on to a single individual. On the other, she distinguishes a form of representation based on unanimity, in which the group represented is nothing but a collection of individuals, the consent of all of whom must still be considered, in accordance with the tag 'What touches all must be approved by all.'

2.   The development of . . . what kind of representation?

In England, the reigns of the three Edwards saw the gradual victory of the majoritarian, 'speaking for somebody' relationship, as the recourse to 'speaking as instructed' was slowly undermined. At first, this was done entirely to the advantage of the king, binding communities to accept what had been agreed, especially concerning taxation, by their appointed representatives. It was in Edward I's reign that it was established in parliamentary writs of summons that knights of the shire and burgesses ought to be sent with *plena potestas* (full power) to bind their community to any decision made in parliament.[13] Although in 1339, the Commons could still argue that they needed to consult again with their communities before consenting to the king's demands, suggesting that they felt they had only a limited mandate to 'speak for' those they represented, this

---

[12] A useful definition suggested by R. Horrox, informal paper, July 2003.
[13] Post (1964); Edwards (1934).

seems to have been the last gasp of such a 'unanimatarian' argument.[14] The development of a majoritarian form of representation established that the gentlemen and burgesses sitting in parliament could be taken by the king to speak for the whole kingdom without the tedious business of negotiating with each community individually. It made the establishment of a common good centred on the king's concerns all the easier, since it was this which was discussed in parliament, not whether or not such and such a policy was in the interests of Yorkshire, or Hertfordshire, or Devon.

The kings of France, by contrast, were rarely successful in getting representatives to acknowledge that they could act without reference back to their communities. This was not for want of trying. As early as 1302, Philip IV was asking for representatives to be sent with full powers to act for their communities.[15] In 1321, Philip V even went so far as to send out royal agents to brief communities of his intentions in advance, in the hope that this would persuade them to grant power to their deputies to act without returning home to consult.[16] In the end, however, the most kings of France were successful in obtaining from large assemblies of estates was preliminary agreement that there was a pressing necessity which obliged his subjects to grant him aid. It seems that, in such assemblies, the right to give consent was considered to be less important to all concerned than the duty to give counsel, and the king's duty to request it.[17] Counsel involved agreeing that an emergency existed and agreeing that something needed to be done. Consent primarily concerned how the subsidy was to be collected, and it was granted locally if it was felt necessary at all. Where large estates assemblies did make specific tax grants, as happened on a number of occasions in the 1340s and 1350s, these grants often proved impossible to collect, and the whole process had to be begun again on a local level.[18] Charles VII's early assemblies of the 1420s and 1430s, called in circumstances of acute military, political and financial crisis, were an exception to this general rule, and even then the actual details of how tax would be raised still had to be worked out with provincial assemblies, municipal councils and local lords.[19] In normal and even disturbed times, towns and provincial assemblies seem to have regarded

---

[14] Harriss (1963). Later protests by the Lancashire knights of the shire in the parliament of October 1491 (*PROME*, Oct. 1491; *Rotuli Parliamentorum*, ed. Strachey et al., 1767, vol. VI, pp. 456–7) that concessions concerning their county made in their absence were not binding do not contradict this. Such an argument could not have been advanced if the Lancashire knights had been present at the contested assembly of parliament.

[15] Post (1964), p. 110.   [16] Taylor (1968).

[17] Langmuir (1958), p. 28; Henneman (1971), p. 327.

[18] Henneman (1971), Chapter 6; Henneman (1976), Chapter 2.

[19] Major (1960), pp. 25–34.

larger gatherings with outright suspicion, as an occasion on which their liberties might be infringed by an individual representative subjected to bribery or intimidation or otherwise suborned.[20] The relative fiscal fortunes of regions which continued to be consulted in provincial estates, as opposed to those which lost such rights or never had them in the first place, would appear (on an anecdotal level, at least) to confirm such fears. The results of a tax inquiry under Charles VIII recorded that the *généralités* of the Languedoïl and Outre-Seine, where there were no provincial estates, paid the *taille* at between a third and a half of the per hearth rate current in Normandy and the Languedoc, where provincial estates continued to give their consent.[21]

From the late thirteenth century, communities in both England and France were subjected to pressure from their monarchs to return representatives with sufficient powers to bind these communities to what had been agreed – often a grant of taxation. It was clear that this exercise was supposed to work entirely in the king's favour. French communities were aware of this, and resisted such initiatives, often with considerable success. Writers who stress the legal aspects of these institutions thus tend to emphasise the extent to which the development of parliament as an institution in England was more of a victory for the king than for his subjects, more a means to impose his will upon them than a conduit by which they could present their grievances to the monarch. Yet if this is conceded, it nonetheless remains clear that even at an early stage, the Commons' acknowledged status as the representatives of their communities did lead them to attract a form of authority which had not formed part of the king's intentions, and which had the potential to work against his interests. The work of Harriss, Roskell and others, tied to the most cursory examination of the Rolls of Parliament, makes it clear that Sayles and Richardson overstepped the mark in minimising the importance of the Commons. The determination of Sayles, in particular, to explain away anything that confirmed the authority of the Commons makes one wonder why anybody bothered with the Commons in the first place. We are left wondering why the exclusive right to give consent to public taxation came to inhere in a body that was nothing more than a clearing house for petitions not resolvable at common law; or why the author of *Richard the Redeless* should exclaim upon the uselessness for their communities of members of parliament in 1397 who 'like a zero in arithmetic occupy a place but contribute nothing' unless it was expected that they

---

[20] Lewis (1962), esp. pp. 5, 8. Cf. the more general concerns of Tournai about the powers of embassies to the king. Small (2000), p. 159.
[21] Major (1960), p. 42.

would, indeed, contribute something.[22] It seems clear that there was more to the importance of parliament than its judicial status as described by the king's lawyers.

Nonetheless, Sayles and Richardson did have an important point which goes beyond their stress on the judicial functions and the king-centred nature of parliament. Their work rightly notes a matter that can be easily passed over, namely that although, in the records of the English parliament, the representatives of the late medieval Commons spoke in the name of the people, and indeed were referred to as if they simply were the people, this representativeness did not, at least in these documents, create an authority which might precede or overrule that of the king.[23] In the often vigorously contested debates of this period, the Commons did not claim superior authority in their arguments with the king and his officials because they represented the people's will. Indeed, there was often a certain ambiguity in their position, in which they both represented the Commons and excluded themselves from that body, sometimes petitioning that the 'people' were impoverished by labourers who asked for excessive wages,[24] sometimes asking for reform lest the commons who had just risen in revolt (and who were clearly not the Commons in parliament) should rebel once again.[25] To this extent, their formal position in some ways resembles that of French estates bodies, who were more concerned with their duty to give counsel, and the king's duty to demand it, than with a right to give consent.

3.   The consequences of representation

Of course, one should not go too far. In the first half of the fourteenth century, the English parliament in general and the Commons in particular had become a far more firmly established part of political life than would ever be the case for provincial or general estates assemblies in France. Regularity was the key. Forty-four assemblies, including both magnates and shire and borough representatives, took place in England between 1297 and 1337. Twenty-one of these assembled in the first decade of Edward III's reign, amounting to two a year. The closest parallel to this in France occurred in the early years of Charles VII's reign. Perhaps twenty-seven assemblies of the Estates of the Languedoïl, or

---

[22] 'Richard the Redeless' in *The Piers Plowman Tradition*, ed. Barr (1993), Passus IV, ll. 53–4.

[23] Sayles (1975), pp. 8–10.

[24] *PROME*, Feb. 1351, item 12; *Rotuli Parliamentorum*, ed. Strachey et al. (1767), vol. II, p. 227.

[25] Tuck (1984); Fletcher (2014).

of the western or eastern Languedoïl, or of the Estates General, met between May 1421 and April 1448.[26] Yet in this last case, a maximum of six of these might be identified as full Estates General. In England, far greater regularity at a far earlier stage enabled the Commons' role to mutate from that of semi-passive approvers of the king's actions, to active supporters of baronial calls for reform, to the primary voice calling for action themselves. Whilst this mutation was occurring, estates assemblies in France retained their role as essentially convenient communications devices to be deployed when the king was 'undertaking risky or unprecedented operations'.[27] Philip IV used large assemblies to justify his dispute with Boniface VIII, or his suppression of the Templars, or to explain why he intended to go to war with Flanders. Local assemblies were used to gain acceptance of the peace treaty in Flanders in 1305 and to ratify the annexation of Lyon in 1307. A number of assemblies of nobles and, less often, of towns, were summoned between 1295 and 1304 to discuss taxation. Experiments continued under Philip IV's sons. Yet after Philip V's failed attempt to raise money in peacetime in 1321 by securing the assent of a large assembly for specific reforms, no large central assembly was asked to consider tax until 1343. It was only in the late 1340s and 1350s that crisis circumstances saw the renewed use of large estates assemblies in response to the English threat. In the meantime, the Commons in parliament had been called to witness every major internal upheaval in England between the last years of Edward I, through the turbulent reign of his son, and on to the unsettled circumstances of Edward III's early reign. Parliament became the regular venue in which not only the king but also his opponents publicised and confirmed their actions in the most public venue possible, such that both the king and his enemies would (in theory at least) feel more bound by undertakings made in such solemn circumstances than at any other time. This role would flourish again during the renewed tensions over taxation, royal government and household expenditure which characterised the reigns of Richard II and Henry IV. In England, not only the king but also the king's subjects had found a way to make use of a body which represented the whole community of the kingdom. In France, by contrast, the king did not summon estates assemblies unless he felt the need of them, and when he did the good people of the *bonnes villes* became understandably concerned for the health of their purses. Both Charles V and Charles VII stopped summoning large assemblies once they no longer needed to do so, and their subjects do not seem to have been unduly put out by this development.

---

[26] Major (1960), pp. 151–2.   [27] Strayer (1981), p. 384.

Given the very different point which the English parliament had reached by the mid fourteenth century from relatively similar origins to the French estates some fifty years before, it might seem rather beside the point to insist upon the similar nature of the theoretical justification for the Commons' importance. Does it matter what the theoretical origins of the Commons' powers were if the limits of their actions were not determined by these ideas? In the end, if they in practice derived power and authority from their representativeness of the people which could be used in opposition to the king, what difference does it make if they did not quite portray it like that? Nonetheless, it is important to note that the failure to recognise how these ideas lent a certain form to contemporary political debate can still lead to some fundamental misreadings of the political discourse of late medieval England.

Take, for example, the controversies of one of the last parliaments of Edward III's reign, which met in 1376 and earned its name – the Good Parliament – through its vigorous assault on the king's ministers, royal financiers and certain prominent courtiers, including Edward's mistress, Alice Perrers. This assembly, above all others, might have been expected to promote the right of the Commons to intervene in central politics, witnessing as it did the emergence of their first Speaker, and the first occasion on which the Commons took the lead in demanding the reform of the kingdom. The proceedings began, as was by then well established, with an address by the chancellor, John Knyvet. After requesting funds for the king's wars, Knyvet went on, as was already the accepted form, to command the knights, burgesses 'and all the commons of the counties' to ask redress for any bad government taking place in the kingdom, and by their *bon avyse* and *conseil*, to ordain a remedy so that the kingdom might be more profitably governed 'to the honour of the king and the profit of the kingdom'.[28] It is perhaps not surprising to hear this loyal form, in which the Commons faithfully advise the king on how to cure the kingdom's ills, coming from the mouth of the king's most senior official. What is rather more telling is the way in which the Commons maintained the same terms in their own debates. In their deliberations on the following day, the Commons swore an oath to keep counsel on what was discussed and decided 'to faithfully treat and ordain for the profit of the kingdom without concealment'.[29] It was then declared that, 'if any one of us knows to say anything which is for the profit of the king and the kingdom' that it would be good to show what they knew, and that afterwards each one after the other could declare what lay at their heart. This loyal terminology – the profit of the kingdom, or the honour of the

[28] Galbraith (1927), p. 80.   [29] *Ibid.*, p. 81.

king and the profit of the kingdom, or the profit of the king and kingdom – was continued by Peter de la Mare when he assumed the role of Speaker. In his initial address to the Lords, requesting an intercommuning committee, he talked of the charge placed upon the Commons by the king 'to treat and ordain for the estate (*lestate*) of him and of the kingdom', and to amend faults insofar as they could. He went on to assert that they had noted many faults which 'it would be the profit of our lord the king and of the kingdom to be amended', and requested 'for the profit of the kingdom' an intercommuning committee to reinforce the Commons' limited knowledge.[30]

Even in the Good Parliament, and in their discussions amongst themselves, the Commons did not present themselves as an independent power, the embodiment of a community whose interests might correspond with or diverge from those of the king. Their role was to fulfil the charge placed upon them, that of determining how best money might be raised for the king's wars, and to report on any unresolved grievances which had not been settled at common law. Their charge was not, in formal terms, to give their opinion on what should be done, particularly not in the king's wars, but only to provide information on how this might be achieved. As representatives of the commons, the people or the kingdom, they at least claimed not to give their advice on policy; they were simply there to give information which would assist the king in the realisation of the profit of the kingdom. Their formal role, even in 1376, still seemed to be conceived of in a comparable fashion to that of the estates of France as discussed by Jean Gerson in his sermon *Vivat rex* (1405), in which it is clear that the nobles, clerks and burgesses were summoned for their concrete knowledge of the kingdom's difficulties, a reinforcement of the king's prudence in taking wide counsel, not because they had the right to refuse consent if they did not feel it would be in the interests of the communities they represented.[31] Although, by the end of Edward III's reign, the Commons in parliament had a far better established, accepted and regular position in the process of government than would ever be the case for estates assemblies in France, the ideological basis of this role had not yet diverged from what it had been at the end of the thirteenth century, and what it had remained in France: they were still in theory the occasional counsellors of the king, called in voluntarily to help him to make his own decisions on how to deal with particular problems in justice, war or the church.

This is not to say that the interests of the localities which they represented were to be put to one side. But such interests entered into debate

---

[30] *Ibid.*, p. 84.   [31] Quillet (1988), p. 549.

only in the second part of the chancellor's charge to the Commons, in the form of petitions for grace. In 1376, the first knight to speak in the Commons' debates began by mentioning the subsidies requested, before continuing that these would be 'difficult to grant', since 'the commons are enfeebled and impoverished by many tallages and taxes which they have paid before now so that they will not be able to support such a charge or pay it this time'.[32] Such an argument on its own, although it might be entered as a plea for clemency, did not exempt the community of the realm from coming to the king's aid. In the course of the wars of the late thirteenth and fourteenth century, it had been established that in case of necessity the king's subjects were obliged to come to his aid.[33] Arguments of impoverishment could not countermand this, but they could be lodged as appeals to grace. This was the form taken by petitions adopted by the Commons in the autumn of 1381 and in 1388 which asked for an end to war. The people were impoverished, so let it please the king and the lords to find some way of honourably bringing unnecessary conflicts to an end.[34] But if the government was intransigent, the Commons could not use their representative role to force through their opinions on policy. Although they had a right to refuse supply, they also had to have a legitimate reason to do so within the discursive system of the 'honour and profit of the king and kingdom'.

In France, such negotiations took place in similar terms, but the fact that they took place on a regional level, even where they had been preceded by a larger assembly, substantially changed their nature. Each community pursued its own interests, often with some success, attempting to have its contribution to a particular levy reduced or commuted either on the grounds of impoverishment, or of the need for the same funds on a local level, to restore defences or raise local levies. Even the twenty parishes which made up France-Alleu were able, on petition, to secure a reduction of their contribution to the *taille* of 1437 from 700 to 500 *livres*.[35] Such negotiations could often take place in overt opposition to the interests, not only of distant provinces, but also of immediate neighbours. Thus in 1427 the town of Lyon, despite the extra weight which would have been derived by sending a single delegation from the Lyonnais as a whole to the Estates to be held at Poitiers, instead insisted on sending separate representatives. The majority in the city's municipal

---

[32] Galbraith (1927), p. 81.
[33] Harriss (1966); Post (1964), pp. 110–27; Kantorowicz (1957), pp. 284–91.
[34] *PROME*, Nov. 1381; *Rotuli Parliamentorum*, ed. Strachey et al. (1767–77), vol. III, pp. iii, 102; *Knighton's Chronicle*, ed. Martin (1995), pp. 444–5, 448–9.
[35] Major (1960), p. 39.

government believed that they would have a better chance of securing special favours for themselves if they went to the king separately.[36]

The English Commons played the same role of humble petitioner in their intervention in the legislation of parliament – for Maude Clarke the only kind of representation which deserves to be regarded as 'political'.[37] Clarke's definition of the political now seems excessively restrictive, and inhibits the formation of a global idea of the role of the Commons in parliament. The Commons petitions, like short-term arguments over requests for taxation, took the form of an approach to the king's grace. The Commons took advantage of parliament to draw the attention of the king to matters, not capable of resolution at common law, of which he might otherwise be ignorant. Such approaches could always be, and often were, turned aside, often because it was considered that a remedy already existed at common law, that existing legislation should stand, or that individuals should sue for restitution of what seemed like too general or vague an issue. In this way, complaints lodged in parliament could drag on for years, with regular repetition producing no resolution, to be intoned with particular fire at the moment of political crises, and even more at royal depositions. Once again the Commons' role was only a supplicatory and informative one. It was whether or not 'le Roi le voet' which counted.

On the face of it, this state of affairs was not so very dissimilar from the situation in France, in which Estates meetings provided opportunities for the submission of *cahiers de doléance* to be submitted, accepted and, often, ignored by the king and his ministers. The practical reality of government in England and France was that, although kings might be obliged to accept the demands of the Commons or issue reform ordinances in times of crisis, it was easy simply to ignore these concessions once the crisis had passed. Committees of reform could only continue to exert influence where abnormal conditions continued to pertain and necessitated the repeated summoning of representative assemblies, such as during the 1340s and 1350s or 1420s and 1430s in France, or in the 1380s or 1400s in England. When the trouble was over, it was relatively easy for an Edward III or a Louis XI simply to ignore the concessions which he had made.

Again, it is possible to overplay similarities as well as differences when comparing the role of representation in legislation in England and France. The *Parlement* of Paris played a role in the registering of legislation, first established under Philip IV, which ultimately became binding on the king as well as his officials, a function which was fulfilled in England by

[36] *Ibid.*, p. 42.   [37] Clarke (1936), pp. 278–316.

parliament. English kings might use this role to their advantage, claiming to the pope, for example, that they could not repeal the statutes of Provisors or Praemunire without consulting with the estates of the realm assembled in parliament.[38] Even if they might in practice ignore what had been agreed in parliament, kings acknowledged on different occasions that they could not go back on a decision made in parliament except in another parliament, especially where, such as in the Statute of Treasons, this had been expressly asserted.[39] French kings had neither this alibi nor this restraint. Again, the concentration of functions in the English parliament which were carried out by a multiplicity of institutions in France produced something fundamentally different, even where the point of departure had not been totally dissimilar. Even the role of the Commons as humble petitioners came to be a right inhering in them as a body, established by custom, ranking with their right to determine the form that taxation would take. In the parliament of 1407, the Commons objected to the king and Lords first deciding what taxation was appropriate, and then passing their decision to the Commons for approval, rather than the Lords and Commons first conferring and passing on their decision to the king through the Commons' speaker. This was described in the petition as 'to the great prejudice and derogation of their liberties'. In the reply granting this petition it was asserted that the king wished to do nothing 'which could at all turn against the liberties of that estate, for which they have come to parliament, nor against the liberty of the aforesaid lords'.[40] The elaboration and close definition of their role as 'petitioners and demanders' is of undeniable significance in a period which also saw the growth of petitions *to* the Commons, asking them to present petitions to the king. That said, even in circumstances of crisis, the practical and institutional weight of the Commons in the fourteenth and fifteenth centuries still appeared through, not despite, the king-centred form of the institution of parliament. What established legitimacy for the Commons was as much their ability to argue in terms of a king-centred common profit as their right and obligation to speak in the name of the localities.

From the thirteenth century, across Europe, rulers made use of representative assemblies to exert a new kind of power over the communities under their authority. In England, the accumulation of competences in the institution of parliament gave it a significance which it never acquired

---

[38] E.g. *Foedera*, ed. Rymer (1739–45), IV, part III, p. 137.
[39] Fletcher (2008), p. 163, n. 62.
[40] *PROME*, Oct. 1407; *Rotuli Parliamentorum*, ed. Strachey et al. (1767–77), vol. III, p. 611.

in France. Nonetheless, it would be reading history backwards to imagine that parliament was already a fully established counter-power by the mid-fifteenth century, whereas the French estates, general or provincial, were mere stooges to the king's ever-expanding claims to authority. Seen in the later Middle Ages, the English parliament appears as an unusually vigorous, well-established version of a kind of mechanism which could be found across Europe. It was still less by reference to the representation of the people than to the representation of the king that political legitimacy was established in late medieval England.

Even when the language of the 'three estates' was deployed, the diversity of the significance attached to this language suggests the need for considerable care. In 1410, for example, when the Commons petitioned for the newly appointed continual councillors to be charged by the king 'in the presence of all the estates of parliament' to do justice and right without delay, it is difficult to see how this differs from similar requests, lacking this terminology, which were issued during the childhood of Richard II.[41] It is the ultimately public nature of parliament which is at issue, ensuring good governance. It is also hard to see how the references to the prorogation of 'the three estates of the realm in this present parliament assembled' fundamentally change the nature of the body in question.[42] It is too much to deduce from the description of parliament as 'all the estates of the kingdom', when consenting to the deposition of Richard II in 1399, that because of this 'the proceedings might have the justification of representing the people of England'.[43] If this were so it would have been made explicit in proceedings which otherwise mobilised every other possible justification for Richard's deposition and Henry IV's accession. Deposing Edward II and Richard II in parliament made these acts more binding, and more likely to be accepted throughout the kingdom, but they did not confer legitimacy on the grounds that the people thereby added its authority to the removal of the king. The language of estates seems rather to be a way of confirming what Chief Justice Thorpe had uncontroversially asserted in 1365, that everybody in the kingdom is held to be aware of what happens in parliament, 'since parliament represents the body of all the kingdom'.[44]

---

[41] *PROME*, Jan. 1410; *Rotuli Parliamentorum*, ed. Strachey et al. (1767–77), vol. III, p. 623. Cf. *PROME*, ed. Given-Wilson et al. (2005), Oct. 1377, Oct. 1378; *Rotuli Parliamentorum*, ed. Strachey et al. (1767–77), vol. III, pp. 7, 15–17, 35–6.

[42] *PROME*, Nov. 1449, Nov. 1450, Mar. 1453, Oct. 1472, Jan. 1489, Oct. 1491; *Rotuli Parliamentorum*, ed. Strachey et al. (1767–77), vol. V, pp. 172, 213, 270; vol. VI, pp. 39, 424, 444.

[43] Myers (1981), p. 152.   [44] Chrimes (1936), p. 76 and appendix 8.

This role of parliament as a public space, an assembly whose deliberations could be held to have taken place in the full knowledge and view of those communities who were summoned to it, was shared with French Estates assemblies and similar bodies both local, regional and general. It was this which first recommended such assemblies to Philip IV and his sons, to secure confirmation for their more controversial actions, or to attempt to secure financial support for specific financial exactions. For similar reasons, later baronial reformers from John the Fearless to Louis XI's opponents in the war of the Public Good invoked an assembly of Estates as the most powerful forum in which the problems of the kingdom might be thrashed out. It was this, too, which inspired kings to make use of such bodies in the course of diplomacy, to confirm an alienation of sovereignty or an annexation to the Crown, or to secure approval for a particularly controversial treaty or change of policy. It was this which led the English and the Burgundians to secure consent to the Treaty of Troyes by a body of representatives summoned from throughout that part of France which was under their control in the autumn of 1420. In such circumstances it was all the more imperative for Charles VII to consult the Estates in the first, insecure decades of his rule. Since the Estates summoned to Paris had seen fit to disinherit him, it was all the more important for Charles to assemble still larger assemblies which, simply by turning up, confirmed his title to rule.

In England, for similar reasons, parliament came to be the most important sphere for the resolution of political crises. That parliament was useful for such purposes was an outgrowth of its ultimately 'representative' role, which had been established with other aims in mind. With the acceptance of *plena potestas*, everything in parliament could arguably be held to be binding on the whole kingdom, since every community had been 'represented' in it. Removed from a legal or fiscal context, the presence of advocates for the whole kingdom made possible the use of parliament as the ultimate public location, a place where the common good could be negotiated and determined such that no one in the kingdom could claim not to have been party to it. Nonetheless, put in this way, it is by no means clear whether things done in parliament gained authority because they were done in the view of (as it were) the representatives of the body of all the kingdom, or *by* those representatives. This ambiguity remains even in the later use made of parliament to authorise claims to the throne which are still, at least in theory, made in terms of the right line of hereditary succession. When in 1484 Richard III made a declaration in the first and only parliament of his brief reign as a usurper, he noted:

how that the court of parliament is of such authority, and the people of this land of such nature and disposition, as experience teaches, that manifestation of any truth or right made by the three estates of this realm assembled in parliament, and by authority of the same, makes, before all other things, most faith and certainty, and quieting men's minds, removes the occasion of all doubts and seditious talk.[45]

In one way, it was still parliament's role as the ultimate form of publicity which was held to be significant in this declaration. Parliament represented the whole body of the kingdom, therefore no one could claim to be ignorant of what took place during its proceedings. Richard III only suggested that any truth or right was less likely to be contested if it was propagated with parliament's authority, not that parliament determined what was true or right through its own authority. His was not a 'parliamentary' title. But at the same time the (to say the least) dubious nature of Richard III's title to rule made it clear that parliament's role lay as much in agreeing to accept his coup as in simply publicising the truth and righteousness of his claim to legitimate succession. Even in these straitened circumstances, no clear statement was made that the Commons, as representatives of the kingdom, the people, or as one of the estates, derived a right to do more than observe, approve and publicise judgments and actions originating (often somewhat obscurely) elsewhere, even as it was clear that their role was rather more significant than that in practice.

The Commons gained no sovereignty, no power in opposition to that of the king by being 'representative' of the people's will. What they did gain, however, was a right of advocacy. It was a limited advocacy, in theory at least, in matters of policy, not concerning what was to be done, but how it was to be made possible. In practice, however, this, tied to their role of petitioners, gave them considerable room for self-assertion. It gave them the space to marshal arguments about the king's and the kingdom's honour and profit whilst still not claiming to *be* the kingdom, nor to embody its will. As expressed in the nineteenth article of the 'record and process' of the deposition of Richard II, every county ought to be free to elect and appoint knights of the shire to attend parliament, there to put forward their grievances and request remedies as seems expedient to them. Richard was alleged to have interfered in the process of selection, ordering the sheriffs to send men he himself had nominated, whom he bribed and threatened 'to agree to things prejudicial to the kingdom

---

[45] *PROME*, Jan. 1484; *Rotuli Parliamentorum*, ed. Strachey et al. (1767–77), vol. VI, pp. 241–2.

and burdensome to the people', notably onerous grants of taxation.[46] His crime was not to have denied the will of the people, but to have refused redress, and to have imposed taxation without proper consent. As elsewhere, his fault was not that he asserted that the king's will was the last word, that he was the ultimate arbiter of law, justice and custom – this was not in doubt – but that his will was arbitrary; that he would not even listen to the advocates of his subjects. This was where the significance of parliament came from. It was judicial in form, but political in impact. Every community had a right to an advocate in parliament. This was fitting, as the very function of a parliament was that anything done in it was to be held to be binding on the whole kingdom, because every community had been 'represented' in it, in this legal sense.

In France, although the idea of the assemblies of Estates, general and provincial, never went away, they never assumed the centrality nor the regularity that parliament did in England. They were instead one aspect of a multifaceted discourse of reform and not, moreover, one which was very popular with the towns, regional assemblies or local lords who were summoned to the various bodies it occasionally gave rise to. Kings or noble rebels might invoke such assemblies as the ideal forum in which to deal with the greatest affairs of the kingdom, but local elites saw in such mechanisms simply another occasion to undermine their customary rights. Recent work has emphasised the variety of means available to local communities who wished to represent their interests to the king, and for the king to represent his wishes to these same communities, even as it has ascribed greater importance to estates assemblies than an earlier generation of writers had done. It would clearly be overstepping the mark to see the seventeenth-century constitutions of England and France pre-figured in the fifteenth century, or even in the early sixteenth century. But it is clear that the English parliament had already become something rather different from any identifiable means of interaction between the French king and his subjects, simply by the way that so many functions had become concentrated in one institution. By the end of the fifteenth century, with the Treaty of Etaples (1492), and in further Anglo-French treaties in 1510 and 1514, it was the English parliament which was used to ratify such major diplomatic agreements, whilst in France it was not the Estates General, as first envisaged, but a variety of regional assemblies who gave their assent to what was done. The fact that Henry VIII was simply repeating late medieval commonplace when he stated that he was never so high in his estate as in parliament makes the sentiments he

---

[46] *PROME*, Oct. 1399, item 37; *Rotuli Parliamentorum*, ed. Strachey (1767–77), vol. III, p. 420.

voiced on that occasion all the more important.[47] The power of the King of England was expressed most effectively in parliament, when his actions were witnessed by the community of the realm, binding them and him to respect what had been agreed in that assembly. The King of France could not have assigned such a central role to any single institution, except to himself, the king.

BIBLIOGRAPHY

1. INTRODUCTION

Clark, L. (ed.), 2004. *Parchment and People: Parliament in the Middle Ages*, Edinburgh.
Hébert, M. (ed.), 2014. *Parliamenter: Assemblées représentatives et échange politique en Europe occidentale à la fin du Moyen Âge*, Paris.
Lewis, P., 1962. 'The Failure of the French Medieval Estates', *Past and Present*, 23, 3–24.
Ormrod, W. M., Dodd, G. and Musson, A. (eds.), 2009. *Medieval Petitions: Grace and Grievance*, Woodbridge.
Roskell, J. S. (ed.), 1993. *The History of Parliament: The House of Commons, 1386–1421*, Stroud.
Small, G., 2009. *Late Medieval France*, Basingstoke.

2. SOURCES CITED

The Anonimalle Chronicle, 1333–1381, ed. V. H. Galbraith, Manchester, 1927.
Foedera, conventiones, litterae, et cujuscumque generis acta publica inter reges Angliae, alios quosuis imperatores, reges, ed. T. Rymer et al., The Hague, 1739–45.
Knighton's Chronicle, 1337–1396, ed. G. H. Martin, Oxford, 1995.
Parliament Rolls of Medieval England (PROME), ed. C. Given-Wilson et al., CD-Rom, Leicester, 2005.
The Piers Plowman Tradition, ed. H. Barr, London, 1993.
Rotuli Parliamentorum, ed. J. Strachey et al., London, 1767–77.

3. FURTHER READING

Brown, A. L., 1964. 'The Commons and the Council in the Reign of Henry IV', *English Historical Review*, 79, 1–30.
—— 1981. 'Parliament 1377–1422' in R. G. Davies and J. H. Denton (eds.), *The English Parliament in the Middle Ages*, pp. 109–40.
Brown, E. A. R., 1970. 'Philip the Fair, "Plena potestas" and the *Aide pur fille marier of 1308*', *Studies Presented to the International Commission for the History of Representative and Parliamentary Institutions*, 39.

---

[47] Koenigsberger (1977).

1971. 'Assemblies of French Towns in 1316: Some New Texts', *Speculum*, 46, 282–301.

Bulst, N., 1984. 'The Deputies of the French Estates General of 1468 and 1484: A Prosopographical Approach', *Medieval Prosopography*, 5, 65–79.

1988. 'Les Députés aux États Généraux de France de 1468 et 1484' in *Mélanges de l'École française de Rome*, 100, 265–72.

1992. *Die französischen Generalstände von 1468 und 1484. Prosopographische Untersuchungen zu den Delegierten*, Sigmaringen.

1996. 'Rulers, Representative Institutions and Their Members As Power Elites: Rivals or Partners?' in W. Reinhard (ed.), *Power Elites and State Building*, Oxford, pp. 41–58.

Carpenter, C., 1983. 'Law, Justice and Landowners in Late Medieval England', *Law and History Review*, 1, 205–37.

Chevalier, B., 1981. 'The *bonnes villes* and the King's Council in Fifteenth-Century France', in J. R. L. Highfield and R. Jeffs (eds.), *The Crown and Local Communities*, pp. 110–28.

Chrimes, S. B., 1936. *English Constitutional Ideas in the Fifteenth Century*, Cambridge.

Clark, L., 1993. 'Men of Law as Members of Parliament', in J. S. Roskell (ed.), *The History of Parliament, 1386–1421*.

Clarke, M. V., 1936. *Medieval Representation and Consent*, Oxford (repr. 1964).

Davies, R. G. and Denton, J. H. (eds.), 1981. *The English Parliament in the Middle Ages*, Manchester.

Dodd, G., 2007. *Justice and Grace: Private Petitioning and the English Parliament in the Late Middle Ages*, Oxford.

Edwards, J. G., 1934. 'The Plena Potestas of English Parliamentary Representatives', in *Oxford Essays in Medieval History Presented to H. E. Salter*, Oxford, pp. 136–49.

Fawtier, R., 1953. 'Parlement d'Angleterre et États Généraux de France au Moyen Age', *Académie des Inscriptions et Belle-Lettres: Comptes Rendus des Séances de l'Année 1953*, Paris, pp. 275–84.

Fletcher, C., 2008a. *Richard II: Manhood, Youth and Politics*, Oxford.

2008b. 'Morality and Office in Late Medieval England and France', in N. Saul (ed.), *Fourteenth-Century England V*, Woodbridge, pp. 178–90.

2014. 'Rumour, Clamour, Murmur and Rebellion: Public Opinion and Its Uses Before and After the Peasants' Revolt (1381)', in H. R. Oliva Herrer, V. Challet, J. Dumolyn and M. A. Carmona Ruiz (eds.), *La comunidad medieval como esfera publica*, Seville, pp. 193–210.

Giancarlo, M., 2007. *Parliament and Literature in Late Medieval England*, Cambridge.

Harriss, G. L., 1963. 'The Commons' Petition of 1340', *English Historical Review*, 78, 625–54.

1966. 'Parliamentary Taxation and the Origins of Appropriation of Supply in England, 1207–1340', in *Gouvernés et gouvernants: Troisième partie, Recueils de la Société Jean Bodin 24*, Bruxelles, pp. 165–79.

1975. *King, Parliament and Public Finance to 1369*, Oxford.

Henneman, J. B., 1971. *Royal Taxation in Fourteenth-Century France: The Development of War Financing, 1322–1356*, Princeton, NJ.

1976. *Royal Taxation in Fourteenth-Century France: The Captivity and Ransom of John II, 1356–1370*, Philadelphia.

Highfield, J. R. L. and Jeffs, R. (eds.), 1981. *The Crown and Local Communities in England and France in the Fifteenth Century*, Gloucester.

Horrox, R., 1989. *Richard III: A Study in Service*, Cambridge.

Kantorowicz, E. H., 1957. *The King's Two Bodies*, Princeton.

Koenigsberger, H. G., 1977. 'Dominium regale or dominium politicum et regale? Monarchies and Parliaments in Early Modern Europe' in P. R. Gleichmann, J. Goudsblom and H. Korte (eds.), *Human Figurations: Essays for Norbert Elias*, Amsterdam.

Langmuir, G., 1958. 'Counsel and Capetian Assemblies', *Studies Presented to the International Commission for the History of Representative and Parliamentary Institutions*, 18.

Lewis, P.S., 1981. 'The Centre, the Periphery and the Problem of Power Distribution in Later Medieval France', in J. R. L. Highfield and R. Jeffs (eds.), *The Crown and Local Communities in England and France in the Fifteenth Century*, Gloucester, pp. 33–50.

1995. 'Pourquoi aurait-on voulu réunir des états généraux en France à la fin du Moyen Age?', in J. Blanchard (ed.), *Représentation, Pouvoir et Royauté à la fin du Moyen Âge*, Paris, pp. 119–30.

McFarlane, K. B., 1944. 'Parliament and Bastard Feudalism', *TRHS*, 4th Series, 53–79.

Maddicott, J. R., 1978. 'The County Community and the Making of Public Opinion in Fourteenth-Century England', *TRHS*, 5th Series, 28, 27–43.

2010. *The Origins of the English Parliament, 924–1327*, Oxford.

Major, J. R., 1960. *Representative Institutions in Renaissance France, 1421–1559*, Madison.

Myers, A. R., 1961. 'The English Parliament and the French Estates in the Middle Ages', in H. Cam (ed.), *Album Helen Cam*, vol. II, *Studies Presented to the International Commission for the History of Parliamentary Institutions*, 24, Louvain and Paris, pp. 139–53.

1981. 'Parliament, 1422–1509', in R. G. Davies and J. H. Denton (eds.), *The English Parliament in the Middle Ages*.

Oliver, C., 2010. *Parliament and Political Pamphleteering in Fourteenth-century England*, Woodbridge.

Post, G., 1964. *Studies in Medieval Legal Thought: Public Law and the State, 1100–1322*, Princeton.

Quillet, J., 1988. 'Community, Counsel and Representation', in J. H. Burns (ed.), *The Cambridge History of Medieval Political Thought*, Cambridge.

Rey, M., 1965. *Le domaine du roi et les finances extraordinaires sous Charles VI, 1388–1413*, Paris.

Reynolds, S., 1984. *Kingdoms and Communities in Western Europe, 900–1300*, Oxford.

Richardson, H. G. and Sayles, G. O., 1927–9. 'The Early Records of the English Parliaments', *Bull. Instit. Hist. Res.*, 5 (1927–8), 129–150 and 6 (1928–9), 129–155.

1930–2. 'The Parliaments of Edward III', *Bull. Instit. Hist. Res.*, 8 (1930–1), 65–82; 9 (1931–2), 1–18.

1931–2. 'The King's Ministers in Parliament', *Eng. Hist. Rev.*, 46 (1931), 47 (1932) 194–203, 377–97.

1946. 'The Origins of Parliament', *Trans. Royal Hist. Soc.*, 4th Series, 28, 137–183.

1981. *The English Parliament in the Middle Ages*, London.

Rigaudière, A., 1984. 'L'essor des conseillers juridiques des villes dans la France du bas Moyen Âge', *Revue historique de droit français*, 4th Series, 62, 361–90.

Roskell, J. S., 1951. 'The Social Composition of the Commons in a Fifteenth Century Parliament', *Bull. Instit. Hist. Res.*, 24, 152–72.

1954. *The Commons in the Parliament of 1422*, Manchester.

1964. 'Perspectives in English Parliamentary History', *Bulletin of the John Rylands Library*, 46, 448–75.

1965. *The Commons and their Speakers in English Parliaments, 1373–1523*, Manchester.

Sayles, G. O., 1975. *The King's Parliament of England*, London.

Scace, W., 2007. *Literature and Complaint in England, 1272–1553*, Oxford.

Small, G., 2000. 'Centre and Periphery in Late Medieval France: Tournai, 1384–1477', in C. Allmand (ed.) *War, Government and Power in Late Medieval France*, Liverpool, pp. 145–74.

Strayer, J. R., 1981. *The Reign of Philip the Fair*, Princeton.

Strayer, J. R. and Taylor, C. H., 1939. *Studies in Early French Taxation*, Cambridge, MA.

Taylor, C. H., 1954. 'The Composition of Baronial Assemblies in France, 1315–1320', *Speculum*, 29, 433–59.

1968. 'French Assemblies and Subsidy in 1321', *Speculum*, 43, 217–44.

Tuck, J. A., 1984. 'Nobles, Commons and the Great Revolt of 1381', in R. H. Hilton and T. H. Aston (eds.), *The English Rising of 1381*, Cambridge.

Watts, J. L., 1996. *Henry VI and the Politics of Kingship*, Cambridge.

2009. *The Making of Polities: Europe, 1300–1500*, Cambridge.

9 Grace and favour: the petition and its mechanisms

Gwilym Dodd and Sophie Petit-Renaud

Many of the chapters in this book consider the themes of governing and being governed from the point of view either of the people who exercised authority or of those who were subject to it. In this chapter we take a slightly different stance, considering these twin themes not in terms of people, but in terms of processes. Of all the different ways in which authority was solicited, expressed and upheld in the late medieval period, the petition was undoubtedly one of the most important. Certainly, it was the least contentious of ways in which the governors and governed crossed paths and interacted with each other, for the act of presenting a petition carried an implicit acceptance on the part of the supplicant that changes to their personal circumstances were entirely subject to the judgement of the person or body who received their request. In a strict sense, a petition could be any form of request, verbal or written; but in this discussion it is defined purely in its written form.

The late medieval period was an age of the petition par excellence: it was a period which saw a remarkable growth in its use, not just within the upper echelons of central government, but also locally, to solicit favours from nobles, to initiate proceedings in law courts and to stimulate business within urban centres. To compare all these contexts, from an English and French point of view, would be impossible in the space available to us. Therefore our discussion focuses specifically on the place of the petition in defining the relationship between the king and his subjects. This is the most promising area to consider from a comparative perspective, for it was at the very pinnacle of political power that some of the most striking similarities – and also differences – become apparent when considering how petitions were used in the respective administrations of the English and French crowns.

1.   The records

Most petitions served private interests; that is to say, they aimed to secure gifts and favours, to obtain new privileges or preserve exisiting rights, or they sought recompense for damages. The petition was also a key mechanism for the king's subjects to gain justice: in France, a petition was necessary to secure the delivery of a *lettre de justice*, addressed by the king to a judge; in England, the petition served a crucial role in allowing the king's subjects to obtain justice from the king and his ministers in cases where they could not obtain redress from the king's ordinary common-law courts. In both contexts, petitions for justice were proceeded on by the Crown by drawing on the principles of equity, custom and law, but only after the facts alleged by the petitioner were shown to be correct.[1] Petitions were also used as a means to contest or challenge the actions of government, for example where an edict or ordinance deliberated in council had damaged private interests. Many petitions were framed to promote the common good or to defend collective interests. In France, fourteenth-century reform ordinances were often based on a petition.[2] In England, petitions promoting the collective interest came to be especially associated with parliament, where common petitions were presented to the Crown by the representatives from the second quarter of the fourteenth century.[3]

Uncovering the precise workings of the petitionary process in France is not an easy task, for whereas in England many thousands of original petitions, as well as enrolled summaries of petitions, survive from the late thirteenth century, and in the Vatican Archives there are thousands of registers recording petitions received from 1342 onwards,[4] the King of France did not keep those which were submitted to him. The few that have survived call for careful handling, particularly since the result they obtained is not always known. Moreover, the ordinances which set down the proper mechanism for the presentation of petitions, and which occur from the reign of Philip V onwards (the first dates from 16 November 1318), are sometimes obscure, despite a 'codification' of procedure in the Cabochienne ordinance of May 1413.[5] The few surviving fragments of the deliberations of the royal council are no help in this matter. Finally, most acts undertaken as the result of a petition do not specify clearly which persons or institutions took part in its examination.

In England, large numbers of the original petitions or bills[6] presented to the king and his ministers survive in various collections in The National

---

[1] Tessier (1940), p. 110.   [2] Gauvard (1988).   [3] Dodd (2007a), p. 5.
[4] Millet (2003), p. 1.   [5] Tessier (1963).
[6] 'Bills' and 'petitions' were essentially the same thing: the words were often used interchangeably by contemporaries.

Archives (TNA). The principal collections are classified as SC 8 'Ancient Petitions' (i.e. petitions addressed to the king and council and presented, in many cases, in the context of parliament from the late thirteenth to the late fifteenth centuries)[7] and C 1 'Early Chancery Proceedings' (i.e. bills presented in chancery, dated mainly to the fifteenth century). There are also large numbers of petitions scattered throughout numerous other TNA series (e.g. C 81, C 49, E 208). This reflects the fact that very often petitions were sent on from the immediate context in which they were presented to authorise action elsewhere in government: a petitioner asking the king for payment of an outstanding debt, for example, might have his petition sent into the exchequer for action; and a petition presented to the council asking for justice could be sent into King's Bench for adjudication. The concentration of supplications in collections associated with parliament and chancery reflects the fact that over time both institutions developed into 'courts of record', where a premium was placed on retaining the petitions and bills in a single location.

Historians of late medieval England are extremely fortunate to have access to such prodigious source material, but the predominance of parliamentary petitions and chancery bills may, nevertheless, distort the impression we gain of where the main weight of petitioning fell in the late medieval period. For neither provide clear evidence of the extent and scope of petitionary business which English kings routinely handled *outside* a formal institutional context. It is not until the early fifteenth century, when an additional class of petitions comes into play (TNA, E 28 – Exchequer: Treasury of the Receipt: Council and Privy Seal Records) that we can begin to appreciate the full scale of the written requests which came before the monarch in his chamber.[8] Large numbers of this type of petition presumably made up the 4,000 petitions which A. L. Brown estimated that Henry IV (1399–1413) personally handled every year.[9] If his figure is accurate, and if Henry IV was typical, English kings were considering an average of ten petitions every day. The implications of this unrelenting flow of requests on the king's time must have been immense. An indication is provided in the treatise on court ceremonial known as the *Ryalle Book*, probably compiled by John Hampton, an usher of Henry VI's (1422–61) chamber, who noted that in the time of Henry IV and Henry V (1413–22) it had been customary after dinner for a cushion to be laid out on a sideboard in the Great Chamber where the the king 'wold lene by the space of an houre or more to resaue [receive] billis and compleynts off whomesoeuer wold come'.[10]

---

[7] Dodd (2009).   [8] Dodd (2008).   [9] Brown (1964), p. 154.
[10] *Antiquarian Repertory*, ed. Grose (1807–9), vol. I, p. 314.

Besides the petitions themselves, there is the possibility of measuring the volume of supplicatory business which the English and French crowns handled by looking for royal letters or grants which indicated that they had a petitionary provenance. Here, however, there are also difficulties. It was from the papal chancery that the French chancery borrowed the distinction between letters *motu proprio*, which were the result of direct initiative from the king and his council, and letters *ad petitionem*, which were prompted by a petition (*requête* or *petitio*). Unfortunately, the French chancery also followed the papal administration's bad practice. Even though the presence of the clause *motu proprio* ought to have embodied only those acts prompted by the king's spontaneous initiative in decision-making, interested parties very soon demanded, with success, that their petition be passed over in silence (i.e. without the note *ad petitionem*), or even that the chancery insert the clause *motu proprio* into the letters subsequently granted. Thus, this clause itself became the object of a petition. These practices, which lasted at least until the seventeenth century, thus effaced the difference between acts of supplication and acts of royal will.[11]

In England, there was not the same interest on the part of petitioners to have the supplicatory origins of grants hidden behind formulae which suggested the act had been the spontaneous result of the king's exercise of royal grace. But the generalised nature of the warranty notes used to authenticate letters issued by the Crown to the king's subjects meant that the petitionary origin of most acts of grace was also usually hidden. The one exception was the warranty note *per peticionem de consilio* – an instrument that was employed on a frequent basis at the end of the thirteenth and beginning of the fourteenth centuries in letters issued by chancery as a result of petitions presented specifically in parliament.[12] Nevertheless, after the middle of the fourteenth century, the use of this warranty note disappeared, and most letters were recorded as being issued simply on the authority of the king, the council, the chancellor or by privy seal. The task of quantifying precisely the contribution which petitions made to French and English government in the later Middle Ages is thus extremely problematical.

2.   The language of petitioning

The petition was not an act of authority, but rather a humble supplication. It is well established that petitioning in a secular context owed much to the tradition of petitioning in a religious and clerical context, especially the

---

[11] Olivier-Martin (1950).   [12] Dodd (2007a), pp. 60–3.

long-established system of papal petitions. Like a prayer, a supplication –
itself a term drawn directly from religious vocabulary – transformed the
petitioner into a humble supplicant 'bowed before majesty as one is before
God'.[13] Very often, petitioners called attention to their devotion, humility
and subordination, whilst concurrently calling upon the *benignitas* of the
pope.[14] In France, the religious connotations of presenting a petition
were echoed by the words 'may it please the king, of his benign grace',
which opened, for example, the petition addressed by the inhabitants of
Amiens to King Louis XI (1461–83).[15] Similarly, in England, petitions
universally drew on the terminology of prayer, often using the verb 'to
pray' [*prie* or *prient*] to describe the petitioner's act of making a request. It
was not uncommon for petitioners to seek 'the grace of the lord king' or
something 'as of his grace'; and many petitions ended with the final appeal
to have the request granted 'for God and in aid of charity' (*pur dieu et en
oev[re] de charite*). In England and France, petitioners frequently stated
their intention to pray for the king and, less often, for his family. The
same linguistic conventions existed in petitions addressed to territorial
princes, such as the petition to the duke of Brittany from the inhabitants
of Guinguamp in 1488, asking for a reduction of tax, in which they
declared that they 'will pray God for [him], that [he] would give him
good and long life, fruit and lineage and paradise in the end'.[16]

The vocabulary of the petition remained essentially fixed, ritualised
and codified, suggesting the existence of formularies which could be used
by supplicants. Indeed, petitions had to be carefully drafted (usually by
an intermediary, such as a clerk or attorney) since they often served
as the basis for the form of royal letters. For example, the instructions
addressed by Louix XI to the tax commissioners (*élus*) of Saint Flour,
ordering them to verify the *taille* assessment for Aurillac, repeats many
elements in a petition presented by that town. The arguments in favour
of a reduction of its contribution (the geographic description of the town,
the sufferings that it had endured, the plague, depopulation and poverty)
are all taken up in almost identical terms by the royal text.[17]

All petitioners, even the most powerful, conformed to traditional
expressions such as '*Plaise au roy*' ('May it please the king'), '*Au roy
nostre seigneur, humblement supplie*' ('To the king our lord, [the petitioner]
supplicates . . . '). Almost all the petitions for office addressed to Louis XI
at the beginning of his reign, for example, open with these words.[18] The
same formulae can often be found in the royal act which reflected the

[13] Millet (2003), p. 8.   [14] Koziol (2003), p. 34.
[15] *Recueil de monuments*, ed. Thierry (1853), vol. II, p. 338.
[16] Morice (1746), col. 584.   [17] Rigaudière (2008).   [18] Mattéoni (2003), p. 292.

petition which lay behind it, for example: 'we have received the humble supplication', 'they supplicate to us' (*nobis supplicarunt*), 'the aforesaid supplicants have very humbly supplicated and petitioned us' (*lesdits suppliants nous ont très-humblement fait supplier et requérir*). On the other hand, the language used may have more closely reflected the supplicant's desire to secure justice: *nous ont monstré en complaignant* ('they have shown to us, complaining'); and *ex gravi conquestione monstrarunt* ('out of their grave complaint they show'). A comparison of letters issued by the English chancery with the originating petitions, similarly highlights the way in which chancery clerks often simply copied out the details of a petition in order to provide the main narrative structure informing a royal grant, commission or pardon.[19] It is easy to see why this was the case: privy seal writs issued in response to petitions handled by the king often explicitly ordered the chancellor to draft letters according to the 'effect' or 'purport' of the original request. This shows why the narrative of a petition was so important, because it could significantly influence and shape the nature of the response.

Petitions displayed a remarkable uniformity in the language they employed and the structure they followed. But over time these attributes developed and changed. A petition presented to the king in the late thirteenth century had a very different appearance to a petition presented at the end of the fifteenth century, though the basic attributes remained the same. In the English context there are a sufficient number of extant petitions to be able to identify with confidence some important trends in the writing style. In the late thirteenth century, petitions presented to the king tended to be short and to the point. No trouble was taken to embellish the request with unnecessary detail: the language was functional and precise. From the middle of the fourteenth century, however, the drafters of petitions began to employ language in a much more elaborate way. The language of petitioning developed in such a way as to emphasise the supplicant's deference and respect for the authority to whom the petition was directed. From the late fourteenth century, it was not uncommon for the king to be attributed with qualities such as *tresexcellent*, *tresredoubte*, *tresnoble* and *trespuissant*. Where petitions were also addressed to the council, the latter was frequently described as *tressage*; and in petitions presented to parliament, the Lords and Commons were commonly described as *tressages* and *tresnobles* (Lords) and *tressages* and *treshonourables* (Commons). It also became common practice for petitioners to ingratiate themselves to the king by identifying themselves as his 'loyal lieges' and by using the adverb *treshumblement* to describe

[19] Dodd (2011b), pp. 236–7.

their act of supplication. As well as highlighting the development of a sophisticated petitionary idiom, the increasingly elaborate use of diction highlighted how petitioning was no longer merely a bureaucratic procedure, but was also being used to articulate and reinforce political and social hierarchy.[20]

It is useful to illustrate these observations with a small selection of petitions presented to English and French kings (the first two are English examples, followed by three French examples). The first is a petition presented in the parliament of 1315, addressed to Edward II (1307–37) and his council. This was a complaint of Roger of Wigginton that he had been prevented from obtaining justice against John of Bloxham, who had secured immunity from prosecution on the false pretext that he was going to Scotland in the king's service. The second example is a petition of William Langeton, who wished to have confirmation of his prebend in Exeter Cathedral. It was presented to Henry IV (1399–1413) in 1402, almost certainly to the king in his chamber. The third example was probably presented to Philip III at the end of the thirteenth century by Pierre Pillart, knight of the county of Beaumont-sur-Oise, who had been accused of beating a cleric and stealing two horses from him. This is one of the rare original petitions for which evidence survives for this period. The next petition was one of those presented to Louis XI in 1461 in the hope of obtaining an office; it can be found amongst the group of documents of this kind mentioned above, which were collected by the king's secretary, Jean Bourré. Finally, the last example is a petition addressed to Francis I, around 1525, by the inhabitants of a castellany in the Gironde, requesting a tax reduction.

Example 1

A nostre seignur le roi et ason conseil se pleint Roger le fiz Gy de Wygynton' qe come il ad suy par un bref de entre vers Johan le fiz Robert de Bloxam par grant temps devant justices le roi du Bancke, issint qe le ple fut seuy jesqes al jugement rendre, a queus l'evandit Johan bota avant une proteccion, en supposant son aler en la service le roi en Escoce, issint qe le ple ad pris delay del terme de Pasche l'an sime tantqe a ore, maliciousement et a grant arerisement de recoverir l'evandit Roger, et par la ou l'evandit Johan nul aler ne service ne fit au roi, mes emprit coverture par my la proteccion, selonc la fourme avandit, en despit nostre seignur le roi, et agrant damage l'evaundit Roger: dont il prie remedie.[21]

---

[20] Dodd (2014).
[21] *Parliament Rolls of Medieval England* (*PROME*), ed. Given-Wilson et al. (2005), parliament of 1315, item 56 (43).

Example 2

Please au Roy n[ost]re tresredoubte et tresgracious souvrain Seignour rat-
ifier et confermer a vostre humble chapellein et continuel oratour William
de Langeton chaignon de l'esglise cathedrale d'excestre et prebender de
la prebdende qui fuist iadys a Henry Brokelond en icelle q'est de la
collacion de le Reverrent piere en dieu l'evesque d'excestre lestate et
la possession lesquex vostre dit chapelleyn ad en lez ditz chaingme et
prebende pur dieu et en oevre de charite.[22]

Example 3

A vostre grant hautesce, très gentieus rois de France, je Pierres Pillart, du
Menil, chevalier de la conté de Biaumont, requier merci por Dieu. Sire,
por Dieu, resgardez se j'é tant atendu merci que je la doie avoir, et sachiez
que ma doleur est si pême que enviiz enquareiz moi ne autrui . . . Sire por
Dieu, voloiz que ceste doleur prengne fin, et si ne vous plet que j'aie
repos, et si me changiez ceste paine a une austre, si vous plet. Et si ne
vous plet, por Dieu, quemandez que droit me soit fet.[23]

Example 4

Plaise au roy nostre sire donner a Pierre de Riviere, povre gentil homme
demourant a Rains, l'une des elections de Rains, Laon ou Chaalons ou
aultre port ou son bon plaisir serat ou aultre office car ledit Riviere est et
a esté leal serviteur et serat toute sa vie et sy prira Dieu pour le roy nostre
sire.[24]

Example 5

Supplient très humblement vos très humbles et très obeissantz subjectz
les habitants de la chastellenie de Didonne, en Xainctonge . . . vous plaise
les soullaiger et abonnir à certaine petite somme de deniers, qu'ils puissent aisément porter leurs tailles, aydes et équivallents qui sont imposés
sur eulz par chacun an, et du surplus les descharger affin qu'ilz puissent
mieulx supporter les autres fraiz et charges susdictes. Et ilz seront tenus
à jamés pryer Dieu pour vostre sacrée majesté.[25]

Although there are obvious points of stylistic difference, the petitions follow a common form of structure and they use vocabulary to roughly the

---

[22] TNA, E 28/15 (no. 6).   [23] Berger (1896), p. 343.
[24] Bibliothèque Nationale, fr. 20497, f. 58°, cited Contamine (1992), p. 139.
[25] *Choix de documents inédits*, ed. Marchegay (1875), p. 99.

same ends. They begin with the address; they identify who is petitioning; some provide a form of narrative to explain the background to the
request; the request is made; and the petitions end with a formulaic plea
to God. That there is such close resemblance should not come as a surprise: both English and French examples drew on a common petitionary
heritage that was rooted in the long-established ecclesiastical tradition
of petitioning within the church hierarchy. These universal diplomatic
conventions were set out in large numbers of theoretical treatises in circulation at the time which articulated the guiding principles of the 'art' of
letter writing; that is, the *ars dictaminis*.[26] But, even without these models
to draw upon, English and French petitionary practice is likely to have
remained close – the petitions adopt the most straightforward and logical
structure to meet the demands and needs of contemporary bureaucracy:
the identity of the key players is given and sufficient detail supporting the
request is provided to allow the king or his ministers to make an informed
decision on whether the petition deserves sympathetic treatment, further
investigation or outright dismissal.

It should be noted that the English petitions were written predominantly in the French language. This was the formal language of pleading
in England in the thirteenth and fourteenth centuries and it remained
the language of petitioning par excellence until the third decade of the
fifteenth century when the English language was increasingly used.[27] It
has been suggested that one of the advantages that petitioning held in
England was that the use of French made the process much more accessible to the general populace. This may be true insofar as the use of Latin
in formal legal proceedings represented a much more formidable barrier
to comprehension and participation; but the continued use of French
to draft petitions at a time when English had become the language of
speech meant that for much of the period in England, at least, petitioning retained a distinct air of formality. In practical terms, this placed
greater weight on the requirement for petitioners to employ the services
of professional scribes, clerks or men of law to write their petitions for
them.

3.   The regulation and control of petitions

The petition was a fundamental aspect of political society which brought
into play patronage, pressure groups and relationships of clientage. It
gave expression to a constant and necessary dialogue between governors and the governed. Beyond the 'institutional' dialogue to be found
in parliament and in the assemblies of estates – the latter becoming

---

[26] Dodd (2011b).   [27] Dodd (2011a).

progressively weakened in the middle of the fifteenth century – the petition permitted the sovereign to keep himself informed about the state of his kingdom. Petitioning undoubtedly facilitated royal government and was a means for the king to 'bed down' his authority, since he expected fidelity and services from the individual or group to whom he accorded his grace. Nevertheless, petitioning was open to abuse. The availability of the king to the solicitations of his subjects presented an opportunity for self-advancement and self-aggrandisement which some of his more unscrupulous subjects could not resist, even if this meant making a request that was less than sincere or truthful. Throughout the fourteenth and into the beginning of the fifteenth century many writers, such as Philippe de Mézières, unceasingly denounced the behaviour of those who led the system off its proper course by harassing the king all day long in order to submit their petition directly to him.[28] An ideal king listened to the requests of his subjects and awarded his favour where a case deserved a positive outcome; but, inevitably, favour and bias could be shown in undeserving cases, especially to the more tenacious and ambitious of his subjects.

Contemporaries would not have voiced their concerns about the abuse of petitioning had this method of approaching the king not become so popular and widespread in the late medieval period. The popularity of petitioning stemmed from the fact that, in simple terms, this was often the quickest, easiest and most direct way for the king's subjects to draw the attention of their sovereign to their needs. Presenting a petition to the king gave suitors the opportunity to bypass lower courts and secure a judgement on the basis of the king's unassailable authority. When obtaining justice in the ordinary law courts was often a protracted and costly affair, and was also sometimes inhibited by an inflexible legal code (for example, the common law in England), submitting a complaint to the king had obvious advantages. Petitions could be very straightforward documents to draft because they were not bound by strict rules of litigation. It would therefore not have been difficult for a supplicant to find a ready and willing clerk capable of writing his/her request. Definitive responses to petitions were also often given by the king in a very short time, sometimes on the day of presentation itself, but perhaps more usually within a matter of days of having the request submitted. If a petition was presented in parliament, it was common practice for answers to be given before the assembly ended. There were also no theoretical restrictions on who could present a petition,[29] so it made the king accessible to a

---

[28] Paravicini (1980).
[29] Though in practice the peasantry tended not to make use of the petitionary system: for discussion, see Dodd (2007a), pp. 208–9.

remarkably wide spectrum of suitors, each hopeful of attracting his attention to their plight. Once systems were in place to handle the requests brought before the king, the capacity of the Crown to process these requests inevitably expanded, which in turn allowed a greater range of people to submit requests than hitherto. In short, fears about the abuse of petitioning stemmed in large measure from the fact that in an age when securing justice or accessing higher authority so often depended on an individual's wealth and connections and on carefully established processes, petitioning (although not at all devoid of these considerations) nevertheless provided a greater measure of freedom to the king's subjects to obtain what they wanted on their own initiative. For some contemporaries this represented an invidious threat to the established norms of government and law.

Disquiet about the negative aspects of petitioning in England was voiced primarily in parliament and in the fourteenth century when the growth of petitioning procedure was most marked. In some cases, the concerns focused on the development of petitionary procedure within the common-law courts. In 1346, for example, the Commons complained that some criminals indicted before the justices of the peace went into King's Bench and chancery, where they maliciously presented bills accusing the justices of changing the tenor of the accusations against them.[30] In 1354 and 1355, similar complaints were made against 'various people of their own malice and deceit [who caused] bills to be made in destruction of the good people of the area', as a result of which, innocent people were said to be indicted before false panels of jurors.[31] The main thrust of the complaint was that bill procedure now opened up to a much wider range of people the possibility of procuring inquests, whereas in truth the Commons felt that such action should only be available to 'the better and most loyal people of the counties'.

The Commons expressed concerns more directly associated with the king in 1352 when they asked that 'no one shall henceforth be taken by a petition or suggestion made to our Lord the king or his council except by the indictment or presentment of good and loyal men of the neighbourhood . . . or by process made on an original writ at common law'.[32] Again, it was the freedom from set processes – the fact that decisions on important cases of law could be determined at the personal whim of the king and his councillors, rather than by the professional scrutiny of royal justices working within an established legal framework – which formed

---

[30] *PROME*, parliament of 1346, item 12.
[31] *Ibid.*, parliament of 1354, item 30; parliament of 1355, item 26.
[32] *Ibid.*, parliament of 1352, item 19.

the focus of anxiety. In 1365, parliament took a more robust stance on those 'who make grievous complaints to the king himself' when it was ordained that if a petitioner 'cannot prove his intent . . . he shall be sent to prison, to remain there until he has made satisfaction to the party of his damages and of the slander that he has suffered for such reason'.[33] This was clearly an attempt to disincentivise the presentation of speculative petitions made in the hope of catching the king on a good day. There is, unfortunately, little evidence that sanctions against rogue petitioners were ever enforced widely.

In France, although the king was not obliged to agree to a petition, it did however sometimes happen that he could not refuse it and therefore ordered the issue of letters 'by inadvertence, by importunity of the petitioner and with the truth of the matter silenced' (*par inadvertance, importunité de requerans et la verite du fait teue*). Indeed, such letters could be contrary to the king's interests or the source of disorder.[34] In France, far more so than in England, the consequences of bad decisions being taken by the king on requests put forward by petitioners were taken extremely seriously. In order to protect the king from over-hasty decisions and to limit access to his person, it was necessary to put in place a body of regulations which were repeated all through the fourteenth and fifteenth centuries. This strongly hints at their ineffectiveness. On one level, ideally, it was the King of France's duty to receive the petitions and the complaints of his subjects in person. The emblematic figure here is, of course, that of Saint Louis (1223–70), dispensing justice under the oak at Vincennes: 'all those who had business came to talk to him, without being prevented by a bailiff or anybody else', so Joinville tells it in his *Histoire de Saint Louis*. Boniface VIII, in one of his sermons delivered in 1297 when he decided to canonise Louis, insisted 'how great was his justice . . . Indeed he sat almost continually on the ground on a carpet to hear judicial cases, especially those of the poor and of orphans, and he had justice rendered to them in its entirety.'[35] In the fourteenth century, Christine de Pizan stressed the exemplary attitude of Charles V who, after mass, let himself be approached by one and all, the greater and the lesser, to hear their petitions. This ideal of direct access to the king remained strong in the centuries that followed. Thus, Charles VIII (1483–98) revived towards the end of his reign the tradition of Saint Louis, establishing a public audience open to all in order to receive their petitions in person.[36]

---

[33] *Ibid.*, parliament of 1365, item 27.   [34] Paravicini (1980), p. 169.
[35] Le Goff (1996), p. 645.   [36] Paravicini (1980), p. 175 n. 35.

But quite apart from the practical impossibility of the king managing single-handed the ever-growing flood of petitions, French royal ordinances insisted on the necessity of preventing the king from making decisions on his own. They set out his obligation to submit petitions for examination in council, in the absence of the interested parties. The objective was to impose an official intermediary between the sovereign and the petitioner. Oral requests (*requêtes de bouche*) were also forbidden, even when the supplicant was a powerful feudal lord, unless they were followed by a written approach. It seemed natural that the petitioners, or their representatives, should present themselves before the king to defend orally a request which they would then put into writing. The same applies in the context of provincial and general estates assemblies. Requests were submitted orally, a common *cahier de doléances* for all three orders was then compiled and submitted to the king or his commissioners. The *cahier* compiled during the assembly of the Estates of Languedoc, in November 1428 includes a request 'which had been made orally and had been omitted by forgetfulness' (*laquelles se devoit faire de bouche et par oubli a esté obmise*).[37]

In England, the way in which patronage was distributed by the king was always a source of interest and concern on the part of the king's subjects, but the way in which petitioning per se could disrupt or destabilise the political equilibrium rarely came under close scrutiny, at least in terms of the petitions which came before the king. In part, this reflected the fact that the ways in which royal authority could be accessed were far less regulated: there was no equivalent ordinance in England to the one enacted in France which forbade oral representations to the king. Consequently, it is very hard to estimate how much of the business of English government which was prompted by the solicitations of the king's subjects actually derived from informal 'off-the-record' requests for favour. It seems likely that those closest to the king did not need to bother with written requests to secure for themselves grants of favour or redress. In England, attempts to control or regulate the access which individuals could have to royal largess focused instead on the person of the king himself, or his favourites, and were usually confined to limited periods of political instability and/or opposition when the king was considered incapable of making sound judgements on his own.

In fact, the only period when petitioning *as a process* became a matter of 'public' or political interest in England was in the reign of Henry VI, when the political community faced a series of extremely difficult circumstances, caused initially by the king's youth and later by his personal

[37] Devic and Vaissete (1885–9), p. 102, col. 2080sq.

failings. In the first instance, a series of ordinances were enacted in the early 1420s to respond to the particular challenges created by Henry VI's minority and the need, in specific terms, to ensure that the council which ruled in his name handled requests in a transparent and regulated fashion. The terms of the ordinances demonstrated the particular anxiety which contemporaries had, now that the realisation of petitioners' hopes and ambitions rested on the judgement of a group of noblemen and prelates substituting for the power of the sovereign. The ordinances included the specification that: 'bills' should be scrutinised by all members of the council, so that no individual council members could grant favour on his own accord; the outcome to a bill should only be enacted where it enjoyed the majority support of council members; the council should not consider bills which could be determined at common law; the clerk of the council should ensure that bills from poor suitors were accorded priority in the order of business; and finally, that the council should draw on the advice of royal justices if bills raised matters which they were not qualified to address.[38]

A further set of ordinances was devised in 1444 in an attempt to monitor and regulate the way in which the king handled requests, now that he was beginning to take a more active part in discharging the duties of government.[39] Amongst these measures was the stipulation that any member of the king's council or anyone else who laboured to have a bill accepted on behalf of others should make their identity known by writing their name on the dorse; that bills dealing with matters of grace should be given to specially appointed readers who would summarise the contents and return them to the king, noting his response; and that all petitions, if they had been accepted by the king, should pass along a set administrative route beginning with his secretary, who would ensure that letters were then issued under the signet letter to the keeper of the privy seal, who would then in turn send instructions to the chancellor. The ordinances highlighted the short-term problems caused by the mechanism of petitioning when the king did not have the personal capacity to discharge these requests in a disciplined and even-handed way; they were not indicative of a long-term structural weakness whereby the petition was undermining the very fabric of royal government. This probably explains why nothing appears to have been done to ensure that the terms of these ordinances were properly implemented: the problem was not the

---

[38] *Proceedings and Ordinances of the Privy Council of England (POPC)*, ed. Nicolas (1834–7), vol. III, pp. 148–51; *PROME*, parliament of October 1423, item 17.
[39] *POPC*, ed. Nicolas (1834–7), vol. VI, pp. 316–20.

petition per se but the king; soon, attention shifted elsewhere and other solutions were devised to make the king's rule more effective.

The situation in France was quite different. One of the essential mechanisms put into place in France in order to deal with illegitimate demands and the importunity of petitioners was the institution of the *maîtres des requêtes*, who served as intermediaries between supplicants and the king. They received petitions addressed to him wherever he was at that time. Such was their importance that in the middle of the sixteenth century, an advocate at the *Parlement* of Paris specified that the 'true place of audience is the king's door, where they [the *maîtres des requêtes*] must be present to receive the petitions which are submitted and presented to the king'.[40] Their origins, attested during the reign of Louis IX (1226–70), lay amongst the judges or clerks 'following the king' (*poursuivants le roi*) who helped the king to provide justice in person during 'pleas at the door' (*plaids de la porte*). In 1305, this institution separated off and became the *Requêtes de l'Hôtel*.[41] The *maîtres des requêtes* received and examined petitions for which ordinances required a written response. They passed on the most important to the king. They could also act for the sovereign in deciding independently requests which did not seem to pose any problem. However, at the end of the reign of Philip VI (1328–50), the king more and more often put in an appearance when the *maîtres des requêtes* assembled to reply to petitions, as is seen by the frequency of the phrase '*Par le roi en ses requêtes*' or '*Per regem in hospicii*'. Decisions taken independently by the *maîtres des requêtes*, without the intervention of the king, marked '*in requestis hospicii*', became more and more rare, before disappearing in the fifteenth century, since the king's council had absorbed the *Requêtes de l'Hôtel*.[42]

The *maîtres des requêtes* were not the only ones involved in the presentation of requests to the king. The chancellor, the members of the council, or commissioners specifically designated to deal with a case could also intervene.[43] If the royal administration imposed few formalities in the matter, texts later appeared which multiplied the rules to obey. Article 19 of the royal ordinance of 27 January 1360 specified that apart from the *maîtres des requêtes*, only the chancellor, the councillors, the chamberlains, the king's confessor and his almoner were permitted to present petitions to the king.[44] The reform ordinance of 1413 (article 212) distinguished between two types of request: on the one hand, those which

---

[40] Cited by Bailhache (1924), p. 227.   [41] Guillois (1909), p. 30.
[42] Bailhache (1924), p. 229.   [43] Bautier (1965), p. 366.
[44] *Ordonnances des roys de France de la troisième race*, ed. de Laurière et al. (1723–1849), vol. III, p. 386, art. 19.

were passed on by the *maîtres des requêtes* to be presented to the king, and which could be dealt with outside the council; and on the other hand, those which could only be granted in council, after having been presented by members of the royal family, sitting councillors, or the *maîtres des requêtes*. A special session of the council, presided over by the king and the chancellor was even reserved for their consideration. This session, called '*pleine requestes*', existed from the reign of Jean II (1350–64). The royal ordinance of 27 January 1360 specified that it should take place twice a week at first, 'or once only if we are prevented from doing so' (*ou une foiz se nous n'avons empeschement*) but it was later held every Friday. The institution was later re-established in the reign of Charles VI (1380–1422). At this point, the chancellor received the power to preside over the assembly in the absence of the king. This special delegation was to be transformed into a general power, and kings no longer attended except on Good Friday.[45] Under Henry III (1574–89), petitions were presented to the king during a special session held on a Saturday, the decision being taken on the following Saturday, although petitions were probably still presented outside of the ordinary session.[46]

Whether in an ordinary session or a special session, it was in his council that the king examined supplications which had to be in writing and which the *maîtres des requêtes* had already examined to ensure that they damaged neither the rights of the king nor of third parties. However, the sovereign did not hesitate to ignore this formality. This is seen in a deliberation of 7 August 1484, by which the regency council ordained that the seigneur de Pons should be freed from a fine. The letters were to contain the words 'provided that the *maîtres des requestes* consent'. But in fact Charles de la Vernade, one of the *maîtres des requêtes* who was present, was ordered to say 'to his companions . . . that they should not give cause for any hindrance' to the grant of this petition.[47]

Other institutions apart from the council proper were called upon to intervene, whether the petitions were directly addressed to them, or their particular responsibilities led them to examine petitions addressed to the sovereign. The *chambre des comptes*, for example, controlled grants which involved the alienation of goods or revenues pertaining to the royal domain. Within the *Parlement*, *lettres de justice* were obtained after examination by the *maîtres des requêtes* of the palace. The latter also had presented to them the cases of individuals who enjoyed the privilege of addressing the *Parlement* directly in the first instance. Moreover, it was not uncommon for litigants, humble or powerful, to address petitions to the *Parlement* in the hope that it would accelerate the treatment of particular cases. As for the chancellor, he was naturally led to intervene when requests concerned judicial organisation. When the ambassadors of the duke of Brittany came and presented 'remonstrances and requests' in 1462 they received the answer that 'it pleases the king to say that these will be submitted by the said ambassadors to my lord the chancellor, who will make a report to him' (*il a pleu au roy dire que elles seroient par lesdits ambaxadeurs remonstrées à Mons. le chancelier, qui lui en feret rapport*).[48]

At the end of the formal process, all decisions of an individual character, obtained by petition, could be subject to judicial recourse through appeal or opposition. The *Parlement* therefore found itself placed by the king himself in the position of verifying the form and content of letters issued by the chancery, both privileges and *lettres de justice*. This applied not only to letters granting privileges to individuals, but also to those aimed at certain categories of person, concerning the general interest, such as those defining jurisdiction, according a municipal statute or regulating a guild. The *Parlement* had first to ensure that the letters which were the intended outcome of a petition conformed to the royal will (ensuring the presence of clauses of derogation, for example). They had to ensure that they had been taken in full knowledge of the circumstances and so to consider the validity of the motives presented by the petitioner. If the summary of the facts was not exact or complete, the act would be placed under the category of letters which were *subreptrices* (if they were inexact), *obreptrices* (if they were incomplete), or *iniques* or *tortionnaires* (meaning that their dispositions were contrary to reason and equity). The court of justice, always suspicious of royal arbitrary discretion, also examined the reality of the formation of the royal will, and made sure that the decision had been made *ex justa causa*. Indeed, even if according to legal doctrine the will of the prince had the force of law, for the judges the case nonetheless had to be just, reasonable and explicit. The intervention of the judge limited the autonomy of the sovereign, just as the importance of the petition did in formal procedure.

In the English royal court, there was no regulation equivalent to that in place in France which ensured due process in the presentation of petitions in the *Requêtes de l'Hôtel*. This highlights an important institutional difference between the two kingdoms. In France, petitioners were able to contribute to the making and amending of law, if they wished to, by presenting their requests directly to the sovereign within the royal court. In England, important changes relating to the law, and other ordinances governing the political and economic life of the kingdom tended, by

[48] Morice (1746), col. 20.

contrast, to be petitioned about only in parliament. In 1444, this principle was articulated explicitly: the king was instructed that 'if thar be billes of justice and co[n]teyne mat[er]e of co[m]mune lawe ... yf plese him to co[m]maunde þeime to be sent to his Counsail þat þei may by þadvis of his said Counsail be remitted to þe co[m]mune lawe and to such places where þe matier is terminable'.[49] Petitioners certainly followed the king wherever he was, to present their requests for favour and redress, but these requests normally only concerned areas where the independent exercise of the king's will was understood to apply, that is to say, where requests required the exercise of royal grace. Typically, these petitions asked the king for grants of patronage (e.g. for lucrative offices or annuities), special dispensation (such as a pardon from a fine or prosecution) or royal permission. These were not areas which were considered to be open to regulation or supervision because they were understood to pertain solely to the royal prerogative. In fact, the only level of 'management' in place to regulate the requests coming into the royal court appears to have lain in the office of royal chamberlain – usually filled by a close and trusted advisor of the king – who was responsible for organising and 'signing off' petitions once the king had given them his approval.

The English parliament, on the other hand, provided a strong measure of regulation and monitoring by virtue of the fact that the power to suggest changes to the law and government of the realm was understood to reside specifically with the representatives of parliament. From the 1320s, members of parliament assumed the role as intermediaries between the king and his subjects on issues which pertained to the common interest of the realm. The petitions which the Commons began to present soon became known as common petitions, not because they were all drafted by MPs (though a large proportion probably were), but because their content was understood to have a general – or common – application. Very quickly, statutory legislation began to be formulated around the lists of common petitions presented by MPs in each parliament, so that in effect, almost all changes to the law were made as the result of an initial consensus reached by the parliamentary knights and burgesses. The petitions were still addressed to the king and were still, crucially, subject to royal approval; but the convention was firmly established that the king could only be approached to make changes to the kingdom's laws in the specific context of parliament, and through the medium of the common petition. The Commons fought to defend and consolidate their grip on the statutory process: in 1348 they affirmed their power to monitor all petitions presented to the Crown as common petitions,

---

[49] *POPC*, ed. Nicolas (1834–7), vol. VI, p. 317.

disavowing any which did not meet with their approval;[50] and in 1414 they demanded that statutes should enact the terms of a common petition word for word, unless the Crown had consulted MPs on any changes.[51]

The English parliament was also an important venue for those of the king's subjects who wished to approach the Crown with requests or grievances of a private nature.[52] This function had its origins in the thirteenth century, when early assemblies heard a modest number of difficult legal cases;[53] but it was as a result of encouragement by Edward I (1272–1307) that 'private petitions' became a truly significant aspect of parliamentary business. Indeed, in the last decades of the thirteenth and early decades of the fourteenth century, the petitionary function which parliament discharged appears to have largely shaped contemporary perceptions of what purpose the institution served. The anonymous author of the tract known as *Fleta* defined parliament at the end of the thirteenth century as a place where 'the king has his court in his council in his parliaments when prelates, earls, barons, magnates and others learned in the law are present and there doubts are determined . . . concerning judgements, new remedies are devised for wrongs newly brought to light, and there also justice is dispensed to everyone according to their desserts'.[54] Again, it is worth stressing that these were petitions addressed to, and (in many cases) considered by the king; only it was the king acting within the setting of parliament. There was no formalised convention, as there was in the case of common petitions, to say that only certain types of private petitions could be considered by the king in parliament; but the presence of all the king's senior ministers, the royal justices, clerks and administrators, plus the political and ecclesiastical elites, inevitably created for parliament a specialised role as the venue for petitions which raised particularly intractable legal cases, faults in royal government or cases of notoriety. In other words, these were cases which the king could not easily address without the expert advice and opinion of the broader political and governmental community.

It was in parliament that an equivalent system of administrative apparatus was created in England to that of the *maîtres des requêtes* in France. Much the same rationale applied: a system was needed to help the king tackle the flood of requests and grievances by reserving for him only those cases which absolutely required his personal intervention, leaving the rest, the more routine petitions, to be handled by his officers and ministers. One notable difference, however, was that in England these intermediary

---

[50] *PROME*, parliament of 1348, item 30 (petition 24).
[51] *Ibid.*, parliament of April 1414, item 22.   [52] Dodd (2007a).
[53] Sayles (1988).   [54] *Fleta*, ed. Richardson and Sayles (1955), vol. II, p. 109.

bodies were not devised explicitly to regulate or limit the ability of the king to dispatch requests of his own accord. Their primary purpose was to assist the king, either by lessening the petitionary burden or by giving him expert counsel and advice. By the turn of the fourteenth century, private petitions were initially handed to 'receivers' (mostly clerks of chancery); those petitions which had not been weeded out by the receivers because they were judged to be unsuitable for consideration in parliament were then passed to the 'triers' or auditors of petitions (i.e. a committee comprising judges, nobles and bishops); and those cases considered to be beyond the competence of the triers were then forwarded to the king and council for final adjudication. It is possible, even at this stage, that council members shouldered the principal burden where petitions required further investigation and hearings. Common petitions, by their nature as requests carrying particular prestige, were automatically considered by the king and council, though they were administered and written up by government clerks (the clerk of the Commons and clerk of parliament respectively).

Although the focus of this chapter is the place which petitioning occupied in shaping the *king's* relations with his subjects, it is important to recognise that the petition also played a critical role in facilitating royal authority in the broader context of late medieval English government. As we have seen, although a majority of petitions presented in parliament in the thirteenth and fourteenth centuries were addressed to the king, many were in fact dispatched by officials and advisors acting on the king's behalf, exercising royal authority, as it were, by proxy. This process of delegation occurred in several other notable contexts. In the first place, the council fulfilled a vital role as a semi-permanent 'troubleshooting' advisory body, tackling cases which the king did not wish to conclude without the advice and opinion of his key counsellors. The mechanics of this process are revealed very clearly in Henry IV's reign, when the king forwarded to his council (normally sitting at Westminster) a small, but continuous stream of problematic petitions which had been handed to him during his perambulations in the localities.[55] In the course of the fourteenth century, the exchequer also began to function as a regular forum for petitioning. J. A. Tuck summed up the significance of this development by pointing out that 'control over the bulk of routine patronage, in which the Crown's interest was mainly financial, was in the hands of the great officers of state, and above all the treasurer'.[56] But, perhaps the most notable manifestation of royal delegation, in terms of petitionary processes, was the emergence of chancery as a court of

[55] Dodd (2003).   [56] Tuck (1971), p. 4.

equitable jurisdiction in its own right. As the king's senior administrator, the chancellor had always exercised a large degree of latitude in the duties he discharged and the authority he commanded, but in the course of the fourteenth century these powers became more formalised and chancery's role as a court of conscience became more sharply defined. By the fifteenth century, chancery had emerged as the principal forum allowing the king's subjects to appeal to the royal prerogative in civil actions, and the chancellor himself became the focus of vast numbers of 'bills' from supplicants seeking resolution to what are sometimes termed as 'offences against conscience' (such as uses, holdings, obligations, debt and bonds).

4.   The petitioners

Theoretically, petitioning was open to anyone who could have their request written down and presented to the king. Apart from those who held servile tenure, there were no restrictions which limited petitioning to individuals of a certain status or wealth. This, indeed, was one factor to explain why the petition was such an attractive means of gaining the attention of the king. The king had a duty to listen to his people and respond to their grievances: it would have been very hard for him to deny access to his subjects simply on the grounds that they were not members of the political or ecclesiastical elites. Nevertheless, it was perhaps inevitable that the vast majority of supplicants making representations to the king would belong to the higher echelons of society.

In France, petitions came from many different origins. It is clear that the division between different categories of petitioners differed according to the nature of the documents solicited, and to whether they concerned acts of a general nature or letters of grace or justice of an individual nature. The petitions presented by individuals accounted for a very large number of royal acts. However, they were rarely the source of acts of a general nature, concerning government or administration. These most often arose out of the individual initiative of a relatively select group of clergy, nobles, and in particular members of the royal lineage, who had easier access to power, especially in the area of justice (i.e. defining the scope of jurisdictional privilege and authority). Likewise, in England, the majority of petitions were presented by members of the gentry, clergy and urban elites (together with a smaller number from the lay and spiritual peerage). It was the relative wealth and status of these individuals which very often explained their need to approach the king, perhaps because their lands had been illegally seized by an unscrupulous neighbour, or because they had sufficient standing to expect a royal grant or special dispensation. It is thus important to distinguish between the rhetoric and reality of a petitioner's stated plight: claims of impoverished status or powerlessness in the face of overwhelming force were useful diplomatic strategies employed to induce a sympathetic hearing, but they did not always match the reality of a petitioner's circumstances.

Collective petitions were amongst the most frequent type of request in France and were also an important subclass of petition in the requests presented to English kings. Petitions were presented by incorporated towns (the most numerous), ecclesiastical establishments, groups of officers, guild communities, the religious orders and, from the fourteenth century, the assemblies of estates (in France) and the parliamentary Commons (in England). Their demands generally aimed to protect their collective interests at local or regional level, often by obtaining confirmation of privileges or statutes, but could also include more general measures. A particularly interesting category of English petition was the supplications presented by abbots and priors on behalf of their religious houses.[57] A large range of subject matter is represented in these cases, from complaints about the infringements of royal officials to requests for assistance in disputes with recalcitrant tenants or hostile neighbours. Occasionally, monks might petition the king against members of their own religious community and/or their abbot.[58] Such cases highlight the reach of English royal authority into the lives of both the king's religious and lay subjects.

Petitions from towns predominate amongst the collective petitions of both England and France, especially those towns which had been interacting constantly with royal government since the thirteenth century. In the fourteenth century, towns, burghs and villages were amongst the king's main interlocutors in their search for privileges and exemptions of all kinds. Typical of the sorts of issues to be raised in petitions presented by English towns were requests seeking the renewal or modification of liberties; royal licence to levy funds for the repair of bridges, pavements or harbours; or the king's intervention in commercial disputes with other towns.[59] In France, numerous petitions came out of municipal administration, such as those which sought the creation, suppression or re-establishment of communes, or even the selection and functions of municipal magistrates.[60] With the onset of the Hundred Years War, requests for authorisation to tax the inhabitants of French towns multiplied, as did petitions concerning the works necessary for fortification. In an English context, there were similar requests to raise funds locally to improve defensive works, especially in coastal towns exposed

---

[57] *Petitions to the Crown*, ed. Dodd and McHardy (2010), esp. Introduction.
[58] *Ibid.*, no. 147.   [59] Dodd (2007a), pp. 266–77.   [60] Petit-Renaud (2003), p. 276.

to French attack or in the north, where communities were vulnerable to Scottish incursions. There were also requests for relief (usually financial) in the aftermath of destructive raids. In 1385, for example, the citizens of Carlisle petitioned for a lessening of the fee-farm due at the exchequer following the destruction of various mills and fisheries belonging to the town and because (as their petition stated) 'all the lands and tenements together with corn, goods and chattels from all parts of the said city are burned wasted and destroyed by the enemies of France and of Scotland' (*et ensement ore tard toutz les terres et tenementz ensemble ove bles, biens et chatealx de toutz parties du dite citee sont arcez, gastez et destrutz par les enemys de France et d'Escoce*).[61]

Finally, some petitions presented by towns concerned the common interests of the kingdom, principally in economic and monetary matters. Both the English and French crowns looked to urban communities for advice and information which could be used to formulate economic or mercantile policies for the whole kingdom. Thus, at the beginning of the fourteenth century, the French king did not hesitate to ask the towns to suggest and prepare the principal measures to be taken in these areas, as a result of their competence in these matters.[62] On the other hand, in the fifteenth century, even if petitions presented by towns are still numerically dominant, there are fewer of them and they concern – aside from requests for the confirmation of statutes and privileges at the beginning of each reign – justice, finance, franchises and the creation of fairs and markets.[63] Except in times of crisis, the exchanges between the state and towns became less frequent demonstrating, that the autonomy of the towns was real, as Bernard Chevalier has shown, up to the seventeenth century. The equivalent in an English context are the numerous requests relating to economic and mercantile matters to be found amongst the common petitions presented in parliament from early in the fourteenth century. We can safely assume that these cases were compiled by the numerous representatives of urban communities who were returned to each parliament.

As in England, where the common petition soon became the principal means for the political community to express its collective will, in France, too, there is evidence, albeit of a less direct nature, of supplications presented in the name of the people. Like their English counterparts, these emerged in the course of the fourteenth century. In a recurrent theme in royal acts, the sovereign explains that he is not indifferent to the suffering of his people, that he governs in their interest, and above all affirms his desire to listen, although he is not obliged to do so. Thus we

---

[61] TNA, SC 8/101/5046.   [62] Rigaudière (2000), pp. 73–101.
[63] Chevalier (1988), p. 76.

see the 'clamour of the people' appearing in these texts.[64] Some traces of it can be found in the acts of the last Capetians. It multiplies in those of the first Valois, and at the same time changes form. This is the demanding voice of the *voluntas populi*, a form of petition which embodies criticism. It expresses discontent, even crisis or revolt, in sometimes violent forms.

Although the king declared that he was disposed to reply favourably to the petitions of his people, many of these texts only claim to speak for a restricted and enlightened public opinion, invoking the 'clamour of the best part of all the common people'. If the clamour of the people pushed the king into action, this was usually considered not to be enough on its own, so the royal act was 'reinforced' in a variety of ways, notably by the rapports or endorsement of those who were 'worthy of faith', or by an inquiry undertaken by the *réformateurs généraux*. The clamour of the people took its place naturally in assemblies of estates which stressed in particular their role in relaying information and opinion to the sovereign on the state of his kingdom.

5.   Intercession and the intercessors

Outside the formal institutional framework which regulated the presentation of petitions, there developed other more informal mechanisms and indirect routes. It is here that we need to consider the importance of the intervention of a third party – of the intercessor – in the petitioning process. Intercession was a function of a social and political system shaped by the needs of patronage and lordship. It was at the same time both an obstacle to good government and a necessary mode of governing. It was an obstacle, since it left much room for arbitrary discretion, for favour and for disorder. Thus Henry III of France was said by one of his secretaries of state to have forbidden princes and lords of quality to talk 'for any but themselves'.[65] It was a necessary mode of governing as a consequence of the contractual nature of social relations and the pervasive force of lordship and clientage in the later Middle Ages. For a petition to have a greater chance of success, it was sometimes important for the supplicant to draw on networks of influence, relying on the 'good word' of a sympathetic spokesman, such as a prominent lord or prelate, a royal councillor or officer, or a courtier or royal favourite – anyone, in fact, who was considered to be capable of exerting some degree of influence over the king (women as well as men). Intercession was an unavoidable aspect of the petitioning process.

---

[64] Petit-Renaud (2003), pp. 289–94.   [65] Boüard (1929), vol. I, p. 71.

Perhaps for this reason, intercession was treated rather ambivalently by the political community in England. In some contexts, the role of the intercessor was regarded with deep suspicion, as though the act of intercession threatened the integrity of the petitioning process itself by colouring or distorting the king's ability to make sound judgements on a request. One type of petition which became the focus of serious concern in this respect was the request from convicted criminals asking for the king to extend his grace to them and grant a pardon.[66] The use (and abuse) of royal pardons by the king became the subject of serious disquiet in the early fourteenth century. From the 1330s onwards, however, attention turned instead to the ways in which pardons were procured and, in particular, to the role played by intercessors in persuading the king to grant undeserved or unwarranted pardons. In a petition presented in the parliament of 1353, the Commons declared that 'our lord the king, by false representation, has often granted his charter of pardon to well-known thieves and common murderers, who led him to believe that they are remaining overseas in his wars, when they have quickly returned to their country to continue their crimes, in deceit of the king and in disturbance of the commonalty of their regions'.[67] The Crown appeared to be receptive to these concerns, for in the preamble to the resulting statute it was acknowledged that the king had often granted charters of pardon 'upon feigned and untrue suggestions of divers people'.[68] From this point onwards, a measure of transparency was brought into the process by the requirement that the name of the intercessor was to be recorded on all charters of pardon.

Later, fines were introduced to discourage the complicity of intercessors in procuring false pardons. From the point of view of historians, one of the great advantages of these new measures is that the charters of pardon recorded in the patent rolls from the mid fourteenth century provide very clear quantitative evidence to show how extensive the practice of intercession was. The work of Helen Lacey has gone far in uncovering the scale of the phenomenon.[69] In general, petitioners seeking intercession for royal pardons aimed as high as they could: amongst the most frequent intercessors used by petitioners wanting royal pardons in Richard II's reign (1377–99) were: Queen Anne (71), John of Gaunt (62), Henry Percy, earl of Northumberland (53), Edward of Langley, earl of Rutland (40), Joan of Kent, the king's mother (31), Nicholas Exton, mayor of London (29), Edmund of Langley, duke of York (29),

---

[66] Lacey (2009).
[67] *PROME*, parliament of 1353, item 41.
[68] *Statutes of the Realm* (1810–28), vol. I, p. 330.   [69] Lacey (2009), pp. 44–58.

Henry Bolingbroke, earl of Derby (24), Thomas Arundel, archbishop of Canterbury (21) and Richard Fitzalan, earl of Arundel (17).[70]

It is important to stress that intercession was not considered to be an inherently bad thing. Had it not been an accepted and important part of the political culture of late medieval England, it is highly unlikely that the leading political figures of Richard II's reign would have given their support to the representations of petitioners so willingly, as this data suggests. In England and France, having the support of a powerful patron to secure the favour of a higher authority was not automatically considered to be sleazy or disreputable, as it might be today. It was more akin to a job reference than subversion of due process. In a society where legitimacy of an action was intrinsically linked to status and position, intercession was an accepted means for supplicants to add weight to their claim to be deserving of the king's clemency. The intercessors, for their part, will have seen their role in general terms as providing good lordship to the recipients of pardons and good counsel to the king to enable him to make the right decisions.

For these reasons, it is very unlikely that the Commons would have seen anything paradoxical in their campaign to curtail the influence of intercession for royal pardons, when they themselves were developing a crucial role in the English parliament as intercessors for private petitioners. A typical example of a petition appealing to the king *via the Commons* was presented by the mayor, aldermen and commons of the city of London in 1429 about legislation passed in 1406 which limited the terms in which apprentices could be taken on in the city.[71] The petition was addressed to 'the most wise and most honourable commons of this present parliament' and it asked them 'to consider the great harm that will befall the inhabitants of the said city because of the said article if they suffer restriction in their liberties and customs . . . [and] to pray our said sovereign lord and the lords spiritual and temporal assembled in this present parliament to ordain and declare by the authority of the same parliament . . . [that] the said long-standing manner and terms of apprentices . . . be upheld and observed forever'. In this case, the petition was fully supported by MPs who presented the request to the king as a common petition (and succeeded in having it subsequently enacted into legislation).[72] The emergence of the Commons as intercessors in the petitionary process almost certainly reflected the increasing difficulty

---

[70] *Ibid.*, Appendix 4.iii.
[71] TNA, SC 8/85/4238; *PROME*, parliament of 1429, item 51.
[72] *Statutes of the Realm* (1810–28), vol. II, p. 248 (c. xi).

with which petitioners were able to secure redress in parliament.[73] It was not necessarily indicative that access to the king himself was becoming increasingly difficult (outside parliament, a steady flow of requests continued to flow into the king's hands); but it did indicate how parliament was changing from an institution in which the king considered requests en masse to one that now spent time on only a relatively small number of high-profile cases.

The importance of a recommendation was also inherent in the life of the French court. It was also found in the territorial principalities,[74] or at the Holy See. Thus, to ensure their success, individual petitions addressed to the pope were most often presented by protectors, relatives or familiars of the pope, persons of high rank – kings, cardinals, bishops – or even lords of lesser importance. A supplication could contain the names of as many as four intermediaries.[75] Individuals – of modest condition or elevated social rank – could moreover address the king of France directly in certain circumstances, as he was going to mass, for example, or as he travelled about his kingdom. For example, Louis XI, in 1481, accorded grace to a woman whom he met whilst praying before the relics of St Hilary at Poitiers.[76] Nevertheless, from the fourteenth century, because of the growth of the distance between the sovereign and his subjects, it became more and more necessary to make sure that each approach was backed up by the aid and mediation of an important person, rewarding his services monetarily as necessary. It became difficult to present a petition directly to the sovereign. Thus, in October 1461, Dauvet, president of the *Parlement* of Toulouse, found it necessary to solicit the aid of the highly influential secretary Jean Bourré in order to approach Louis XI:

I recommend myself to you as much as I can. I arrived here yesterday to go to meet the king to take leave of him to go to Tholoza and to know what he would please command and order me, and also I would much like to talk to him on my own small account . . . And for this reason I send you my gift, praying of you that you will command me if it would be appropriate to go presently to the king and if I would indeed have access to speak to him.[77]

It was just as necessary for towns and professional bodies to find an intermediary. The Venetian or Castillian merchants settled for nothing less than the intervention of their sovereign, who supported their appeals

[73]   Dodd (2007a), pp. 191–3.
[74]   For the county of Hainault, see Cauchies (1982), pp. 99–101.
[75]   Gorochov (2003), p. 151.   [76]   Gauvard (1997), p. 283.
[77]   Devic and Vaisette (1885–9), vol. XI, col. 62.

to the king of France.[78] The inhabitants of more humble communities preferred to let their lord act in their place to obtain favour with the king. It became rarer and rarer for town representatives to approach the king directly, except whilst he was travelling through his kingdom. Thus, all those at the court who carried out a function of some importance were approached, such as the members of the council, of the *Parlement*, or the chancery, as well as all those who had the opportunity to approach the king regularly. In 1472, in order to renew a safe-conduct (*sauve-garde*), Amiens made sure that it could count on the intervention of the chancellor of France, Philippe de Morvilliers, on account of his local attachments. It was said that he had originated from amongst 'the notable people of the said town of Amiens and [had] offered before to maintain them with the king'.[79] In the same year, Louis XI granted letters for a fair 'in favour of and on the request of our well beloved doctor and astrologer Master Pierre Choynet'.[80] It was to a correspondent well-placed in the court that the inhabitants of Rennes addressed a very pressing letter on the 11 February 1554 in order to prevent the translation of the *Parlement* of Rennes to Nantes:

We send to the court to make remonstrance to the king concerning the damage and ruin [if this decision is taken], in which, Monseigneur, your aid and favour will be greatly required and necessary . . . we supplicate to you, Monseigneur, to do us such honour and such good to the public, to wish to hear our interests and reasons, and to lend us your hand in this with recommendation such that the honour of our defence remains yours, Monseigneur, the confidence which we have to be numbered amongst your very humble and obedient servants, emboldens us to present this request to you, and to supplicate to you to be willing to command us, praying to the Creator to give you, Monseigneur, in health a long and very happy life.[81]

In England, similar processes are evident in urban records, which not infrequently recorded payments for 'services rendered' in support of particular economic agendas. The research of Matthew Davies into the London companies of the fifteenth century reveals a world in which financial inducements and backhanders were perfectly normal and acceptable methods of securing a favourable response to a petition.[82] Moreover, it is interesting to observe that it was not just the great men of the realm whose influence was solicited in this way: exploiting connections with clerks and bureaucrats who worked in the central administration and knew 'how to get things done' was evidently regarded as an equally promising way of

---

[78] *Ordonnances*, ed. de Laurière et al. (1723–1849), vol. IV, pp. 110, 421.
[79] Cited by Gauvard (1991), p. 70, n. 70.   [80] Cited by Boüard (1929), p. 70, n. 5.
[81] Morice (1746), col.1123ff.   [82] Davies (2004).

strengthening one's case in the eyes of the Crown. A good example is the lengths taken in the parliament of 1497 by the Carpenters' Company to repeal an act which limited the wages and working hours of the city's craftsmen. To ease the passage of their supplications, payments were made to the porter of the parliament chamber, to the clerks of the Commons, to the clerk of parliament, to the sergeant-at-arms and, finally, to the king's attorney. There were other key people in parliament who were equally well placed to help petitioners: in 1485 the Pewterers' Company lobbied the Commons' Speaker to support their campaign against itinerant craftsman, setting aside the princely sum of 26 *s.* 4 *d.* for 'garnysshe large vessell newe fascioned counterfeit for Maister Speker of the parliament'. The support of individual MPs might also be solicited: in 1455 the Mercers' Company paid John Whittoksmead 6 *s.* 8 *d.* 'to be our friend in parliament'.

In France, towns also sent accredited commissioners to act as intercessors. They were embassies whose solemnity can be seen without too much trouble through a discourse delivered at the end of the fifteenth century before Louis XII by the representatives of the town of St Malo in order to attract his attention to the difficult financial situation of the town:

> Very high, very powerful, very excellent and very Christian king, your very humble and very devout orators, subjects and servants, men of the Church, nobles, bourgeois, dwellers and inhabitants of your royal town and city of St. Malo send us presently before your majesty, [and charge us] to say to you that with all their heart and affection they recommend themselves very humbly to your very-good and very-desired grace . . . praying our Lord Jesus Christ that he will grant to you who persevere to prosper in this very high and very triumphant reign, long and good life, and paradise in the end. They have placed upon us and commanded us to speak, that you might willingly hold excused, considering the little understanding of I who am not worthy nor adequate to be nor to present myself before you, such a great, such a noble, such a powerful king, and the greatest in the word in this low age, so accomplished, so provided, so well-instructed in all knightly matters, that the whole world knows it and speaks of it. But having confidence in your great benignity and clemency, in fear I have accepted this burden placed upon me which would be bearable by one more powerful than I, very humbly supplicating to your majesty to tolerate my faults.[83]

Petitioning was also testament to a relationship of power, a negotiation, or even an exchange based on established procedure and reciprocity. So it appears in the letters of the duchess of Burgundy who, in 1472, sent the town of Dijon a request from her husband in order to provide for the

---

[83]   Morice (1746), col. 797ff.

charge of the *procureur* of the town, without waiting for the death of the *procureur* in office:

> We who have not yet made a request to you as we remember since we came to lordship, write now to you and pray and request you as certainly as we can, that to this our first request which, if it is reasonable, which it is, you ought not to resist us.

The ducal couple were acting as intermediate petitioners, in the interests of one of their familiars, charging the duke to respond favourably to requests presented subsequently by the town, 'that we should have reason similarly to accord to you the next petition that you make to us'.[84] Although, according to Derville, the autonomy of the towns of Burgundy tended to recede in all areas at the end of the fifteenth century,[85] this petition remained without effect. Everything depended on the capacity of the towns to resist in the face of pressure from princes, notably in the case of provision to municipal offices. Such promises of reciprocity were also made by the king himself, such as when Louis XI wrote to the chapter of Lyon on the subject of the grant of prebends: 'And in doing this you will do us the greatest and most agreeable pleasure that you could do for us in this case, which we will remember when you require anything for yourselves or the business of your church.'[86]

6.   Responding to petitions

Like the pope, the King of France could give his response directly on the letter of the request, very often beginning with the word *Fiat*, if it were positive; *Non potest fieri* or *Non fiat* if negative. This was the case in a petition presented to Charles VIII, 'so that [he] might make provision for it' (*afin qu'[il] lui plaise y donner provision*) in August 1484, by two ambassadors of the duke of Lorraine, read by the chancellor and copied into the registers of the council. It contains eight articles, in the margin of which the responses of the council are noted individually.[87] A petition addressed to Louis XI by the inhabitants of Amiens shows the same structure. Although some articles received no reply, the king inscribed his approbation next to others – 'The king has ordained that it shall be done' (*Le roy a ordonné que ainsy sera fait*), and 'The king has granted it according to the contents of the article' (*Le roy l'a ottroyé selon le contenu de l'article*) – in anticipation of letters which would confirm the

[84] *Correspondance de la mairie de Dijon*, ed. Garnier (1868–70), vol. I, no. 77.
[85] Derville (1974), p. 341.
[86] *Lettres de Louis XI*, ed. Vaesen et al. (1883–1904), vol. I, p. 35.
[87] *Procès-verbaux des séances du conseil*, ed. Bernier (1836), pp. 29–31.

royal decision.[88] In the petitions presented to the English king in his chamber, the king's assent to requests was usually recorded by the words *Le Roy ad grante*.

A similar procedure is shown in the *cahiers de doléances* (general petitions) submitted by the estates in France, and in the common petitions in England. In France, the king, his council or his commissioners responded article by article, whether the response was positive (*'Placet '*; *'Il plait au roy'*; *'Le roy y consent et en est d'accord '*), negative (*'Il ne peut se faire'*, *'Nichil'*), that an inquiry was necessary, or, as became more and more frequent in the fifteenth century, that the king's commissioners had promised to refer the content of the articles to the king himself.[89] In England, the standard response given to a petition presented by the Commons, which the king had accepted, was *Le roy le voet* (the king wills it); the formulaic response to a petition which he had rejected was *Le roy s'advisera* (the king will consider this further).

Petitions made at the highest level were no different. Take, for example, the replies made to petitions addressed to Philip IV, king of France, by Edward II in his capacity as duke of Guyenne (or presented in his name by his agents), around 1310. These concerned cases first heard by judges in the duchy which had been appealed to the court of France. After each article, a reply was given by the French king, which was either evasive or lengthily argued when the request had not been met: 'May letters be issued' (*Litera fiet*); 'It is doable and shall be done' (*Il est fesable et sera fait*); 'It cannot be done without injustice' (*Non potest fieri sine injuria*); 'This request, the king, in a land which is governed by custom, he will not do that, since he could not without doing wrong to his subjects nor without sin' (*Ceste requeste, li roi, en la terre qui se gouverne par costume, ne fra pas ceo, car il ne porroit sanz tort fere aux sogetz e sans peché*); 'In a land governed by written law, he will do as written law wills' (*En la terre qui se governe par droit escryt, il le fra solom ceo que droit escrytz veut*), to name some of the answers given in the name of the king of France.[90]

It was frequently the case in both the French and English contexts that the king or his council reserved or delayed their response, often on the grounds that the result of an inquiry undertaken by competent institutions was required to verify the implications of the *petitio*. For example, replying to a request for the payment of his pension submitted by the duke of Lorraine, the regency council of Charles VIII replied that 'concerning this matter it will be communicated and written to those of the finances who will come to make a report of it' (*a ceste matier sera*

[88] *Recueil de monuments*, ed. Thierry (1853), p. 338.   [89] Quéré (1997), p. 213.
[90] *Lettres de rois*, ed. Champollion-Figeac (1839–47), vol. II, pp. 39–58.

communicqué ou escript à ceulx des finances qui en viendront faire le rapport);[91] much the same was done concerning appeals from the duchy of Guyenne to the *Parlement* of Paris: 'it will not be done except by order of the court' (*non fiat nisi de mandato curie*).[92] This was particularly the case in petitions which asked for the king's adjudication in complex legal matters or royal intervention to resolve local difficulties: straightforward requests for patronage tended by contrast to be treated in a more perfunctory way. Numerous acts compiled in response to a petition evoked this request for information, the verification of facts, of rights or of law, an inquest *de commodo et incommodo*, directed by men of the council or by local agents.

Private petitions presented in the English parliament frequently raised matters relating to injustices or local problems and so similarly elicited 'holding' replies from the king. It was often the case that petitions presented in parliament would be referred elsewhere, such as the chancery, exchequer or King's Bench (or a combination of these three), where the king's officers and judges were instructed to accumulate further information and possibly interview the parties concerned, before referring back to the king for a final decision. A good example is the reply given to a petition presented by the abbot of Bury St Edmunds in 1326 who sought confirmation of his abbey's right to remain unmolested by royal ministers. The reply read: 'A writ is to be issued to inquire into the contents of this petition, and when the inquisition has been returned the king will speak his will on the matter' (*Fiat breve de inquirendo super contentes in peticione, et inquisicionem retornatum, dicat rex inde voluntatem*).[93] Petitions from towns and other local communities which drew the king's attention to important regional problems frequently resulted in the appointment of a special commission charged to investigate the accuracy of matters raised by the petition to provide the king with the information necessary to make a sound judgement. Certain acts, very often those which concerned the regulation of guilds or municipal organisations set down the procedure to be followed for the inquiry. In France at least, if these prescriptions were not respected, and the letters granted nonetheless, it was forbidden for the chancellor to seal them and for competent judges to put them into practice.

Although the *petitio* was an essential element in the procedure of drafting letters patent, its study is still the source of difficulties. As has been said, the king of France did not preserve the petitions which were addressed to him. It is thus impossible to establish the ratio of petitions

[91] *Procès-verbaux des séances du conseil*, ed. Bernier (1836), p. 30.
[92] *Lettres de rois*, ed. Champollion-Figeac (1839–47), vol. II, p. 44.
[93] TNA, SC 8/234/11700.

granted to petitions partly or totally rejected. Even where large numbers of petitions survive, as they do in the case of parliamentary petitions presented in England, it is very difficult to make quantitative assessments of successful petitions to failed petitions, because very often failed petitions were simply thrown away, there being no requirement to keep them for filing. With far fewer extant petitions to hand in France, it is also impossible to determine to what extent the text of the petition was taken up by the royal act which followed it. Furthermore, it is clear that the distribution between different categories of petitioner varied according to the nature of the documents envisaged, that is, according to whether they were acts of general import, or letters of grace or *lettres de justice* of individual significance.

Nonetheless, there are ways around these difficulties. In France, many acts drafted by the notary-secretaries of the king bear the trace of the initial petition in their preamble or *exposé*. On the basis of the collection of acts edited in the collection *Ordonnances des rois de France*, it is possible to calculate that, for the reigns of the first three Valois (Philip VI, John II and Charles V) more than 50 per cent of these followed explicitly from a petition. For the reign of Charles VII, F. Olivier-Martin has shown that 61 per cent of laws were the result of petitions.[94] Clearly, these statistics must be handled with care. Beyond the fact that certain letters do not mention a petition which is nonetheless likely to have existed, the collection used constitutes only a minority of all the acts produced by the kings of France. However, certain significant tendencies are there to be seen.

In England, the link between common petitions and new laws – or legislation – is much easier to discern and more straightforward to measure. In broad terms, the overwhelming majority of new statutes promulgated in the fourteenth and fifteenth centuries originated from common petitions, and most reproduced the wording of the original petition faithfully. It is less frequently recognised in an English context that a small but steady stream of new acts were also issued on the initiative of the Crown – the Statute of Labourers of 1351 is perhaps the best-known example.[95] This did not violate any constitutional principle: the Commons appear to have accepted that some statutes had an 'official' origin so long as these were passed by them for approval.

In an English context, it is also easy to measure the ratio of petitions presented to statutes promulgated. Indeed, historians often use this crude

---

[94] Olivier-Martin (1997), p. 133.
[95] *PROME*, parliament of 1351, item 47; *Statutes of the Realm* (1810–28), vol. I, pp. 311–13.

formula to measure the political climate and to indicate how receptive the Crown was to the difficulties facing the kingdom. In the final years of Edward III's reign – a period characterised by political malaise and tension – only thirteen statutes were enacted in the six parliaments which met between 1369 and 1377, and this in spite of the fact that very large numbers of common petitions were submitted (the largest total for a single parliament in the late medieval period – 126 – was recorded for the Good Parliament of 1376). By contrast, King Henry IV was much more assiduous in addressing the grievances of the political community in the initial parliaments of his reign – almost a hundred statutes were promulgated in the first four assemblies alone. This no doubt reflected the king's desire to be seen to be responsive to the concerns of the political community, because of his urgent need to attract political support following his recent usurpation of Richard II. As regards private petitions, it is much harder to measure the success rate of these requests, not least because (as we have seen) many petitions did not achieve a definite solution during parliament, but were referred onwards for further investigation and deliberation. However, the Crown's commitment to addressing these requests is shown to good effect by the unique list of petitions presented to the parliament of October 1318 where it was recorded that out of a total of 336 petitions presented in this assembly, only 29 (9 per cent) failed to be expedited because of difficulties they raised (*Peticiones non plene expedite propter aliquas difficultates*).[96] Even if the petition did not receive a positive response, there was at least a good chance that it would receive consideration.

Conclusion

Comparing the phenomenon of petitioning in France and in England presents quite a challenge given the fundamental institutional differences between the two kingdoms. Kings of France and England were, like any territorial prince, subject to a constant flow of supplicatory traffic, but the way these petitions were handled differed greatly as a result of the different structures and cultures of English and French government. The petition, a means of gaining acts of grace of all kinds, could, in France, also direct or limit the action of the king as a legislator, whereas in England the normal route for legislation passed through parliament, with its own powers and its own institutional permanence. In this context it becomes easier to understand the specific issues which led in France to various attempts to regulate direct access to the king, since it was neither

[96] *PROME*, parliament of October 1318; TNA E 175/1/22.

possible nor desirable to prevent such access entirely. In later medieval France, the king was still open to direct approach, although everything possible was done to make such personal interactions more difficult. This helps us to understand the tension between, on the one hand, the reality of forms of mediation which became more and more necessary as the bureaucratic machine became more complicated, and, on the other, the ideal of a king who was expected to be close to his people and accessible to all. In England, this same tension existed, but attempts to divert petitioners away from the king, or to place intermediaries between him and his petitioning subjects were more usually the result of pragmatic considerations rather than a legal or political agenda. In England, elaborate bureaucratic processes were created and large numbers of petitions were dealt with by proxy, but the king still handled huge numbers of complaints and requests in person throughout the late medieval period. Even in parliament, the king remained at the very heart of the petitionary process. As a general rule, only petitions which the king did not wish to deal with were delegated elsewhere. It may, therefore, have been the case that Englishmen had a greater chance of gaining access to their king than Frenchmen did to theirs, and it may even be true that English kings consequently had a clearer vision of conditions in their kingdom. This inevitably placed much greater emphasis on the personal qualities and judgement, as well as industriousness, of English monarchs, which meant that whilst the English petitionary system might have been a more effective tool of royal power, it also had greater capacity to expose the weaknesses and failings of an English king's rule.

BIBLIOGRAPHY

1. INTRODUCTION

Bautier R.-H., 1964–5. 'Recherches sur la chancellerie royale au temps de Philippe VI', *Bibliothèque de l'Ecole des Chartes*, 122 (1964), 89–176 and 123 (1965), 313–459.

Dodd, G., 2007a. *Justice and Grace: Private Petitioning and the English Parliament in the Late Middle Ages*, Oxford.

Millet, H. (ed.), 2003. *Suppliques et Requêtes: Le Gouvernement par la Grâce en Occident (xiie–xve Siècle)*, Rome.

Ormrod, W. M., Dodd, G. and Musson, A. (eds.) 2009. *Medieval Petitions: Grace and Grievance*, Woodbridge.

Petit-Renaud, S., 2003. *Faire loy au royaume de France de Philippe VI à Charles V (1328–1380)*, Paris.

Rigaudière, A., 2000. 'Un enjeu pour la construction de l'Etat : penser et écrire la loi dans la France du xive siècle', in A. Padoa-Schioppa (ed.), *Justice et législation*, Paris, pp. 73–101.

2. SOURCES CITED

Antiquarian Repertory, ed. F. Grose, 4 vols., London, 1807–9.

Choix de documents inédits sur l'Aunis et la Saintonge, ed. P. Marchegay, Les Roche-Baritaud, 1875.

Correspondance de la mairie de Dijon, ed. J. Garnier, Dijon, 1868–70.

Devic, D. Cl. and Vaissete, D. J., *Histoire générale de Languedoc, tome 10 and tome 12, Preuves*, Privat (ed.), Toulouse, 1885–9.

Fleta, ed. H. G. Richardson and G. O. Sayles, Selden Society 72, London, 1955.

Histoire de Bretagne, ed. D. G. A. Lobineau, Paris, 1707 (repr. Paris, 1973).

Lettres de Louis XI, roi de France, ed. J. Vaesen, E. Charavay and B. de Mandrot, Paris, 1883–1904.

Lettres de rois, reines et autres personnages des cours de France et d'Angleterre depuis Louis VII jusqu'à Henri IV tirées des archives de Londres par Bréquigny, ed. M. Champollion-Figeac, Paris, 1839–47.

L'ordonnance cabochienne (26–27 mai 1413), A. Coville, Paris, 1891.

Morice, D. H., 1742–6, *Mémoires pour servir de preuves à l'histoire ecclésiastique et civile de Bretagne*, Paris (repr. Paris, 1974).

Ordonnances des roys de France de la troisième race, ed. E. de Laurière, D.-F. Secousse, L. G. de Vilevault, L. de Bréquigny, C. de Pastoret, J.-M. Pardessus, Paris, 1723–1849.

Parliament Rolls of Medieval England (PROME), ed. C. Given-Wilson et al., Leicester, 2005.

Petitions to the Crown from English Religious Houses, c.1272–c.1485, ed. G. Dodd and A. K. McHardy, Canterbury and York Society 100, Woodbridge, 2010.

Proceedings and Ordinances of the Privy Council of England, ed. N. H. Nicolas, 7 vols., 1834–7.

Procès-verbaux des séances du conseil de régence du roi Charles VIII, ed. A. Bernier, Paris, 1836.

Recueil de monuments inédits de l'histoire du tiers Etat, ed. A. Thierry, Paris, 1853.

Statutes of the Realm, 11 vols., London, 1810–28.

3. FURTHER READING

Autrand, F., 1969. 'Offices et officiers royaux en France sous Charles VI', *Revue Historique*, 242, 285–338.

Bailhache, G., 1924. 'Les maîtres des requêtes de l'hôtel du roi depuis l'avènement de Jean le Bon jusqu'à l'édit de Compiègne, 1350–1553', thesis, Ecole des Chartes.

Berger, E., 1896. 'Requête adressée au roi de France par un vétéran des armées de Saint Louis et de Charles d'Anjou', in *Etudes d'histoire du Moyen Age dédiées à Gabriel Le Bras*, Paris, pp. 343–50.

Boüard, A. (de), 1929. *Manuel de diplomatique française et pontificale*, Paris.

Brown, A. L., 1964. 'The Authorization of Letter under the Great Seal', *Bulletin of the Institute of Historical Research* 37, 125–56.

Cauchies, J.-M., 1982. *La législation princière pour le comté de Hainaut. Ducs de Bourgogne et premiers Habsbourg (1427–1506)*, Brussels.

Chevalier, B., 1988. 'L'Etat et les bonnes villes en France du temps de leur accord parfait (1450–1550)', in N. Bulst and J.-P. Genet (eds.), *La ville, la bourgeoisie et la genèse de l'Etat moderne (XIIe–XVIIIe siècles)*, Paris, pp. 71–85.

Clark L. (ed.), 2004. *Parchment and People: Parliament in the Middle Ages*, Edinburgh.

Contamine, P., 1992. *Des pouvoirs en France 1300-1500*, Paris.

Coville, A., 1888. *Les cabochiens et l'ordonnance de 1413*, Paris.

Davies, M., 2004. 'Lobbying Parliament: The London Companies in the Fifteenth Century', in L. Clark (ed.), *Parchment and People: Parliament in the Middle Ages*, Edinburgh, pp. 136–48.

Derville, A., 1974. 'Pots-de-vin, cadeaux, racket, patronage. Essai sur les mécanismes de décision dans l'Etat bourguignon', *Revue du Nord*, 56, 341–64.

Dodd, G., 2001. 'The Hidden Presence: Parliament and the Private Petition in the Fourteenth Century', in A. Musson (ed.), *Expectations of the Law in the Middle Ages*, Woodbridge, pp. 135–49.

2003. 'Henry IV's Council, 1399–1405', in G. Dodd and D. Biggs (eds.), *The Reign of Henry IV: The Establishment of the Regime, 1399–1406*, Woodbridge, 95–115.

2007b. 'Diplomacy, Sovereignty and Private Petitioning: Scotland and the English Parliament in the First Half of the Fourteenth Century', in M. Penman and A. King (eds.), *England and Scotland in the Fourteenth Century: New Perspectives*, Woodbridge.

2008. 'Patronage, Petitions and Grace: The 'Chamberlain Bills' of Henry IV's Reign', in G. Dodd and D. Biggs (eds.), *The Reign of Henry IV: Rebellion and Survival, 1403–1413*, Woodbridge.

2009. 'Parliamentary Petitions? The Origins and Provenance of the "Ancient Petitions" (SC 8) in the National Archives', in W. M. Ormrod, G. Dodd and A. Musson (eds.), *Medieval Petitions: Grace and Grievance*, Woodbridge.

2011a. 'The Rise of English, the Decline of French: Supplications to the English Crown, c. 1420–1450', *Speculum*, 86, 117–50.

2011b. 'Writing Wrongs: The Drafting of Supplications to the Crown in Later Fourteenth-Century England', *Medium Ævum*, 80, 217–46.

2014. 'Kingship, Parliament and the Court: The Emergence of "High Style" in Petitions to the English Crown, c. 1350–1405', *English Historical Review*, 129, 515–48.

Ehrlich, L., 1921. 'Proceedings Against the Crown (1216–1377)', in P. Vinogradoff (ed.), *Oxford Studies in Social and Legal History*, Oxford.

Etchechoury, M., 1991. *Les maîtres des requêtes de l'Hôtel du roi sous les derniers Valois (1553–1589)*, Mémoires et documents de l'Ecole des chartes, 33, Paris.

Gauvard, C., 1980. 'Les officiers royaux et l'opinion publique en France à la fin du Moyen Age', in W. Paravicini and K. F. Werner (eds.), *Histoire comparée de l'administration ive–xviiie siècle*, XIVe colloque historique franco-allemand, Beihefte der Francia 9, Munich, pp. 583–93.

1988. 'Ordonnance de réforme et pouvoir législatif en France aux xive siècle (1303–1413)', in A. Gouron and A. Rigaudière (eds.), *Renaissance du pouvoir législatif et genèse de l'Etat*, Montpellier.

1991. *"De grace especial"*. *Crime, Etat et société en France à la fin du Moyen Age*, Paris.

1997. 'Les clercs de la chancellerie royale française et l'écriture des lettres de rémission aux xive et xve siècles', in K. Fianu and D. J. Guth (eds.), *Ecrit et pouvoir dans les chancelleries médiévales: espace français, espace anglais*, Actes du colloque international de Montréal (7–9 septembre 1995), Louvain-la-Neuve, pp. 281–91.

Gorochov, N., 2003. 'Le recours aux intercesseurs. L'exemple des universitaires parisiens en quête de bénéfices ecclésiastiques (vers 1340–vers 1420)', in H. Millet (ed.), *Suppliques et Requêtes: Le Gouvernement par la Grâce en Occident (XIIe–XVe)*, Rome, pp. 151–64.

Gray, H. L., 1932. *The Influence of the Commons on Early Legislation: A Study of the Fourteenth and Fifteenth Centuries*, Cambridge, MA.

Guillois, A., 1909. *Recherches sur les maîtres des requêtes de l'Hôtel des origines à 1350*, Paris.

Harding, A., 1975. 'Plaints and Bills in the History of English Law, Mainly in the Period 1250–1350', in D. Jenkins (ed.), *Legal History Studies 1972*, Cardiff, pp. 65–86.

2002. *Medieval Law and the Foundations of the State*, Oxford.

Harriss, G. L., 1963. 'The Commons' Petition of 1340', *EHR*, 78, 625–54.

1975. *King, Parliament and Public Finance in Medieval England to 1369*, Oxford.

Haskett, T. S., 1991. 'The Presentation of Cases in Medieval Chancery Bills', in W. M. Gordon and T. D. Fergus (eds.), *Legal History in the Making: Proceedings of the Ninth British Legal History Conference, Glasgow 1989*, London, pp. 11–28.

1993. 'County Lawyers? The Composers of English Chancery Bills', in P. Birks and T. S. Haskett (eds.), *The Life of the Law: Proceedings of the Tenth British Legal History Conference, Oxford 1991*, London, pp. 9–23.

1996. 'The Medieval English Court of Chancery', *Law and History Review*, 14, 245–313.

Koziol, G., 2003. 'The Early History of Rites of Supplication' in H. Millet (ed.), *Suppliques et Requêtes: Le Gouvernement par la Grâce en Occident (xiie–xve Siècle)*, pp. 21–36.

Lacey, H., 2009. *The Royal Pardon: Access to Mercy in Fourteenth-Century England*, Woodbridge.

Le Goff, J., 1996. *Saint Louis*, Paris.

Mattéoni, O., 2003. '"Plaise au roi." Les requêtes des officiers en France à la fin du Moyen Âge', in H. Millet, *Suppliques et Requêtes: Le Gouvernement par la Grâce en Occident (xiie–xve Siècle)*, Rome, pp. 282–96.

Myers, A. R., 1937. 'Parliamentary Petitions in the Fifteenth Century', *English Historical Review*, 52, 385–404, 590–613.

Olivier-Martin, F., 1950. 'Quelques exemples de l'influence du droit canonique sur le droit public de l'Ancien Régime', in *Actes du congrès de droit canonique, Paris, 1947*, Paris, pp. 362–8.

1997. *Les lois du roi*, Paris.

Ormrod, W. M., 1990. 'Agenda for Legislation, 1322–c.1340', *EHR*, 105, 1–33.

Paravicini, W., 1980. 'Administrateurs professionnels et princes dilettantes. Remarques sur un problème de sociologie administrative à la fin du Moyen Age', in W. Paravicini and K. F. Werner (eds.), *Histoire comparée de l'administration (ive–xviiie siècle)*, XIVe colloque historique franco-allemand, Beihefte der Francia 9, Munich, pp. 168–81.

Pollard, A. F., 1942. 'The Clerical Organization of Parliament', *English Historical Review*, 57, 31–58.

Quéré, S., 1997. '"Qu'il plaise au roy faire bailler lettres patentes . . . "': les Etats de Languedoc et la chancellerie royale française (XIVe–XVe siècles)', in K. Fianu and D. J. Guth (eds.), *Ecrit et pouvoir dans les chancelleries médiévales: espace français, espace anglais*, Louvain-la-Neuve, pp. 205–21.

Rayner, D., 1941. 'Forms and Machinery of the "Commune Petition" in the Fourteenth Century', *English Historical Review*, 56, 198–233, 549–70.

Richardson, H. G. and Sayles, G. O., 1981. *The English Parliament in the Middle Ages*, London.

Rigaudière A., 2008. 'Requête des habitants de la bonne ville d'Aurillac pour une révision de l'assiette de la taille royale en 1480–1481', in J.-C. Cassard, Y. Coativy, A. Gallicé and D. Le Page (eds.), *Le prince, l'argent, les hommes au Moyen Age. Mélanges offerts à Jean Kerhervé*, Rennes, pp. 387–402.

Sayles, G. O., 1988. *The Functions of the Medieval Parliament of England*, London.

Scase, W., 2007. *Literature and Complaint in England 1272–1553*, Oxford.

Tessier, G., 1940. 'Lettres de justice', *Bibliothèque de l'Ecole des Chartes*, 101, 102–15.

1962. *Diplomatique royale française*, Paris.

1963. 'La chancellerie royale française d'après l'ordonnance cabochienne (1413)', *Moyen Age*, 69, 679–90.

Tuck, J. A., 1971. 'Richard II's System of Patronage', in F. R. H. Du Boulay and C. M. Barron (eds.), *The Reign of Richard II*, London, pp. 1–20.

Wilkinson, B., 1924. 'The Authorisation of Chancery Writs under Edward III', *Bulletin of the John Ryland's Library* 8, 107–39.

10 The masses

Vincent Challet and Ian Forrest

The majority of the population of late medieval England and France did not have an institutional or official voice, nor a meaningful right to be involved in the governance of the realm. Even as political society expanded and drew in the lower gentry, clergy, and (on an ad hoc basis) sections of the peasantry, the majority of the population in each realm was still excluded from the decision-making and administrative activity of government, and from meaningful representation or consultation. And yet these excluded people, whether so lowly as to be always beneath the radar of governance, or of some intermediate status that meant they were sometimes useful and sometimes a nuisance, always considered the king as their lord, and they looked to him as the guarantor of peace and justice in the realm, and in their lives. Conversely, late medieval kings were encouraged to see themselves in exactly this role, although little direct contact was necessarily envisaged between them and these, the least of their subjects.

This chapter is concerned with the attitudes and actions, vis-à-vis government and governance, of those who had no personal place in its structures. Whether this subject is seen as a stage in the long-term integration of the masses into the modern state, or merely as the relationship between the powerful and the powerless that pertained in one particular historical period, it is clear that 'the masses and governance' constitutes both a neglected and a difficult theme. The neglect is familiar, but the difficulties are worth discussing in some detail, since new horizons are currently appearing. We will proceed from a definition of terms and an examination of how the histories of England and France have responded to the question of popular politics, to a description and analysis of the ways in which the masses could conceivably speak to and act upon royal government, looking at prophecy and rebellion as symptoms of pressure exerted by the masses on a political system that excluded them.

1.   Problems of definition

The masses

The study of the masses in both England and France has, to date, largely been concerned with the economic and material conditions in which they lived. Early pioneering work on peasants conducted by Postan, Kosminsky, Chayanov, Bloch and others, has been greatly augmented, and criticised by historians such as Guy Bois, Monique Bourin, Pierre Charbonnier, Georges Duby, Christopher Dyer, Robert Fossier, Rodney Hilton, James Ambrose Raftis, Zvi Razi and many others who aimed to reconstruct the contours of peasant life from the records of seigniorial administration and land transactions. The study of the lower classes in medieval towns has received less thorough historical treatment, but there has recently been some fascinating work on the politics of urban life, building on the foundational studies of Rodney Hilton, Susan Reynolds, and Bronislaw Geremek. The findings of this boom in social history provide the basis for much of what we will say in this chapter, but the study of the masses is now at an interesting juncture. Whereas the agenda for the study of popular politics set by Marxists revolved around class conflict and focused on a few iconic rebellions, it has recently become more common to talk about the politics of everyday existence, and notions of peasant ideology have consequently become more complex. The work of Paul Freedman,[1] and other English-speaking historians and literary scholars, has been particularly important here. However, there is still a great deal of scope for historians to marry the techniques and findings of social and economic history with new developments in the writing of political history over the last thirty years. Questions of popular political aspirations and knowledge, the ideological as well as the social basis of collective action, of communication, imagery and emotion, are all wide open.

Most significantly, perhaps, the time may be ripe for a reclassification of social status on political grounds. Rather than categorising the masses in terms of economic activity, legal status, or tenurial position, and then studying the politics of that group, we suggest that it can be profitable to make one's initial classification of a social group in terms of political activity. Essentially we wish to urge an understanding of the masses that is political and not determined by social class or economic status. Class was the analytical starting point for a generation of French medievalists influenced by the Marxist Boris Porchnev's studies of

[1] Freedman (1999).

peasant revolts under Louis XIV,[2] using the phrase *masses populaires* to indicate a homogenous class. For British students of Hilton the exploitative relationship between lord and tenant was thought to be the determining feature of late medieval society. Now, however, the focus of social historians has shifted from lord–peasant relations to inter-peasant relations, and we are much more aware of the importance of social stratification within the urban and rural masses. By privileging politics above class we wish to emphasise that exclusion from the institutions of governance was not predicated entirely on wealth or economic position. Many of the individuals whom historians would place among the 'upper peasantry', the 'yeomanry', or the *coqs de village* are better – that is, more precisely – described according to their political activity.[3]

These people were often described by church and state authorities as the *maior et sanior pars*, the *boni et graves*, *boni et probi homines*, or *viri fidedigni* of their communities. They were the collaborators with outside authority, sometimes acting as representatives of their excluded neighbours in secular and ecclesiastical courts, and sometimes acting as the agents of authority in the same contexts. This group was not, however, primarily distinguished from the rest of peasant society by wealth, but by compliance, trust (both within the community and with authority), and knowledge of administrative procedure. For the people who were never part of this privileged group, the distinction between them and the *boni et graves* mattered a great deal and could be the nub of local politics, but for those in power, the distinction was less important, or less visible. When threatened, those in power were happy to group these humble collaborators with the state along with the greater body of permanently excluded *populares* or *pauperes et minuti*. These less discriminating Latin terms for the lowest stratum of society correspond to the French *commun* and *menus*, the Occitan *menutz*, and the Middle English *pouere*.[4]

Literate members of the governing classes used such words to describe the total body of people who would not normally be involved in politics or governance as they saw it, but these terms were often ambiguous, concealing diversity as much as describing reality. In Montpellier between 1321 and 1331, for example, conflict between the consulate and the so-called *populares* over taxes and expenses seemed to pit an urban oligarchy against 'the masses'. However, a list of *populares* who contributed

---

[2] Porchnev (1963) for the French edition. Against Porchnev's positions, see Mousnier (1967).
[3] Menant and Jessenne (2007); Masschaele (2008); Forrest (2013).
[4] Boglioni, Delort and Gauvard (2002).

towards the legal costs of prosecuting their case, while revealing over 130 ploughmen and many artisans, also shows that their leaders were lawyers and merchants.[5] The thirteenth-century jurist Beaumanoir thought that all collective actions should involve some of the wealthier inhabitants of a place, so that the poor would not run roughshod over the interests of their betters. Such diversity, however, was more routinely disguised when chroniclers, lawyers, notaries or poets wrote about the masses. For example, in Middle English words such as *rustics*, *knaves*, *churls*, and even *villeins*, elided social distinctions in order to create a politically excluded category, combining negative moral associations with extremely malleable social descriptors, while a similar simplification and denigration took place in the description of late-medieval Parisian labourers as the 'inutile au monde'.[6] Late medieval rulers, gentry, merchants and clergy had very strong instincts with regards to those with whom they did *not* wish to govern.

Where does this leave 'the masses' as a term of historical analysis? There are two possible approaches, it seems. Either, one may nuance one's use of the term to exclude those of the *populares* or *menutz*, who were clearly socially superior to their fellows – burgesses, merchants and so forth – on the grounds that people with economic and social status should not be lumped together with people who had neither. This creates a problem of method in that it is not always possible to distinguish between the actions and motives of a group whose behaviour is usually discussed in the vague and generalised terms referred to above. There were, of course, very real political differences of interest between producers and merchants in French and English towns, and the civic elites of a guild merchant or town council were far from being excluded from national politics. However, many poorer merchants and burgesses did not enjoy routine access to power, and their political interests did not always depend on economic interest. We will proceed with a political definition of the masses: those people deprived of an institutional voice in normal circumstances.[7]

In recent years historians of political thought have gradually moved their attention from what people thought, to what they said they thought. This change in the focus of elite political history has major implications for how we approach the political history of the rural and urban masses. Is it possible to write the history of popular political thought, of self- and collective representation? The answer is yes, but the process is more

---

[5] Combes (1972).   [6] Barr (2001); Freedman (1999); Geremek (1976).
[7] Which does not mean that they did not have any voice. See Challet, Dumolyn, Haemers and Oliva Herrer, 2014.

protracted than for elite history, and the results will be different. Much remains to be done in this respect and it is not our intention to present detailed local findings here, but to provide a partial overview of themes and problems.

Community

To begin with: is it possible to study the masses independently of the communities in which they lived? Many of our sources, such as legal and tax records, either treat individuals as members of a community, or refer only to communities and not to individuals. The royal governments of England and France were most comfortable dealing with the masses at arm's length in this way, but in England the theoretical possibility for freemen to plead in the central common-law courts means that on occasion we can study the actions of an individual peasant or townsman. However, this individuality may be misleading, as the social status of the masses, their political ideas and actions in relation to government, were determined in large part by the social circumstances of the communities in which they lived. There is the danger, in accepting the division of the masses into communal categories that we find in government or official sources, that one merely repeats a simplification at the expense of providing analysis. While we are keen to eschew an individualism that would prevent us from saying anything meaningful about the social groups and networks within which people experienced government – as passive victims or beneficiaries, by collaborating or by resisting – it is necessary to remain mindful that an individual can inhabit many different, overlapping or even contradictory, communities at the same time. Some of these were institutional and recognised by government, but others were informal, like families and the friendship groups that lay behind feuds and oath-helping, and the groups described by David Nirenberg as 'communities of violence', or by Barbara Rosenwein as 'emotional communities', as well as some forms of economic cooperation.[8]

Having established that communities are necessary to the analysis of the masses' relationship with government – because this is how social life was experienced and how government imagined the masses – we have to face the differences in 'community' between England and France, and between English and French historiography. In the south of France many villages and small towns enjoyed a corporate legal identity from the thirteenth century, largely as a result of the policy of Louis IX and his brother Alphonse of Poitiers. Consulates and syndicates represented towns and

[8] Nirenberg (1996); Rosenwein (1998); Dyer (2004).

villages at regional assemblies, and even those settlements that had neither consulate, syndicate, nor commune, could appoint proctors to give
themselves an institutional voice.[9] For example, in 1360 an assembly was
convoked by the king's lieutenant of Languedoc, John count of Poitiers,
to meet at Pézenas. Of the settlements in the *viguerie* of Gignac, two
towns (Lodeve and Clermont) and fourteen villages sent representatives.
Most of the villages sent someone who was described as a consul, while
others sent someone without a formal position. This legal and institutional identity, in part a legacy of the Roman law traditions of the south
of France, gave the community a formal existence that was recognised by
those in authority, and could not always be ignored. This situation was
less common in the north of France, where only one in six settlements
could be called communes, possessing a charter of liberties, but as many
as one in two settlements had some form of political organisation.

In England only boroughs, and in the later Middle Ages, some non-
burghal towns, achieved this formal communal status, with charters of
liberties, a degree of self-government, and some measure of corporate
identity. In the countryside and in many small towns corporate identity was only achieved by proxy. In many places, guilds and fraterni-
ties came to represent the collective power of a local elite, and in 'seigniorial boroughs' the judicial and administrative prerogatives of the lord
were frequently leased to a group of leading burgesses.[10] The differences
and similarities with France can be seen if we compare the representation of the English vill at the hundred court with that of French village
communes at regional *états*. The composition of the representation was
perhaps similar, with each English vill sending its reeve and four other
men and each French commune sending a *consul*, *juré*, or *échevin*; the
contact with public authority and the tacit acknowledgement that the
acquiescence of peasant communities was necessary for local government was also similar; but the institutional identity of many French
settlements was a major difference, as was the higher political level
at which French rural communities could be represented. One reason for the *relative* institutional weakness of English communities was
the strength of English lordship. Although, in England, manorial lordship regularly cut across settlement boundaries and other jurisdictional
boundaries like the parish, and one village could contain more than one
manor, in France, outside the *bastides* and other planned settlements
of the eleventh to thirteenth centuries, the situation was much more
fragmented, with one village often containing not one or two lords, but
many. At Hermonville in Champagne, for example, the break-up of the

[9] Bourin-Derruau (1987).   [10] Bailey (2011).

seigneurie in the early fourteenth century left eight or nine minor lords, each operating his own court, and in parts of the south, many lords possessed only one sixteenth, or less, of any given village. Eventually, to reimpose some order onto agricultural activities, the commune appointed its own officers, ignoring the petty lords. Despite the leasing of seigniorial authority noted recently by Mark Bailey, the strength of private lordship in England was, by contrast with France, sufficient to be an impediment to the development of strong formal communal institutions.

These historical differences are translated into historiographical differences. While French historians are quite comfortable talking about communities as settlements with recognised geographical, social and institutional boundaries,[11] English historians tend to use community as an abstract noun indicating the sociability of places and other groups. Some historians are deeply cynical about the existence of community, although this is mostly the result of an a priori rejection of communities as anything but ideological constructions. Communities as groups of people bound by common interests and a degree of common identity are made and maintained by social interaction, for good or ill.[12] In agricultural settlements this interaction primarily took place in the cooperation necessary to organise the distribution of field strips, regulate grazing (*vaine pâture*), plan crop rotations (*assolement triennial* in the north of France), mobilise the labour of the plough team and enforce the maintenance of common land, irrigation and drainage ditches and village buildings. Affective community – feelings of common interest and identity – can only be based on interaction: this is what Peter Blickle means when he envisages *Kommunalismus* on the basis of *Zusammenleben*.[13]

Over the course of the late medieval period, the relative importance of the various institutions of communal life shifted. In southern France the parish was evolving as a corporate institution only as late as the fifteenth century, while in northern and eastern France and in England, the parish had been firmly established as a focus of community by the later twelfth century. During the next three centuries, parishes in these areas gradually took over some of the governmental functions of the vill relating to tax assessment, musters and proclamations. This happened in a piecemeal fashion over time and space. In 1296, Langham in Essex was described as a parish rather than a vill for the purposes of a land transaction; in 1377, the poll taxes in Cornwall and Middlesex were collected by parish rather than by vill; and in the fifteenth century the practice of splitting by-law fines between the parish and the manor court became widespread.

---

[11] Fossier (1992).
[12] Contrast Carpenter (1994) with Davies (2001).   [13] Blickle (1997).

In northern France, parishes were being used for the assessment and collection of taxes by the mid fourteenth century, and increasingly people began to identify themselves as being 'from' a particular parish, rather than a commune. This was a style of identification that would have seemed quite out of place in the south of France, even at the end of our period. As seigniorial authority declined in both countries after the Black Death, the parish and associated religious associations like guilds also became the focus for communal self-government, social control and moral regulation.

All of this took place within an increasingly centralised governmental structure, most noticeably in England, but also to some extent in France, with royal institutions replacing local feudal institutions. Landlords in both countries increasingly looked to central government for the enforcement of labour laws (both kingdoms saw labour legislation in 1351 after the Black Death) and the maintenance of the social order; peasants likewise looked to the king to guarantee their rights against rapacious landlords. The English common law was opened up to more people as greater numbers of the peasantry achieved free status; the assessment of taxation was more frequently placed in the hands of government agents than communities themselves; military array was moving away from the feudal levy towards contracts and indentures; law and order was becoming more concentrated in the hands of royal justices; and local officers collaborating with government officials now made decisions that had once been made by the community. France was, in this respect, moving at a slower pace than England, given the resistance that the Crown encountered when encroaching on the territory of provincial dukes and princes. In both realms, these changes took place over a long period of time, and not all at the same time, but the institutional landscape of 1450 was significantly changed from that of 1250.

The entry of central government into areas previously the preserve of local lords and communities was matched by the extension of the rhetoric of community to more and more of the population. In England the kingdom was defined in the broadest possible sense as the community of the realm, given temporary reality in, for example, *le commun de Engleterre* established by the oaths of the baronial rebels in 1258. When the communal idea achieved a degree of permanence its will was thought to reside in parliament and in the king's personal consultation with his leading subjects. By the fifteenth century, however, many historians now agree that the English saw themselves as part of a regnal community to which some historians have attached an incipient national identity. This developed partly in response to the propaganda for war and partly in people's acknowledgement of their role as taxpayers. In France, however, the idea of the masses being *regnicoli* was a rather empty, academic one, although this did not hamper the formation of what might be called 'public opinion' in response to war. Bernard Guenée, for example, dates the emergence of public opinion as a force in French politics to the propaganda efforts surrounding the allegiance of Charles II of Navarre in 1357.[14] Periods of civil war also saw concerted propaganda campaigns in England, with the bills and manifestos particularly important in *creating* a public during the Wars of the Roses.[15] Alongside this abstract regnal community, the idea of the community of the faithful also became much more of a reality as the language of theological community (*corpus Christi, communitas fidei*) became ever-more familiar to the laity through using the church courts, and from preaching and religious instruction, embodied in England by John Pecham and in France by Jean Gerson. This meant that communication between the king and his subjects was becoming more of a possibility, as the language of politics and community extended to more and more of the population. The masses were also becoming more of a direct concern to central government, whether they represented taxable wealth or a threat to law and order, but the developments by which they were incorporated into the 'modern state' did not constitute an improvement in their own access to government. Their involvement was expected to be obedient and to conform to allotted roles: labourer, juror, soldier; but conversely, no king was powerful enough to levy taxes without at least tacit consent.[16]

To what extent then, and in what ways, did the masses desire and achieve influence on the governments of England and France?

2.   The masses and the king: direct or indirect links

An institutional and judicial voice?

The idea that the king was responsible for justice and peace throughout the kingdom was an essential attribute of royal power in both England and France, constantly reiterated by all political writers during the Middle Ages, and consequently perhaps, an expectation shared by many. The myth of Saint Louis, seated under an oak tree and always ready to hear the grievances of his subjects remained vivid during the entire period. As the embodiment of his people, the king was supposed to feel their tribulations as his own. In England, parliament was also supposed to reflect the interests of all the king's subjects. This does not mean, however, that

[14] Guenée (2002).   [15] Watts (2004), pp. 176–9.
[16] Scordia (2005); Ormrod (2010).

any individual person, let alone illiterate peasants or labourers, could automatically have direct access to royal justice.

The English and the French masses had a roughly comparable juridical relationship with royal government. Both had some theoretical access to royal justice, yet both were severely constrained by the costs involved. In England, however, even this theoretical access was limited to free men, while the un-free population was limited to pursuing grievances in the manorial courts, most of which operated both as the lord's private court, and as a communal forum for the settlement of disputes. While manor courts increasingly adopted the actions and language of the common law in the fourteenth century, this did not make King's Bench in any sense a court of appeal from seigniorial jurisdiction.

A comparison with France depends on the point of view adopted. It seems obvious that most individual peasants were similarly deprived of the financial means that would give them access to the central courts, represented by the *Parlement* of Paris. But at the beginning of the fourteenth century, this institution was recognised as a court of appeal from any seigniorial jurisdiction in the kingdom, whether ecclesiastical or secular, in addition to being a court of appeal from any lower royal jurisdiction, such as those of the *baillis* or *sénéchaux*. In spite of this possibility, individual appeals to the *Parlement* from people belonging to the masses were rare and quite exceptional, mainly because poor peasants or workers had a cheaper alternative to lawsuits, which was the letter of grace delivered on direct appeal to the king. French letters of grace have been analysed for the fourteenth and fifteenth centuries by Claude Gauvard, who demonstrated that even if the price of such a letter was still high (32 *sous* in the fourteenth century), it was quicker and cheaper than appealing to the *Parlement*.[17] Much of what we know about the individuals involved in the Jacquerie of 1357 derives from these letters, many of them delivered to people describing themselves as *povres laboureurs*.

One alternative to individual contact with royal government was collective action in a formal *universitas*. In France, from the beginning of the fourteenth century, many communes or consulates began to plead against their own lords or even royal officers before royal courts. Their position as *universitates* gave communities a juridical existence and the potential to bypass the level of lordship, going direct to royal government. But the juridical identity of French communes was by no means purely for their own benefit. In Languedoc from the beginning of the thirteenth century, consulates were founded both by the king and his officers. The Crown's objective in promoting legal communities in the region was to

---

[17] Gauvard (1991).

strengthen its relationship with those communities, and to weaken the local seigniorial powers in their own lands. Philip II had already used such a tool, creating communes in northern France in return for military service against the Plantagenets, or at the Battle of Bouvines. The political importance of these communities to Philip IV, for example, was the support that they could lend to his suppression of the Templars, and the leverage their backing could have on the Avignon papacy. Philip IV also used new communes, across France, as a source of money during the Flemish wars.[18]

As the fiscal demands of the war grew and the Italian banks could not cope with the Crown's borrowing requirements, the English government also looked to the wealth of urban communities, demanding loans from the whole community of a town instead of from a small group of rich merchants. This change meant that artisans demanded consultation on matters like loans and the election of civic officers, since they were now contributing to their towns' fiscal relationship with government. In 1351, for example, a loan to the Crown from the city of London was refused because it had been made 'without the consent of the community'. As a consequence of this fiscal and political change, some English towns underwent changes in their political structure during this period. For example at York in the 1370s, the commons came to be represented in a council of forty-eight, which was called upon to endorse or criticise important decisions made by the councils of twelve and twenty-four that represented the old urban elite. In Norwich in 1404, a new charter made the city into an urban county, with two sheriffs and, for the first time, a mayor who was to be popularly elected. These changes did not, however, make the urban commons partners in government, as oligarchical rule became even more firmly entrenched.

More interesting was the possibility that people not represented in communes or consulates might band together and hire a proctor or advocate to pursue their case in the royal courts. For those members of the masses without any institutional recognition, this was the only route open to them. At Lavaur in 1357, the *populares* forced the consuls into a fair distribution of the taxes amongst the population, by first addressing themselves to a royal judge and then to the court of the seneschal of Toulouse. In this case, the judicial decision went against them, but a subsequent riot frightened the richer citizens so much that it led to a compromise: a new consulate charter was promulgated by royal order, decreeing that the consuls be elected by a general assembly of the entire population. In the years 1390–3, the workers in the vineyards of the

---

[18] Petit-Dutaillis (1947).

abbey of Saint Germain in Auxerre entered into conflict with the abbey over the length of the working day. First of all they gathered together and launched a strike, then, when nothing changed, they collectively hired a lawyer and launched an appeal to the *Parlement*. The judgement of the *Parlement* was that 'even though they are poor people, one cannot force them to work like horses or oxen'.[19]

In England, the masses could also, on occasion, take action in the royal courts by banding together to hire a proctor or advocate. The cause in pursuit of which they most famously did this was the mirage of ancient demesne. Feeling oppressed by the exactions of landlords, tenants on some manors once believed to have been part of the ancient demesne of the Crown attempted, from the mid thirteenth century onwards, to reassert this status, believing that it would free them from customary labour services and high rents. They did this by suing in the royal courts for an exemplification from Domesday Book, which would prove the status of the manor of which they were tenants.[20] Tenants acting in this way could not appear in court themselves as a *universitas*, but this became a more realistic option as the Court of Chancery developed from the 1380s. This court, which operated until the 1530s, accepted pleas that did not easily fall within the common law, and it practised a so-called equitable jurisprudence, partly based on canon law. It was in this context that parish communities could use the legal fiction of 'enfeoffment to use' in order to hold property without the corporate legal personage possessed by French communes.

The pursuit of ancient demesne status and the use of the Court of Chancery by parishes and guilds illustrate an upward pressure on the institutions of government and law in the late Middle Ages. The masses were largely excluded from these institutions, but they were increasingly seeking to access government and law more directly. Even if such a movement as 'ancient demesne' did not arise in France, references to the rules of the kingdom, the *coutumes* or the law, were not absent from the claims of rebels: the insurgents of Rouen in 1381 refer to the *Charte aux Normands* delivered in 1315 by Charles IV, and the captains of the Tuchins in Languedoc wanted a return to the last decisions of Charles V. In all of this, as we say above, the masses looked to the king, or an idealised kingly figure, to guarantee justice and peace for all.

While neither seigniorial justice, common law, statute law, nor canon law provided a means by which the masses could easily and directly get involved in governance, it is possible to see a quite different picture by changing our point of view. If the evolution of justice during the later

[19] Stella (1996).   [20] Faith (1984), pp. 69–74.

Middle Ages is not only understood as a process of top-down legislation and enforcement, but as the interaction between enforcement and collaboration, then the masses may be seen to have had a crucial role to play. As John Watts has suggested, rule 'was less a force imposed by the king upon the realm than a reaction which his proper functioning elicited from it'.[21] This would give to the masses a passive, but crucial, role in determining the course and success of governance. Even if this does not amount to the more active connotations of Peter Blickle's idea of 'state-building from below', we must build the masses into our picture of governance in this period.[22] As jurors in inquests and parish representatives at visitation, peasants and poor townsmen could alter the course of government policy to some degree, albeit passively and only by multiplying individual acts of resistance or compliance many times. To some extent, this was recognised by legal concepts such as *fama publica*, which elevated social relations inside a community to the defining standard of truth before the law. The masses did not often play an active role in which resistance to a particular measure could be organised and made to change government policy, but a passive role did emerge from the beliefs and actions of those who filled local offices and sat on juries. Particular judicial campaigns like the enforcement of the Statute of Labourers, or the fight against heresy, stood or fell on the degree to which this group from among the masses were (i) willing to cooperate, (ii) respected by their fellows, and (iii) sufficiently well-informed in order to do the job. So while direct access to government was restricted to a few examples in a number of limited spheres, the indirect, cumulative importance of the masses cannot be underestimated.

The prophetic voice

Prophecy was one rhetorical conduit for contact between the masses and the king. In France, the importance of close contact between the king and the people was thought to derive from the sacral nature of French kingship, something which was less pronounced in England. The thaumaturgic powers of the heirs of Saint Louis, which required the physical touch of the king, were much more central to royal power in France than in England, although 'touching for the king's evil' was practised by English kings in times of crisis.[23] Differences between the two realms in terms of direct approaches to the king are therefore often differences of emphasis and degree, rather than differences of type.

---

[21] Watts (1996), p. 29.
[22] Blockmans, Holenstein and Mathieu (2009).   [23] Bloch (1924).

Addressing the king through prophecy was an initiative that was more often individual than it was communal, but the existence of an excluded voice or platform from which to make complaints or seek redress, indicates a wider awareness that the masses were a significant presence lurking in the background of late medieval political discourse. Prophetic speech relied upon the repetition of shared words and phrases, making it (in the way of all political speech) collective. Prophecy came to the fore in times of political crisis, and was often closely associated with the type of demands made by rebels. In France, this voice is well illustrated by Hug de Montpellier, Constance de Rabastens, Marie Robine, and Jeanne d'Arc, and in England by popular prophets such as Thomas of Erceldoune, millennial preachers like John Ball, and religious visionaries like Elizabeth Barton. The prophetic voice came from the margins of society and the frontiers of the realm. Erceldoune, or Thomas the Rhymer, supposedly came from Melrose in the Scottish borders, while other prophecies were located by later commentators in the Welsh Marches, Cheshire and Cornwall. Marie Robine, Marie Constance de Rabastens and Pierre Hug all originated from the southern provinces of France, while Jean de Gand and Jeanne d'Arc came from the eastern borders of the kingdom.[24] Social marginality was also emphasised by the gender of the prophet. The model is of a poor and humble woman who comes from the margins of the kingdom and makes her way to Paris or to London to speak to the king and deliver a message from God.

The political content of this message might be very strong. Prophets claiming to speak for the nation or the masses combined loyalty to the king with predictions of disaster if the people's grievances were not heeded. For instance, in 1388, Pierre Hug, who came from Montréal d'Aude, bearing stigmata on his right arm in the shape of a cross, went to Paris to meet the young Charles VI. In spite of the opposition of his uncles, the king agreed to receive the prophet, who told him that God was angered by the sufferings of the people, predicting that if Charles were not attentive to the sufferings of his subjects in Languedoc and did not ease their fiscal burden, his children would not have long lives. This visit is supposed to have had a marked influence on the king, playing a role in his decision to make a trip to Languedoc the next year, and in obliging his uncle, the duke of Berry, to give up his lieutenancy of the king in Languedoc.

In England, political prophecy was rarely so direct. The medium of Thomas the Rhymer and other popular prophets was more of a riddle than a specific demand, asking questions rather than stipulating policy.

[24] Beaune (2004); Hiver-Bérenguier (1984); Vauchez (2012); Coote and Thornton (2001).

Verses such as, 'Wha sall be kynge, wha sall be none, / And wha sall welde this north countre?' expressed only general concern about the person and qualities of the king. The prophetic letters attributed by English chroniclers to John Ball at the time of the Peasants' Revolt are also highly coded, relying on the shared religious imagery of *Corpus Christi* and the symbolic figure of *Piers Plowman* to predict the millennial return of Christ who would 'pay for all'. These prophecies were only generally connected to the more specific demands of the 1381 rebels.

The marginal voice, strongly linked to popular opinion (criticising heavy taxes and the expenses of the royal court, paying attention to the sufferings of the poor and the ravages of war), tended to operate at the fringes of heresy. As is shown by the examples of Jeanne d'Arc and John Ball, one's opinion as to whether a prophet was truly inspired by God or by the devil would be conditioned by one's political position. It may also have been in part conditioned by the wider political culture, as the prophetic voice seems to have occupied an acceptable, if not welcome, position in French political culture that it did not possess in England, where prophets were usually condemned as traitors or heretics. This is perhaps due to the sacral nature of kingship in France, which may have encouraged political society to accept inspired speech and direct links with divine or secret knowledge more easily than England, where statutes on treason (1352), scandal/slander (1285 and 1378), and heresy (1401 and 1414) imposed firm limits on these marginal voices. On the contrary, in France, not only the masses but also the king and even major ecclesiastical figures such as Jean Gerson, chancellor of the University of Paris – who defended Jeanne d'Arc and elaborated the theory of *discretio spirituum* – did believe in the reality of mediation between God and the king through a humble medium. The importance of this humble prophet-leader is shown by Jeanne's replacement in the armies of Charles VII by a poor shepherd of Gévaudan (who was soon captured and executed by English troops).

The French monarchy always considered this prophetic voice to be a part of the necessary, albeit frequently symbolic, dialogue between the masses and their king, and a reminder from God that the sovereign must never forget his duty to protect the poor. Prophecy was also a way to remind the king that sovereignty, in some theoretical formulations, lay in the hands of the people, and that he enjoyed power only by delegation and grace. In England, prophecy was less acceptable, even symbolically. Maybe the difference lies in ecclesiastical attitudes, as well as in the character of the two monarchies. French prophets did not issue from the clergy (as John Ball and Elizabeth Barton did in England), and they did not contest the church and so it was *possible* for the authorities to recognise and control them. In England, the association of radical political agendas with the claims of lollards to divine inspiration arguably hindered prophetic voices from establishing an orthodox platform from which to speak.[25]

An emotional voice

Related to the use of prophecy as an indirect channel for the masses to speak to government, is their use of set-piece emotional rituals. Barbara Rosenwein has ensured that the use of emotions in medieval politics and governance is treated as a serious historical subject, but the political use of emotion by the masses does not figure in this reorientation of historical attention. While the king may be pious, indignant, generous, haughty, for medieval writers, and for historians if they are not careful, the masses are merely angry without reason, and loving without explanation. But there was a highly developed emotional voice available for popular use, cultivated by the masses into a political tool in its own right. In France, theorists of royal government repeatedly told the following anecdote about Philip II. As the king was entering a royal palace, he was approached by an old woman seeking justice. Irritated by this spontaneous petitioner, he said that he had no time to hear her complaints because he had to deal with public affairs. She replied: 'If you have no time to hear me, then you shall not be the king!' Whether this anecdote is true or not, it reflects the widespread opinion that it should be possible for subjects to make complaints directly to the king and that he should answer them. The introduction to Chaucer's *Knight's Tale*, for example, has Theseus returning to Athens after defeating the Amazons, when he is halted by a group of crying women. Theseus asks them 'who hath yow mysboden or offended?' and he asks how he can amend the wrong they have suffered. An emotional appeal by individuals or groups of people possessed something of the popular quality that made prophecy a compelling political voice. Bound together by the expectations of peace and justice that could not always be fulfilled through the institutions of government and law, monarch and people met in circumstances where emotional appeals were considered important. Though they had always been stylised, and to some extent fictionalised, such direct contact between the king and his subjects was gradually replaced by more ritualised royal appearances. Nevertheless, these occasions were still governed by the old expectations of an emotional, mystical, bond between king and people, partially created by the monarchy, as Arlette Farge has suggested, but

[25] Kerby-Fulton (2006).

also actively encouraged by spontaneous, if orchestrated, groups of the king's subjects.[26]

One of the best-known examples of such an 'emotional ritual' created by the monarchy is the royal entry. These entries created a space of dialogue which was both desired and feared by the monarchy, as the site where the king's rule could receive popular approbation, or fall foul of the unpredictable emotions of the masses. The masses could use collective displays of emotion (or a lack of emotion) when the king made a formal entry into a city, or made a procession through a city, and the civic authorities could try to assert their own agenda as well.

In France, the ritual of royal entries developed from the beginning of the fourteenth century but gained in favour from the reign of John II. The most important ceremony took place in Paris when the new king came back from Rheims after the coronation ceremony. The king was welcomed by the bishop, the main authorities of the town and the crowd (especially children) shouting 'Noël' and 'Montjoie' which were the traditional shouts of joy and praise to the king (*laudes regie*). But there was a counterpart to this, as the king was supposed to confirm the ancient privileges of the town and grant new ones (especially fiscal concessions), as well as to grant favours to everyone who asked them. The force of this ritual was so strong that, after the coronation of Charles VI, the trip back from Rheims to Paris avoided the major towns so that the monarchy would not have to give up the taxes it received from them. A major innovation took place in 1389 when for the first time in the kingdom a 'ciel', or canopy of the type carried above the eucharist in Corpus Christi processions, was carried above the king during his entries into the towns of Languedoc. This ritual assimilated the king to Christ himself and His very first entry into Jerusalem. The king likewise took on the messianic responsibility to feed his subjects and grant their wishes. There was often a communal feast after the entry, and even the lowest people could obtain favours from the king at this moment: in 1389, Charles VI made some concessions to the prostitutes of Toulouse who petitioned him as he entered the town.[27]

These rituals could only be efficient if a crowd was present and was willing to share the emotional space opened by the monarchy. Thus, silence from the masses is always interpreted as a bad sign for the government. For example, in 1404, the duke of Berry, brother of Charles V, and then very sick, asked the clergy to organise processions in Paris, hoping that people would join in and pray for his recovery. But, because he was very unpopular, only a few people attended and the processions

[26] Farge (1997).   [27] Guenée and Lehoux (1968).

failed. A similarly salutary tale is told in the Great Chronicle of London about Henry VI's procession through London in 1471: an attempt by his friends to rally the citizens to support Henry against the approaching Edward IV. The procession took place on Shrove Tuesday, and Henry walked through the streets with the archbishop of York holding his hand. The chronicler wrote that this 'was more like a play than the showing of a prince to win men's hearts, for by this act he lost many and won none or right few'. It is likely that this was intended to be a penitential procession, but in any case it failed to impress the Londoners. In these examples, emotional rituals reveal a political and social fissure between the prince and the masses.

Conversely, the masses could also use these rituals to demonstrate their own emotional–political positions, even if they were not expected by authority. In 1408, the Duke of Burgundy, John the Fearless, was welcomed by the Parisians with the shouts of 'Noël! Noël!' which were normally reserved for the king. This was a sign of his great popularity at that moment. It is possible that these were speculative cries of enthusiasm, prompted by much the same political uncertainty that caused the civic officers of York in 1485 to carefully stage-manage Henry VII's first entry into that city by placing children to shout out 'King Henry!' when he appeared. More spontaneous, perhaps, was the way that Parisians in 1422 used the funeral of Charles VI to express their own feelings: they wept to show the great loss represented by the death of the king, but whispered when the duke of Bedford made his entry in the town with king's sword in front of him, to show their dissatisfaction at having the duke of Bedford as regent. On these occasions, public acclamation meant a great deal to the ruling power, and some ritual meetings, such as Richard II's appearance amongst the London crowds after his coronation, were organised by royal government with the hope of a favourable emotional response in mind.

In spite of the close relations between the French and English monarchies, and the mutual influence they had on one another (the entry of Henry VI in Paris was made according to the French model; the funeral of Charles VI used the English model with the first appearance of a wax effigy of the king), this emotional voice does not seem to have had in England the importance it had in France. This was due to differences at the regnal level, particularly the sacred character of the French monarchy which obliged him to be in direct contact with his subjects, a duty that in England was discharged through the common law, an institution revered almost as much as the memory of Saint Louis, and through petitioning. Another occasion on which individuals did occasionally approach the English king was when seeking a pardon for homicide. A long Latin poem composed on the occasion of the restoration of the liberties of

London in 1392 describes such an appeal to the king as he approached the city. However, these appeals for mercy were nearly always personal in England, and they did not pertain to the general quality of the king's rule, except insofar as they provided an opportunity for the king to demonstrate publicly his authority. No general appeal for better governance seems to have been attached to them.

3.   Rebellion as a political language

What is a popular rebellion?

If all else failed, rebellion remained as a means of last resort by which the masses could communicate their dissatisfaction to the king. Medieval rebellions must not be regarded as desperate expressions of blind violence, but as part of continuous strategies elaborated by the masses according to their capabilities, and in response to the reactions and initiatives of those in power.[28] They represent the upward pressure on government that characterised the later Middle Ages.

Continuing our political exploration of who 'the masses' were, it is necessary to ask a series of questions about the identity of rebels and the character of rebellions. In his analysis of the social origins of the English rebels of 1381, Chris Dyer has argued that those rebels prosecuted for their part in the rising came from the upper levels of village society. They were bailiffs, jurors, reeves, warreners, collectors of taxes, and were amongst the larger landowners of peasant society. Nonetheless, they were still peasants. However, we also know that members of the clergy, the gentry, and the urban masses took part, which has led to questioning whether 1381 should in fact be called a 'peasants'' revolt at all. Similar questions have been raised about rebellions in the French kingdom. While some historians have been content to label the leaders of the rebels of Flanders who stood up against their count between 1323 and 1328 as peasants, the implications of this are not clear. The rebels chose as their leaders Nicolas Zannekin and Jacques Peyte, who, far from being poor, miserable peasants were in fact quite prosperous tenants. Indeed, the greater part of these rebels were free and wealthy peasants rather than poor ones, the rebellion taking place in a prosperous region that produced corn and livestock for the markets of Ypres and Bruges.[29] Exactly the same could be said for the rebels of Kent and Essex in 1381, whose prosperous economy was geared towards supplying the needs of London, and of the Jacquerie in the well-to-do Île-de-France, where clergy and craftsmen also played

---

[28] Neveux (1997).   [29] TeBrake (1993).

a part in the rising. Still, drawing distinctions between different levels of peasant (as with Pirenne's false distinction between the prosperous Flanders peasants of 1323–8 and the 'starving' Jacques of 1358) is ultimately unhelpful for present purposes, since we are still dealing with the political action of those largely excluded from any other form of expression.

The complexity of the leadership and identity issue has been addressed by Steve Gunn, who has argued that gentry leadership in the northern English risings in 1536 can variously be seen as the result of coercion, as a sign of sympathy with the rebel cause and as an attempt to control and ultimately defuse the actions and aims of the rebels. In other rebellions, such as that of the Tuchins in Languedoc between 1381 and 1384, peasants did not hesitate to elect local noblemen as their captains,[30] but in common with their gentry counterparts in the Pilgrimage of Grace, these nobles later claimed that they had been coerced into leadership by the peasants with threats of murder. We cannot really take this at face value, as the nobles hoped to obtain royal grace and a pardon for their part in a rebellion. The participation of nobles, clergy, merchants and gentry in rebellions does not automatically mean that they were the leaders of the peasants and labourers. Since there is little evidence of political initiative on the part of the knights and nobles in these revolts, we can interpret their presence in other ways: the most compelling of these being that rebels across Europe had a strong sense that the natural unit of collective action was the community – however they defined it – and so uncooperative members of the community should be coerced into participation.

As Paul Freedman has suggested in the case of 1381, rebellions which focused their demands on villeinage must in some measure have been peasants' rebellions. It is all too easy to forget the mass of participants and focus on the smaller numbers of knights and nobles who provide a bridge to the familiar world of court politics. Nor must we divide the participants from one another. Thinking of rebellion in terms of community was second nature to the medieval masses. Rodney Hilton argued that because rebellions so often sprang from and spoke for communities, we should not be surprised to see priests, craftsmen, yeomen, farmers and even members of the gentry or noblemen involved, as long as they considered themselves, or were considered, as members of the rebellious community. This can be illustrated by the role of the nobility in the Jacques and Tuchin rebellions. During the Jacquerie, the nobility failed to protect their communities and so were attacked; during the Tuchinat they were seen as the natural leaders of their communities. It was normal

---

[30] Gunn (1989); Challet (1998).

for peasants to look to the gentry and nobility as participants, protectors, figureheads and fellow rebels, and their role should be seen in this light.

Another way in which we can address the identity of rebels, and the political role that they sought to fulfil, is by looking at the language in which they were described. The claims of English rebels to represent the 'true commons of England' has sometimes been taken to support the idea that the leaders of the rebellions in 1381 and 1450 were the lower gentry. Being electors to parliament or petitioners to parliament gave this group a corporate identity that could be stimulated when they saw their representatives, the MPs in parliament, failing to protect their interests. However, the language of 'the commons' was at this time coming to be used by a much wider constituency as a way of expressing popular political ideals. In the 1536 rebellions across northern England, for example, rebels identified themselves as the 'commonalty' of Beverley or Pontefract and so on. When the Jacques rose up in 1358 the chronicler Jean le Bel reported it as a rebellion of the 'communes' or the 'communities'.[31] Although there are different implications in the English words 'commons' and 'commonalty', and the French 'communes', the language is indicative of a desire for inclusion, sometimes on the basis of communities as social units, and sometimes as idealised publics. The Jacquerie occurred in a moment of political tension between the heir of John II – the future Charles V – and the general Estates, where peasants were not really represented. After all, peasants could, with a certain legitimacy, claim to be part of the 'community of the realm' and have their voice heard in discussions between Charles and the representatives of the kingdom. The language of community was a common political language shared between royal power, elites and the masses, even if the exact significance of the words differed slightly for each group.

There is a growing consensus among historians that 'high' and 'low' are no longer as useful as they once seemed in the lexicon of political history. Paul Freedman has argued that we should not underestimate the capacity of the masses to use the ideological discourses elaborated by elites to legitimate their domination, turning it back against them when government or elites failed to live up to their responsibilities. We may, certainly, expand Raymond Cazelles' concept of a fairly limited 'political society' which reused concepts made familiar during the fourteenth century through royal letters and orders, to include the masses as well as the elite.[32] The constant use by royal power of such ideas as *communitas regni*, or 'taxes in exchange for security', made it possible for the masses

---

[31] Watts (2007); De Medeiros (1979).
[32] Cazelles (1958); Challet, Genet, Oliva and Valdeon (2007).

to reuse them in rebellions. Perhaps the most striking example of the feedback loop between elites and the masses is the claim of the Tuchins that they were acting for *lo profieg e la honor del realme* (for the profit and honour of the kingdom) which seems to be an approximate translation of the Roman law concept of *utilitas rei publice et regni*. At a more practical level, rebels also often claimed to be following royal orders, as with the authorisations for peasants in the Île-de-France in 1357 and Languedoc in 1369 to take up arms in self-defence against plundering soldiers. In 1450, Cade's rebels in England claimed to be acting on Henry VI's orders to round up traitors when they murdered the bishop of Salisbury.[33]

The grammar of rebellion

We learn most about the communal basis of rebellion from the grammar of rebellion: the words rebels used, the places where they first gathered, the flags they used, the way they formed contacts with other villages, elected leaders or captains and rang church bells. Every action of medieval rebels speaks of the mobilisation of a community (whether that was achieved or not), and across Western Europe this 'grammar of rebellion' in words, flags and actions, was remarkably similar.

An examination of the grammar of rebellion reveals that it was part of a political language that had to be spoken in the correct way, just as petitioning, and in its own way prophecy, had to conform to recognised patterns in order to register on the political scene. In other words, rebels had to act as rebels to avoid being considered as criminals and traitors, which is how they were usually described by contemporary chronicles. This was a fine line to tread, and so the words and actions of rebels had to conform to tradition to ensure that there was no confusion. But confusion was likely, since rebellion used the threat of force as a bargaining tactic, and force against the king was treason. The first 'rule' of the grammar of rebellion was not to use the words 'rebel' or 'rebellion'. Because the king was an untouchable figure, no one was expected to proclaim himself a rebel. On the contrary, rebels had to demonstrate their loyalty to the community, the king and the kingdom. At the risk of over-simplifying this paradox, one could say that in order to appear as rebels in the king's eyes, the masses should use violence, deny that they are rebels and proclaim their allegiance to the king. The fact that the French Jacques in 1357 bore flags with the royal symbol, the fleurs de lys, is clear evidence of this necessary allegiance to the king.

---

[33] Harvey (1991).

Linked to claims of loyalty were claims of inclusivity. When the 1381 English rebels claimed to be the true commons or loyal commons they were tapping into a rhetorical position also claimed by vernacular poets who sought to represent the 'common voice', to criticise without condemning and to seek reform without revolution. Similar claims were made by the rebels of Kent in 1450 who sought the 'common profit' or 'common weal' of the realm, language which was repeated in 1536 when the Lincolnshire and Yorkshire pilgrims asked for reforms to secure the 'common wealth'. Inclusivity and loyalty were also indicated by the choice of Corpus Christi festivals for the rebellious marches on London in both 1381 and 1450. Christ's body signified the whole community, unified, and the rebels may have been trying to advertise their support for national unity and the true religion, quite the opposite of the motives imputed to them by hostile chroniclers.[34]

The signal for rebellion was often given on an important church festival, especially when rebellion proceeded from a *conjuratio* – a sworn association between rebel leaders which might establish a list of enemies to kill. At Béziers in 1381, the leaders of a rebellion gathered in the Church of the Madeleine, swore on the altar of Saint Antoine and decided to act on the 8 September, the date of the Virgin Mary's birth. At Clermont-l'Hérault in 1379, rioting broke out on All Saint's Day. Not only did the rebels generally choose a feast day, they sometimes (at Béziers and Rouen in 1381) acted at vespers, the first canonical hour of prayer, in the dark of night, or just during the night (midnight in Paris in 1418). Whether the timing of rebellion indicates an attempt to exploit religious days and hours for their 'official' meanings of orthodoxy and inclusivity, or an attempt to invert sacred time, as argued by Claude Gauvard, must be left open to further investigation.[35] The use of churches as the gathering places for rebels combined practicality (a well-known place), with the inference of community (church as communal meeting place and symbol), the possibility of communicating with neighbouring villages (sounding the alarm with church bells), and the creation of an atmosphere out of the ordinary. Bells were rung in parish churches by the Jacques in 1357, but in 1379 it was the bells of consulates' houses that were rung in Montpellier, and those of guildhalls in Ypres, Bruges, and Ghent during the 'wapenings' of the fifteenth century. In 1379 at Pont-Saint-Esprit, some rebels went to the town's Cluniac priory and tried to force the monks to ring the bells.

Insofar as the ringing of bells may have contributed to an atmosphere of anticipation and resolve, so did the cries of rebels which suddenly invaded

[34] Aston (1994).   [35] Gauvard (1989).

the streets, such as the 'Haro!' which gave the Harelle in Rouen its name, or the cry of 'Hoo!' with which John Ball encouraged the 1381 London rebels to begin their action. Rebels also used more meaningful slogans, such as the 'Moyran los traidors' (Death to the traitors!) found in many southern French towns, or the exhortatory passwords used in England: 'With whom haldes yow?'; 'Wyth kynge Richarde and wythe the trew communes.' Sometimes the cries of rebels reflect the celebratory feeling that rebellion was its own reward, as with the 'A revelle!' reported in the Westminster Chronicle for 1381.[36]

Communication between rebel groups, across short and long distances, also form part of the grammar of rebellion, since letters, proclamations and messengers brought rebellion into the public sphere, providing the common platform on which all rebels could stand, as well as being of great practical importance in mobilising rebels over large areas. The letter of John Ball included by Thomas Walsingham in his *Historia Anglicana* encourages fellow rebels to stand firm, maintain solidarity and remember the example of Piers Plowman, a reference to William Langland's fictional ploughman-Christ figure. Then follow verses that may be interpreted as a mnemonic call-to-arms, or an instruction about the timing of the rising on Corpus Christi day, with references to a miller grinding his corn and the king's son of heaven, which may mean the Eucharist. The texts of these letters bear a great resemblance to the genre of popular prophecy in that they are cryptic and deal with global concerns of governance and salvation. This would seem to mark rebel communication out from official governmental culture, but the media of communication – letters, oral proclamations and messengers – are basically the same, and would have been recognised by elites. The use of written communication by peasant rebels may be peculiar to the English context, since the examples we have of rebel letters from France are those sent by bourgeois leaders such as Étienne Marcel in 1358, and the consuls of Montpellier, who, after the town rebelled against the duke of Anjou in 1379, wrote to the consuls of surrounding towns asking them to join the rebellion. Written messages may have been used by peasants during the Flanders rebellions between 1323 and 1328, given that peasant captains assumed the duties of comital officers at a local level, rendering justice or collecting public revenues, but Jacques, Tuchins or the peasants who rose against the English troops in Normandy seemed to communicate by oral messages, ringing bells and so on.

There were of course more informal modes of communication. When rebellion occurred the normal currents of news flowed speedily around

---

[36] Lecuppre-Desjardin and Van Bruaene (2005); Dobson (1983).

the country. Following Jack Cade's rebellion, for example, a captured cloth dyer stated in his trial that he had been travelling on the road in Dorset in August 1450 when he had met a merchant riding along. The merchant asked him 'What news of Normandy?', and the dyer replied he had heard it was lost. The merchant then said to the dyer that England too would soon be lost, and he persuaded him to meet with like-minded people who wanted to alter the government of the country. What happened next adds an important aspect to the grammar of rebellion. Like the English barons in 1258, these Dorset rebels bound themselves to each other with an oath. For the Tuchins and the Norman peasants under English rule, taking an oath was the first step in binding together a rebellion, and in 1381 the burgesses of Paris swore an oath of mutual support on bread. In 1536, the Yorkshire pilgrim-rebels also put the swearing of oaths at the centre of their political action, highlighting the threads of a common political culture that was comprehensible to king and peasant alike. Oaths were central to rebellion, whether of urban movements or rural ones, giving purpose and form to collective action, and making it recognisable as rebellion – as a political action, rather than mere disorder.

The words and sounds of rebellion were complemented by the unfurling of flags which might belong to parishes, urban districts or guilds, or have been specially made as rebel flags. Flags emphasised the military character of rebellion, and according to Cohn, they provided a focal point for rebels, who felt the raising of the standard, and the loss or destruction of the standard, as keenly as any chivalric army.[37] During the Tuchins' rebellion in Languedoc, the armed peasant companies entered several towns with flags at their head and a band made up of bagpipes, drums and trumpets. The leader of rebels in St Albans in 1381 raised 'his standard' in front of the abbey church 'and ordered everyone to follow it closely, as in battle'. His standard, in common with that carried by the rebels in London, bore the arms of St George. The importance of emblems and symbols was always well understood by rebels. In Paris, where rebellion could quite easily reach the king, the crowd was very sensitive to the colours worn by the king. In 1358, Étienne Marcel put his own red and blue hat (the colours of Paris) on the head of the Dauphin Charles, and in 1413 during the Cabochiens movement, Charles VI wore the white hat, symbol of the Burgundian party. English rebels frequently used religious imagery on their flags, and not only the cross of St George. In 1414, John Oldcastle was discovered to have made a flag depicting a chalice and a loaf of bread and others showing Christ's cross with whips,

---

[37] Cohn (2006).

nails and a spear, which were to have been carried during the so-called 'lollard' revolt. In 1536, famously, the pilgrim-rebels wore badges and marched behind banners bearing the five wounds of Christ in reference to their defence of Catholic religion.

The grammar of rebellion must also be taken to include violence against property and people, which even when horrific and seemingly unplanned, contained political meaning. In 1379 at Alès, the *populares* gathered and forced the king's officers to accompany them to the houses of the consuls, who were accused of embezzling public funds, where they sold the consuls' possessions in the street. A similar, if less polite, gesture was made against goods paid for from the profits of unpopular subsidies in Paris in 1381, when the Maillotins (Hammer men) took the doors off tax-collectors' houses, threw their furniture out of the windows onto the street and broke open wine casks to signify the return of the goods to the masses. Symbolic destruction in the face of economic injustice was also found in England, as in the smashing of millstones on the estates of the abbey of St Albans in 1381, but during this rebellion, as in others, it was the targeted destruction of documents relating to serfdom and taxation that carried the greatest symbolic weight.

Violence against people could also be invested with political meaning. Rebel leaders often made decisions about 'marked men', typically hated ministers of the king held responsible for bad governance, and carried out their murders as political assassinations. This was the case with the murders of Archbishop Sudbury (chancellor), Robert Hales (treasurer) and John Cavendish (Chief Justice of the King's Bench) in 1381, and of Bishop Aiscough and the duke of Suffolk (royal councillors) in 1450. The treatment of the victims' corpses also belongs to this grammar. In 1379, royal officers were killed in Montpellier, their naked corpses pulled through the streets and thrown into wells, and ritual cannibalism was also reported. In 1418, during the civil war between the Armagnacs and Burgundians, Armagnac corpses lay unburied in the street, among them that of the *connétable* Bernard d'Armagnac. The sphere of legitimate political action in the late Middle Ages was circumscribed by universal agreement about the need for obedience to authority, and this was a political ideology shared by the masses, even when in rebellion. Rebel demands were always couched in terms of saving the king from evil counsellors, and many rebels swore loyalty to 'their sovereign lord'. When Richard II agreed to meet Wat Tyler's rebels outside London in 1381 he presented himself as their captain, which to a large extent neutralised their threat by appearing to give them what they wanted: no lordship but that of the king. Similarly, in France in 1357, while John II was being held prisoner in London, the Parisians invaded the king's palace and murdered two of the Dauphin's close counsellors in front of him, without ever threatening his life. In 1413, rebels led by the butcher Caboche presented Charles VI with a list of evil counsellors who should be excluded from government, including the king's chancellor, and his brother-in-law, the duke of Bavaria. Jack Cade's rebellion was characterised by various schemes for the replacement of ministers around the king, who was thought to have been dominated by malevolent forces. All these rebellions occurred during the reigns of kings who failed to build up a theatrical and magisterial persona that would hold together the centripetal forces at work in the medieval state. The gap left at the centre of politics by the youth of Richard II and the incompetence of Henry VI in England or by the defeat and capture of John II and the madness of Charles VI in France could be filled by the imagination of rebels for whom the king was the miracle-working guarantor of peace and justice.

The aims of rebellion

Still, the identification of these patterns does not answer a fundamental question: why, in a given moment, did peasants and craftsmen take arms and choose the path of rebellion, endangering their goods, their families and their lives? What did they hope to achieve by challenging their lords, their church and, sometimes, even their king? Did they really have anything that could be called a programme, and did they pursue rational goals? A long historiographical tradition has denied most rebels (with the significant exception of the English in 1381) any political or social programme. Michel Mollat and Philippe Wolff, for example, wrote in 1970 that the Tuchins had no programme other than to survive,[38] and because rebels rarely wrote any documents, it is quite difficult to reconstruct their ideas. Even now, the idea that peasant communities could shape their own political vision without being advised or manipulated by elites is denied by some historians. Even if there are similarities in the language of rebellion in England and France, it seems that the aims were slightly different, partly because of the different positions of the king and the church in the two kingdoms, but mainly because of the effects of the Hundred Years War being fought on French soil.

It has often been argued that medieval rebellions were conservative in their political and social meaning. Rebels often sought to return to a hypothetical 'golden age': the France of *Monseigneur Saint Louis*, or perhaps the England popularly associated with the Statute of Winchester in 1285. The idea of conservative rebels should be abandoned.

---

[38] Mollat and Wolff (1970).

Did French peasants really wish to return to the reign of Louis IX, during which the king's officers crushed the Crusade of the shepherds, hanging or killing many of them, and did the English peasants really want to return to the late thirteenth century, a time when seigniorial control was at its strongest? How clear was their historical vision? The fact that parvenus (especially men who became noblemen by the king's decision and thus did not pay taxes any more) constituted one of the favourite targets of rebels is not evidence for conservative aims. Consider the case of Pons Biordon, a citizen of Pont-Saint-Esprit who in the 1370s became one of the richest men in town through involvement in collecting the salt tax and was then ennobled by the king, bought a castle and became Lord of Aiguèze. When the Tuchins rebelled they forced him to flee, attacking his house and occupying his castle, seizing large amounts of wheat. He was not targeted because he was a parvenu, but because he was accused of embezzling the revenues of salt taxes while being exempt from taxation himself. We would suggest that the idea that public officials should be accountable to popular control was from a fourteenth-century perspective actually quite modern, and not conservative at all.

Neither, we would argue, is the expression of rebel demands in terms of ancient liberties and privileges necessarily conservative. The appeals for 'ancient demesne status' by the tenants of a large number of manors in southern and western England culminating in 1377, involved attempts by groups of peasants to obtain exemplifications from the Domesday Book of 1086. Although these peasants thought in terms of ancient rights, they demanded these because it seemed that they would provide the best protection against current difficulties. They were not turning back the clock, but making imaginative use of law and documents to secure privileges for the future. In Normandy, the legal basis of every opposition to royal power (including the Harelle de Rouen in 1382) was always the 'Charte aux Normands' delivered by Louis X in 1315, and confirmed by each new king, granting the province some control of royal officers and guarantees about royal taxes. Rebels used it to try to limit the financial demands of the king. The same phenomenon also appears in Languedoc, where the Tuchins were said to have risen up to save the *antiqua libertas patrie*, but in reality the revolt had more to do with taxation. In the wake of the urban revolts in Languedoc, Charles V conceded that all royal expenses in the province would be strictly controlled by a treasurer chosen by the Estates of Languedoc, alongside the royal treasurer. Claims for popular control of public funds and expenses was both a popular demand and a concern of the urban elites. In France, local populations valued provincial liberties, while although in England taxation was much more of a national issue, popular control of tax collection, or at the very least involvement in the process of raising levies, was a political ideal in both kingdoms. The peasants and townsmen who rose in defence of this ideal were not conservatively resisting state-building; they were demanding that they be included in the process.

Such remarks can also be made about the social programme of most rebellions. Even though both Jacques and Flemish peasants may have wanted the extinction of the nobility, this was not simply because 'nobles were nobles', but because they failed in what they were supposed to do. The counterpart to noble and clerical privileges and wealth was a general expectation that royal and comital officials should not be corrupt, and that the burdens of supporting the state and its wars should be spread fairly. We would suggest that this feature of rebel programmes was also 'modern' in late medieval terms rather than conservative: demanding that the state should operate in a certain way, pushing the building of states in a particular direction. From a completely different perspective, the English demand of 1381 that there be 'no lordship but that of the king' and that the church should be disendowed, may also be seen as very 'modern' ideas. Freedom from villeinage and the separation of church and state may have been imagined in terms of ancient liberty and apostolic poverty, but these were demands for radical change in society, not resistance against change.

In May 1358, when a small group of armed nobles appeared in the small village of Saint-Leu d'Esserent and tried to plunder it, the peasants not only took arms to defend themselves and to kill the nobles, they also rang bells to call neighbouring villages to join them. This was the starting point of the Jacquerie, which was remembered, thirty years later, as the *commocion des non nobles contre les nobles*. If the Jacques first took arms to protect their goods and homes, they soon launched attacks against castles, burning them, killing noblemen and their families, raping their wives and so on. Even though Froissart was likely to have been exaggerating when he told of Jacques roasting a knight and forcing his wife to eat him, we cannot deny that class-hatred was involved.[39] Such hatred did not seem to appear during the Tuchin revolt in Languedoc, where numerous local noblemen were freely elected as captains by peasants for their military experience and because noblemen were still considered as natural leaders. Many of those noble captains betrayed the rebellion in the end by joining the royal repression, but some of them remained faithful and were finally beheaded. To begin with, the Tuchinat was a self-defence movement aimed against the ravages of the 'Great Companies' active in Languedoc after the treaty of Brétigny, but a social programme can also be discerned

[39] De Medeiros (1979).

in the very form the rebellion took. By organising small groups in which each member, except the captain, was equal to the others (especially when sharing the spoils), the Tuchinat became a social protest.

In England the modes of organisation and mobilisation, and the language of rebellion, had much in common with France, so that the social groups and identities formed during rebellion were similar to a certain extent. The experience of rebellion was likewise often a martial one, with rebels organised along the lines of local musters, including leadership by village constables and gathering at hundred muster sites such as Blackheath outside London in 1381. Some rebellions marched under the leadership of knights and gentry, who could provide valuable strategic advice, and others rejected, or were not able to sustain, gentry leadership. Most rebellions, however, combined both social features. The Cornish tax rebellion of 1497 was initially led by a lawyer and a blacksmith, but later acquired the support of Lord Audley, who was acclaimed as captain and led the march towards London. In 1381, knights were coerced into leading groups of rebels in Essex, and in 1536 the gentry and nobility of Yorkshire were for a time willing leaders of the Pilgrimage of Grace. Even so, the relationship between peasants, townsmen and nobles was uneasy, as their economic interests were not always the same. What is most remarkable about English rebellions is the autonomy with which the masses were capable of acting, at the national level. This can be taken as proof that new social forms were being created in the crucible of revolt: new allegiances, new bonds amongst peasants from different villages and even regions. So far, so similar to the French experience, but the absence of prolonged militarisation, and the long years of peace enjoyed in England (as opposed to the wars it fought with France, Scotland, Wales and Ireland) must have made for differences in the social experience of revolt, and consequently its aims and ambitions.

The other main difference between English and French rebellions lies in the relative importance of religion. As we have already seen, the fact that prophecy was in France considered an acceptable way to speak to the king seemed to remove religion from rebellions. Signs of anti-clericalism are hard to find: Jacques Peyt, one of the captains of Flemish peasants, was, after his death, condemned for heresy by the bishop of Thérouanne and his bones exhumed and burnt, but he is the only example of a rebel leader considered a heretic. It is difficult to detect simple anticlericalism in English rebellions, since the clergy were prominent rebel leaders in 1536 when rumours spread that Henry VIII wanted to destroy parish churches as well as monasteries, and in 1381 it was lawyers, rather than clergymen, who attracted the most hatred. The attacks on the property of St Albans Abbey were against the monks as landlords, rather than as religious, and the murders of bishops in 1381 and 1450 were motivated by their roles in royal government.

The Pilgrimage of Grace was distinctive in being a rebellion partly launched in defence of religion and the church. Nothing of this sort seems to have occurred in France. The 'lollard' revolt led by John Old-castle in 1414 is also distinct from the French experience in being a revolt associated with the condemned heresies of John Wyclif. But the major difference in terms of the importance of religion is in the millenarian tone of 1381 in England. Perhaps surprisingly, in France after the Shepherds' Crusade, there was scarcely any further sign of millenarianism in revolts. One very interesting isolated trace came in the lawsuit brought by the proctors of Lunel around 1380 against noblemen who refused to con-tribute to local taxes. The proctors asked: 'If Adam is our father and Eve our mother, why are we not all equal in nobility?' This, famously, was the theme taken up by John Ball in England in 1381: 'When Adam delved and Eve span, who was then a gentleman?' The expectation that 'The Kynges sone of heuene schal paye for al', amending the wrongs of a time of pride and greed, lechery and gluttony, and the ambition of an end to serfdom, speaks of deeply held assumptions about politics being played out in eschatological time. The Wycliffite agenda of disendowment of the church should also be connected with this.

To try to explain this huge difference, we can point out two things. First of all, French peasants had to deal with much more concrete and imme-diate problems. For many French rebels, the main objective was peace and the end of the English presence in France, that is, their very survival. Secondly, French prophecies were mainly concerned with peace, and the almost permanent plundering may have slowed down the development of millenarian and egalitarian ideas in France.

In England, one of the perennial demands of rebels – justice – changed in character during the late Middle Ages. There is a great difference, for example, between the reaction in 1381 against the sheer bureaucratic effi-ciency of the English state's tax-gathering commissions, and the reaction in 1450 against its partiality, corruption and inefficiency. This difference illustrates the contingent nature of rebels' complaints – their complaints were not unchanging, but were reactions to current political issues, while showing that the language of loyalty, inclusion, community and justice was a tradition that can hide real political differences from historians. In 1450, the groups who could claim this access by right had grown to include many more peasants who had grown wealthy and might by this time be called yeomen. There was such confidence in Jack Cade's ranks that they took over the organs of royal justice that had in fact been established to try *them* and *their* crimes. The increasing impregnability of state bureaucracy over the next century meant that the alternative justice of rebels in 1549, notably Kett's followers in Norfolk, was limited to symbolic parallel justice. Over the course of the late medieval period, the claims of rebels for justice became more inclusive as society changed and royal justice came within reach of more people. As the machinery of the state grew, however, royal justice was less open to challenge.

Such developments do not seem to have taken place in France, where royal justice remained untouchable, in spite of numerous reproaches addressed to the *Parlement* of Paris or the king's officers. When rebels did manage to take control of justice, as in 1413, they did not hesitate to sentence their enemies to death. Popular trials to judge traitors also took place in 1358, when the Jacques captured a messenger of the King of Navarre and the rebel captain decided to execute him, an event attended by about 200 people. Nevertheless, there seems to have been less confidence amongst French rebels about gaining real access to the organs of justice. On the contrary, a captain of the Tuchins decided to deliver to the urban authorities two of his followers who, for personal and greedy reasons, had murdered a merchant. These men, even amongst rebels themselves, were considered as murderers who should be treated as such. It seems that, in the kingdom of France, to dispense justice was considered by rebels to be a usurpation of one of the major prerogatives of the king himself: as long as the king remained untouchable, his justice could not be questioned. In addition, the most popular concern in France was not really justice at all, but peace. Only after having restored peace, could the king rule with justice.

Last but not least, the final, and perhaps greatest, divergence between France and England lies in the scale of rebellions and the link with the king. Whereas most French rebellions remained local, English revolts were able to develop at a variety of scales up to that of the kingdom. The phenomenon of the march on the capital, seen in 1381 and 1497, was unknown in France. In spite of the pre-eminent position of Paris, only Parisian rebels themselves seemed to give any importance to the occupation of the capital and to a direct connection with the king, as during the rebellion led by Étienne Marcel. Besides the fact that most rebels could simply not walk on Paris, it may also have been unthinkable, because for most of them, the king was less a person than an idea. When English rebels sought an audience with the king or his representatives, they wanted to extract political concessions or pardons, but in France, despite the keen need felt for direct contact between the king and the masses, this contact was reserved for prophets who told God's truth, and penitents asking for a 'grace', which was always considered something of

a miracle: 'utens exemplo Christi' were the words used when forgiving
the rebels of Languedoc in 1384.

Conclusion

At the end of the Middle Ages, both in England and France, the masses
were not engaged in a head-on struggle with the state – except maybe
during short phases – but in a long, subtle and complex process of integration into the state by trying to establish a global political space able
to include and answer to their grievances. One of the goals pursued by
politically active sections of the masses was simply to be considered as
members of political society, by negotiation through representatives as
well as rebellion. For a long time historians have denied the masses any
political ideas, or have described a simple process of resistance to domination. But it is obviously much more than that. Changes in the state –
in representation, taxation and expenditure, military organisation, social
control – cannot be divorced from the upward pressure of those who
were excluded from government, but whose behaviour set limits upon it.
   A political definition of the masses, as those excluded from governance, reflects the increasing political confidence of large sections of
the population in England and France during the late Middle Ages.
Better communication, the growing demands of the state, the widen-
ing fiscal base of government, and changes in social structure, all made
the masses more important to those in power. The fact that these were
people with whom kings, nobles and clerics did *not* wish to govern produced a dynamic of assimilation, exclusion, negotiation and conflict that
characterised the relationship between government and the masses in the
late Middle Ages. England and France had different experiences of this
dynamic. In France, kingship was more sacral, while in England the state
was more integrated. France had had to accommodate provinces which
already possessed their own political culture, whereas England emerged
quite early as a single nation. As Colette Beaune has shown, the building
of the French nation was a long-term process which ended only at the
close of the Hundred Years War.[40] While the King of England had to
deal with a single community, the King of France had to deal with many
political, cultural and linguistic communities, each with their own prox-
ies or representatives. The dynamic relationship between those in power
and those excluded from power has to be seen within this framework.

[40] Beaune (1985).

BIBLIOGRAPHY

1. INTRODUCTION

Arnold, J. H., 2009. 'Religion and Popular Rebellion, from the Capuciati to Niklashausen', *Cultural and Social History*, 6, 149–69.

Blickle, P. (ed.), 1997. *Resistance, Representation and Community: The Origins of the Modern State in Europe*, Oxford.

Bourin, M., Cherubini, G. and Pinto, G., 2008. *Rivolte urbane e rivolte contadine nell'Europa del Trecento. Un confronto*, Florence.

Brunel, G. and Brunet, S. (eds.), 2009. *Haro sur le seigneur! Les luttes anti-seigneuriales dans l'Europe médiévale et moderne*, Cahiers de Flaran, 29, Toulouse.

Cohn, S. K., 2006. *Lust for Liberty: The Politics of Social Revolt in Medieval Europe, 1200–1425*, Cambridge, MA and London.

Cohn, S. K. and Aiton, D., 2013. *Popular Protest in Late Medieval English Towns*, Cambridge.

Fletcher, A. and MacCulloch, D., 1997. *Tudor Rebellions*, 4th edition, London.

Freedman, P., 1999. *Images of the Medieval Peasant*, Stanford.

Hilton, R. H., 1973. *Bond Men Made Free: Medieval Peasant Movements and the English Rising of 1381*, London.

1975. *The English Peasantry in the Later Middle Ages*, Oxford.

Masschaele, J., 2008. *Jury, State, and Society in Medieval England*, Basingstoke.

Mollat, M., and Wolff, Ph., 1970. *Ongles bleus, Jacques et Ciompi. Les révoltes populaires en Europe aux xive et xve siècles*, Paris.

TeBrake, W. H., 1993. *A Plague of Insurrection: Popular Politics and Peasant Revolt in Flanders (1323–1328)*, Philadelphia.

Watts, J. L., 2004. 'The Pressure of the Public on Later Medieval Politics', in L. Clark and C. Carpenter (eds.), *The Fifteenth Century IV: Political Culture in Late Medieval Britain*, Woodbridge, pp. 159–80.

2. SOURCES CITED

Dobson, R. B. (ed.), *The Peasants' Revolt of 1381*, 2nd edition, Basingstoke, 1983.
'Thomas of Erceldoune's Prophecy', in J. M. Dean (ed.), *Medieval English Political Writings*, Kalamazoo, 1996.

3. FURTHER READING

Aston, M., 1960. 'Lollardy and Sedition, 1381–1431', *Past and Present*, 17, 1–44.
1994. 'Corpus Christi and Corpus Regni: Heresy and the Peasants' Revolt', *Past and Present*, 143, 3–47.

Attreed, L., 2001. *The King's Towns: Identity and Survival in Late Medieval English Boroughs*, New York.

Bailey, M., 2011. 'Self Government in the Small Towns of Late Medieval England', in M. Bailey (ed.), *Commercial Activity, Markets and Entrepreneurs in the Middle Ages: Essays in Honour of Richard Britnell*, Woodbridge, pp. 107–28.

Barr, H., 2001. *Socioliterary Practice in Late Medieval England*, Oxford.

Beaune, C., 1985. *Naissance de la nation France*, Paris.

2004. *Jeanne d'Arc*, Paris.

Bloch, M., 1924. *Les Rois thaumaturges. Étude sur le caractère surnaturel attribué à la puissance royale particulièrement en France et en Angleterre*, Strasbourg.

Blockmans, W., Holenstein, A. and Mathieu, J. (eds.), 2009. *Empowering Interactions. Political Cultures and the Emergence of the State in Europe, 14th to 19th Centuries*, Aldershot.

Boglioni, P., Delort, R. and Gauvard, C. (eds.), 2002. *Le petit peuple dans l'Occident médiéval: terminologies, perceptions, réalités*, Paris.

Bois, G., 1976. *Crise du féodalisme*, Paris.

Bourin-Derruau, M., 1987. *Villages médiévaux en Bas-Languedoc: genèse d'une sociabilité (xe–xive)*, Paris.

Carpenter, C., 1994. 'Gentry and Community in Medieval England', *Journal of British Studies*, 33, 340–80.

Carpenter, D., 1992. 'English Peasants in Politics', *Past and Present*, 136, 3–42.

Cazelles, R., 1958. *La société politique et la crise de la royauté sous Philippe de Valois*, Paris, Argences.

1962. 'Les mouvements révolutionnaires du milieu du xive siècle et le cycle de l'action politique', *Revue Historique*, 228, 279–312.

Challet, V., 1998. 'La révolte des Tuchins: banditisme social ou sociabilité villageoise?', *Médiévales*, 34, 101–12.

, Genet, J.-Ph., Oliva Herrer, H. R. and Valdeon, J. (eds.), 2007. *La société politique à la fin du XVe siècle dans les royaumes ibériques et en Europe. Élites, peuple, sujets?* Paris/Valladolid.

, Dumolyn, J., Haemers, J. and Oliva Herrer, H. R. (eds.), 2014. *The Voices of the People in Late Medieval Europe*, Studies in European Urban History, Turnhout, Brepols, Studies in European Urban History, 33.

Clanchy, M., 1970. 'Remembering the Past and the Good Old Law', *History*, 55, 165–76.

Combes, J., 1972. 'Finances municipales et oppositions sociales à Montpellier au commencement du xive siècle', in *Vivarais et Languedoc : XLIVe Congrès de la Fédération Historique du Languedoc Méditerranéen et du Roussillon, Privas, 1971*, Montpellier, 99–120.

Les Communautés rurales: Recueil de la Société Jean Bodin pour l'histoire comparative des institutions, 4e partie, Europe Occidentale (Italie, Espagne, France), Paris, 1984.

Les Communautés villageoises en Europe occidentale du Moyen Âge aux Temps Modernes: Journées de Flaran 1982, Auch, 1984.

Coote, L. and Thornton, T., 2001. 'Merlin, Erceldoune, Nixon: a Tradition of Popular Political Prophecy', in W. Scase, R. Copeland, and D. Lawton (eds.), *New Medieval Literatures*, Volume IV, Oxford, pp. 117–37.

Crane, S., 1992. 'The Writing Lesson of 1381', in B. Hanawalt (ed.), *Chaucer's England: Literature in Historical Context*, Minneapolis, pp. 201–21.

Davies, C. S. L., 1973. 'Peasant Revolt in France and England: a Comparison', *Agricultural History Review*, 21, 122–34.

De Medeiros, M.-Th., 1979. *Jacques et chroniqueurs: une étude comparée de récits contemporains relatant la Jacquerie de 1358*, Paris.

Davies, R. R., 2001. 'Kinsmen, Neighbours and Communities in Wales and the Western British Isles, *c*.1100–*c*.1400', in P. Stafford, J. Nelson and J. Martindale (eds.), *Law, Laity and Solidarities: Essays in Honour of Susan Reynolds*, pp. 172–87.

Dyer, C., 1984. 'The Social and Economic Background to the Rural Revolt of 1381', in R. H. Hilton and T. H. Aston (eds.), *The English Rising of 1381*, Cambridge, 9–42.

1994. 'The English Medieval Village Community and its Decline', *Journal of British Studies*, 33, 407–29.

2004. 'The Political Life of the Fifteenth-Century English Village', in L. Clark and C. Carpenter (eds.), *Political Culture in Late Medieval Britain*, Woodbridge, pp. 135–58.

Faith, R., 1984. 'The "Great Rumour" of 1377 and Peasant Ideology' in R. H. Hilton and T. H. Aston (eds.), *The English Rising of 1381*, Cambridge, pp. 69–74.

Farge, A., 1997. *Des lieux pour l'histoire*, Paris.

Forrest, I., 2013. 'The Transformation of Visitation in Thirteenth Century England', *Past and Present*, 221, 3–38.

Fossier, R., 1968. *Les hommes et la terre en Picardie jusqu'à la fin du xiiie siècle*, Paris-Louvain.

1992. 'Les "communes rurales" au Moyen Âge', *Journal des Savants*, 2, 2, 235–76.

Fourquin, G., 1964. *Les campagnes de la région parisienne à la fin du Moyen Âge*, Paris.

1972. *Les soulèvements populaires au Moyen Âge*, Paris.

Gauvard, C., 1989. 'Les révoltes du règne de Charles VI: tentative pour expliquer un échec', in F. Gambrelle and M. Trebitsch, *Révolte et Société*, Paris, vol. I, pp. 53–61.

1991. *'De grace especial': Crime, État et Société en France à la fin du Moyen Âge*, Paris.

Geremek, B., 1976. *Les marginaux parisiens aux XIVe et XVe siècles*, Paris.

Gilles, H., 1965. *Les États de Languedoc au xve*, Toulouse.

Green, R. F., 1992. 'John Ball's Letters: Literary History and Historical Literature', in B. Hanawalt (ed.), *Chaucer's England: Literature in Historical Context*, Minneapolis, pp. 176–200.

Guenée, B., 2002. *L'opinion publique à la fin du Moyen-Âge d'après la 'Chronique de Charles VI' du Religieux de Saint-Denis*, Paris.

and Lehoux, F., 1968. *Les entrées royales françaises de 1328 à 1515*, Paris.

Gunn, S. J., 1989. 'Peers, Commons and the Gentry in the Lincolnshire Revolt of 1536', *Past and Present*, 123, 52–79.

Harriss, G.L., 1993. 'Political Society and the Growth of Government in Late Medieval England', *Past and Present*, 138, 28–57.

Harvey, I. M. W., 1991. *Jack Cade's Rebellion of 1450*, Oxford.

Harvey, P. D. A., 1989. 'Initiative and Authority in Settlement Change', in M. Aston, D. Austin and C. Dyer (eds.), *The Rural Settlements of Medieval England: Studies Dedicated to Maurice Beresford and John Hurst*, Oxford, pp. 31–43.

Hilton, R. 1992. *English and French Towns in Feudal Society*, Cambridge.

Hiver-Bérenguier, J. P., 1984. *Constance de Rabastens, mystique de Dieu ou de Gaston Fébus*, Toulouse.

Jouet, R., 1969. *La résistance à l'occupation anglaise en Basse-Normandie (1418–1450)*, Cahier des Annales de Normandie, no. 5, Caen.

Justice, S., 1994. *Writing and Rebellion: England in 1381*, Berkeley and London.

Kerby-Fulton, K., 2006. *Books Under Suspicion: Censorship and Tolerance of Revelatory Writing in Late Medieval England*, Notre Dame.

Lecuppre-Desjardin, E. and Van Bruaene, A.-L. (eds.), 2005. *Emotions in the Heart of the City (14th–16th Century)*, Turnhout.

Leguai, A., 1982. 'Les révoltes rurales dans le royaume de France du milieu du xive siècle à la fin du xve', *Le Moyen Age*, 88, 49–76.

Liddy, C., 2005. *War, Politics and Finance in Late Medieval English Towns: Bristol, York and the Crown 1350–1400*, Woodbridge.

Maddicott, J. R., 1984. 'Magna Carta and the Local Ccommunity', *Past and Present*, 102, 25–65.

Masschaele, J., 2008. *Jury, State, and Society in Medieval England*, Basingstoke.

Menant, F. and Jessenne, J.-P. (eds.), 2007. *Les élites rurales dans l'Europe médiévale et moderne*, Cahiers de Flaran, 27, Toulouse.

Mousnier, R., 1967. *Fureurs paysannes: les paysans dans les révoltes du xviie siècle (France, Russie, Chine)*, Paris.

Neveux, H., 1997. *Les révoltes paysannes en Europe xive–xviie siècles*, Paris.

Nirenberg, D., 1996. *Communities of Violence: Persecution of Minorities in the Middle Ages*, Princeton.

Ormrod, W. M., 2010. 'Parliament, Political Economy and State Formation in Later Medieval England', in P. Hoppenbrouwers, A. Janse and R. Stein (eds.), *Power and Persuasion: Essays on the Art of State Building in Honour of W. P. Blockmans*, Turnhout.

Petit-Dutaillis, C., 1947. *Les communes françaises. Caractères et évolution des origines au XVIIIe siècle*, Paris.

Porchnev, B. 1963. *Les soulèvements populaires en France de 1623 à 1648*, Paris.

Powell, E., 1989. *Kingship, Law and Society: Criminal Justice in the Reign of Henry V*, Oxford.

Reyerson, K. and Drendel, J. (eds.), 1998. *Urban and Rural Communities in Medieval France. Provence and Languedoc (1000–1500)*, Leiden.

Rogozinski, J., 1982. *Power, Caste and Law: Social Conflict in Fourteenth-Century Montpellier*, Cambridge, MA.

Rosenwein, B. (ed.), 1998. *Anger's Past: The Social Uses of an Emotion in the Middle Ages*, Ithaca, NY.

Scordia, L., 2005. *'Le roi doit vivre du sien.' La théorie de l'impôt en France (xiiie–xve siècles)*, Paris.

Stella, A., 1996. 'Un conflit du travail dans les vignes d'Auxerre aux XIVe et XVe siècles', *Histoire et Sociétés rurales*, 5, 221–51.

Strohm, P., 1992. *Hochon's Arrow: The Social Imagination of Fourteenth-Century Texts*, Princeton.

1998. *England's Empty Throne*, New Haven.

Vauchez, A. (ed.), 2012. *Prophètes et prophétisme*, Paris.

Walker, S. J., 2000. 'Rumour, Sedition and Popular Protest in the Reign of Henry IV', *Past and Present*, 166, 31–65.

Watt, D., 1997. 'Of the Seed of Abraham: Elizabeth Barton, the "Holy Maid of Kent"', in D. Watt, *Secretaries of God: Women Prophets in Late Medieval and Early Modern England*, Cambridge, pp. 51–80.

Watts, J. L., 1996. *Henry VI and the Politics of Kingship*, Cambridge.

2007. 'Public or Plebs: The Changing Meaning of "the Commons", 1381–1549', in H. Pryce and J. Watts (eds.), *Power and Identity in the Middle Ages: Essays in Memory of Rees Davies*, Oxford, pp. 242–60.

Whittle, J., 2010. 'Lords and Tenants in Kett's Rebellion 1549', *Past and Present*, 207, 3–52.

Wood, A., 2002. *Riot, Rebellion and Popular Politics in Early Modern England*, Basingstoke.

2007. *The 1549 Rebellions and the Making of Early Modern England*, Cambridge.

Wright, N., 1998. *Knights and Peasants: The Hundred Years War in the French Countryside*, Woodbridge.

11   In the mirror of mutual representation: political society as seen by its members

Franck Collard and Aude Mairey

How did the actors of political society see each other in England and in France? This important question, which to a certain extent allows them to speak for themselves, is not so easy to answer. 'Official' discourses directed from one group to another, or even the expression by one part of the governing strata of their opinion of the others, are rare in both France and England at the end of the Middle Ages. For instance, speeches delivered in the English parliament are not addressed to one estate in particular, since the English parliament was not an assembly of estates, but a 'representative' assembly, including both the 'lords', lay and ecclesiastical, and also the 'Commons', the representatives of the counties and the towns. The opening speech was addressed to all the members of the parliament. If these speeches were often delivered by a prelate, and if they sometimes turned into a veritable sermon, the prelate in question, in general the chancellor (a function which was most often fulfilled by clerics up until the end of the Middle Ages) nonetheless spoke in the name of the king he represented. By the same token, in the address delivered by the speaker of the Commons, it is often ambiguous whether it is the king, the first object of communication, or the 'lords' who are being addressed. Overall, the texts to be considered here from both sides of the Channel were rarely produced in the name of a specific social category, nor did they concern a particular category of members of political society so much as the 'estates' or groups of society in general.

In fact, for the people of the time, 'political society', a modern historians' concept, was not readily distinguishable from society considered as a whole. In the work of the Anglophone historians whom we here follow in preference to their French contemporaries, 'political society' is not restricted to the 'counsellors' of the king (as in the restrictive definition of Cazelles),[1] but extends to include all those of significance or with a direct or indirect influence on the government. Changes in the political societies in the two monarchies in the fourteenth and fifteenth

[1] Cazelles (1958, 1982).

centuries provoked reflection in both, although these reflections took different forms. In France, men of power, in the broad sense, saw themselves and described each other most often in terms of legitimacy and ability to take up the affairs of an unstable royal state. In England, one of the most striking characteristics of numerous sources from the late fourteenth and early fifteenth century is the impression they give of social and political fluidity, despite all the weight of convention, rather than any attempt to deal with questions concerning the state (which had largely been settled). Although the king and his titled nobility appeared 'above the *mêlée*' without their place at the summit of the hierarchy of power ever being put into question, more and more numerous voices can be heard – essentially amongst the 'gentry' – in a dynamic system in which relatively open elites were concerned both with their own interests and those of the government, and never the one without the other. These voices suggest hierarchies and interactions of great complexity.

To understand better the functioning of these reciprocal perceptions, it is not enough to limit oneself to describing their content. It is also necessary to consider the context of the written culture in which these texts were made, the problem of their origin, larger systems of classification and the images of the composite members of political society in order to be able to consider the different purposes of these acts of representation.

1.   The sources

The sources which we can consult in order to begin our inquiry are abundant and varied, with, in the two kingdoms, similarities and differences. It is obviously not possible to consider, in the limited space of this chapter, all the available material. Iconography will be left to one side, despite its immense intrinsic interest, and certain types of writing will be brought to the fore.

Amongst the sources available on both sides of the Channel, political speeches take the first place. In England, they are abundant, in particular parliamentary addresses, whether they were delivered in convocation (often delivered by clerics – but clerics in the service of the king) or, from 1376 on, by the speaker of the Commons (who was always a layman). It is also possible to place the petitions of the Commons under the heading of political discourse. These are a very significant source, as much from the point of view of volume as content. Other more isolated, but nonetheless significant, texts need to be considered too, such as the tracts issued by the Lancastrian and Yorkist camps during the civil wars of the second half of the fifteenth century (the 'Wars of the Roses'). The petitions of Richard of York in 1450, for instance, are a precious example of the discourse of the English high nobility. In France, a vision of governors and governed was also expressed in addresses to assemblies or sermons for particular occasions. In the first case, the assemblies of the estates served as the opportunity for depictions of certain groups as they were and as they ought to have been. In the second case, works compiled in the aftermath of the French defeat of 1356, such as the anonymous *Complainte sur la bataille de Poitiers* and the *Tragicum argumentum* of the Benedictine François de Montebelluna gave much space to criticism of those responsible for the disaster. In the time of Charles VI, the sermons of Jean Gerson overflowed with judgements on many different groups amongst the powerful.

Normative legislation can also show an unexpected richness, although its sheer mass makes it difficult to handle. In England, the different sumptuary laws issued on repeated occasions from 1337 are of great interest for the evolution of social perceptions and classifications. Practical legal material also contains useful descriptions, for example judicial sources or contracts which provided the occasion for the elaboration of different classes of identity. All the hate, all the prejudice of one category concerning another often came out in the course of litigation.

Historiographical production is not negligible in its importance, either. On the one hand, certain chroniclers who are themselves engaged in political action describe and catalogue the ruling classes. On the other, historiographical accounts report how the antagonistic groups evolving in the corridors of power perceived one another. The chronicle of the monk of Saint Denis is extremely rich from this point of view, as is the work of Thomas Walsingham in the England of Richard II.

Other forms of expression are more specific to each kingdom, which does not mean that they are exclusive to them. In England, collections of letters, abundant in the fifteenth century and which emanate essentially from the gentry (the Paston letters are the most famous) are rich in information on social relations, and hence on contemporary social types. One marked particularity is that 'political literature', in contrast to France, for the most part appeared in poetic form, including 'mirrors' addressed directly to the prince. This poetry was increasingly written in English, in the context of the exponential increase in textual production in this vernacular language, above all after 1350. If this abundant literature, notably at the turn of the fourteenth and fifteenth centuries, is illustrated by several important names such as Geoffrey Chaucer, William Langland, John Gower, Thomas Hoccleve and even John Lydgate, whose works were widely diffused, there is also a mass of anonymous poems, which are generally quite short. Most of these only survive in one or two copies, but their accumulation is in itself indicative of the taste in

England for this type of writing. It is, however, necessary to be careful of chronology. The flourishing of English 'political literature' took place above all between the middle of the fourteenth century and the end of the first quarter of the fifteenth century. In the years 1430–50, it becomes less abundant. There are many reasons for this exhaustion, and it is not easy to unravel them. It is possible to distinguish, amongst other factors, the general political crisis which hit England in the central and final decades of the fifteenth century (the minority of Henry VI, the Wars of the Roses). Whatever the reason for these developments, the essential part of the texts which we will consider here were written before 1430.[2]

These vernacular texts considered many subjects, but social and political preoccupations are very present in them, notably as a result of the concerns of the 'literature of estates', which was more popular in England than in France. This literature has been defined by Jill Mann, as 'First, an enumeration of the "estates" or social and occupational classes, whose aim seems to be completeness. Secondly, a lament over the shortcomings of the estates; each fails in his duties to the rest. Thirdly, the philosophy of the divine ordination of the three principal estates, the dependence of the state on all three, and the necessity of being content with one's station. And last, an attempt to find remedies, religious or political, for the defects of the estates.'[3] These different aspects are more or less marked in the texts in question, but their relationship to each other needs to be refined. In fact, English authors, in the relationship which they maintained with the tradition of the literature of estates, often show a subtlety which reveals much about the society in which they evolved, about its social types and social transformations. In France, by contrast, it is denunciation and complaint that predominates: in the fourteenth century *Les mélancholies* of Jean Dupin stands as a typical example.

Texts written in France emerge above all from a more theoretical genre, even if a work such as the *Roman de Fauvel*, composed between 1310 and 1318, put flesh on the ideas transmitted and if poetic or chivalric literature includes useful descriptions: late *chansons de gestes* such as *Ciperis de Vignevaux, Dieudonné de Hongrie*, the *Chanson d'Hugues Capet, Florent et Octavien*; or poems concerning the present day by Guillaume Machaut or Eustache Deschamps. Certain texts did not have, or no longer really had, an equivalent in England. The literature of 'mirrors' continued to depict groups which participated in public affairs. Its methods passed, as in the case of Philippe de Mézières or Pierre Salmon addressing Charles VI,

---

[2] This is not to say that there is nothing after 1430, simply that the writings before this date are particularly rich regarding the representations of the society.
[3] Mann (1973), p. 3.

through the representation of the ideal arrangement of the kingdom and so by the attribution to each group of a definite function. In a newer development, the debates of these works put the actors of political society face-to-face concerning the situation of the monarchy or the kingdom exposed to a threat – theocracy at the beginning of the fourteenth century, the English war and civil wars later on. When these perils had passed towards 1480, it was the fiscal or socio-economic situation which this kind of text evoked: this can be seen in the *Débat du prêtre, du laboureur et du gendarme* written by the Trinitarian humanist Robert Gaguin, who probably knew the famous *Quadrilogue invectif* composed by Alain Chartier a half-century earlier. But writings like these, often composed in the vernacular in the fifteenth century, put at the centre of the debate the state of the kingdom, more than of its estates, which were themselves described less in terms of their strictly political activities than of their moral comportment.

The formal framework of a debate (which also slipped into the theatre, itself becoming 'political' from 1434, vivaciously depicting the powerful) was taken up in quite a different way by a new genre of tracts, more concrete than the 'mirrors', of which the best known is the *Songe du Vergier* written by Évrard de Trémaugon for Charles V (1378). Inspired by the *Dialogus inter militem et clericum* of Philip le Bel's time, although coming from a very different angle, the author dramatises an encounter between a clerk and a knight who 'debate' concerning the best organisation of the government of the kingdom. The import of their words goes well beyond the reciprocal perception of virtues and vices which the two categories in the king's service lend each other through the mouth of those who represent them. The golden age for the production of this kind of treatise, which was contemporaneous with the liberation of 'political thought' and of its diffusion through the translation into the vernacular of the *Policraticus* of John of Salisbury by Denis Foulechat (1372) and of Aristotle's *Politics* by Nicole Oresme (1370–4), stretched from the middle of the fourteenth to the middle of the fifteenth century, but the need to describe the 'polity' lasted much longer, as witnesses the *Grant monarchie de France* offered by Claude de Seyssel to François I in 1519.

2. The social perspective of satire and political commentary

In a substantial proportion of the political texts produced in the fourteenth and fifteenth centuries the speaker is placed outside the world he describes. This literary artifice or subterfuge directly affects this inquiry and complicates it since it obscures the social theory of those who construct these social typologies, these *représentations*. The allegory (it is

Faith who criticises those who govern in the *Livre de l'espérance* of Alain Chartier) or the dream vision makes it possible to outline and depict particular groupings of 'men of power' from a social point of view which is literally utopian. In fact, many points of observation are superimposed: that of personages whose speech is supposed to reflect the average opinion of the group which they represent concerning this or that other group; that of allegories, which look on the estates from outside and on high, somewhat as the king sees them when they are assembled; that of the authors of these texts, which comes through despite their efforts to extract themselves from the tableau they have painted.

In England, for some authors, and in particular laymen (but also those who, like Langland, had taken minor orders), this extraction from the world and this multiplication of points of view took place at the price of a certain distancing from their discourse which was sometimes accompanied by a real anxiety. In many texts, in fact, the narrator (or sometimes the narrators), and thus in a certain way the authors, deliberately positioned themselves at the margin of centres of power. This led them to look within their narrative scheme for an authority able to support them in their project. These authorities were moreover, and this fact is striking, often laymen. In the early fifteenth-century poem *Mum and the Sothsegger*, for instance, the narrator, who violently but often subtly criticises all the categories of political society, finds a point of reference in a beekeeper. Much the same is done by Thomas Hoccleve, a clerk of the privy seal, in his poetical 'mirror' entitled *The Regement of Princes* (1411–12). In the course of a prologue which makes up more than a third of the entire text, Hoccleve takes care to have his enterprise validated by an old man, who is not only a layman (or in any case an ex-layman) but poor as well, even though the work directly addresses the future Henry V. Other writers take a different tack, but one with finally rather similar objectives, multiplying the number of narrators and authorities to demonstrate the multiplicity of points of view and, at the same time, the difficulty of having their own voice heard. It is this that Chaucer expresses in a magisterial manner in the *Canterbury Tales*, where every tale is told by a different narrator, a pilgrim who has previously been described in the *General Prologue*.

These poetical works were for the most part composed by authors taken from that dynamic social milieu which we have already evoked, at a more or less elevated level on the social scale. Chaucer (d.1400) was perhaps the poet with the closest links to the court at the end of the fourteenth century, in that he had exercised relatively important functions within the royal administration and had links with John of Gaunt (the third son of Edward III). Chaucer originated, however, from a family of London merchants, and his attainment of the status of esquire in itself attests to upward social mobility within English society. Gower (d.1408) was a member of the gentry who had apparently been a lawyer. Hoccleve (d.*c.* 1426), whose origins are unknown, was a clerk of the privy seal, and so an administrator, and thus not in the highest spheres of society either, even if he seems at one period to have enjoyed quasi-official recognition as a poet. Langland (d.*c.* 380) and Lydgate (d.1449), on the other hand, were clerks but, whereas the second was a Benedictine monk at Bury St Edmunds and was one of the few to have approached the official position of court poet, the first had only received minor orders and perhaps worked as a scribe. We thus have a sample of authors from different social groups and who met with greater or lesser degrees of success. But all of them were part of the intermediate levels of English society, with the possible exception of Lydgate (who nonetheless often left his monastery to undertake diplomatic missions for the government). What is striking, however, is the importance of administrative careers, or jobs related to the development of administration or the state, above all at the central level, since all these men lived all or part of their lives in London. Their point of view is thus by no means neutral, even when they write for the king (as is the case, for example, with Hoccleve).

Alongside these authors, some writers from traditional elites were still to be found in England. In general, however, the clergy and the nobility are not our only sources of social typology, above all after 1350. The 'Commons' need to be taken into account, and this in all domains. Here, indeed, it is necessary to be careful about what is being discussed, for there are many difficulties with this term. For in fact, the term 'Commons' possessed connotations which were at the same time political and social, and which are not entirely possible to separate out. In parliament, in the second half of the fourteenth century, the Commons constituted a group with a collective identity, symbolised by the appearance in 1376 of the spokesman or 'Speaker' of the Commons. But despite this very tangible identity in parliament, the Commons were an extremely composite group of categories which are nevertheless often differentiated: members of the gentry, merchants, lawyers – the very groups which demonstrated the greatest dynamism within society. The matter is all the more complicated by the numerous crossovers between groups: the nobility and the gentry are so connected that in literary texts, for example, they are often dealt with at the same time; many lawyers, moreover, were part of the gentry. The frontiers between these groups are in general relatively blurred. But the 'commons' were also the 'people' who, for their part, were required to stay silent and obey. The problem is that it is not always possible to tell in what sense this term is being employed. This concept in itself seems to sum up the whole problem of the portrayal of the different ruling strata of English political society at the end of the Middle Ages. Its very ambivalence, which authors use and abuse, suggests the fluidity of political society beyond the king and the high nobility.

In France, the clergy and nobility were for a long time the main milieus from which social typologies emerged. The clerical point of view had for a long time been the only one to exist for reasons of culture and *auctoritas*. It remained predominant at the end of the Middle Ages, despite the incursion of laymen into the activity of textual production. It was a Bourbon monk, Jean Dupin, who, around 1340, described the estates of the world somewhat in the style of Rutebeuf, incorporating within his description the categories of political society. It was also a prelate, Claude de Seyssel, who described the 'men of power' at the end of the reign of Louis XII. Between the two, the great political thinkers from the time of John II and his successors took the point of view of the clerks, above all in the university sense of the term, whether they were jurists, philosophers or theologians. The 'men of knowledge' were very interested in the 'men of power'. This preponderance, itself inherited from Carolingian times when only the clergy had been permitted to reprimand other groups, was overturned from the twelfth and above all the thirteenth century by the emergence of the lay and, in particular, chivalric point of view, without allowing other groups to speak in the process, as in England.

When the direction of the war put the nobility and chivalric class in question, their heralds, whilst defending their values, put forward the vision they had of the other members of political society. Although himself a canon, Froissart embodied this group, represented also by the Burgundian historians (such as Georges Chastellain, Olivier de la Marche), and the Berry herald, otherwise known as Gilles le Bouvier, or also Robert Blondel. It is more difficult to see Commynes as the spokesman of a social group, even though he pertained to the Burgundian nobility, since his point of view is such a singular one. Properly political literature also stylised noble discourse. The *Songe du Vergier* and the debates of the fifteenth century spoke for this group, with, however, the ambiguity that those who expressed the opinion of the chivalric class do not necessarily represent that section which participated in government, but sometimes only the knightly class at war, whether provided with a command or not. The 'gendarme' of the debate written by Gaguin at the end of the reign of Louis XI is a man 'following arms' who does not involve himself in affairs of state. If he attracted the hatred of the people, as Claude de Seyssel indicates, it was because of his warlike way of life.

In the case of those who pertain to neither of the groups mentioned above, it is more difficult to find an unmediated spokesman to judge the members of political society, with the possible exception of estates assemblies, such as in 1347 (the remonstrance of the towns) or in the time of Étienne Marcel. Moreover, it is necessary to proceed with caution: in 1484, according to Neithard Bulst, two-thirds of the representatives of what was beginning to be called the Third Estate were royal officials, which some found less than representative (such as those from Lyon)[4] and in whom it would be dangerous to see the opinion of the people of the towns. The 'people' of political treatises express more the supposed ideas of the 'labourer', the third character to speak in the debate of Robert Gaguin, than that of a non-noble office-holder. Ennoblement or entry into the church did not alter the particular perspective on the political personnel of their time found in the visions of Pierre d'Orgement or Jean Juvénal des Ursins. The Bourgeois de Paris may well have been identified as a canon of Notre-Dame, and probably a Doctor of the University, but his perception of the 'men of power' of the first half of the fifteenth century nonetheless gives evidence of its probably popular origins.

3.   Imagining and ordering political society

Discourses concerning the members of political society rested on a general and ordained vision of that society. In France, for instance, in the work of the St Denis chronicler, two visions were retained, one binary the other tripartite, inherited from the functional partitions of earlier centuries. Translating Aristotle, Oresme distinguished between 'priestly men and men of arms' (*gent sacerdotal et gens d'armes*).[5] The debates of the fifteenth century distinguish the three points of view of the three orders. Without doubt, 'institutions' maintained this simplified perception until the end of the Middle Ages, for instance in the two-way division between clergy and laity in the great body of the monarchy – Charles VIII would demand that parity be respected and Seyssel still reasoned within this framework – or in the tripartite system which for a long time structured the Estates General and the regional estates, where political society represented itself. On 10 February 1484, before the assembly gathered at Tours, Jean de Rély, canon of Paris, theologian and spokesman for the three estates, did not know how to describe those who were responsible for the disorders which burdened the kingdom except by mentioning one after the other the nobles, clerics, then the people, the *plebeius status* or *status populi* depicted by Masselin in his *Journal des États* of 1484.

Although still alive in England, the schema of three orders was often seriously attacked. The three estates of the nobility, the clergy and the

---

[4] Bulst (1982).   [5] Guenée (2002).

labourers appear in many sources, notably in poetry and in sermons which present a very conventional vision of society. However, two points can be observed. First, where it survives, the schema often underwent certain variations. Secondly, more precise classifications were generally made which were very varied, at least for all those below the level of the 'lords', to such an extent that the schema sometimes disappeared entirely. This was the reflection of the mobility referred to above.

One noteworthy characteristic of this variation in the presentation of the tripartite schema is the way in which, in some cases, a social hierarchy which is supposed to be eternal is more or less closely refined. These refinements concern above all the place of the clergy with regard to the other estates. The most extreme case is that of certain texts emanating from the lollard heresy, the only heresy to become at all widespread in England at the end of the Middle Ages which, under the auspices of John Wyclif, had notably put into question much of the power and role of the clergy, to the benefit of a greater role for the lay authorities. According to Helen Barr, the lollards, without denying the tradition of the three orders, wanted to realign it, re-evaluating the role of the Third Estate in order to reduce the worth of the second, held to be corrupt and, in part, outside of society.[6] Other redirections of the established scheme are found in more orthodox texts, although they do not go so far in contestation. Langland, for instance, also puts the secular nobility before the clergy and re-evaluates the order of labourers by insisting on interdependence more than on hierarchy.[7] Chaucer does much the same, in a certain fashion, in the *Prologue* to the *Canterbury Tales*. He puts into relief the knight, the priest and the peasant, but he does this in order to insist upon the social diversity of all the pilgrims. The three idealised portraits seem to drown in this diversity. Furthermore, his pilgrims are not presented in a well-defined hierarchy, to such an extent that the author apologises for it.

Turning to the second point, it is possible to see that even in sermons, often quite conservative ones, important nuances are found from the end of the fourteenth century. For example, in a famous sermon probably delivered in London in 1387 or 1388, Thomas Wimbledon considered in particular merchants and urban elites, even if he had previously evoked the traditional framework of the three estates.[8] And these groups were no longer systematically condemned, as we shall see, even if they were still the object of great suspicion. In a more general fashion, the descriptions of the estates in literary texts became more and more varied. These

---

[6] Barr (2001).   [7] Mairey (2007).   [8] Horner (1998).

descriptions can be organised around a certain number of elements used in different ways by the poets:

1. The hierarchical arrangement of society was not always respected in the enumeration of different groups. This is the case with Langland and Chaucer, but also with the poem *Mum and the Sothsegger*. This does not, however, indicate that the poets put this hierarchy into question, even if it does in part come back to our remarks about the manipulation of the schema of the three orders. It is rather, in our opinion, indicative of the recognition of a more complex society which is more difficult to put into order.

2. The distinction between clergy and laity was no longer primary as a matter of course. Langland and Chaucer, again, freely mixed the two categories, which are equally varied in their subdivisions.

3. Wealth became a determining criterion. Langland began his description by noting that he was going to distinguish between the rich and the poor on the one hand, the workers and the lazy on the other; Lydgate, some years later, put the rich next to the king, the bishops, the lords and the judges in his *Advice to Several Estates* (in *Historical Poems of the XIVth and XVth centuries*).[9]

4. Finally, the political and economic activities of members of different groups became more and more significant. These were added to social status and wealth in order to define categories. If Chaucer refers to some groups by their status, such as the knight, the squire and the yeoman – although the last of these raises a number of problems – most of the pilgrims were defined first of all by their profession. Many of these professions were, moreover, urban, and the town took an increasingly important role in all of these texts.

Not all of these criteria appear in all the poems which deal with social and/or political questions, far from it. In truth, it is necessary to recognise that Chaucer and Langland, who are the only ones (to our knowledge) to use and combine all these criteria, might be thought to be somewhat exceptional cases. However, a certain number of clues suggest that many, in England, were conscious of the diversity of the criteria of social distinction, in particular at the level of the ruling classes.

This coming to consciousness seems to us all the more real in that it is also manifested in normative sources, in which the trifunctional schema had become totally obsolete. Sumptuary laws are rich in information of this kind. It has been shown that these laws – probably ineffective, to judge by their frequent repetition – were the product both of economic anxiety (to protect English commerce) and a desire to control

---

[9] Edited in Robbins (1959).

social hierarchies, as much on the moral level as the political. But the arrangement of these different categories, and above all the numerous exceptions which were set out, say much about the manner in which the authors of these acts perceived these evolutions and represented them to themselves. This was particularly so for the ruling classes, which were the object of the greatest attention. In the case of the two most complete laws, those of 1363 and 1463, social categories below the lords (who were not considered) were defined by social status and wealth. The specified levels of wealth are more detailed in the Statute of 1363, with distinctions within each group. It is worth noting that urban elites had to have far greater wealth than gentry groups to obtain the possibility of the appearance of equality. The arrangement of the hierarchy is very clearly dominated by the nobility, even if some nuances are recognised. This arrangement was again well represented in the ordinance of 1463, as is suggested by the refinement of internal classifications of the gentry. The term bachelor appeared, as does 'gentlemen', the term henceforth fixed to designate those below the rank of squire. But the greatest novelty was the place given to political activity in the social definition of each stratum. Service to the king (whether in the household or the great administrative departments) and the urban political elites in particular, are the most represented amongst the exceptions. It seems to us that this says much about the evolution of the ruling classes: political activity had become a recognised and important social marker, in particular service to the king.

In England at the end of the Middle Ages, it is possible to observe great diversity in the criteria defining each individual's place within society, at least at the level of those who were part of the direction of the kingdom at the centre and in the locality on an everyday level. In addition to statutory denominations, which were also refined considerably in the course of time, wealth and political activity (and also economic activity) come out as determinant. These elements are found as much in literary sources as normative ones. In numerous judicial texts, in contracts for example, people are presented under many identities (status, profession). This diversity did not put into question the hierarchical arrangement of society, which still remained just as strong. It served only to make it more complex.

In France, too, complexity caused traditional visions of society to become in part outdated. Thinkers acknowledged this by subdividing the appropriate categories or by forging different groupings. More precise subdivisions, certainly more social than political, came into being. They can be found in sumptuary ordinances, for example. Those of 1294 distinguish between 'bourgois et bourgoises', clerks with particular dignities (deans, archdeacons, priors) or without dignities, prelates, dukes, counts and barons, knights, squires, '*garçons*', *bannerettes* and castellans. The refinement of classification was also expressed in the treatises of the fourteenth and fifteenth centuries, which tried to embrace all of society and which worked hard to take account of its diversity. Philippe de Mézières thus distinguishes between twelve estates forming the city. Those who took part in its government and its functioning were detached as particular groups.

Within the nobility, following the canonisation of St Louis (1297), princes of the lily were proud to have his blood in their veins and they progressively formed a special category (well described by Andrew Lewis)[10] and the object of a specific discourse, in particular in the first decades of the fifteenth century, despite the great diversity of political choices made by various ones amongst them. The 'princes of the blood', *principes et proceres*, were seen as promoters of discord by the university (remonstrance of 1413), by Alain Chartier around 1430, Juvénal des Ursins in the 1440s and certain deputies in 1484 – influenced, it is true, by the clan Beaujeu, to speak ill of the duke of Orléans. More generally, the nobility gave rise to lively criticism. The chivalric class appears either as the cowards who flee from the battlefield rather than 'dying for the country' – this is the complaint of the people against the *proceres* delivered by Montebelluna and even signalled by Froissart – or else as the pillagers who rob the people instead of defending them. The latter image is above all found, and primarily amongst clergymen, in the fifteenth century, from Alain Chartier or Michel Pintoin (who depicts the reciprocal hatred of the nobles and non-nobles in 1417) to Robert Gaguin. This 'disfunctionality' with regards to the traditional ideal is reinforced with another, newer, complaint related to the new demands of the monarchy: the man-of-war, the captain in particular, defrauds the king by demanding wages with no relation to his real military contribution (a fault denounced under the first Valois and still being condemned by the officer of the king, Robert de Balsac, around 1490); by youthful impulse, he puts individual exploits before the common good, disobeying orders (Honorat Bovet, *The Tree of Battles*). The image of the nobility thus emerged very devalued, even discredited, from the misadventures of 1346, 1356 and 1415, from their straying into the struggles of civil war, and its prolongations (Praguerie, Bien Public, Guerre Folle), which worsened the situation still further.

As early as the twelfth century, John of Salisbury had 'isolated', so to speak, the group of people at court whom he saw pressing about the person of Henry Plantagenet. The 'courtiers' (*curiales*) were to constitute a lasting subject for a discourse which was certainly more moral than

---

[10] Lewis (1986).

political, inspiring also literary writers and poets. Composed around 1422, the *Curial* of Alain Chartier was the work of reference for all the fifteenth century on this subject. This group of *curiales* transcended the old tripartite categories. There were court abbots as well as household nobles and even individuals of low origins such as the 'dogs of the palace' which Thomas Basin considers in his *Histoire de Louis XI*, without in truth showing great originality (a century before, François de Montebelluna, taking his inspiration from Boethius, stigmatised the *canes palatini* and other *curie parasiti*). Those closest to the prince received generic names, some of which were destined to survive through to the modern era. Philippe de Mézières speaks of 'mahommets' in speaking of favourites. At the beginning of the fifteenth century, as Philippe Contamine has shown, the term 'mignon' appeared, showing the degraded image of these courtiers.[11] Indeed, they are depicted as flatterers, plotters and self-interested hypocrites, veritable inverse types of virtue described by the *Fauvel* or the *Dit de Franc Gontier*, amongst many other texts.

Originating from 'court', in the institutional sense of the word, royal counsellors constitute another grouping which was the object of particular concern within political society, and even beyond, as is proved by the criticisms lodged by a labourer punished in 1417 by the *Parlement*. In his translation of the *Politics* of Aristotle, Oresme speaks of the 'men of counsel' (*gens de conseil*), competent to deal with public affairs alongside the men of arms and the sacerdotal class, but the expression does not designate all the counsellors, only those who we would now call experts specialising in law and finance. The term 'counsellor' (*conseiller*) in fact covers a wide spectrum going far beyond simple attendance, on a continuous or sporadic basis, of the royal council, and the individuals who lightly appropriated this flattering title. But even without official status – the council of the king being no more nor less than the always-changing sum of the individuals who made it up – the 'men of counsel' appeared to certain observers to form a particular group, attacked at critical moments (such as the defeats of Philippe de Valois and his son; the madness of Charles VI, imputed to the overwork imposed by the *marmousets*) and frequently holding the attention of the thinkers of the years 1380–1450, when they concerned themselves with the question of the 'counsellors whom the prince ought to have'. Much the same was seen at representative assemblies. At Tours, in 1484, Jehan Masselin execrated the *rectores inutiles* whom the monarch had around him. Moral criteria (age, experience, wisdom, virtues) had already been seen as more important than birth for some time in the ideal selection of counsellors, even if a dazzling rise still seemed ill-considered when it was accomplished in

---

[11] Contamine (1994).

contempt of the providential order which had decreed that an individual should be born into the minor nobility (such as Marigny) or the 'people' (such as Olivier le Daim or Jean de Doyat under Louis XI). In the *Confort d'ami* written for Charles the Bad, King of Navarre, Guillaume de Machaut stigmatised the men of humble origins who had climbed to the summit by the grace of a prince for whom they represented a permanent danger.

Perceptions of the clergymen in government are scarcely more complimentary. One early image is that of prelates as bad counsellors, who presume to promote their opinion in military matters (Eustache Deschamps, *Lay de plour*). Preoccupied above all by plots for advancement, they are avid for the favours to be obtained by assiduous courting of the monarch, who in consequence is flattered, rather than led along the path of good faith. Some theoreticians – heirs of thirteenth-century anticlericalism, influenced by Marsilius of Padua or partisans of a fundamental reform of an ecclesiastical establishment which needed to be extracted from worldly concerns – even went so far as to reject the principle of ecclesiastical participation in government, despite a tradition which had reached its high point during the 'regime of the abbots' put in place for a time under Philip VI. The government prelate, retained far from his flock, seemed to them to betray his primary function, his pastoral duties, in favour of 'lay works' (*The Lamentations of Mattheolus*; Alain Chartier; *Livre de l'Espérance*) which were even less appropriate to clerical status in that they concern finance. After Oresme, who had rejected absolutely the idea of the participation of men of the church in financial affairs (in his translation of the *Politics* of Aristotle), whilst all the time admitting their presence in the council, Jean Gerson railed against those officers of Christ who became officers of the fisc. A letter of advice addressed to Yolande of Aragon around 1425, stigmatised these 'men of the church who stop serving God to embroil themselves in the finances of the kingdom, which does not pertain to their estate'.[12] Juvénal des Ursins thought as much in his epistle of 1430 to the three estates and in his epistle of 1445 to his brother, who was then chancellor. This uncomplimentary vision, inspired by Christian morality and the reforming spirit which was then blowing through the very ranks of the clergy (the clerk as official of the royal fisc appeared as an avatar of the pontifical tax collector), joined another which criticised the clergy in the cultural sense of the term and as an influence group. This critique attacked the clerics who presumed to monopolise the exercise of counsel to the king in the name of the knowledge they had (it is this system, ancestor of the 'think tank', that Gerson

---

[12] *Advis à Yolande d'Aragon*, ed. Boudet and Sené (2012).

and the university masters defended), notwithstanding their inexperience in concrete matters. Delivered to them, the *res publica* approached catastrophe, as in 1356–8 and in 1413. Heir to Trémaugon, who nonetheless admitted the usefulness of the presence of wise clerks in the council, Jean de Montreuil, a humanist of Charles VI's time, took this position along with Michel Pintoin, then Robert Gaguin. For them, the history of the kingdom showed that the exercise of public affairs by clerics always ends in catastrophe.

Their rivals before the monarch, the men of law, were also portrayed in the worst possible light. The exclusive mastery of a complicated and tortuous science, the intensive exploitation of its resources for ends which are at best political, at worst personal, sketched out a collective personality which did not necessarily correspond to effective cohesion or great influence in reality (the historians of Philip the Fair, Strayer and Favier first and foremost, have said what ought to be thought about the supposed ascendancy of the legists of the iron king).[13] Instead, their image emerged from a vision which could be fantastic (the leagues of 1314–15) or more reasoned (Oresme, Seyssel). They commonly passed either for the usurpers of the true nobility (the 'knights at law' so named around 1350, claiming to possess noble characteristics around 1400); or for evil influences imbued with formulae from the *Codex* which justify tyranny (*Songe du vieil pèlerin*) and forget mercy (the exhortation of Juvénel to Charles VII during the trial of the duke of Alençon, 1458); or for political 'idiots', in the sense that they lacked knowledge of human affairs and of philosophy. Giles of Rome had already said all this before 1280, although in a letter written to a friar preacher he differentiated between learned jurists and legist-practitioners with their mechanical use of the law. After Oresme, Gerson and Pierre d'Ailly relaunched the attack against evil-doing jurists around 1400. The echo can be heard once again in a short work from the reign of Louis XI concerning royal officers (*An officiarii sint multiplicandi*) and then again in the Estates of 1484.

In part treated together with the lawyers, the group most directly tied to the genesis of the modern state was, of course, that of royal officials, those *officiarii* who processed under that title at the funeral of Charles VII. However, the generic term for officer emerged late on, towards 1320, under the pen of the clerks of the *Parlement* and it remains rare amongst writers who did not pertain to the workings of the state.[14] To what extent this category was perceived as a coherent ensemble remains an open question. Indeed, there was a whole world of difference between a local agent of the king and a great officer of the Crown, even if the common

[13] Favier (1969).   [14] Telliez (2004).

denominator was service to the monarch, to be proudly recalled on tomb monuments. A Eustache Deschamps, for instance, never specifically took into account royal officers on their own. All the same, according to a composite process into which the monarchy, officers and those who describe political society all entered, a collective perception progressively formed. The status given by royalty to those who they considered to be part of it (an idea consecrated by an ordinance of 1467 but in force as early as the end of the fourteenth century) and therefore progressively furnished with privileges (such as immunity and irrevocability) gave an undoubted visibility to this group, as did their solidarity and their *esprit de corps* (which was more or less underlined at different moments, but undeniable nonetheless). In 1389, Philippe de Mézières made of it one of the four 'hierarchies'. A short work from around 1470 edited by Philippe Contamine (*An officiarii...*) clearly considers the *officiarii regis* as one. In 1519, Claude de Seyssel went so far as to conceptualise a 'fourth estate'. Eminent historians nonetheless doubt the subjective consistency of this group or its perception as such, because of the attraction of nobility for the servants of the king. This fourth estate would only be a transitory stage, an entry bay into the noble caste, which is what Seyssel himself implied when he remarked that officers kept passing into the nobility. But from the outside the perception was of a determinable grouping of men of power who were neither nobles by heredity nor clerics.

These office-holders, great or less great, are depicted as tyrants or wolves, denounced with a virulence packed with images by Guillaume le Maire, bishop of Angers, during his clash with the bailiff of Anjou under Philip the Fair, or by the Thomas Basin of the *Apologie*, full of his rancour as a bishop of Lisieux in exile. At the time of Claude de Seyssel still, the officers are depicted as the persecutors of the nobility: 'Since whoever would lightly believe the royal officers in it, one would at any moment put the greater part of noble men on trial for the supposed rights of the king, by which they would be destroyed and crushed.'[15] The accumulation of multiple offices was denounced with virulence in 1484. Men of justice repulsed the preacher Olivier Maillard by their venality and their corruptibility. The men of the *Parlement* or of the *Chambre des comptes* suffered from the image of a caste which put private interests before the common good, like those *généraux des finances* who raised the indignation of Eustache Deschamps. A war treasurer of the lowest origins could strike a more impressive figure than a duke, according to a scandalised Philippe de Mézières. Clientage, nepotism and prevarication

---

[15] Seyssel (1961), p. 157.

were the generic vices of these categories who protect themselves (so said Robert de Balsac), reproduced amongst themselves (endogamy amongst the families of men of the *Parlement* is denounced by the reformers of 1413 in the remonstrance to the king from the town and university of Paris). Not even their competence was certain, because of their venial and cooptive system of recruitment against which many theoreticians opposed the wholesome principle of election following the verification of aptitude. The petition of the clergy in 1413 violently attacked the excessive numbers of men of finance and justice, calling the first 'men of no worth and of small estate who are raised and enriched'[16] and labelling the second incompetents. The petition of the Parisians targeted the royal *prevôt* of Paris, Pierre des Essarts. In his letter to Jean Jouvenel (1418), the monk of Saint Denis, Pierre de Versailles, stigmatised those predatory officers who, coming up from nothing, made their fortune in two years and raised superb houses which were subsequently doomed to be assaulted by crowds exasperated by their avidity. In 1484, the Estates of Tours attacked the 'king's men' (*pars regia*), notably the men of justice and of finance who, far from being associated with the suffering of the other parts of the body politic (the three traditional estates), broke solidarity with them and took a scandalous profit from doing so (in the discourse of one noble, Philippe de Poitiers). Seyssel believed he could see jealousy conceived by the nobility of the sword against the world of office: 'and this seems good to no one in the first estate' (here he does not mean the clergy, which he puts to one side, but the nobility) 'that this one should be better treated than theirs'.[17] Criticism of wages, of favours and above all of the powers granted to these men who took the place of traditional elites lay behind this claim, which the author found to be baseless in part.

Nonetheless, the common perception of this milieu remained the sum of separate characteristics ascribed to them in particular cases. The global image of the odious *fonctionnaire* was only on the way to being formed. What was in any case an exaggerated perception of their excesses, which were held to be unpunished or even protected, tended to give place, amongst certain social thinkers concerned with the interests of royalty, to the vision of their insufficiency for their task. This much is clear with Jouvenel des Ursins, who found the local agents of the king quite incapable of defending his rights, for want of a good knowledge of the law. The image was even relatively favourable in the writings of a nobleman such as Commynes: certainly, he says, officers are avid to accumulate offices, but their irrevocability is a good thing well defended by the *Parlement*

---

[16] *Rapport sur les doléances*, ed. Marion (1845), p. 282.   [17] Seyssel (1961), p. 123.

where, for some bad counsellors, there are many good ones: 'so it is in every estate'.

As in England, but probably with less precision, the refinement of the perception of political society contributed in the end to distinguishing within the third estate a group concerned with public affairs on a local level. These are those whom Christine de Pizan calls the 'citoiens', or the monk of Saint Denis the *cives notabiles*, who formed together the ruling elites of cities and were made up, depending on the place and period, either of merchants and traders (in the capital) or of the men of law (in Lyon in the first half of the fifteenth century). Further down still are found the 'people', as they are conceived of by the clerk Jean de Rély at Tours in 1484: 'I call the "people" a multitude of men who are neither nobles nor men of the church, such as secretaries, scribes, sergeants, tax collectors for the *taille*, quartermasters, commissars in the matter of the salt [tax], clerks who pay men-at-arms and men-at-arms who are not nobles.'[18] It is no longer the holders of major offices who are in question (the Latin text says: *verum hic populum appello quamdam gentium multitudinem quae non ex nobilibus ecclesiasticisve consistit nec ex aliis publico fungentibus officio*) but ordinary agents. The orator seems in this way to extract officers of high rank from the 'people'.

One further category calls for remark, that of the *cives*, which only corresponded to the 'civic' part of the people and did not include the working *plebs* of the town and the fields. This category did not emerge solely from observation but also from an intellectual movement which was particularly marked between 1350 and 1420, and then again after 1460. This movement, humanism, was concerned to find in the present time, if necessary forcing the sense of words, the terminology of the texts of Aristotle, Cicero and the Roman historians.

As for the *plebs*, it was their pretensions to intervention in public affairs which were denounced as illegitimate or subversive, fruits of pride and cupidity. The image of the 'poor people' who are worthy of compassion was mixed with the hideous figure of the insurgent and bestial *plebs* who usurped, as with the Cabochiens of 1413, a role which nature had not given them. According to Oresme in his French translation of Aristotle's *Politics*, Philippe de Mézières and Christine de Pizan, labourers and craftsmen did not have any aptitude or vocation to involve themselves in public affairs, occupied as they were with their *negocium* and disqualified by their ignorance of the laws and of rhetoric. The spectacle of certain Italian cities delivered into their power inspired Christine to this statement in the *Livre du corps de policie*: 'and believe well indeed that

---

[18] Masselin (1835), p. 207.

such governance is not at all profitable to the *res publica*'.[19] Urban elites, admitted for their part into the management of city government, discredit themselves by their frequent collusion with the populace, a collusion which Christine de Pizan also denounced. The Cotentin noble Robert Blondel had only contempt and hatred for the fury of the Parisians unleashed in the massacres of 1418. An interesting division is found in his writing, one with a rich future, between the good provinces and the evil capital, 'Paris who administers us/All ills':[20] a critique not only of the *plebs* but also no doubt of the bourgeois elites of the capital, whom this worthy noble knight despises.

The English situation presents a number of points in common, but also a number of important differences. Amongst the clergy, first of all, the distinction went far beyond the traditional division between regular and secular clergy. That made between high and low clergy, and in a more subtle manner between beneficed and non-beneficed, became more and more common. Within this opposition, 'subgroups' were numerous and significant (Chaucer's different pilgrims, for instance). We are concerned especially with the high clergy, an integral part of the ruling classes, generally placed alongside the nobles. They were regularly the object of traditional critiques, even by those who were themselves part of this group. The principal complaint was against the usurpation of the style of life of noble laymen, the absence of an exemplary comportment, and more generally, the failure to fulfil the essential mission with which they were charged, tied in with charity in the fullest sense of the term. But other criticisms are significant for our present subject, which concerned the place of the high clergy within the government. They recall the French critiques. In most of the sources under consideration, notably in sermons and poetry (although for different reasons), it was said that the high clergy should not participate directly in temporal government, nor sate their thirst for power within ecclesiastical institutions. There is, however, a certain unanimity on the fact that prelates should give counsel, even if the nature of this counsel varies. For Langland, for instance, this counsel ought to be of a purely spiritual nature, whereas for the author of *Mum and the Sothsegger*, it covers a wider range of subjects. Prelates are thus clearly perceived as being complete members of political society, and not only of ecclesiastical institutions, even if the links between the two are strong.

Laymen as a group are the object of more varied reflection. The different ways in which the English nobility were represented were, to begin with, very complex. In fact, they varied greatly according to whether

[19] Pizan (1967), p. 170.   [20] Blondel (1891–3), p. 67.

the nobility was considered in terms of values and ideals, or on a more pragmatic level.

From the first of these two perspectives, the nobility, defined in its widest sense, is often envisaged as a single unit, whether it is being praised or criticised. In this perspective, the critiques are often rather conventional, notably concerning the pride and corruption of the nobles. But common values and ideals are observed as much amongst the lords as amongst knights and gentlemen considered generally. In fact, as in France, the chivalrous ideal was still very present, and it was espoused to a great extent by the nobles themselves. The examples to be found in literature are innumerable. There are the *Vie du Prince Noir* by the Chandos Herald or the texts written in the wake of Agincourt, for instance, without even mentioning romances (for the latter, the situation is, however, more complicated). This ideal also passed by way of the Crusade, still very much alive at the end of the Middle Ages. However, the accent was placed more and more strongly on the responsibility of nobles to maintain justice and peace within the kingdom. The examples are again numerous. They were certainly inspired by the tradition of 'mirrors for princes', although they must also be put in political context. It is necessary to evoke here significant productions made at the moment of changes of dynasty. Even if he supports the new Lancastrian dynasty, Hoccleve insists strongly on peace and the government of the kingdom. Sometimes genuine critiques are found of the behaviour of nobles in the war, even in texts written by nobles who had themselves been soldiers. The most striking example is that of Sir John Clanvowe, household knight of Richard II, who wrote a poem entitled *The Boke of Cupid* and a religious treatise, *The Two Ways*. Nigel Saul has shown how Clanvowe put forward lively critiques of his own milieu, in particular concerning behaviour towards non-combatants and the inhumanity of war.[21] Saul notes, however, that this type of accusation became very rare once more after the victories of Henry V in France. On the other hand, the call for noble responsibility within the kingdom survived and developed.

If we leave aside the realm of ideals in favour of the realities of government, the distinctions are clearer between the higher nobility and the gentry, which itself is a composite group of sometimes ill-defined contours.

Titled nobles occupied a quite distinct position, as we have already suggested. Their power was never contested, much like that of the king. On the contrary, the most lively critiques concerned their tendency to misuse their power, acting solely for their personal interest and not for the

---

[21] Saul (2002).

common good. An essential criticism in this matter concerned 'maintenance', linked to the system of retinues, which appears in literary sources as well as in the petitions of the Commons. 'Maintenance' consisted of applying pressure through retainers, whether this was in the law courts or through violence. It was vigorously and repeatedly denounced, and was even the object of statutes, notably in 1390.

The situation of the 'gentry' is complicated by the problems of defining this group. The volume of historians' work on this subject is considerable. We have seen how this period was marked throughout by efforts to delimit with greater precision its different subgroups. We have also noted how wealth and, more and more, political activity, constituted important criteria. Without going into the details, it can just be remarked that many squires were equally – indeed more – rich and renowned than many knights. In fact, in literary sources, the gentry was never considered as a coherent group, except when included in nobility in general. Those of Chaucer's pilgrims who pertain to the gentry are not all dealt with together. On the one hand there is the knight (who is the object of one of the rare ideal portraits of the *Prologue*), followed by his son the squire and by his yeoman. The latter is not logically part of the gentry, but his status is not free of ambiguity, as Chaucer's portrait, and also the personage of Robin Hood, suggests.[22] On the other hand, the franklin is described after the sergeant-at-law (at the top extremity of the judicial profession) and his company. This term 'franklin' leads once more into hazy areas, since it denoted, in the second half of the fourteenth century, the inferior grades of the gentry. But Chaucer's Franklin appears to be a particularly dynamic gentleman, who forms part of the local elite of his county: he is described as a knight of the shire (i.e. a representative to parliament), a sheriff and controller. Finally, he is even ascribed the quality of 'vavasour'. The frontiers were thus extremely fluid between different categories within and at the fringes of the gentry.

A large number of criticisms of members of the gentry are concerned with the functions which they fulfil. This appears, for instance, in the principal uses which the author of *Mum and the Sothsegger* makes of the term 'knight'. This term is used above all to designate the members of the gentry who serve the king and who are concerned with government, and in particular to underline their responsibilities (and their incapacities). He also attacks the representatives of the counties in parliament, from the same point of view. Indeed, in this poem, as in other sources, the gentry appear to oscillate between the nobility and the commons. This once again suggests the complexity of the ways in which the ruling

---

[22] Almond and Pollard (2001).

classes were represented, to include considerations of status as much as of wealth and function. This leads on to the study of categories which are above all defined by their political activity, dominated by the gentry but including also people who do not altogether belong to that group.

The group of the courtiers, clearly very linked to the nobility, was not as distinct as in France, especially in the fifteenth century, to such an extent that certain historians have even gone so far as to ask if there really was a court in England.[23] In fact, poetic texts as much as the petitions of the Commons evoke instead the people of the 'household' (as much for the king as for the great nobles), the term referring to an institution situated halfway between the court and the lord's domestic administration. 'Households', that of the king in particular, were the object of numerous attacks. Many concerned the problems of 'maintenance' already invoked when discussing the nobility. For the rest, it is possible to discern two main groups of critique, divided according to those who made them, although poets tend to cut across this division. On the one hand, there was the attack, originating from the Commons, on the excessive expenditure of the royal household, above all at the end of the fourteenth century and the beginning of the fifteenth, relayed by certain poems such as *Mum and the Sothsegger*. On the other hand, the accusation of the appropriation of royal power, regularly raised, came particularly from the great nobles, such as the Appellants under Richard II in the late 1380s, or Richard of York and his partisans under Henry VI in the 1450s. This was the question of the king's 'favourites'. But in fact, the latter are primarily criticised for their excessive grip on government, as Richard of York's petition suggests. This question was closely linked to the problem of counsel and counsellors.

The group of 'counsellors' was very much in evidence in these texts (indeed, omnipresent), although they too were the object of many different definitions – when they were defined at all. In fact, they can be situated at the intersection between numerous categories, which must be linked in part to political 'reality' (we refer here to the many different studies on this question). The magnates, first of all, saw themselves as the natural counsellors of the king, which they were. This is apparent, for example, in the accusations of the Appellants or of Richard of York, which we have just evoked. Richard insisted strongly on this point. In fact, this role of counsellor was never put into question by other groups: it was an integral part of their ruling function. The great nobles were generally criticised for their bad counsel or for their failure to provide counsel. In this matter, Sir John Fortescue perhaps went the furthest, criticising all

[23] Watts (2003).

the great nobles for their inability to provide correct counsel to the king because they are themselves too tied up in their personal interests or in the interests of their networks of associates. But other types of counsellor also appear: the 'favourites' of the king, who were in general members of the household such as the knights of the chamber, strongly criticised by the author of *Mum and the Sothsegger*, as we have seen; or administrators, in particular men of law. That said, whatever the point of view adopted or the group attacked, many common critiques are found which came out of convention (youth, the lure of gain), even if these conventions were frequently turned about in order to stick, so to speak, to the reality of the moment. The author of *Richard the Redeless*, for example, employed these criticisms as part of accusations against specific individuals (those close to Richard II). By contrast, the counsellor had to be a wise and experienced man, who did not hesitate to speak, whatever his origins.

Administrators are also found amongst the courtiers, although this group covers a far broader reality. We prefer this term to 'royal officials' for England, in that a significant system of commissions – temporary and specific charges – rounded off that of offices. These administrators were generally members of the gentry, but it is also necessary to take into account persons of lower rank. What was, for example, the status of Thomas Hoccleve, clerk of the privy seal and by that token close to the government, but at the same time of rather obscure origins? As for counsellors, criticism was directed above all against the way in which different functions were fulfilled. In this, a certain evolution can be noted in the period under consideration. Tax collectors and purveyors, criticised with the greatest enthusiasm in the first half of the fourteenth century, cede to a far more varied range of targets, amongst whom more and more men of law and local urban elites are found. But it must also be noted that some groups were forging their own identity. Clerks of the privy seal, to stay with Hoccleve, lived and worked together, and developed a common culture, a little like the notaries and secretaries of the king of France.[24]

Within the category of administrators, men of law were a group of growing importance, as a result of the evolution of the common law, the principal law of England. There again, things are complicated, because many were part of the gentry, although they nonetheless formed a distinctive group, with a strong collective identity. This identity was perceptible both from within and from outside this group. Men of law themselves, at least at the highest levels (those in the central courts at Westminster) formed a group which was increasingly conscious of its competences and its specificity. This comes out, amongst other ways, in the fifteenth

[24] Killick (2010).

century, in the institutionalisation of the inns of court, but also, for example, in the work of Sir John Fortescue (who was Chief Justice of the King's Bench before being exiled with Henry VI) which constitutes a vibrant panegyric for men of law. However, Fortescue is the individual who tied together most strongly the culture of men of law with that of members of the gentry. In his description of the inns of court, he points out that the students who frequented them were first and foremost noble, and that the complete education which they were given was not to be solely juridical. This identity was expressed also in the continuous use of French – which had become a technical language – whilst it was increasingly replaced by English in other domains. Seen from the outside, the recognition of this group was equally strong, whether in a positive or negative way. As has been seen with sumptuary laws, men of law, at least those at royal courts, were at the end of the fifteenth century the object of very particular attention, since they were completely dispensed from the obligations of the ordinance of 1463, just like the other great officers of the king. By contrast, criticisms of men of law do not disappear, but rather become more and more strident throughout our period. They focus first of all on their cupidity, but can sometimes avoid straightforward denunciation, since their corruption is sometimes perceived in the light of the power which their competences ascribe them. At the end of the fourteenth century, for instance, a line appears in Langland's poem declaring that lawyers should not make profits from their knowledge since this is a gift from God. It also appears far more brutally in the revolt of 1381. Men of law were a particular target for the rebels, who executed many of them, including the Chief Justice of the King's Bench of the time, Sir John Cavendish. The insurgents destroyed numerous judicial archives, in particular those of the Temple in London. The importance of specific competences in the construction of social typologies is particularly fertile in the case of men at law, but this phenomenon is also appropriate for other groups (including the clergy).

Finally, as in France, urban elites were growing in importance and were duly recognised as an integral part of political society. We have seen that merchants were increasingly integrated into the literature of estates, even when they were also the object of great suspicion. Despite this, certain authors tried more and more to ascribe them a place within the economy of salvation. More important for our subject, however, is the greater and greater recognition bestowed on urban elites in political matters in several different types of source. Mayors, aldermen and in general all those who were involved in the government of the towns were the object of a renewed attention in the sumptuary law of 1463. On a more critical level, they were increasingly singled out in poetic works from the end of the fourteenth century. Langland and the author of *Mum*, for instance, strongly criticised mayors and their counsellors, but this is once again because they considered their responsibility to be fundamental. The mayor was an intermediary between the king and the townsmen, just like members of the gentry in their counties. Thus overall, the English ruling classes were primarily criticised because of their increased responsibilities.

4.   Representing and promoting the common good

These descriptions were not only meant to give an account of a particular state of affairs. They were intended above all to propose an ideal configuration for political society leading to the accomplishment of the Common Good. But this configuration differed a little in the two kingdoms.

In France, one of the aims of these social typologies was to furnish, by contrast with reality, a description of what ought to be the role of each group in power, linked to its 'natural' or providential condition. 'Just as each keeps to his estate / So much will he have no cause for remorse' (*Si que tien chascun en son ordre/ Si bien qu'il n'i ait que remordre*), thought Eustache Deschamps. Providence had established clerks to pray and knights to fight. Let them return to this path, but let them follow it in the higher interest of the king and kingdom, with discipline, obedience – according to the Roman model – and piety reinforced with wisdom. Those who work had no role to fulfil but to obey since they were not capable of undertaking high functions. As for courtiers, they had to be put in their proper place, which was to provide domestic service to the prince, without political interference and without attempting to obtain favours or offices for associates. Officers should limit themselves to executing royal orders with moderation but efficiency, whilst rendering accounts, as envisaged in endlessly reiterated ordinances of Saint Louis.

With Providence, the argument of nature, explored by Jacques Krynen from this angle, also served to ascribe a place and a comportment which was unchanging, since it was founded on nature, to the many different members of the political body. This metaphorical vision was itself very old, and was consecrated by *Policraticus*. It was also more functional than the excessively broad and general schema of the orders. The depiction ceaselessly present, in the treatises of the years 1340–1430, of the various groups of society as members or organs of a body, fixed the role of each in turn. Conformity to the natural order derived all initiative from the head or 'chef', which symbolised the monarchy, and reduced the rest to the rank of docile functionaries, without at all abolishing hierarchy, since there were members and organs which were more noble than others. This organicist vision enumerating the categories of society made it possible to integrate new ruling social strata. The hands or arms corresponded to the aristocracy and the knighthood (Guillaume de Digulleville or Christine de Pizan in her 'corps de policie'), whereas the men of law were often compared to the thighs. But the direction of these descriptions remained for the most part turned towards the past and the restoration of a perverted or 'inverted' order. It is there that all the substance of the *Quadrilogue invectif* lies.

In England, beyond the question of moral reform which remains present in numerous texts, very many sources also insisted on the necessity of the common good, even whilst they denounced traditional moral vices such as cupidity. This expression appears in the texts in many forms ('common good', 'common wele', 'common profit') which we have analysed elsewhere.[25] In any case, all those who attended to the government of the kingdom, whether directly or indirectly, were asked to put the common good before their personal interests, to put their various powers and competences at its service, under the enlightened direction of the king.

In this context, many authors (probably more than in France) attempted to take into account the social and political transformations which they witnessed, and in which they participated. All the remarks which we have been able to make concerning the difficulties of providing precise definitions for numerous categories, beginning with the widest, the commons, seem to suggest a perception of a relatively open society, although this does not exclude a very strong hierarchy, which is found in the perceptions of these same commons. Indeed, whatever sources are considered, it seems that this term was above all used in its political sense, as an integral part of the ruling classes. John Gower, in whose work the duality of the term is particularly perceptible, could insist on the importance of the 'common voice' to justify his works and notably his *Confessio Amantis*, which includes, amongst other things, a 'mirror for princes' (Book VII) and counsels for the different categories of (political) society. In this sense, his appeal to the commons in the prologue to the *Confessio* is very representative. But this openness had its limits. When it was the common people who were being considered, those excluded from the everyday government of the kingdom – peasants, artisans and others, but also often the lower clergy – things went very differently. They were asked to remain silent, to stay in their place, as suggests, amongst many other examples, Lydgate's short poem concerning the different estates which we have already mentioned. When in a period of crisis,

[25] Mairey (2010).

they made their voice heard, perhaps because they were better informed than the elites had thought, the predominant sentiments they inspired were those of fear and usurpation. Gower is the most vibrant spokesman of this tendency when he describes the bestial savagery of the rebels of 1381 in his Latin poem *Vox Clamantis*. In this matter, only a few isolated voices were raised, amongst them Chaucer and Langland (who, as we have already been able to see, ought to be situated a little apart from their contemporaries) who understood better than others the aspirations of the common people, without recognising any validity in their independent activity. These voices are also found, sometimes, amongst the Commons, as is suggested by the example of the Speaker Richard Waldegrave. In his discourse to parliament in the autumn of 1381, just after the revolt, he insisted on the necessity of taking account of the needs of the community.[26]

Another essential point to underline is the increasing importance of activity and competence within the government (in a broad sense) in defining each of these groups, even if land, and more generally wealth, remained essential. Participation in the royal government, in particular at the central level, was increasingly perceived as an important social and cultural marker. Much the same can be said of the government of the towns. The best source for this is the parallel between the two sumptuary laws promulgated with exactly one century of separation between them; but other sources, as we have seen, confirm this impression.

Finally, two essential traits seem to characterise the motivations of particular groups when they speak of themselves or others. Certain groups showed a real desire to construct their own identity, even if this is made very complicated in England by the fluidity discussed above, a fluidity which meant that often the men who made up political society could define themselves in terms of several different identities. Men of law furnish an example, but not the only one. It was perhaps because the frontiers between social groups had not yet crystallised that the Commons in parliament were able to forge their own identity on the basis of groups which were in the end rather disparate, and that Langland and Chaucer were able to envisage, even in a disguised manner, societies where horizontal relationships have their place alongside vertical ones. Certainly, these instances remained relatively isolated and they are no longer apparent at all at the end of our period. But they existed nonetheless and they were widely diffused (the manuscripts of *Piers Plowman* and the *Canterbury Tales* survive in several dozen manuscripts, of which the majority date from the fifteenth century).

---

[26] *PROME*, ed. Given-Wilson et al. (2005), parliament of 1381.

This conception is all the more rare in France, where the tone of the texts is essentially reactionary. Nonetheless, it is necessary to move on from the initial impression of the inertia of schemes of thought.[27] Political society had to demonstrate its flexibility in order to give satisfaction in the service of the king. Taking the example of Normandy as a depository of the traditions of the English monarchy, Oresme, in his translation of Aristotle's *Politics*, consider that men-at-arms can serve very well as judges even if their tendency by temperament is to depart from the moderation necessary for justice. The hierarchy of estates is put into question more or less radically. The author of the complaint on Poitiers, probably a Parisian clerk, boldly wondered, after the 'discomforture' of 1356, whether the people had the better aptitude to wage war rather than the nobles. Was he considering the communal militia of Flanders with their painful reputation against French chivalry, or the Swiss soldier-peasants who would so fascinate Commynes later on? Behind the critique of the nobility of blood and of the sword lay also the hopes and expectations of educated milieux for whom nobility was acquired by merit and by the test of service to the king, and for whom leaving one's estate was not forbidden. Oresme considers, in his translation of the *Politics*, that there is a possibility of raising oneself up and participating in the life of the city, even for craftsmen. For Christine de Pizan, after Évrard de Trémaugon, birth does not confer or remove all the qualities necessary to serve the king.

Typologies of the various categories of political society were rich and abundant at the end of the Middle Ages in France and England. In reaction to the crises and the development of royalty and its princely equivalents, as well as by reason of the growing autonomy of political reflection and a new interest in antique institutions, discourses concerning the ruling classes were put into action, partly following paths traced out long before. The denomination of members of these groupings, the generic traits which were assigned them, came out of this flourishing of 'political communication'.

But the discourse of one category concerning another was rarely taken up overtly, for reasons which were finally honourable: it was less a question of advancing in disguise than of proposing an overarching vision in service of a peace that membership of a certain camp would make it impossible to promote, in particular at a time of civil war. The Common Good was not invoked from the standpoint of a single sector of political society. It emerged precisely from the abstraction of certain particular interests tied to a certain social position. The university men of 1413 said

---

[27] Blanchard and Mühlethaler (2002).

it well in their remonstrance to Charles VI: they did not presume to speak in the name of particular and hence hateful interests, as certain ones in the royal entourage sought to have it believed, but rather as simple, good subjects aiming for the good of the whole kingdom.

Finally, in France as in England, the portrayal of those who governed and administered the kingdom, in competition more than in concord, finished most often in contesting their legitimacy and thus either in the promotion of their own milieu, or, more altruistically, in the demand for the reform of the kingdom, which ought to be conferred on rulers more in conformity with the divine and natural order. The difference between the two countries lies above all, it appears, in the nature of the groups which expressed themselves, which were perhaps newer and more varied on the island than on the Continent. In the mirror of mutual representation, French political society seems more rigid and less symbiotic with the *communitas regni*. But that reflects less a direct refusal of evolution than a desire to put them back into an appropriate framework. In the two kingdoms, what was at issue was the need to master disquieting change.

BIBLIOGRAPHY

1. INTRODUCTION

Blanchard J. and Mühlethaler J.-Cl., 2002. *Écriture et pouvoir à l'aube des temps modernes*, Paris.

Coleman, J., 1981. *English Literary History 1350–1400. Medieval Readers and Writers*, London.

Genet, J.-P., 2003. *La genèse de l'Etat moderne, Culture et société politique en Angleterre*, Paris.

Krynen, J., 1993. *L'empire du roi. Idées et croyances politiques en France, XIIIe–XVe siècle*, Paris.

Lachaud, F. and Scordia, L. (eds.), 2012. 'Au-delà des miroirs: la littérature politique dans la France de Charles VI et Charles VII', *Cahiers de Recherches Médiévales et Humanistes*, 24.

Mairey, A., 2007. *Une Angleterre entre rêve et réalité. Littérature et société en Angleterre au XIVe siècle*, Paris.

Mann, J. L., 1973. *Chaucer and Medieval Estates Satire*, Cambridge.

Simpson, J., 2002. *Reform and Cultural Revolution, 1350–1547*, Oxford.

2. SOURCES CITED

Advis à Yolande d'Aragon, ed. J.-P. Boudet and E. Sené in *Cahiers de recherches médiévales et humanistes*, 24 (2012), 67–84.

Balsac, Robert de, *Traité*, ed. P. Contamine, *Annuaire-Bulletin de la Société de l'Histoire de France* (1983–4), pp. 139–71.

Barr, H. (ed.), *The Piers Plowman Tradition*, London, 1993.

Basin, Thomas, *Apologie ou plaidoyer pour moi-même*, ed. and trans. C. Samaran and G. de Groër, Paris, 1974.

Blondel, Robert, *Œuvres*, ed. A. Héron, Paris, 1891–3.

Chartier, Alain, *Livre de l'Espérance*, ed. F. Rouy, Paris, 1989.

Quadrilogue invectif, ed. F. Bouchet, Paris, 2011.

Chaucer, Geoffrey, *The Riverside Chaucer*, ed. L. Benson, Oxford 1987.

Clanvowe, Sir John, *Works*, ed. V. J. Scattergood, London, 1975.

'Complainte sur la bataille de Poitiers', ed. C. de Beaurepaire, *Bibliothèque de l'Ecole des Chartes*, 12 (1851) 257–63.

Contamine, P. (ed.), '*An officiarii regis sint multiplicandi*. Une réflexion scolastique sur la nature et les limites de la puissance du roi de France à la fin du Moyen Âge, à propos des officiers de sa Chambre des comptes', in P. Contamine and O. Matteoni (eds.) *Les Chambres des comptes en France aux xive et xve siècles*, Paris, 1998, pp. 19–28.

Des Ursins, Jean Juvénal, *Écrits politiques*, ed. P. S. Lewis, 3 vols., Paris, 1978–92.

Fortescue, Sir John, *On the Governance of England*, ed. C. Plummer, Oxford, 1892.

Gaguin, Robert, 'Débat du prêtre, du laboureur et du gendarme', ed. L. Thuasne, *Epistole et orationes Gaguini*, Paris, 1903, pp. 350–65.

Historical Poems of the XIVth and XVth centuries, ed. R. H. Robbins, New York, 1959.

Hoccleve, Thomas, *The Regement of Prince*, ed. C. R. Blyth, Kalamazoo, 1999.

Journal des Etats Généraux réunis à Paris au mois d' Octobre 1356, ed. R. Delachenal, Paris, 1900.

Langland, William, *The Vision of Piers Plowman, Version B*, ed. A. V. C. Schmidt, London, 1978 (repr. 1987).

Masselin, Jean, *Journal des Etats généraux tenus à Tours en 1484*, ed. and trans. A. Bernier, Paris, 1835.

Mézières, Philippe de, *Le songe du vieil pelerin*, ed. G. W. Coopland, 2 vols., Cambridge, 1969.

Montebelluna, Francois de, 'Tragicum argumentum de miserabili statu regni Francie', ed. A. Vernet, *Annuaire-bulletin de la Société de l'Histoire de France* (1962–3), 131–63.

Morrison, S. and Mairey, A. (eds. and trans.), *Dialogues et résistances : une anthologie de textes anglais de la fin du Moyen Âge*, Turnhout, 2010.

Parliament Rolls of Medieval England (PROME), ed. C. Given-Wilson et al., CD-Rom, Leicester, 2005.

The Paston Letters, ed. N. Davis, 2 vols., Oxford, 1971–6.

Pizan, Christine de, *Livre de Paix*, ed. C .C. Willard, The Hague, 1958.

Livre du corps de policie, ed. R. H. Lucas, Geneva, 1967.

'Rapport sur les doléances du clergé aux États généraux de 1413', J. Marion, (ed.), *Bibliothèque de l'Ecole des Chartes*, 6 (1845) 281–8.

Remontrances de l'Université et de la Ville de Paris à Charles VI sur le gouvernement du royaume, ed. H. Moranvillé, *Bibliothèque de l'Ecole des Chartes*, 51 (1890) pp. 420–42.

Statutes of the Realm, ed. A. Luders, 12 vols., London, 1810 (repr. Buffalo, NY, 1993).

Trémaugon, Évrard de, *Songe du Vergier*, ed. M. Schnerb-Lièvre, Paris, 1982.

Wimbledon, Thomas, *Wimbledon's Sermon: Redde rationem villcationis tue*, ed. I. K. Knight, Pittsburgh, 1967.

3. FURTHER READING

Almond, A. and Pollard, J., 2001. 'The Yeomanry of Robin Hood and Social Terminology in Fifteenth-Century England', *Past and Present*, 170, 52–77.

Arabeyre, P., 1992. 'La France et son gouvernement au milieu du xve siècle d'après Bernard de Rosier', *Bibliothèque de l'Ecole des Chartes*, 150, 245–85.

Autrand, F., 1991. 'La déconfiture: la bataille de Poitiers (1356) à travers quelques textes français des xive et xve siècle', in Ph. Contamine, G. Giry-Deloison and M. H. Keen (eds.), *Guerre et société en France, Angleterre, Bourgogne, XIVe–XVe siècle*, Paris, pp. 93–122.

Avril, J., 1987. 'La conception du pouvoir politique d'après les écrits de Guillaume Le Maire, évêque d'Angers (1291–1317)', in *Eglises et pouvoir politique. Actes des journées internationales d'Histoire du droit d'Angers (1985)*, Angers, pp. 117–34.

Barr, H., 2001. *Socioliterary Practices in Late Medieval England*, Oxford.

Bulst, N., 1982. 'Vers les états modernes: le Tiers État aux états généraux de Tours en 1484', in R. Chartier and D. Richet (eds.), *Représentation et vouloir politiques*, Paris, pp. 11–24.

Cazelles, R., 1958. *La société politique et la crise de la royauté sous Philippe de Valois*, Paris.

1962–3. 'Une exigence de l'opinion depuis saint Louis: la réformation du royaume', *Annuaire-bulletin de la Société de l'Histoire de France*, 91–9.

1982. *Société politique, noblesse et couronne sous Jean le Bon et Charles V*, Geneva and Paris.

Collard, F., 1998. 'La pensée politique d'un clerc humaniste de la fin du xve siècle: Robert Gaguin (1433–1501)', *Revue française d'histoire des idées politiques*, 7, 3–45 and 155–64.

Contamine, P., 1994. 'Pouvoir et vie de cour dans la France du xve siècle', *Comptes-rendus de séances de l'Académie des Inscriptions et Belles Lettres*, 541–54.

Coss, P., 2003. *The Origins of the Gentry*, Cambridge.

Coss, P. and Keen, M. (eds.), 2002. *Heraldry, Pageantry and Social Display in Medieval England*, Woodbridge.

Favier, J., 1969. 'Les légistes et le gouvernement de Philippe le Bel', *Journal des Savants*, pp. 92–108.

Gauvard, C., 1980. 'Les officiers royaux et l'opinion publique en France à la fin du Moyen Age', in W. Paravicini and K. F. Werner (eds.), *Histoire comparée de l'administration (ive–xviiie siècle)*, Munich, pp. 583–93.

Gower, John, 2000. *Confessio Amantis*, vol. I, ed. R. Peck, Kalamazoo.

Griffiths, R. A., 1991. 'Duke Richard of York's Intentions in 1450 and the Origins of the War of the Roses', in R. A. Griffiths, *King and Country. England and Wales in the Fifteenth Century*, London.

Guenée, B., 2002. *L'opinion publique à la fin du Moyen Age d'après la Chronique de Charles VI du Religieux de Saint-Denis*, Paris.

Harris, G. L., 2005. *Shaping the Nation. England, 1360–1461*, Oxford.

Harte, N. B., 1976. 'State Control of Dress and Social Change in Pre-Industrial England', in C. Coleman and A. H. John (eds.), *Trade, Government and Economy in Pre-Industrial England*, London, pp. 132–65.

Hilton, R. H. and Aston, T. H. (eds.), 1984. *The English Rising of 1381*, Cambridge.

Horner, P., 1998. 'Preachers at St Paul's Cross: Religion, Society and Politics in Late Medieval England', in J. Hamesse (ed.), *Medieval Sermons and Society: Cloister, City, University*, Louvain-la-Neuve, pp. 261–82.

Ives, E. W., 1983. *The Common Lawyer of Pre-Reformation England*, Cambridge.

Hudson, A., 1988. *The Premature Reformation*, Oxford.

Killick, H., 2010. 'Thomas Hoccleve as Poet and Clerk', unpublished PhD thesis, York.

Lewis, A., 1986. *Le sang royal. La famille capétienne et l'Etat, xe–xive siècles*, trans. J. Carlier, Paris.

Mairey, A., 2009. 'Qu'est-ce que le peuple? Quelques réflexions sur la littérature politique anglaise de la fin du Moyen Âge', *Médiévales*, 57, 53–74.

2010. 'Le bien commun dans la littérature anglaise de la fin du Moyen Âge', *Revue française d'histoire des idées politiques*, 32, 373–84.

Middleton, A., 1978. 'The Idea of Public Poetry in the Reign of Richard II', *Speculum*, 53, 94–114.

Mohl, R., 1933. *The Three Estates in Medieval and Renaissance Literature*, London.

Owst, G. L., 1961. *Literature and Pulpit in Medieval England*, Oxford.

Robbins, R. H., 1959. *Historical Poems of the XIVth and XVth centuries*, New York.

Saul, N., 2002. 'A Farewell to Arms? Criticism of Warfare in Late Fourteenth-Century England', in C. Given-Wilson (ed.), *Fourteenth-Century England II*, Woodbridge, pp. 131–46.

Scase, W., 2007. *Litterature and Complaint in England, 1272–1553*, Oxford.

Scattergood, V. J., 1987. 'Fashion and Morality in the Late Middle Ages', in D. Williams (ed.), *The Fifteenth Century: Proceedings of the 1986 Harlaxton Symposium*, Woodbridge, pp. 255–72.

Seyssel, Claude de, 1961. *La Grant monarchie de France*, ed. J. Poujol, Paris.

Strohm, P., 1989. *Social Chaucer*, Cambridge, MA.

Telliez, R., 2004. 'Le contrôle des officiers en France à la fin du Moyen Age: une priorité pour le pouvoir', in L. Feller (ed.), *Contrôler les agents du pouvoir*, Limoges, pp. 191–211.

Verger, J. and Boutet, D. (eds.), 2000. *Penser le pouvoir au Moyen Age, viiie–xve siècle: Études offertes à Françoise Autrand*, Paris.

Watts, J. L., 1996. *Henry VI and the Policy of Kingship*, Cambridge.

2003. 'Was There a Lancastrian Court?', in J. Stratford (ed.), *The Lancastrian Court*, Donington, pp. 253–71.

2007. 'Public or Plebs: The Changing Meaning of "the Commons", 1381–1549', in H. Pryce and J. Watts (eds.), *Power and Identity in the Middle Ages: Essays in Memory of Rees Davies*, Oxford, pp. 242–60.

12   Conclusion

John Watts

The aim of the project from which these essays have arisen was a double one. First of all, we wanted to understand more about the culture and exercise of governance in later medieval kingdoms: to look at the personnel through whom royal authority was transmitted; to consider the institutional, formal and informal means at the disposal of producers and consumers of that authority; and to think about the ideas and practices that informed governmental behaviour and its reception. Secondly, we wanted to do all this in a highly comparative way: not simply comparing the kingdoms of England and France in the fourteenth and fifteenth centuries according to some predetermined agenda, but asking pairs of English and French scholars to look at particular themes in ways that made sense to them. In this way, we hoped to arrive at comparisons derived not from one single point of view, but – somewhat in the spirit of *histoire croisée* – from the combined perspectives of English and French historiography and from a number of different vantage points within the broad space of political society. Given that the kingdoms of England and France have often been presented as polar opposites in grand narratives of state-formation – the one destined to be a low-tax, mercantilist, small-state constitutional monarchy; the other to be a high-tax, large-state, large-army absolutism – and given that they were not just neighbours but were profoundly involved in each other's affairs, especially in the fourteenth and fifteenth centuries, this approach seemed likely to produce some fresh insights.

In these few pages, I shall try to draw out some common themes from the rich set of studies that the project has generated. In the first section that follows, I shall attempt some broad conclusions about the frameworks of government and political society in the two countries, identifying parallels and differences and speculating about their causes. In the second section, I shall turn to the relationship between these frameworks and the course of politics, recognising – as several of the contributors point out – that this was an iterative relationship: while the structures of power in each country helped to shape the dynamics of political life,

351

those dynamics in turn affected the development of the structures. But before embarking on these analyses, it would make sense to say a little more about the historiographical and methodological questions raised by these papers, or reflected in them. After all, whatever they tell us about England and France in the later Middle Ages, they also tell us quite a lot about the practical difficulties of comparative work across national boundaries.

The authors of this book have been engaged in a difficult task of translation – both literally, since all but one of the pairs was Anglo-French and very few members of the group can realistically be described as bilingual, and also figuratively, since the formations and assumptions of British and French historians are so different. For all the transnationalism of today's historical community, and for all the significance of Anglophone scholarship on France and (in less quantity) Francophone scholarship on England, and notwithstanding the large number of travelling scholars, translations and synthetic works that have helped to transmit English and French learning across the Channel, it remains the case that political and governmental history is studied in rather different ways in each of the two countries. Some of the differences of perspective in the essays above can, of course, be put down to the specialisms of the collaborators, and some derive from the radically different source material – the very substantial and accessible archives of the English Crown, for example, against the wealth of literary materials in France or the superiority of certain records of local or regional power (in the Burgundian domains, for instance, or in Languedoc) – but some of the differences seem to stem from historiographical biases.

It is striking, first of all, that there is more convergence between our English and French partners in some areas than in others. Where it has been possible to write a combined essay on the relatively new subject of the role of 'the masses' in political life, for instance, or on visions of political society, most of the other essays alternate between treatments of the English and the French material. In some chapters, such as those on public finance, military institutions and networks, petitioning and office, the treatments are closely paralleled – even if the last essay necessarily has much to say about French princely bureaucracies, for which no precise counterpart existed in England. But in others, there are stark differences – between discussions of French *juristes* and of the English judicial system, for instance, or in the juxtaposition of the English church and churchmen with French *gens de savoir*. However frustrating for the reader who wants to see a series of direct comparisons, these apparent mismatches are actually highly informative and productive, both because they expose more localised interpretative assumptions and because they offer insights into real differences in the societies we are examining. English histor-ians have thought a lot about the development of the legal system and its interaction with social power, especially that of lords; but we have thought much less about the spread of juristic conceptions across gov-erning cadres, and about the possible influence of those conceptions on the formation of royal policy, whether in the specifically judicial sphere or more broadly. And yet one *could* write a study of the impact of juristic learning on English political culture, just as – on the French side – one could attempt to work outwards from Bernard Guenée's masterly study of the bailliage of Senlis to characterise the French judicial system as a whole.[1] Equally, a British tendency to think in terms of 'church' and 'state' shapes our reading of English government personnel in particular ways, heightening the difference between one clerisy (medieval prelates) and another (early Tudor 'new men'): but these *gens de savoir*, as Jacques Verger might call them, came from a fairly similar social background and possessed a fairly similar education; the fact that one group were clergy and the other laymen masks many continuities. Since French kingship has often been seen in terms of 'a welter of divinity', it is rather salutary to be reminded that so many of its architects were scholars – in fact, students of Roman and canon law – rather than divines, and that the presence of actual prelates around the king was quite limited.[2] While smooth comparisons, where both sides correspond tidily, may help us to identify common patterns in medieval European political society, rough ones – where like is not compared with like – force us to think in fresh ways about our evidence.

There is a dynamic element to historiographical differences too, of course. Historical writing is characteristically reactive, but British and French historians are reacting against different things. We share an inherited rejection of the nineteenth-century nationalist narratives that form the basis of our discipline, but just as these narratives were dif-ferent – whig–liberal in England, republican–statist in France – so was the mid-twentieth-century reaction. Influenced by Namier and McFar-lane, English historians began to see noble lordship as legitimate and to study the informal operations of royal and aristocratic power; influenced by the *Annales* movement, meanwhile, French historians turned away from political history altogether. Since the 1980s, British historians of later medieval politics have been taking a cultural turn, trying to recover the underlying ideas and mentalities of political life, and to deploy these alongside a recovered interest in the structures and institutions of gov-ernment to create what has sometimes been called a 'new constitutional

---

[1] Guenée (1963).   [2] Quotation from Lewis (1968), p. 94.

history'.[3] French historians, meanwhile, have returned to politics, and while some of them are certainly interested in political culture – *le pouvoir*, as well as *les pouvoirs* – a notable feature of many of the French contributions to this volume is an interest in networks and prosopography.[4] In some respects, therefore, the two national groups have been moving in different, even opposite, directions in the last twenty years or so, and this was reflected in two different titles adopted for the project – 'Governing' on the English side, and 'With whom to govern?' on the French. While much was shared by the contributors – a concern with how institutions, whether social or governmental, actually worked in practice, an emphasis on grounding generalisations in empirical detail – this basic difference of approach was a challenge for all of us.

I

What, then, can we conclude from these studies about the frameworks of government and political society in later medieval England and France? Much, of course, was shared between the two kingdoms, as it was with other polities in this age of the *genèse de l'état moderne*.[5] Both royal governments saw a considerable expansion of their operations from the later thirteenth century onwards. While the establishment of England's common law from the mid twelfth century lent the island kingdom a certain precocity, establishing effective royal jurisdiction over the whole realm from an early point and laying the foundations for Magna Carta and a plenipotentiary parliament, the timing of many other developments was roughly similar. The growth of central government personnel, the expansion of legislation, representation and the beginnings of mass taxation, the development of large tax-funded armies: these were prominent features of the later thirteenth century in both kingdoms, and the encouragement of appeals from the great fiefs in the *Parlement* of Philip IV and his successors parallels the pressure levied by Edward I on the rulers of Wales and Scotland and on the franchise holders of England and the Marches. While the growth of the state took increasingly different forms in England and France over the course of the fourteenth century – a greater emphasis on jurisdiction, national representation and taxes on trade in the former kingdom, against a greatly increased incidence of taxation and a flourishing system of local representation in the latter – both governments faced resistance to their expanded activities and struck

---

[3] Britnell and Pollard, ed. (1995), p. xvii, referring to Carpenter's essay in the same collection.
[4] Cf. Contamine (1992).   [5] Genet (1990).

different, though parallel, compromises with other power-groups in their realms, such as magnates, churches and towns.

Out of these processes of political dialogue came a strong consciousness of political community and national identity, again developing at roughly the same time, and captured in a shared – or at least overlapping – set of discourses and images of political authority, society and order. While Franck Collard and Aude Mairey find more emphasis on community and on wealth as a determinant of social status in England, and a more traditional sense of the social order, coupled with a more developed critique of officers and councillors, in France, the similarities in these thought-worlds seem more prominent than the differences. Each kingdom was also subject to contingencies – the age and quality of the monarch, the fortunes of war, the impact of epidemic disease, food crises and monetary problems – but, while these played out slightly differently on either side of the Channel, and had distinctive effects on the pattern of military and fiscal development, they could be seen as broadly comparable over the long term, and not so very different from the ups and downs experienced by other kingdoms and statelets in Europe. None of this should surprise us. For all their differences, European kingdoms shared a great deal – Roman and Canon Law, the institutions of the Western church, the classical literary inheritance and its various refashionings by friars, schoolmen and *dictatores*, widespread conventions of landholding and clientage, kinship and warfare. England and France, the former, of course, profoundly shaped by invasions from Normandy and Anjou, shared more than most places, and the essays in this volume are full of more specific instances of copied forms and techniques – in fourteenth-century courtly arrangements and the changing format of petitions, in orders of chivalry and the formation of small retained military companies in the 1350s, 60s and 70s, in the forced loans adopted by Louis XI and Edward IV a century later.

At the same time, it is not hard to identify differences. England was both more centralised and more tightly integrated, its people bound together in a genuine political community – above all through the common law, to which almost all of them had some kind of access by the end of the fourteenth century, but also by regular and uniform taxation, which was paid in some manner by a large cross-section of society, and by the routines of a parliament which met very frequently between about 1275 and 1475 and enabled the conversion of complaints and requests into legislation. This is reflected time and again in the essays above – in the prominence of the idea of community and the distinctive notion of a 'commons' that could incorporate everyone but the nobility; in the tendency for English popular revolts to have a national agenda and impact; in the acceptance of what might be called public–private partnerships in justice and military leadership, both of them normally contained within royally controlled structures of law and finance; in the frequency of conflicts over the quality of royal government, especially in periods of high taxation; and perhaps, too, in the relative atrophy of the English tax system after the 1410s. While the kingdom of France pretended a similar uniformity, it was in reality very different. Here, a large network of royal officers – perhaps ten or more times the size of the English king's – imposed a measure of central control while allowing copious opportunities for localised groups and powers to negotiate concessions and compromises on an individual basis. So it was that, as Graeme Small has recently emphasised, France was vastly more variegated – a patchwork of semi-independent communities and lords, bearing different kinds of jurisdiction and authority, in different customary and cultural settings, but remaining conscious of the desirability of good relations with the royal centre.[6] In the spirit of Peter Lewis, Chris Fletcher points out that the subjects of the French king generally resisted representative projects that threatened to lump them together and erase their individual liberties and privileges; they enjoyed a different kind of representation at the royal centre – through proctors, patrons and networks.[7] This system carried a price-tag, in the tendency for taxation to grow unchecked, the persistent and hard-nosed interference from royal officers, and the general failure on the part of the Crown to coordinate either defence or justice; but there were also significant benefits for princes and communities, as they gained shares in royal assets (often sizeable ones) and a measure of influence over the local operations of the *gens du roi*.

In all, then, the two kingdoms allowed for dialogue in different ways, and with different results. While there were certainly parallels between the English common law and French taxation – both of them powerful means of inserting royal power into every corner of the kingdom, both of them operable only through compromises with local elites – it is clear that there were important differences too. For one thing, more was delegated in France: it is estimated that only two-thirds of the taxes due to the king were reaching the centre in 1390, and the large noble class was generally exempted from paying them.[8] For another, the developing recognition that the common law bound the entire realm affected the way the English treated their kings, lords, serfs and – ultimately – their church. Only under rare and specialised circumstances – notably in the 1410s – did

---

[6] Small (2009), esp. Chapter 1.   [7] See esp. Lewis (1981), as well as Lewis (1962).

[8] Potter (2003), p. 175. This rate of local absorption seems to have been typical for the period before the later fifteenth century.

French taxation funnel resistance to the centre in this way; more commonly, in this less integrated realm, it was the nobility who bore the brunt of taxpayer anger. These different political dynamics are discussed more fully in the next section.

This distinction between integrative institutions in England and rule by network in France should not lead us to see the former kingdom as more formal than the latter one. For one thing, the variety of French judicial and fiscal arrangements, together with all the complexities introduced by exemptions and privileges, was backed up by the activity of armies of administrators, often legally trained, who recorded and exercised rights and powers on behalf of a myriad of authorities. Although, as in any medieval society, much was negotiated in practice, the outward forms of authority had to be respected, and this meant that the French king's discretionary powers – which alone cut through the net of local jurisdictions – were elaborately managed. This is very clear in the chapter by Gwilym Dodd and Sophie Petit-Renaud: the French king's grants had the quality of laws; they thus required expert handling at every stage – by *maîtres de requêtes*, who received and adjudicated petitions, by the *Chambre des comptes*, which checked that the *domaine* was not compromised, and by the *Parlement*, which registered the resulting letters and entertained legal challenges against them from those whose rights were newly infringed. While none of this activity prevented the ruler from exercising his will, it somewhat officialised royal grace, tending to rescue the king from personal responsibility for his actions and focusing the conflicts of the great on the control of leading officers and courtiers. The English royal centre, in contrast, was smaller and much less formal: while matters of justice and potential legislation were handled at one or more removes from the king – in the law courts (including the new resorts of chancery and council) or in parliament, petitions for grace and pardon were a matter for the king in person, and the political consequences of his decisions came home to roost with him and his personal advisers. Informality, then, could have its disadvantages, and one could say the same about the English way of raising and managing men-at-arms through ad hoc contracts with the leading nobility: while this arrangement allowed great flexibility, and rescued the king from all sorts of administrative difficulties, it created a highly intense and interpersonal politics of military leadership, with serious consequences when the king played his hand badly. The more formal French systems – whether in the era of the *arrière-ban*, or that of the fifteenth-century *compagnies d'ordonnance* – had other weaknesses, and were certainly modified by the quality of political leadership coming from the Crown, but they enabled the mobilisation of much larger resources, more consistently and with lower political costs.

In these ways, and no doubt others, the compounds of formality and informality, bureaucracy and social power, in each country were subtly different. The overall balance may have been roughly equivalent – and Peter Lewis especially has drawn attention to the interpersonal dealings behind the façade of French public power[9] – but the differences, as we have begun to see, help to explain the different patterns of politics in each place.

It might make sense to close this section with two factors that help to explain some of the variations noted here, factors which were themselves further differences in the political make-up of the two kingdoms. The first of these is obvious, but important all the same: France was a great deal bigger than England. It took more than three weeks to cross the fourteenth-century French kingdom from north to south, and more than two weeks to get from Lyon to the tip of Brittany; in contrast, news of the Scottish king James III's murder in 1488 travelled the 440 miles from Perth to London in less than a week.[10] A kingdom on the French scale, with all its associated ethnic, linguistic, socio-economic and political diversity, could not be unified in the way that a small, primarily lowland, kingdom like England could be unified; it was certain to contain alternative centres, some of which would serve as the focus for regional solidarities that could threaten the integrity of the whole. But this did not mean that France could not be ruled. If the royal *domaine* was smaller than the kingdom, it was still a great deal larger than the ordinary revenue-base of any of the king's competitors, including the King of England for most of the period. Its resources, in land, rights and taxes, gave the king the wherewithal to sustain a network of officers capable of ensuring that his authority was, at the very least, taken into account across his kingdom. While royal authority was often less complete than its propaganda and prerogatives implied, and while this network could be swayed or suppressed by other powers – especially on a local basis – it proved a remarkably flexible and resilient means of maintaining a royal stake in the affairs of every part of the kingdom. Indeed, it did more than this. The French king's *mouvance* exceeded France itself, extending into Scotland, Spain, the western reaches of the Empire and northern Italy, and his networks of allies radiated further still. If we set the 'imperial' enterprises of the English king against this background, the limitations of the English political system become clear. However effective was English government in the small space of the kingdom, it was not particularly well adapted to ruling a larger congeries of territories. English kings could intervene to devastating effect; they could often prevent, disrupt or slow down the

---

[9] Notably Lewis (1996).   [10] Autrand (1995), p. 429; Armstrong (1983), pp. 112–13.

formation of alternative polities in the external regions where they sought control; but they were much less successful at ruling these areas over long periods of time – poor at providing local lieutenants with the resources they needed, and (on the whole) poor at developing and maintaining dialogue with the inhabitants of their extra-English territories.[11] In all, it is tempting to suggest that, for all the similarities in the expansion of the kingdoms based on Wessex–Mercia and Paris–Orléans–Burgundy between the tenth and the fourteenth centuries, the latter kingdom was much better designed for large-scale government than the former.

The second factor shaping differences of governance in the two kingdoms spins off from the first: France was a war-zone for much of this period, and England was not. Even if actual fighting and raiding was often fairly localised, there were long periods when it engulfed large parts of the country – the 1340s, 50s and (in the South) the 60s and 70s; also the 1410s and 20s – and there were other periods of skirmishing or jockeying for power in which political insecurity was almost as marked as in wartime. This state of affairs had a significant impact on French fiscal and military arrangements, justifying the great extension of taxation in the 1350s and 60s and facilitating the creation of a permanent army, fleetingly under Charles V and more lastingly under Charles VII. As Challet and Forrest explain, it influenced the character and agenda of French popular demonstrations, and – as in the Collard/Mairey chapter – it shaped the perceptions of the princes and other nobles. While the structures of French government help to explain the causes and modalities of the so-called 'Hundred Years War', they also developed in response to it, and, while the same can be said of English government in this period, the fact that England was only glancingly and intermittently affected – by coastal raids, and a handful of invasion threats – helps to explain the overall tendency of representatives to prioritise domestic concerns and set limits to royal initiatives. Here too, then, structures and contingencies were interwoven in the shaping of governance.

II

In both England and France, the fourteenth and fifteenth centuries have traditionally been regarded as a period of disorder, conflict, and 'crisis' or 'decline', falling between a long age of economic, social and governmental 'formation' or 'growth', which culminated in the later thirteenth century, and a putative 'recovery', associated with the Renaissance and the regimes

---

[11] Brown (2013), but for a more positive take on the efficacy and persistence of English imperial rule in the period, see Crooks (2011).

that emerged from mid-fifteenth-century civil wars. While there are now a number of more positive narratives – of the *genèse de l'état moderne*, or the *naissance de la nation France*, or of the 'growth of government' or 'shaping [of] the nation', or 'making of polities' – these scarcely deny the turbulent politics of the era; rather, they explain those politics in the same terms of constitutional development that have more commonly been applied to earlier and later periods. So it is that the frequent confrontations, coups and civil wars of later medieval England and France can be seen as the responses of a changing political society to a changing governmental order, just as that order, in turn, can be seen as developing in response to social and political action. The question before us in this section is how different the political narratives of later medieval France and England are (or ought to be), and what, in the make-up of the two kingdoms, accounts for those differences. To clarify what is inevitably a large and complex topic, it might be helpful to begin by establishing the main outlines of what happened, focusing (as elsewhere in this book) on the regnal level, the politics of the kingdom as a whole – and on the interplay of periods of relative political stability and disorder.

In England, there were three quite lengthy periods of internal conflict between 1300 and 1500, each of them beginning in public reaction against oppressive and/or incompetent royal rule and deepening into crises which divided the political elite, brought down the king, and gave rise to usurpations. The first of these began in the late 1290s, against the background of Edward I's single-minded extension of his fiscal, juridical and military rights in the context of a three-front war in Scotland, Wales and France. It persisted into the early fourteenth century, worsening under Edward II, as the king continued to extract heavy taxes while failing both to prosecute the war effectively and to maintain order in the localities. Edward's divisive promotion of his supporters at the expense of leading noblemen provoked outright civil war in 1321–2 and 1326–7, and led to his deposition in favour of his son in the latter year. While Edward III was drawn into a serious confrontation in 1340–1, which centred on the obligations owed by king and realm in the context of high taxation, he had broadly succeeded in restoring royal authority and reuniting the political community by the early 1330s, and up to the end of the 1360s he presided over the development of effective systems of taxation, representation and justice without major conflict.

The second sequence of troubles began in the 1370s, and once again centred on a combination of high taxation and royal fiscal and administrative negligence, this time caused by the retreat of Edward III into dotage and the succession of a 10-year-old, Richard II, in 1377. Against a background of popular ferment and outright revolt in 1381, the knights and burgesses of a series of highly critical parliaments joined forces with leading noblemen to assert control over royal finances and the king's council. Since Richard and his supporters fought back, there was conflict bordering on civil war in 1386–8 and 1397–9, which culminated in the king's deposition and the usurpation of the throne by Henry, duke of Lancaster in 1399. As the usurper lacked universal authority and was unable to rule more cheaply and effectively than his predecessor, division and disorder continued for much of the following decade, including a major rebellion in Wales (1400–c.1408) and risings against the king in 1403 and 1405. Not until the 1410s were political and financial order restored, though Henry V was able to unite the kingdom in a major war against France, and the after-effects of his efficient rule held the polity together during the minority of his son, Henry VI, in the 1420s and 30s.

The third period of conflict broke out in the 1450s, chiefly as a result of a combined failure of royal government – financial, military and judicial – which was attested by MPs in 1449–51 and by the commons of the South East in another major popular demonstration in 1450. Once again, the nobility divided over how best to resolve the situation, and the ensuing decades witnessed a series of usurpations and dynastic divisions, resulting in several periods of civil war (1455, 1459–64, 1469–71, 1483–7), combined with recurrent local disorder, intermittent popular uprisings and plots. Not until the accession of Henry VIII in 1509 was it clear that these conflicts, known as the Wars of the Roses, were at an end, though there was some recovery of royal authority and political stability in the 1470s and again after 1487.

In France, the pattern of conflict was rather different, featuring large amounts of territorial warfare, combined with mostly short-lived political crises involving the king and his government. The attempts of Philip IV and his successors to assert royal authority in Flanders and Gascony produced localised fighting in the former territory 1297–1305 and 1314–28, and in the latter 1294–7, 1302–3 and 1323–4. The expense of these wars, combined with jurisdictional pressure, produced reaction across many parts of France, first in 1303–5 and then, more seriously, in 1314–15 when leagues of nobles rose up in almost every province of the kingdom, demanding an end to unjust taxation and the concession of charters of liberties. Further tensions over taxes were contained by a mixture of negotiation at meetings of the Estates and resort to expedients such as coinage manipulation, and the failures of the royal bloodline in 1316 and 1328 were managed with few immediate problems.

The causes of the first major sequence of troubles, which broke out in the late 1330s, have been much debated by historians, but they seem to have lain in a series of contingencies, against a background of royal over-extension. Problems mounted for Philip VI, as Edward III of England, resenting Valois policy in Gascony and Scotland and conscious of his descent from Philip IV, joined forces with Flemish rebels, disgruntled Normans and the disappointed parties in succession disputes in Artois (1334) and Brittany (1341) to launch a campaign for the French throne. The first phase of the so-called 'Hundred Years War' (1337–60) was partly a war between kingdoms – Edward's numerous invasions of Normandy, Brittany and Gascony in the 1340s and 50s, and his raids into the centre and the Île-de-France were funded by English taxes – but it was also a French civil war. Not only was Edward also duke of Gascony, he was backed by dissenting factions in many parts of northern and western France, including, from 1354, another claimant to the French Crown and major landholder in Normandy, Charles of Navarre. While some of this backing was opportunistic, some of it reflected local, factional or even national grievances – notably over taxation (which had fallen particularly heavily on Normandy) and over the Crown's persistent failure to fight the English effectively and its shocking readiness to put certain lords to death for treason. Regular meetings of the Estates of Languedoïl in the 1340s and 50s turned highly critical in 1356–7, following the defeat of Poitiers and the capture of King John II; as rebellion broke out in Paris (1356–8) and across the Ile-de-France (1358), the Crown was forced to seek peace, and a huge bloc of territory in south-western France was handed to the English in the Treaty of Brétigny in 1360. By this time, a (royalist, but effectively autonomous) league of towns had formed in the south, and over the next decade large parts of southern, central and eastern France were ravaged by mercenary companies in circumstances bordering on anarchy; in the north, meanwhile, fighting continued in Brittany and Normandy until 1364–5. But the tide was turning for the Valois Crown: drawing on greatly enhanced tax incomes, together with military muscle from the royal dukes of Berry, Burgundy and Anjou, Charles V gradually restored control. In 1368–9, he was able to foment resistance to the English in Gascony, and, converting the mercenaries into tax-funded royal troops, he overran the Brétigny lands between 1369 and 1374, and forced the English to a truce in 1375. This was not quite the end of the period of troubles which had begun almost forty years earlier, however: fighting continued in Brittany in 1378–81, and broke out in Flanders in 1379–85; equally, the reversal of Charles' deathbed promise to cancel the high taxes of the previous two decades prompted angry meetings of the Estates of Languedoïl, and uprisings in Languedoc, Paris, Rouen and other northern towns in 1380–2. Even so, in striking contrast to the situation in England at the same time, the uncles and ministers of the child-king Charles VI were able to restore control, and the kingdom remained fairly orderly for the next two decades.

While France's fourteenth-century struggles had begun in reactions to the Crown's overbearing jurisdiction and had been sustained by a mixture of fiscal pressure, factional division and English intervention, the difficulties of the fifteenth century arose from a combination of inadequate kingship and divisions among the royal princes, with the accumulating experience of taxation as an important backdrop. Although Charles VI's madness was first manifested in 1392, it was not until 1407 that tensions between 'Burgundians' and 'Armagnacs' reached the point of murder, and not until 1411 that outright civil war began. The next few years featured a major reformist uprising in Paris, linked to the Burgundians (1413), together with revolts and disorders across many towns of the kingdom, fuelled by a mixture of factional discord, concern over the state of the realm and pressure to reduce taxes. From 1415, French divisions were further complicated by a series of military interventions by the English, which resulted in the conquest of Normandy and parts of Maine and Ile-de-France, together with the establishment of an Anglo-Burgundian regime at Paris (1420–36). The Dauphin, later Charles VII, retreated to Bourges following his murder of the duke of Burgundy in 1419, and began to rebuild royal authority via a mixture of military intervention, diplomacy and tax negotiations with the revived Estates of Languedoïl and Languedoc. By 1435–6, with the help of factors beyond his control, he had succeeded in breaking up the Anglo-Burgundian alliance and regaining Paris. Within a few years, he was able to collect taxes without needing the Estates, and in the 1440s, he went on to crush a couple of princely revolts (1440, 1442), to form a tax-funded standing army (1445) and then to reconquer all the English-held territories except Calais (1449–53). The 1430s and 40s had not been easy decades all the same: there was fighting along all the borders of English-held areas, and the allegiance of many princes, their forces swelled by mercenaries and adventurers from the civil wars, remained uncertain. Although order returned in the 1450s, the dukes of Brittany and Burgundy remained more or less detached from the realm, and the Dauphin Louis was a focus for discontent.

As king from 1461, Louis XI inaugurated a third period of instability by repudiating his father's establishment and policies, and quickly found himself facing a coalition of discontented princes in the *Ligue du Bien Public*. The conflict which followed was mainly a cold war, involving only sporadic fighting (1465, 1467–8), but it lasted into the 1470s and nearly turned nasty when the Crown was threatened by a large English invasion in 1475. The causes of trouble were a mixture of factional competition, tensions over regional autonomy and urban feeling about levels of taxation, which had remained high and rising since the 1430s. The Crown's eventual victory, in 1477, owed much to the partly fortuitous destruction of Charles the Bold, duke of Burgundy, in his war against the Swiss, but the huge resources at the king's disposal and the difficulty faced by the princes in sustaining and coordinating resistance were also important factors. The Crown faced further challenges from leading magnates later in the century (notably during the minority of Charles VIII in 1483–4). It also had to continue fighting against the Burgundians and, on a smaller scale, the English. But it was able, between the 1470s and the 1490s, to regain most of the remaining great fiefs and *apanages* by making prudent marriages, exploiting dynastic failures and using the law of treason against recalcitrants. By 1494, as Charles VIII prepared to open a new chapter in French history with his unprecedented invasion of Italy, he was master of a larger and more stable kingdom than any of his predecessors.

The fact that it takes twice as much space to narrate French political history reflects the greater size and complexity of the French kingdom. While political crises involving the monarch were mostly short-lived – in sharp contrast to the situation in England – trouble, even warfare, in the regions was much more common. As suggested above, this is partly because our comparison is between England and France, not between the territories that the two kings of these kingdoms generally sought to rule. If France-plus-Flanders were to be set alongside the British Isles and Plantagenet lands, the two narratives would look more similar, though the English Crown would look rather less impressive, since beside its prolonged internal struggles would be set a record of 'imperial' failure, the latter supplying a further set of causes for the former. On the other hand, for all that English kings sought to unify the Plantagenet territories in the early part of our period, when – as Mark Ormrod has shown – they collected taxes from Ireland and Gascony, and coordinated resources across a large west-European domain, it is striking that they rarely lost control of the core of their polity, whereas the French Crown was unable to exploit the wealth of Normandy for roughly a quarter of the period and enjoyed only patchy control over home territory to the north and east of Paris for much of the fifteenth century.[12] These differences will be explored further below, but first of all, let us note how much is shared in the political history of the two kingdoms.

Not surprisingly, France and England followed a roughly similar trajectory to other European polities across the two centuries. As noted in the

[12] Ormrod (2000).

previous section, the decades around 1300 witnessed a hard-nosed assertion of jurisdiction by the two kings over potential subordinates whose autonomy had been more willingly tolerated in the past. This inevitably provoked conflict of the kind experienced in England under Edward I and Edward II and in France under Philip IV and his immediate heirs. Representatives of the classes most directly affected rose up to set limits to royal assertions and/or to subject them to forms of public control. Over the fourteenth and fifteenth centuries, the scope of governmental activity continued to grow – above all fiscally, but also in terms of regulation, justice and official supervision – and with that came further processes of conflict, negotiation and political integration. While the integration of government and political community went further in England, and is a more prominent feature of English historiography, it clearly advanced in France too: as Graeme Small has recently pointed out, what really differentiates the civil war of the 1410s from the Valois–Plantagenet–Navarre struggle of the 1350s is the direct involvement of a much larger political nation – not just princes, nobles, Paris and the commons of the Ile-de-France, but the municipalities of large parts of the country, who were now active partners in a fiscal and petitionary dialogue with the Crown, and felt its failure keenly.[13] This kind of centralisation increased both the chances and the duration of crises of monarchy, as unfit kings struggled with a more demanding political and governmental portfolio, and leading subjects divided over the difficult question of how to preserve (and exploit) an authority on which everyone increasingly depended, while also amending its shortcomings. It is striking that these crises lasted longer in fifteenth-century France than they had before, and easy to see parallels between the long periods of English disturbance c. 1369–c. 1410, c. 1447–c. 1471 and the French troubles of c. 1405–35 and c. 1465–77.

At the same time, however, the political experience of France was profoundly and distinctively conditioned by the presence of warfare in many parts of the kingdom between the late 1330s and the early 1380s (and again, in a more localised way, between 1411 and 1453). War was part and parcel of a story of political and governmental evolution in both countries, as we have seen, but big differences arose from being the defender and host, rather than the aggressor: royal taxation, for instance, offered benefits as well as costs to the subjects of both kingdoms, but much more so in France, where its relationship to the defence of tax-paying communities was direct and obvious. The effective ending of the Hundred Years War in the early 1450s has helped to differentiate a further phase in French history – an era of 'recovery', which partly paralleled, but

---

[13] Small (2009), pp. 133–4 and *passim*.

also preceded, the so-called 'New Monarchy' that developed in England from the 1470s.[14] While the end of continuous fighting was certainly a real change, it is not clear whether the governmental developments of the later fifteenth century should be detached from the long period of administrative growth and political negotiation that preceded them. In France, as suggested above, the Crown obtained a more complete and lasting control of the kingdom than it had possessed at any time before; in England, on the other hand, the Crown that emerged from the Wars of the Roses exercised a more direct control over aristocratic society and was less vulnerable to the kinds of crisis that had engulfed it three times in the fourteenth and fifteenth centuries, but its military and extractive capacities had not kept pace with its competitors. In each kingdom, there was a stronger sense of its specific historical and constitutional identity, but this reflects the progress of generations as much as the experience of the previous few decades.

It will be clear from the above that both French and English politics featured some common themes – territorial assertion and consolidation, shading into the management of the localities; the varying capacity of individual kings to meet the demands of royal office; debates about the proper scope of royal rights and powers, whether fiscal, judicial, official or military, and their relationship to the *bien public*, 'common weal' or *status regni*. If we look more closely at these, taking them in turn, then we see both similarities and differences between the two kingdoms.

The kings of England and France were both frequently engaged in a politics of territorial assertion, and were often drawn into that politics by the inhabitants of the regions concerned, but this was largely an external matter for the former ruler while being both an external and an internal matter for the latter one. By 1300, there were few substantial regional lordships within England itself, and those, as Christine Carpenter points out above, were mainly in the hands of the Crown. Even in the Marches of Wales and on the northern border, royal authority was very present: the Marcher lordships fell to the king over the fifteenth century, but even prior to this they were highly vulnerable to royal intervention; the major northern families – notably the Nevilles and the Percies – were checked by one another, by their dependence on Crown office and also by a strong Lancastrian presence, closely linked to the Crown for a century before 1399.[15] It was unusual for English kings to have to devote much energy to controlling territory within the kingdom, though, in periods of weakness, such as the years following usurpations, or in the depths of disorder, such as the late 1310s and early 1320s, or the 1450s, they could be found

---

[14] Lewis (1971).   [15] Carpenter (1997), pp. 54–7.

setting up new structures of regional rule or intervening in local conflicts which had begun to take on the character of land wars.[16] As in the French kingdom, royal cadets were characteristically endowed with regional lieutenancies, but this was usually intended to allow them to project power into Ireland, Scotland or France, rather than to supervise the English localities.[17] The management of local society was very largely a matter for local lords and the legal system, supplemented by the king's personal attention, both formal and informal, whenever disputes threatened to get out of hand or involved figures of political significance. It is hard to feel that any of the English political crises of the period were driven primarily by regional revolts or tensions, though it is certainly true that each of the three periods of trouble identified above was accompanied by serious disorder and violence in the localities, and that it took time for the Crown to restore its authority. It is hard to know how seriously to take the Percies' tripartite indenture with Owain Glyn Dŵr and Edmund Mortimer in 1405, when a division of the kingdom into three parts was proposed, but it is not insignificant that the rebellion that accompanied it was an utter failure, with even its Welsh component running into trouble by 1406–7: even in the twelfth-century 'anarchy' of Stephen's reign, it had become clear that it was not plausible to divide up the kingdom in this way.[18] It is just about possible to imagine a Richard of Gloucester based in Scotland and joining his 1483 palatinate of Cumbria to the Scottish throne, but it is equally easy to imagine such quasi-Burgundian behaviour producing results similar to those of 1477, and – in any case – Gloucester could not conquer Scotland, and preferred influence at the centre to power in the regions.[19] In essence, then, the politics of the English kingdom were not regional; nor, on the whole, were they local. While the management of local order was a significant task for the Crown, and the failure of judicial arrangements could be a prominent political issue, trouble in the localities was almost always caused by more general failures of royal government, and not the other way around.[20]

The situation in France was very different: from the beginning of the Capetian dynasty in the tenth century, the French Crown had been dealing with more or less autonomous lordships and provinces in varying states of nominal subjection to itself, and this remained a prominent concern throughout our period. It was also, as we have seen, a significant source of antagonism. The king and the greatest lords could co-exist

---

[16] Maddicott (1970), Chapter VI.i; Watts (1996), p. 337ff.
[17] Griffiths (1986), pp. 20–1.   [18] Brown (2013), p. 237ff.
[19] Horrox (1989), Chapter 1 and p. 71ff.
[20] Carpenter (1997), pp. 61, 65–6 and chapters 2–3, *passim*.

perfectly happily, it is true – indeed, this was the norm in relations with both Brittany and Burgundy during the thirteenth century – but the potential for jurisdictional disputes was ever-present, given the imperial fantasies and self-interested assertiveness of the Crown's advisers and officers, and the ill-defined, but substantial, power of princes, towns and local lords. Tensions inevitably mounted in an era of governmental growth: as the Crown developed new powers, its relationships with the other lords and corporations of the kingdom were affected, particularly as they, too, were able to exploit new political and governmental technologies. This was arguably the single biggest cause of French political crises, underlying the wars in Flanders and Gascony in the 1290s, the affair of the Leagues in 1314–15 and the more substantial series of interconnected conflicts that broke out in 1337: in all of these cases, the assertion of royal jurisdiction (often in response to serious disorders, pleas from tenants or the erection of alternative jurisdictions by vassals) was a major factor producing conflict.[21] The Crown was usually ready to do deals – to grant privileges, to offer quid-pro-quos, to concede territory or rights on new terms – but, partly thanks to the zeal of its officers and the absoluteness of its theoretical claims, it was also ready to override them. Equally, its concessions helped to define and authorise the provinces, principalities and municipalities with which its rights potentially conflicted, encouraging the outbreak of further troubles in the future.

Of course, the kings of the period were not without resources to help them manage the regions, but it is important to recognise that these resources reinforced, rather than diminished, the geographical element in French politics. Since the work of Raymond Cazelles, it has often been argued that the French royal network had a regional character – typically, in fact, that it drew on the 'men of the east', viz. those from the Burgundian sphere of influence to the east of Paris, while the 'men of the west' were more vulnerable to Plantagenet influence and could be downright alienated, as were the Montfortians and Godefroy de Harcourt in the 1340s, both of them enemies of the Blois–Penthièvre–Melun/Tancarville network that was influential around the king.[22] Later on, it was the westerners who dominated, notably around Charles VII, and the Burgundians who were in the cold: Louis XI's rejection of both camps helps to explain the trouble he faced in Normandy, Brittany and Burgundy from an early point in his reign.[23] While some form of factional tension is difficult

---

[21] Jones, 'The Last Capetians and Early Valois Kings, 1314–1364', in Jones (2000).
[22] Cazelles (1958), Chapter 4; Small (2009), p. 97ff. Of course, as the names suggest, there were also Norman and Breton members of the royal network: the distinction between 'west' and 'east' should not be pushed too far.
[23] *Ibid.*, p. 145ff; Favier (2001), pp. 213ff, 447ff.

to avoid in any interpersonal and monarchical system, it is striking that French factions were directly connected to regional power-blocs, in a manner that was only matched in England in the very depths of political crisis. The existence of these networks was the flip-side of the provincial isolationism seen in the early fourteenth century – like the *apanages* created by John II for his sons in the early 1360s, they acknowledged the mutual interests of the Crown and regional potentates. In the right royal hands and the right circumstances, a powerful relationship might be forged between king and princes, fuelled by the sharing-out of the new taxation revenues and maintained by a lighter touch in the prosecution of royal rights. But the solution of the 1360s was a major cause of the second great sequence of French troubles in the 1400s, as John II's sons became Charles VI's uncles, and sought to direct royal policy and resources towards their divergent interests.[24] Clearly enough, it was the vacuum of power on the throne that allowed the conflict of Burgundians and Armagnacs both to take hold of the royal administration and to become so bitter, but the recreation of powerful regional lordships with a stake in the centre contributed an important element to the conflicts of the fifteenth century. As the English once again became involved in French affairs, the threat of princely autonomism – or 'princely polyarchy', as Bernard Chevalier has called it – was dramatically exposed, particularly in circumstances when the English had some control over the Crown, and particularly for those princes at the peripheries of the kingdom (though even the dukes of Anjou and Orléans flirted with English alliances, as late as the 1440s).[25] At the same time, it is important to recognise that the Crown was usually able to overcome princely leagues, even before the military ordinances of 1445: for one thing, the princes found it difficult to coordinate their actions; for another, they preferred, wherever possible, to work with the king rather than against him; and for a third, he possessed many points of entry to their domains, such as key allies in their entourages, prominent towns and the support of public opinion.[26] These factors were decisive in the *Praguerie* of 1440, the *Guerre du Bien Public* and the *Guerre Folle* of the 1480s; while France's politics were profoundly regional and territorial in character, the king could usually keep on top of his subjects.

If we turn to the other common themes in the politics of the two kingdoms, we can see how they are conditioned by the same issues of integration and regionalism. In England, 'bad kingship' was ultimately

---

[24] Autrand (2000).
[25] Allmand (1998), p. 408; Watts (1996), p. 222ff; Favier (2001), pp. 92–4.
[26] Caron (1994), Part 4; Favreau (1971); Richard (1971).

about a failure or inability to perform a handful of key tasks: above all, making decisions which appeared both representative and independent; and secondarily (though the two are related), transmitting authority to those who acted in the king's name – officers and councillors, judges and military commanders.[27] It is in these respects that Edward II, Richard II, Henry VI and intermittently other kings went wrong, but it is important to note that the crises which stemmed from these failings blew up in particular circumstances: that is, amid a widespread public perception of misgovernment, typically attested in parliament (and/or by the 'commons') and typically associated with a significant failure of financial management, usually against a backdrop of high taxation. Misgovernment was not only, in the public eye, a matter of paying too much for too little – it also entailed failures in the defence of the realm, in the preservation of order and justice and, increasingly, in the protection of trade and industry – but, in this period of frequent parliaments and regular taxation, it was arguably the implicit fiscal contract between king and subjects which was most prominent and which provided the main basis for imposing councils and other restraints on the errant king.[28] As each crisis deepened, the financial focus became less important, and the breakdown of relations between the king and leading magnates moved to centre stage. From here, with charges of treason and threats of deposition in the air, it was a short step to civil war and the raft of battlefield killings and judicial murders to which it gave rise. This was the situation in which, notoriously, the English killed their kings, though it is worth noting that the kings usually managed to kill a good few Englishmen first.[29] In all, then, these crises were about the inner dynamics of a highly centralised political system and about the publicly attested evidence that the king had failed to manage those dynamics. There was perceived to be a direct connection between kingship, good government and the condition of the realm or 'common weal', and, in fact, there *were* some direct connections in this area: unless the king did his small but important job properly, nothing else worked. Unfortunately, none of the devices typically put forward to deal with that problem – from imposed councils, to supervision of the royal finances, purges of the royal household, or, ultimately deposition and usurpation – had positive results: only the king himself, voluntarily, could rescue the situation, and this he was unlikely to do if his prerogatives were being infringed. It is for these reasons – coupled with the difficulty faced by usurpers in exercising an

---

[27] Watts (1996), pp. 74–80 and Chapter 8.   [28] Harriss (1993), pp. 40–6.
[29] For this well-known French trope ('The English kill their kings'), see Lewis (1964).

independent and representative authority – that crises over kingship were so bitter and prolonged in England.[30]

In France, once again, the situation was different. Of course, there were unsatisfactory kings – besides the mad Charles VI and the imprisoned John II (1356–60, 1363–4), the sneaky and mercurial Louis XI is a plausible candidate – but they did not end up dead at the hands of their subjects and they do not seem to have generated the same kind of political response. This was because none of the steps that linked the English king so directly to his leading subjects, to his parliament and to the adjudication of a wider public, existed in France, which made the French king a less personally threatening figure, and hence a less vulnerable one. The king's grace, as we have seen, was managed by his officers on his behalf; the leading magnates may have enjoyed access, but they had large domains to rule elsewhere in the kingdom and dealt with the king mainly through proctors and intermediaries; the Estates, which could ventilate the concerns of the tax-paying public but not control taxation, met only rarely on a quasi-national basis (hardly at all between the 1370s and c.1420, or after the end of the 1430s), and were in no position to bind or correct the king – only in 1355–7 and in 1413 did they even attempt that, both times in the context of uprisings and both times unsuccessfully.[31] Only rather late in the day did magnates become vulnerable to accusations of treason for challenging the king or accroaching his powers, and this took some heat out of the upper reaches of French politics, even if it did not prevent the murders of 1407 and 1419.[32] On that note, it is true that there are marked parallels between the reign of Charles VI and that of his English grandson Henry VI: in both cases, ministers and magnates maintained a simulacrum of royal authority during the minority and on into the king's adult years, when it was much harder; in both cases, divisions grew between leading subjects with alternative visions of how the king's rule should be made effective; in both cases, there were attempts to capture public opinion; and in both cases, divisions among the magnates led haltingly but inexorably towards war. Equally, Charles the Bold's capture of Louis XI at Péronne in 1468, looks rather like the earl of Warwick's capture of Edward IV in Oxfordshire a year later: a sign that it was important for a prominent magnate to have some kind of purchase on the king's person. But there are important differences, too. Even allowing for historiographical biases, it does seem as if the conflict between

---

[30] These issues are explored at more length in Watts (2005).
[31] Small (2009), pp. 113–17, 124–5, 137, and see now Hébert (2014), Chapter 1.
[32] Cuttler (1981).

Burgundians and Armagnacs was more directly a struggle for control of royal resources than was the conflict between Richard of York and his opponents; it was also a struggle between regional interest groups with solid power-bases in different parts of the realm.[33] These elements were certainly present in the Wars of the Roses, but to begin with, at least, they were secondary to a public debate over the government of the realm. A similar debate took place in early fifteenth-century Paris, and no doubt in other towns, but it seems that the duke of Burgundy's willingness to reduce taxes related more to his access to Flemish revenues and to the withdrawal of his royal pension than to genuine upward pressure; while the duke of Orléans concentrated more on trying to seize royal assets, such as the duchy of Normandy and the person of the Dauphin, than on defending the government's record. Moving later, the episode at Péronne did not greatly alter, still less destroy, the relationship between Louis XI and his most powerful subject, whereas Warwick's transgression led rapidly to the showdown of 1470–1. In all, while English and French politics look more alike in the fifteenth century than before, and while these parallels certainly deserve further exploration, there are important differences, and they reflect the greater size and looser framework of the French kingdom.

Drawing all this together, it is clear (if not surprising) that the patterns of political life reflect the structures of power and government in each kingdom. England, tightly integrated and closely governed, was vulnerable to prolonged crises of kingship, but there was no real problem over the control of the regions by the centre. France, multipolar and governed in a much less uniform way, was vulnerable to revolt and prolonged disarray in the regions, but, while outbreaks of trouble were partly caused by the Crown and its agents, they did not result in damage to the king, nor, in any lasting way, to his rights – indeed, in fiscal terms, at least, quite the reverse. Analysis of French politics is greatly complicated by the fact that one French prince was also king of England and had a plausible claim to the throne. It has sometimes been tempting to believe that the problems of later medieval France stemmed from this simple fact, and that the removal of the English in the second half of the fifteenth century inevitably produced recovery. But episodes such as the rising of the Leagues in 1314–15, the struggle of Burgundians and Armagnacs, the *Praguerie* and the *Guerre du Bien Public* – however minimised in French historiography – demonstrate that there were autogenous tensions within the kingdom, just as there were in every other sizeable political unit in later medieval Europe. The possibility of English intervention surely

---

[33] The most accessible and up-to-date overview of this conflict is in Small (2009), pp. 135–46.

increased the chances of regional fragmentation and provided options even at the heart of France for princes and towns to gather forces and resources and to strike hard bargains with the Crown. But even when this intervention was most devastating, as in the 1340s and 50s, or in the 1410s and 20s, France did not disintegrate: the king retained 'enclaves', contacts and allies everywhere; it was easier for any prince to rule with his grace than without it; and he alone held the key to taxation within the kingdom, however much he had to share the proceeds. So it was that France, forever on the brink of flying apart, never actually did so; while England, so closely drawn together around its king, spent half its time at odds with him.[34]

BIBLIOGRAPHY

1. INTRODUCTION

Allmand, C. T., 1998. *New Cambridge Medieval History VII. c.1415–c.1500*, Cambridge.
Brown, M., 2013. *Disunited Kingdoms: Peoples and Politics in the British Isles, 1280–1460*, Harlow.
Carpenter, C., 1997. *The Wars of the Roses*, Cambridge.
Genet, J.-Ph., 1990. 'L'État moderne: un modèle opératoire', in J.-Ph. Genet (ed.), *L'État moderne: genèse*, Paris, 261–81.
Guenée, B., 1967. 'État et nation en France au moyen âge', *Revue Historique*, 237, 17–30.
1968. 'État et espace dans la France du bas moyen âge', *Annales ESC*, 23, 744–58.
Gunn, S. J., 1995. *Early Tudor Government, 1485–1558*, Basingstoke.
Harriss, G. L., 1993. 'Political Society and the Growth of Government in Late Medieval England', *Past and Present*, 138, 28–57.
2005. *Shaping the Nation: England, 1360–1461*, Oxford.
Jones, M. (ed.), 2000. *New Cambridge Medieval History VI. c.1300–c.1415*, Cambridge.
Lewis, P. S., 1968. *Later Medieval France: The Polity*, Oxford.
Ormrod, W. M., 1995. *Political Life in Medieval England, 1300–1450*, Basingstoke.
Small, G., 2009. *Late Medieval France*, Basingstoke.
Watts, J. L., 2009. *The Making of Polities: Europe, 1300–1500*, Cambridge.

2. FURTHER READING

Armstrong, C. A. J., 1983. 'Some Examples of the Distribution and Speed of News at the Time of the Wars of the Roses', in C. A. J. Armstrong (ed.), *England, France and Burgundy in the Fifteenth Century*, London, pp. 97–122.

---

[34] I am most grateful to Malcolm Vale and Chris Fletcher for their helpful comments on a draft of this Conclusion.

Autrand, F., 1995. *Charles V le Sage*, Paris.

2000. 'France under Charles V and Charles VI' in M. Jones (ed.) *New Cambridge Medieval History VI. c.1300–c.1415*, Cambridge, pp. 422–41.

, with Barthélémy, D. and Contamine, P., 1991. 'L'espace français: histoire politique du début du xie siècle à la fin du xve', in A. Balard (ed.), *L'Histoire médiévale en France. Bilan et Perspectives*, Paris, pp. 101–25.

Beaune, C., 1985. *Naissance de la nation France*, Paris.

Britnell, R. H. and Pollard, A. J. (eds.), 1995. *The McFarlane Legacy*, Stroud.

Caron, M.-Th., 1994. *Noblesse et pouvoir royal en France, xiiie–xve Siècle*, Paris.

Carpenter, C., 1992. *Locality and Polity. A Study of Warwickshire Landed Society, 1401–1499*, Cambridge.

1993. 'Political and Constitutional History: Before and After McFarlane', in R. H. Britnell and A. J. Pollard (eds.), *The McFarlane Legacy*, Stroud, pp. 175–206.

Cazelles, R., 1958. *La société politique et la crise de royauté sous Philippe de Valois*, Paris.

1982. *Société politique, noblesse et couronne sous Jean le Bon et Charles V*, Geneva.

Contamine, P., 1972. *Guerre, État et société à la fin du Moyen Âge*, Paris.

1976. 'De la puissance aux privilèges: doléances de la noblesse française envers la monarchie aux xive et xve siècles', in P. Contamine (ed.), *La noblesse au Moyen Âge, xie–xve siècles*, Paris, pp. 235–57.

1992. *Des Pouvoirs en France, 1300–1500* (collected essays, 1976–91), Paris.

Crooks, P., 2011. 'State of the Union: Perspectives on English Imperialism in the Late Middle Ages', *Past and Present*, 212, 3–42.

Cuttler, S. H., 1981. *The Law of Treason and Treason Trials in Later Medieval France*, Cambridge.

Davies, R. R., 1990. *Domination and Conquest: The Experience of Ireland, Scotland and Wales, 1100–1300*, Cambridge.

2000. *The First English Empire*, Oxford.

Favier, J., 2001. *Louis XI*, Paris.

Favreau, R., 1971. 'La Praguerie en Poitou', *Bibliothèque de l'École des Chartes*, 129, 277–301.

Fletcher, C., 2008. *Richard II: Manhood, Youth and Politics, 1377–99*, Oxford.

Griffiths, R. A., 1986. 'The Crown and the Royal Family in Later Medieval England', in R. A. Griffiths and J. Sherborne (eds.), *Kings and Nobles in the Later Middle Ages*, Gloucester, pp. 15–23.

Guenée, B., 1963. *Tribunaux et gens de justice dans le bailliage de Senlis à la fin du Moyen Age (vers 1380–vers 1550)*, Paris.

2002. *L'Opinion publique à la fin du Moyen Âge*, Paris.

Harriss, G. L., 1975. *King, Parliament and Public Finance in England to 1369*, Oxford.

1985. *Henry V: The Practice of Kingship*, Oxford.

Hébert, M., 2014. *Parlementer: assemblées représentatives et échange politique en Europe occidentale à la fin du Moyen Age*, Paris.

Henneman, J. B., 1971. *Royal Taxation in Fourteenth-Century France. The Development of War Financing, 1322–1356*, Princeton.

1976. *Royal Taxation in Fourteenth-Century France: The Captivity and Ransom of John II, 1356–1370*, Philadelphia.

1978. 'The Military Class and the French Monarchy in the Late Middle Ages', *American Historical Review*, 83, 946–65.

1983–4. 'Nobility, Privilege and Fiscal Politics in Late Medieval France', *French Historical Studies*, 13, 1–17.

Holt, J. C., 1992. *Magna Carta*, 2nd edn, Cambridge.

Horrox, R., 1989. *Richard III: a Study of Service*, Cambridge.

Krynen, J., 1993. *L'Empire du roi: idées et croyances politiques en France, xiiie–xve siècle*, Paris.

1995. 'La rébellion du bien publique (1465)', in M. T. Fögen (ed.), *Ordnung und Aufruhr im Mittelalter*, Frankfurt, pp. 81–97.

Leguai, A., 1967. 'Les états princiers en France à la fin du moyen âge', *Annali della Fondazione Italiana per la Storia Amministrativa*, 4, 133–57.

1987. 'Fondements et problèmes du pouvoir royal en France (autour de 1400)', in R. Schneider (ed.), *Das Spätmittelalterliche Königtum im europäischen Vergleich*, Sigmaringen, pp. 41–58.

Lewis, P. S., 1962. 'The Failure of the French Medieval Estates', *Past and Present*, 23, 3–24.

1964. 'Two Pieces of Fifteenth-Century Political Iconography', *Journal of the Warburg and Courtauld Institutes*, 27, 317–20.

1981. 'The Centre, the Periphery and the Problem of Power Distribution in Later Medieval France', in J. R. L. Highfield and R. M. Jeffs (eds.), *The Crown and the Local Communities in England and France in the Fifteenth Century*, Gloucester, pp. 33–50.

1996. 'Reflections on the Role of Royal Clientèles in the Construction of the French Monarchy (mid-14th/end-15th centuries)', in N. Bulst (ed.), *L'État ou Le Roi?*, Paris, pp. 51–67.

(ed.), 1971. *The Recovery of France in the Fifteenth Century*, London and Basingstoke.

McFarlane, K. B., 1973. *The Nobility of Later Medieval England*, Oxford.

Maddicott, J. R., 1970. *Thomas of Lancaster, 1307–22*, Oxford.

2010. *The Origins of the English Parliament, 924–1327*, Oxford.

Ormrod, W. M., 2000. 'The English State and the Plantagenet Empire, 1259–1360: a Fiscal Perspective', in J. R. Maddicott and D. M. Palliser (eds.), *The Medieval State: Essays Presented to James Campbell*, London, pp. 197–214.

2011. *Edward III*, New Haven and London.

Potter, D., 1995. *A History of France, 1460–1560*, Basingstoke.

2003. 'The King and his Government under the Valois, 1328–1498', in D. Potter (ed.), *France in the Later Middle Ages*, Oxford.

Richard, J., 1971. 'Royal "Enclaves" and Provincial Boundaries: The Burgundian Elections', in P. S. Lewis (ed.), *The Recovery of France in the Fifteenth Century*, London and Basingstoke, pp. 216–41.

Small, C. M., 1977. 'Appeals from the Duchy of Burgundy to the Parlement of Paris in the Early Fourteenth Century', *Mediaeval Studies*, 39, 350–68.

Vale, M. G. A., 1974. *Charles VII*, Berkeley and Los Angeles.

Vaughan, R., 1979. *John the Fearless*, 2nd edn, London.

Watts, J. L., 1996. *Henry VI and the Politics of Kingship*, Cambridge.

2005. 'Usurpation in England: a Paradox of State-Growth', in F. Foronda, J.-Ph. Genet and J.-M. Nieto Soria (eds.), *Coups d'État à la fin du Moyen Âge?*, Madrid, pp. 115–30.

Wolfe, M., 1972. *The Fiscal System of Renaissance France*, New Haven and London.

Index

Note. To keep the length of the index manageable, and also reflecting the comparative nature of the work, entries below for institutions that existed in both England and France do not differentiate between the two kingdoms.

Printed in the United States
By Bookmasters